RIKERS

An Oral History

GRAHAM RAYMAN

and

REUVEN BLAU

RANDOM HOUSE

NEW YORK

Published in the United States by Random House,
an imprint and division of Penguin Random House LLC, New York.

RANDOM HOUSE and the HOUSE colophon are registered trademarks
of Penguin Random House LLC.

Hardback ISBN 978-0-593-13421-4
Ebook ISBN 978-0-593-13422-1

Printed in the United States of America on acid-free paper

randomhousebooks.com

2 4 6 8 9 7 5 3 1

First Edition

Book design by Edwin Vazquez

For those who made it out and those who didn't

CONTENTS

RIKERS

PROLOGUE

On a chilly autumn day, Vincent Gilroy, a candidate for public office in New York City, gave a speech blasting the penal colony on Rikers Island. The shiv of an island at the confluence of the East River and the Bronx River, he declared, was awash in narcotics, corruption, and violence.

"Is it not a fact," Gilroy boomed, "that heroin and other drugs are freely 'railroaded' into Rikers Island, and that from May to the middle of August of this year the night rioting and fighting continued uninterruptedly and that no effort was made to remove this disgrace? Is it not a fact that [guards] on Rikers who point out inmates actually using needles and drugs on their cots at night are invariably told: 'Mind your own business, what can I do?'

"Is it not a fact," he expounded, "that drug addicts leave Rikers Island far worse than when they entered because of the absence of control and the ease with which they get drugs while committed there?"

If all of that sounds familiar, it's because that speech could have been given yesterday.

But it was given in 1921.

It was given more than a century ago.

FIRST DAY

"A City Within a City"

There's only one way to get on Rikers Island and one way to get off—a narrow, forty-two-hundred-foot-long bridge spanning a part of the East River. At the ribbon cutting in 1966, Mayor John Lindsay called it the "Bridge of Hope." Forty years later, in 2006, the rapper Flavor Flav dubbed it the "Bridge of Pain."

Purchased from the Rikers family in 1884 for $180,000 (about $5.1 million today), it began life in the nineteenth century as a motley assortment of jails and "workhouses," or debtors' prisons. Using fill from the construction of the Manhattan street grid, the city expanded the island from 87 acres to roughly 415 acres.

It was also a massive garbage dump. Residents of Hunts Point in the Bronx could smell it from their homes a mile away, and Upper East Siders could easily see the flames from the burning of mountains of trash. Enormous clouds of rats populated the dump to the point where they challenged dogs, and humans, for control of the island.

Even today, Rikers remains landfill to a depth of roughly ten feet, based on borings conducted in 2009. "They drilled a bunch of holes and all ten feet were garbage, mixed sand with pieces of glass and brick, pieces of wood—everything you can imagine that would be thrown away as materials from a construction site was in there," explained Dr. Byron Stone, research geologist with the U.S. Geological Survey.

The first jail at Rikers, in the modern understanding of the place, was born in the spirit of reform. In July 1928, seven years after Vincent Gilroy's broadside, the city fathers unveiled their plan for the Rikers Island Penitentiary. *The New York Times* described it as a model prison that would correct the evils of the past.

The inscription, placed in 1933, read, "Those who are laying this cornerstone today . . . hope that the treatment which these unfortunates will receive in this institution will be the means of salvaging some lives which would otherwise have been wasted."

As the decades passed, this purported icon of penology became a forbidding place indeed. Detainees were thrown or jumped from the upper tiers to their deaths, so those floors had to be closed.

Violence ruled.

And over time, it became known by the jailed as the "House of Dead Men."

But the city stuck with Rikers as the place to leave the people society had deemed worthy of incarceration, the vast majority poor and of color. It was out of sight, hard for visitors to reach, closed, and foreboding.

For some of the hundreds of thousands of souls who have made the passage over the past five decades, a trip to Rikers may be the first time they will sleep somewhere away from home. For others, it's their only chance for a bed and a warm meal. For some, it might be the place where they find themselves fighting for their lives. And still others may never make it out. The memories of their first day on Rikers are ingrained in the minds of the people who worked, visited, and served time there.

It's an experience no one forgets.

—

GRACE PRICE, detained 2011: They literally arraigned me at midnight. It was me and three other people on the bus to Rikers. There was this little crackhead lady falling asleep on my shoulder on the way across the bridge. She was nasty, but I just let her sleep there because it somehow made me feel like I was actually in control of my situation.

COLIN ABSOLAM, detained 1993 to 1996: Going back and forth on those DOC buses over that bridge was traumatic. The bridge is very narrow, and you're caged up, shackled. If the bus happened to go off that bridge and fall into the water, everyone would die. I mean the correction officers would get out, but you're in a cage. They would have to open the cage and get the shackles off. There wouldn't be enough time to do that before you drowned.

GRACE PRICE: The guards on the bus were horrible, and I just kind of sat there quietly sobbing. The guards hated me for that because they don't like to hear a hysterical woman.

YUSEF SALAAM, detained 1989 to 1994, Central Park 5 case: I can't really describe in words this horror and this horrible feeling coupled with that horror, but it had a lot to do with the smell of the place. We're talking about a place that smelled like death, vomit, urine, feces, and like the bad train stations in New York City all wrapped up in one. And one of the first encounters I had with somebody coming up to me while I was inside the holding cell, they were asking me to check out my watch, and I didn't realize this, but they were trying to steal the watch from me.

And I remember [the Central Park 5 co-defendant] Antron [McCray] saying, "No, don't let them check your watch out, man. You know what I'm saying? Like they're trying to get you, this is a trick, you know?"

DONOVAN DRAYTON, detained 2007 to 2012: I was nineteen years old. I'd never been through prison before. I've been through some difficult things, but walking into the unknown and not knowing what's waiting for you, it's one of the scariest things. And once you actually get inside and see how it's running and operating, the environment and all the chaos, you're just like, "Wow, this is a whole nuther world."

Donovan Drayton was nineteen when he went to Rikers, where he spent nearly five years pretrial.

EDDIE ROSARIO, detained 1990: When people ask me, what is being locked up like, the most horrible thing about being locked up is that you are being dehumanized on a daily basis. They practically stamp a number on you. In order to navigate the experience, you have to normalize the dehumanization. You have to buy into it in order to survive. That is the most horrible thing about being locked up. You're never the same person again. Once you internalize it, you project it outward. If you are being dehumanized, that's how you treat other people. That to me is the essence of incarceration: having to buy into the dehumanization.

STANLEY RICHARDS, detained 1986 to 1988: I was addicted to crack and on a methadone program and was out on the street robbing for my addiction. When I went to jail after I got arrested, I was in the most emotional pain in my life. And I find myself now in a bullpen with people that I'm going through it with. I'm going through it 'cause I haven't been able to get my crack, haven't been able to get my medication, and I am hearing my name being called through the various cells as they process you. So from the point of arrest to the point of getting a bed on Rikers could be something like five days. It's that intense. No shower. No hot food, none of that. There's no phone 'cause you're all in bullpens. You're basically shoved into a small cell like fifteen by ten and there's anywhere from like twenty to thirty men shoved in there. So you're lucky to get a seat. Most are staying on the floor. And most of the people are dope sick. Some are mentally insane or having other medical issues not treated 'cause they're on the streets.

BERNARD KERIK, correction commissioner, 1998 to 2000: When I got to Rikers the first time, when I crossed that bridge, I thought, God, this is a nightmare. I couldn't imagine what it would be like to, you know, work there. Instead of one jail (where I previously worked in New Jersey), there's ten and it looked like a city within a city. And then getting through the process, getting into the facility, meeting the guys on the island, waiting for the inmate. It was just a mess. It was uncoordinated. It was filthy. It was what the reputation was.

KATHY MORSE, detained 2006: I remember being in the holding cell in reception, the one they first put people in when they arrive. There were women in there who were getting dope sick. They were fighting over space to lie on the floor. Another woman had multiple layers of clothing on. I couldn't figure out why. It was because at that point, when I was there, you could wear your own clothes if they met the criteria in terms of non-gang colors and things like that. So she came to court that day prepared for going to jail. She was wearing enough clothes for her stay. I realized I was unprepared.

DONOVAN DRAYTON: I went in November. It was cold. I remember just being in intake, man. It's like, "Yo, I'm really stuck in jail, son." Seeing everybody with their bags and all their stuff. Like your whole life packed up in a bag in a waiting cell, getting ready to be shipped off somewhere. You don't know where the heck you at, where you going, and they don't tell you where you're going until you actually go.

ROBERT CRIPPS, retired warden, 1983 to 2013: The first couple of weeks I literally had trouble sleeping 'cause you have to get accustomed to working on Rikers Island, you know, with all the gates locking behind you, all the violence, and everything else. Tough job.

DR. HOMER VENTERS, correctional health services chief medical officer, 2015 to 2017: My first day on the island was in November 2008. It was snowing heavily. And it was just incredibly surreal to hear all the guys yelling out of the [solitary unit called the] Bing. You get out there and all these guys are yelling out. It never stopped. Really. It was just kind of a constant.

KATHY MORSE: I just remember how medieval the reception cells were. The toilet didn't flush, but people were still using it. They were going to the bathroom or to vomit. It was just a mess. I don't do drugs so I have never been exposed to that. There were women on the floor throwing up, getting violently sick because they were withdrawing. One woman in the cell had crack hidden in her hair, and it fell out. And they all scrambled around the floor, like it was a piñata that had been opened. That was the first time I had ever seen crack in my life. It was just a horrible experience. And the officers were trying to figure out who brought it into the cell. They did take away what they could, but they only got a portion.

KANDRA CLARK, detained 2010: We were in the bullpen, hadn't even been through intake. And it was dinnertime, so correction officers were eating outside food. Really good-smelling food. A young lady came in and it was right after everybody in the bullpen had been served sandwiches. So she kept saying she was hungry, she was hungry. Correction officers refused her because they said she had just missed the cutoff for dinnertime. Mind you, this is the bullpen so she doesn't have any other options to get food. The officers were just laughing and eating their own outside food.

She was a young woman. She pushed her hand outside through the bar and she grabbed the garbage can that was sitting next to the bullpen and she pulled it closer to the bars and she reached her hand in and she grabbed out pieces of half-eaten baloney. And she just started eating it out of the garbage. And there had to be ten officers sitting around who just watched her. I was so angry because it was very frustrating to see so many human beings laughing at someone who was just hungry and having no care for her.

You kind of knew this was how it was going to be. There was definitely not relationships being built between correction officers and incarcerated people. It was an us-versus-them kind of thing.

ANNA GRISTINA, detained 2012: The judge decides they were going to put me in protective custody. This experience was coming off the Rikers bus from court. I was told I had three minutes to pack up my stuff. I didn't get a pillowcase or a bag. I had no way to carry my stuff, so I had to wrap everything in my blanket.

They took me down to the condemned psychiatric ward. This was a place that had been deemed unfit for human occupancy, I learned later from my psychiatrist. I was in there alone. The windows were fused shut. The heat was turned up to 102. I got heatstroke. They had a guard six feet away from me 24/7. They had three men in the Bubble [a glass-enclosed booth where an officer sits to observe the unit]. Every time I took a shower, there were two-inch water bugs and it reeked of cat urine, because there was a cat colony under there. There was no water source other than the orange juice or milk they gave me at meals. When I complained, they leaked a story about wanting to put me in diapers. It was a derogatory story.

Later, it came out I was telling the truth.

There was no air-conditioning, and these were cinder-block cells. I tried to get on the phone but kept getting cut off, so I had no phone access and I couldn't leave. And there's no commissary. I couldn't pick out what food I could eat. One night it got so hot that I was getting a severe heat migraine. I told the guards, but I didn't even get Advil. I vomited from the heatstroke. There was no cool water. They could see me when I was in the toilet too. There was a row of eight toilets. I had to clean the toilet with shampoo. It was covered in feces.

KENNY GILMORE, detained 1971: Going through Rikers Island helped me to forget about what I actually had to deal with because it was atrocious. It was in 1971. Being in a holding cell with sixty, sixty-five, seventy people and some were there days before you. Someone was always sick, throwing up, dope sick. The toilets are not flushing, and people are not bathing. It's crazy.

SIDNEY SCHWARTZBAUM, retired deputy warden, union president, 1979 to 2016: I was twenty-five. I was a street kid, though. In the academy, I was told to be fair, tough, and consistent and give the inmates what they deserve legally by law, but you are the authority figure. You control your housing area and work with adolescents. I was told you have to make sure that nobody assumes the role of authority figure in the inmate population because that's when the inmates don't eat, they starve them. They'll come up and take your tray.

You make sure everybody gets a phone call. Make sure nobody's getting bullied. Make sure nobody gets seriously hurt. Make sure nobody escapes and nobody hangs up [takes their life].

STANLEY RICHARDS: And then when you get to the housing area and now you start getting a little normal. You can start making your phone calls. You can start getting a shower. You get your three hot meals; now you're figuring out, how do I survive in this environment? So from the moment you go into the house, you're figuring out who's running the place. Back then we used to call them the house gangs. The guys who controlled all the food, phones, and TVs. They had relationships with the officers.

DIMITRI ANTONOV, detained 2020: The biggest thing was the phone. As soon as I walked in, people started asking me about using the phone. Everybody on Rikers sells their PIN numbers for commissary or other stuff. But you shoot yourself in the foot. You give out your PIN number, and if you're moved, the guy is going to change your PIN number and take all your minutes. At first, I was giving it out. This one guy kept hitting me up over and over. And I was letting him use it.

Another Russian guy says to me, why are you letting him use it for free? I said I was being diplomatic. He goes, what are you talking about? Every five minutes is a dollar. You are going to end up running out of calls. That's a bad idea. These guys are going to use up your minutes you could have used to call your lawyer. I was still thinking I would be released any second. But after about two weeks, I realized that wasn't going to happen, and I stopped giving out free minutes. One guy actually said he felt bad for asking, so he stopped.

His friend came to me and said, yo, you remember giving my boy free minutes? What's up? He goes, I'll give you a soup and chips, but you gotta give me the call right now. And he would make the call and take off. And of course I was chasing him to get the soup and the chips. It would always be this big thing [to get paid back].

JERRY DEAN, detained 1987, 2003: Okay, so I remember 1987. I remember I was going to Rikers Island and I had my nice clothes in the court and my father brought my old clothes just in case I was going to get sentenced that day. I didn't want to go to Rikers Island with new clothes, 'cause they rob you. They didn't want to send me to Rikers Island, because that Howard Beach case had just happened and there was a lot of racial tension on Rikers Island. And I said no. I said, I want to go to Rikers and start doing my time. And they sent me to Rikers.

The first day I was there, I was on the phone with my girlfriend. This Dominican kid comes over and hangs the phone up on me, and I knew right then and there I had to fight. I had just turned sixteen, so I was in [the teen jail, the Robert N. Davoren Center]. And I got into it with this Dominican kid, and then we went to the back [where] correctional officers used to let you fight for five minutes. As long as you kept it clean and no weapons, they let you get it off your chest. So me and this kid go in the back and we started fighting. I was a pretty good fighter.

I hit him with some blows and he went down and he said he wanted to take a nap to sleep it off. So he went to take a nap and I said to myself, I was gonna show these kids what happens the next time when one of these little motherfuckers hangs the phone up on me when I'm talking to my girlfriend. I wanted to gain my respect. He was sleeping, so I went over to him and quietly took toilet paper and wrapped it around his legs. Then I set him on fire. He jumped up and he was screaming. But I got my respect, and all of a sudden the correction officers liked me, the other inmates liked me, and they put me on the house gang.

JACQUELINE MCMICKENS, correction commissioner, 1984 to 1986: Correction officers are mean to inmates, and inmates are mean to correction officers. A man doesn't haul off and hit a man if he thinks there's a consequence.

ROBERT CRIPPS: During lunch, there was an alarm and there were inmates fighting. The correction officers had to restrain them and march them down the corridor. I wasn't involved in it, but that was my first day. It was like, what did I get myself into? They were being marched down the corridor and the inmates were all bloodied up and one of the officers got bloodied up too. It was all pretty violent.

COSS MARTE, detained 2010: I was eighteen. I went to the adult facility. I remember as soon as I walked in the dorm, there were people banging on the glass waiting for me to get in. It was called Broadway because my bed was in the middle. I was the new guy. A couple of gang members came up to me and asked me what I was claiming. If I was part of a gang or not. I told them I'm NFL, which back in the day stood for Neutral for Life. There was a riot that first day. Someone got stabbed with a broomstick on top of my bed. There was so much blood. I remember trying to get new sheets because mine were covered in blood.

EDWARD GAVIN, retired deputy warden, 1982 to 2001: So there was an orange alert, and what that meant was the count was off, which means there may have been an escape attempt. The captain at the time of the academy, Mendoza, he said, you're stuck. Go over there now on overtime, being that you're going to be assigned there Monday. So I walk over there, this captain in the control room, he picks his nose; he has a snot on the end of his nose. He goes, "Six lower B, rookie." I must have looked like New Jack City. I'm walking down there with white gloves in my lapel jacket. I'm walking a quarter mile to the post. I'm brand-new. Right out of graduation. You would think they would say, go home and have a nice graduation day. But no, you're stuck. Imagine that! They would never do that in the Police Department.

It was my first day. I'm white. I start taking the count. It's like 3:00 p.m. I've got all of six minutes on the job. They [detainees] go, "Yo, punk white boy from Long Island!" I was from Rockland. "New Jack motherfucker!" They were all making fun of me. I'm walking by the cells. The inmate goes, "Yo, New Jack, you, CO, you know that Jamaican CO you just relieved?" I thought about it. I go, "No, what Jamaican CO?" He goes, "CO, you're Jamaican my cock hard, motherfucker!" I really got into how they talk, the lingo.

So, anyway, the next thing you know, we gotta get them ready for a meal. I don't even know if I should say this—if I'm going to get in trouble thirty-six years later—but I'm just brand fucking new, so they crack all the cells, sixty on the A and sixty on the B. We put them in the dayroom.

They're all in there. And everything is fine. Then this Black guy comes on the post. He's a big guy. He's got like ten years on the job. And I got like ten minutes on the job. He goes, "Crack the dayroom." He brings a big kid out. This kid was huge. They start having words. Apparently, this kid disrespected him two hours earlier in a corridor. He's coming back to tell this kid what time it is. This is how you maintain order. They are now fighting and going at it to the point where my guy's losing. And I'm thinking, this is not good.

So I go behind the huge kid and jump on him and put him in a full nelson. I take him to the ground. They are still fighting. He was getting the better of my guy until I jumped on him, but now my guy is getting the better of him: *boom, boom, boom.* In the end, my guy broke his arm and his elbow and the inmate had a broken jaw. Ten minutes into my first day.

EVE KESSLER, director, DOC public affairs, 2014 to 2017: When I got the job, it was very late 2014. I saw [the political consultant] Hank Sheinkopf at a holiday party. I said, "Oh, hey, uh, you know, I got a job. I'm the new director of public affairs in the New York City Department of Correction." He said, "Congratulations, you won't make a difference. Correction has been a corrupt department for thirty-five years." And that proved to be true.

JOHN BOSTON, retired director, Legal Aid Prisoners' Rights Project: People were getting into fights all the time. Sanitation was not maintained. The food service operation was incredibly badly run. The level of chaos, the level of dirt, just the squalor of the housing areas where you've got double bunks all over the place. I mean, you've seen photographs from Mississippi and Alabama when they were at their most overcrowded or California before they got their population cap. And it was the same story.

KENNY GILMORE: You don't want to sit down; you don't want nobody to touch you. You really have to establish yourself. You're looking at the madness of it. And then you go from the holding pens to Rikers Island, and this is where we were corralled. That's a good word. We're corralled into a reception area. And they'll say, "Okay, everybody take their stuff off. We are processing you in now," and to be processed was so degrading because they strip-search you, and when they strip-search, you've got to take everything off to check for contraband. If we're carrying any contraband, no one is checking for any diseases or anything like that. It's all about security. They check you, they talk to you dirty, they try to humiliate you. They don't care who you are. In fact, most of them don't even know.

MARTIN HORN, correction commissioner, 2002 to 2009: It was all about bullying. If you were a single guy and walked into a cell-block, somebody is going to walk up to you and say this is a Blood house. Joey is our leader. We're loyal to Joey. Here's the deal. If you want to sit on this chair to watch TV, you gotta give us a blow job or we're gonna fuck you in the ass.

KENNETH SAMUELS, detained 1994 to 1996: My first night in Rikers, I got surrounded by some gang members. They thought I was a member of the Bloods. At that time I didn't know what that was. They thought I was joking around. They asked me if I was a Five Percenter. Then I saw somebody I went to school with, and he told them he knows me and I wasn't part of a gang or anything like that. You had to ask to be on the phone and I didn't understand that. I got into a couple of fights over that. On Rikers Island, you gotta basically help yourself. There was no counseling at that time or anyone you can really talk to.

SIDNEY SCHWARTZBAUM: The first day, I did my job. I was happy. I got through it; there were no incidents, no fights. But I remember one day taking it personal, about an inmate who beat the crap out of another inmate and bloodied him up really bad. And over the course of a few months, I started to see more blood and violence, and I could see that my mind started to adapt as a defense mechanism, to deaden, because I was starting to take it personal that if it happened on my tour, I wasn't doing my job. I'm not protecting them. But after a while you realize that it's inevitable, that it's a high-crime area. These guys are going to hurt each other, that's what they do, you know? So I started to create defense mechanisms in my head to allow me to deal with it.

LINUS

"There Was No Plan B"

The sculptor Linus Coraggio came of age in the Rivington School movement in the Lower East Side art scene of the early 1980s. Notably, he was a founder of the Gas Station on Avenue B and East Second Street, a legendary avant-garde art space and nocturnal happening. One snowy night in 2015, he found himself in jail.

—

LINUS CORAGGIO: It was winter 2015. I was on the Upper West Side bicycling over to my friend's house on 107th and Amsterdam. I get to 106th Street, and it's shorter to go north against traffic for a half block. It was snowing and slushy. There was a police van. I couldn't tell what they were saying. And then I heard something like "Stop, cyclist!"

I went up on the sidewalk to disappear into the crowd. Then I realize I'm being pursued. One of the cop vans has done a 360 with the objective of corralling me.

I get into Riverside Park. I throw the bike behind these bushes and lie low. They somehow spot me and this white cop gets out. And then this other van with this Spanish cop rolls up, and they get into a fight about whose arrest it is.

Linus Coraggio, a sculptor of recovered metal, spent a harrowing night in the Tombs for riding his bike the wrong way.

The cops were both in Central Park Precinct vans. So what they were doing tooling around the Upper West Side, ready to bust a bicyclist for any minor violation, is an interesting question.

They put the bike in the van and then drive me to the Twenty-Fourth Precinct to get the mug shot. After about three hours there with no bathroom break, I'm in this cubicle on the ground floor. Coraggio was charged with "reckless endangerment."

I'm still asking for a bathroom. And there are file cases in this makeshift holding cell. At this point I really have to pee. So I wait for people to gravitate away from that corner of the floor and I piss behind this file cabinet, where it looked like other people had pissed.

Finally they bring me out and they're saying, "We have to take you to 123rd Street because their photo machine works."

I still haven't been able to call anybody. We get the picture taken. I'm in handcuffs. It's probably 10:30 p.m. Now it's a ride down to the Tombs with the Spanish cop.

I was complaining about the cuffs. I said, "You gotta loosen these. I have high blood pressure." Suddenly the cops are real happy. "Oh, you do? Okay. We'll take you to the hospital." 'Cause it means more overtime, of course.

So we rolled by Bellevue, and they take you into a room in the basement and make you wait. And the cop was like, "Do you want some water?" And he comes in while I'm still rear cuffed and puts it on a counter next to me and walks out.

I'm looking at this water and the cops are twenty feet away. So rather than yell to them and get ignored, I picked up the water cup with my mouth and *glug, glug, glug.* There are three cops at the door, popping their heads in. *Ha, ha, ha, ha.* They were waiting for me to do that.

Finally the doctor comes in and puts the blood pressure thing on me and writes something down on a clipboard, walks out. The cops come get me. They never released the cuffs. On the way out, at the nurse's desk, they hand me a bill for $1,800.

We get to the famous roll-down gate at the Tombs. A cop walks you down a narrow flight of stairs. At this point you're hearing shrieking reverberating down this long hallway.

Then it's down this other stairway into a side room where they let you out of the cuffs. There's two guys in there. One who's gonna search you again and turn you to the wall and do a preliminary pat down.

Then the other guy sits you down at an optical projector and he said, the mayor says you gotta do this laser retina scan. I'm looking at this machine; it looks like it's set up to fry your eyeballs.

Then it's a long walk underground to get to this low-ceiling hallway. The diameter of the bars were three inches. I remember thinking, this is built for King Kong. I was picturing a film with a fourteen-foot version of King Kong in there going up against the bars like, *grrrrr.* They were just so ridiculously wide.

By then, it was after midnight. They gave you no clue about how long you were going to be there. They were doing that bullshit thing, like, "Oh, you just need to do a desk appearance." And "We'll call you in a little while for night court." So, it starts to fill up on a Saturday night. And the first guy in there was a teenage Black kid who hopped the train.

And the food cart came by with the milk and the cereal and the peanut butter sandwiches. They weren't really watching. So I took something like four sandwiches and three milks, even though it seemed really disgusting.

The sandwiches were sort of mashed-down whole wheat, Wonder Bread–type loaf, with peanut butter, sorta smashed in a circle in the middle. You had to reach through the bars.

So I thought, well, this is pretty mellow. I just heard doors clanging in the distance and muffled discussions, and it seemed like the whole night would go like that.

And then around one, this really built Puerto Rican guy comes in. He's distraught and he's muttering to himself about his latest crime, like it was a holdup of some kind, and it became clear that he'd been in jail for six years previously. He knew he was going to be in for a long time.

Ten or fifteen minutes later, they bring in these two other Spanish guys. So they're talking to each other in English and Spanish. Almost shoptalk. They didn't know each other personally, but they knew the deal with each other.

And then, within a half hour, they bring in six other guys, Spanish and Black. Everybody's hooded out in Timberlands. They took the laces, and their jeans are hanging out of the tops of the boots. Big down jackets. They got the sweatshirts and the down jackets. Everybody's kind of jabbering, letting go of the night's excitement.

There's a bench on two sides of it. Maybe ten feet by fourteen feet. And then in the corner, there's one partition wall, low, for the toilet. There's a pay phone that's been busted for decades. The receiver's ripped off at the nub.

I'm lying on the bench, watching shit. I had my coat on. I had several layers, luckily. I used one of them for a pillow. This Puerto Rican robber guy said something about food. So I offered him a sandwich, which he took in a weird way. I was like, uh-oh.

I felt pretty weird taking up all that space lying down. I was just trying to conserve energy and not be interactive with them, being the only white guy in there. What the fuck was I going to start talking about? Only that first teenage kid was easy to talk to.

So it's getting to be 2:30 a.m. Some of these guys don't even scam the bench. Within ten minutes they're lying down curled up. And I had gotten off the bench a few times to take a piss. I could tell from my sneakers the whole floor was caked in piss. It was like, *shhh-plunk. Shhh-plunk.*

These guys were lying down with their fresh North Face jackets, turning, and I could hear a little *shick* from a jacket sticking to the urine-soaked floor. They didn't seem to give a shit.

The floor is filling up. Now there's five guys standing up talking and one guy saying, "Shit, this dude taking up that whole bench like that," talking about me, you know, "lying on that bench." Somehow it fades out and gets ignored. So I don't feel compelled to move.

I'm kind of holding my ground because at that point I'm pretty sure it's going to be all night. It now takes on this kindergarten vibe when it's nap time. Everyone's lain out and there's snoring. None of these guys have insomnia or are too freaked out to sleep.

There's still doors opening and closing, and voices get more animated and then die out. Around 3:30 a.m., when it's almost quiet and almost feels peaceful, this Black guy comes in and he's got this voice that's just like Jimi Hendrix.

It's almost magical to listen to, but it's got this grating harsh edge that's also nothing like Jimi Hendrix. So it's sucking you in, and then it's so abrasive to listen to.

I was extremely edgy. You could tell these guys were going up for a few years at least the way they were talking. And they were all dejected and pissed at the same time. Their body language was steroided out.

At that point I was just really trying to be invisible because it occurred to me if there was any fighting, you could yell your ass off and nobody would come. It was not a feeling of the jail overseers being there in a protective capacity. It felt really dangerous for a good two hours.

I'm there with my milks and my sandwiches on a napkin under the bench, not so hidden, but sort of in the corner—*how about a milk instead of fighting?* There was no plan B. It was just ride out whatever this animal is.

So way earlier than breakfast, 5:15 a.m., this crazy Puerto Rican church lady comes through with the food cart. And she's shrieking, "Mail! Sandwiches! I got peanut butter! I got baloney!"

Somehow in the morning, the sound of the doors opening and closing is crisper and louder. Meanwhile, they haven't let out anybody from this cell with the fourteen motherfuckers in it. There could have been twenty. Every body was next to every other body, barely an inch or two in between.

Finally they're reading names at the cell: we're going to take so-and-so out to court or to be moved to Rikers. And so people are shuffling out.

It's nine-ish and they came for me. I'm led upstairs. You meet the public defender. I'm unsure what the process is, if this is just a meeting and then they're going to bring me back for more detainment.

I'm trying to impress upon this twentysomething girl with a clipboard, the public defender, what I've been through. I've been in there twenty-five hours. She takes some notes. Two hours to get into a courtroom. They take you back to a holding cell, just within twenty feet of the courtroom.

And then I had to take a shit and it's this public hallway and the stall is small and guys can see in. I take a shit, and even before I even started shitting, they're like, "Flush that shit, flush that shit." They want you to flush like twenty times. And I'm kind of straining to shit and they're getting pissed that I'm not flushing the second they say flush that.

I get led back in the courtroom and the judge says, "Okay, don't get in trouble for a year. Dismissed. No fine. Here's a Metro-Card."

I was held after that morning appearance 'til almost dark, and somehow I didn't get out of there 'til eight, nine o'clock at night.

I thought I might walk home from down there just to air all the piss and fucking vomit off my body. And I'm coming up Mulberry Street and I see a bicycle on the street leaning up by some trash. I get on it and it's rideable. So I ride myself home through Chelsea and up Broadway.

I'm home in the shower, and at this point I'm getting pretty pissed off. I remember throwing away the sneakers. Man, everything had piss on it.

I tried a couple lawyers and it was either "Oh, you have a terrible case" or "You have a great case and I need X amount of money." Then I got this letter in the mail saying, have you recently been incarcerated, call the law offices of blah, blah, blah. And so, I call him up.

I happened to bring the hospital bill. He pulls it out of my hand and says, "I'll take care of this." He was saying this is outrageous excessive detention and the rate is $100 per hour of excessive detention. So that worked out to $2,700.

Somehow it came out to fifteen grand. So he took $5,000. I took $10,000. When I told my brother the story, he said you probably made more that night than the hottest call girl in Manhattan.

It took weeks of calling to get my bike back. They wouldn't even tell me where the bike was held. They said it was going to be at One Police Plaza and I should show up there. So I did and they say you have to go back to the Central Park Precinct and get it from the cop who arrested you.

So finally I caught up to him. And I remember him rolling the bike out of some storeroom. I did a piece to remember it. I called it *City Dog*. He's in a cage. It's a lead cast of a dog with a long tail, which signifies being pulled back into the system.

BULLPEN THERAPY

"A Life Sentence, Thirty Days at a Time"

Anyone who has spent time on Rikers is familiar with the term "bullpen therapy." The city's criminal justice system—driven by factors like the logistics of bringing inmates to court from the distant environs of Rikers, overcrowding, jammed dockets, and constant case delays—has raised the process to a form of torture.

The term emerged during the late 1980s and early 1990s, when the jail population hovered near twenty thousand. The influx of inmates was partly due to widely available cocaine that was cut with baking soda and cooked into little rocks. Crack was cheap and highly addictive and hit the city's neighborhoods like a tsunami.

"Crack had just arrived," recalled Richard Koehler, correction commissioner from 1986 to 1989. The police commissioner, "Ben Ward, who was a genius and one of the smartest guys I ever met, he said, 'I went out to California and they got this crack out there. It's crazy how many people are getting robbed or locked up and how many people shooting one another. It's going to come here. And we're not going to be able to handle it.'"

———

The ordeal of bullpen therapy begins with something called intake, or the journey from central booking to a bed on Rikers—a trail crisscrossed in red tape and delays that can take days. And then there are the court appearances. A typical trip to court begins as early as 4:00 a.m. and stretches through the day. Packed in fetid cells, detainees sit hour after hour in a sort of endless holding pattern. Violence sometimes erupts when, for example, rivals cross paths. Often as not, the expected court appearance is postponed. It's often dark by the time they get back to Rikers. It's not uncommon for detainees to simply refuse to go to court or even plead guilty to escape the misery.

On top of that, the criminal justice system defaulted to sending people arrested on low-level charges, often with substance abuse or mental health problems, to Rikers, meaning that detainees would be sent there again and again and again. This Kafkaesque torment became known as the Revolving Door.

—

PAUL WOOSTER, detained 2016: The biggest problem they have on the men's side is intake. The guards are so lazy, all the way up to the captains. It's so crowded. Legally you must have a bed, or housing as they call it, within twenty-four hours. But you can go as long as nine to eleven days. That's on the highest end, but at least four or five without getting a bed, which is unheard of anywhere else. That's like you're going back to archaic times. You're in a dungeon essentially. We used to call it the seven chambers of hell because you go from one room to another to another and don't get anywhere. Basically you just suffer.

VALERIE YOUNGBLOOD, public defender, 1982 to 1996: What really was particularly awful with the misdemeanor population was practically everybody had bails set on them. I mean $250, $200. I mean $500 was actually kind of high, but it didn't matter. It could have been $5,000 because these folks, who were largely substance-abusing offenders, didn't have $200, didn't have $500.

And so these poor people, mostly men, would sit on Rikers and inevitably take pleas because they had been sitting there long enough that they could essentially get time served.

And going up with the prosecutor to the bench, I was saying, this is ridiculous. The offense was nothing, like a criminal trespass, let's say. But the prosecutor said, "He got five days last time. And so he has to get ten days this time, or ten last time and fifteen this time." It was like some sort of formulaic approach to prosecution. It was just ludicrous. And he said to me, "Well, what's the difference to you, between ten and fifteen days?" I said, "Why don't you spend an extra five days on Rikers Island and see if you come up with that same question?"

PAUL WOOSTER: So one place will be 90 degrees, and there'll be like sixty men in a ten-by-twenty with a toilet that completely overflows with crap on the floor. It's really inhumane, and you'll have to sleep there for twenty-four hours in those conditions. And it can be either 90 degrees or 20 degrees. It depends what season. And then you'll sit there for a day, and then they'll move you to another. They'll actually take your picture, which is one part of fifty things they have to do to get [you to] your house, and you think you're getting somewhere, but you'll sit there and it'll be a fifty-by-fifty. It's a bigger cell and it'll be ice cold if the other one was hot and there'll be a hundred men. It's just crazy.

ROBERT GANGI, director, Correctional Association, 1982 to 2011: When you think about it, that is out-fucking-rageous. Some people were held three or four days in these really harrowing conditions. No phone call. No ability to change clothes, wash yourself, brush your teeth, often no real accommodations for any kind of thing that approached comfortable sleeping. And often the toilets and sinks weren't working. They were clogged up. And often there was vermin and the places stank. The lights weren't working, and these were people not just presumed innocent; they weren't even officially charged with a crime. Part of it was that nobody cared and nobody was watching.

PAUL WOOSTER: You're supposed to get three trays [of food] a day no matter what, any prison or jail in the country. Well, they're so backed up and they're lazy. They won't feed you for four days sometimes. And if they do feed you—I've seen them [do this] at least ten times on ten separate occasions—they will feed you through the hole in the cell. It'll be like forty men waiting for food, and they'll put a gloved hand through the cell door with a piece of fish and people have to fight to grab that. Then they'll put water in those plastic gloves and hand the water through the hole. That's been going on for a long time. They've been doing this for years.

No medication, either. I've heard men who are sixty or seventy years old and they are sitting there with me for three or four days and they have like a heart condition and they can't get their nitro and they're fucking screaming to a captain who's walking by and they literally ignore you hundreds of times in a row.

VALERIE YOUNGBLOOD: When I was a misdemeanor lawyer, primarily a misdemeanor lawyer, I was in the AP5 courtroom. And the sign over the judge was "In Go We Rust." The *d* and the *T* had fallen off. And nobody ever fixed it. Then in the back were what they so charmingly called the pens, like they were describing animals. And the court officers wrote stuff on the walls that was really offensive.

One of the worst things I saw firsthand was the "Sub BAPU." There were different levels of storing people once they'd been brought to the courthouse and the DA had done the papers. There was BAPU, the Brooklyn Arraignment Processing Unit, below the first floor of the courthouse where various paperwork and other stuff was done.

But then there was Sub BAPU, where they went initially and would be kept for days. The first time I went there, the stench of urine and feces and body odor was gagging. People were half dressed, basically on top of each other. It was worse than how animals are treated.

ROBERT CRIPPS, retired warden, 1983 to 2013: I was the tour commander on the boat that was moored on Rikers Island. So, you know, the increase in the population [during the crack years] was dramatic. And twenty-two thousand prisoners in New York City alone was a huge population.

[Crack addicts] throwing up all over the place. Being locked up, it was better for them. 'Cause they would eventually break the addiction. Unfortunately, when they were released six months later, they would go right back. I remember one inmate came in and I'm looking at his rap sheet. It was like a book. We took his rap sheet in AMKC [Anna M. Kross Center], which has the longest intake area of any facility, and we stretched his rap sheet from one end all the way to the other. I mean it must've been like fifty feet long or more. And that's how many times he was arrested. How crazy is that? Talk about a revolving door.

GREG BERMAN, co-founder, Center for Court Innovation: I moved to New York in 1992, and I was doing this fellowship called the Coro Fellowship. One of my assignments was to work for this guy, John Feinblatt, who was planning the Midtown Community Court.

He assigned me to sit in the holding cells in Midtown North and Midtown South [Precincts] and interview people who had just been arrested on misdemeanor offenses to ascertain what their social service needs were. This was my first exposure to criminal justice in New York City. And it was an eye-opening experience for me because so much of what I learned in my civics textbooks turned out not to be true.

In those days, Times Square was the misdemeanor capital of the world. They were making these busts all the time. The thing that hits you in the face is race. Almost everyone I talked to was Black or Hispanic. I think that I went in expecting to see really hardened dudes that were engaged in serious criminal mischief. That's not who these people were.

You could just talk to them for two seconds and see that these were homeless individuals. These were drug-addicted individuals. These were mentally ill individuals. And it was that experience that made me want to go work on creating alternatives to incarceration for people.

ERVIN "EASY" HUNT, detained, various stints, 1970s to 2010s: My recidivism went from 1970 to 2010. My recidivism rate was just like going to school. I kept going back and forth. I've gone back and forth to Rikers from the age of eighteen between the drugs and things of that nature. Rikers, the familiarity of it for me was HDM, the first building on Rikers Island. That was the House of Detention for Men. And it just smelled of death. It was just like, in my spiritual mind, I could hear the voices of death. You know what I mean?

So at eighteen, my first time, you only do two-thirds of your time, depending on what you get sentenced to. If you get thirty days, you only have to do twenty. When I saw that it wasn't anything like I imagined, I said this is nothing. I can do this. I can do this over and over and over and over. There was no fear factor.

I became affected in so many other ways behind my recidivism, you know what I'm saying? I wonder if had I not been part of that time in my life, of that round and round and round and round and round, what kind of person would I be today?

Ervin "Easy" Hunt cycled in and out of Rikers many times before finding his way. He used to perform his comedy to get by.

GREG BERMAN: Part of the time I had the opportunity to sit on the bench with a judge in Manhattan Criminal Court at 100 Centre Street to observe how these cases were handled. Again, it just kind of upset the preconceived notions that I had. These rose-colored notions based on *To Kill a Mockingbird* or civics textbooks of what criminal court was like, because what I expected to see was something like Gregory Peck giving impassioned speeches on behalf of their client. Prosecutors arguing about the harm done to the community. Judge Learned Hand weighing these arguments.

That's not the reality of 100 Centre Street or Schermerhorn Street or any of the other places. What I saw instead was no one wanted to spend any time on the cases. They wanted to adjudicate them as quickly as they possibly could. There was an underlying assumption I felt, and in some cases I felt this was true even of the defense bar, that if you were there, rather than there being a presumption of innocence, there's a presumption of guilt that you must've been a fucking knucklehead and done it if you were stupid enough to get caught.

At that point, you were seeing a lot of misdemeanor defendants sentenced to Rikers Island for five days, ten days, fifteen days, twenty days, twenty-five days, and it's those types of sentences that were useless on any metric. They were useless as incapacitation 'cause you were taking people off the streets for a minimal amount of time. They were beyond useless as deterrent. And they were beyond useless as rehabilitation. Nothing happens on Rikers Island that points in that direction and particularly over the course of a week or two. And so really those kinds of cases were what struck a chord with me.

ERVIN "EASY" HUNT: I sent my sister something for an anniversary or something. Something jail-made. And she said, "Don't send me nothing. I don't want my name on anything going to jail or coming from jail. You come home? It's a different story. But while you are doing this shit that you're doing, don't send me nothing." My sister has always provided me with that tough love and clarity. You want to do that shit, you go ahead, but you keep this shit away from me and my children. And she was adamant about that.

GREG BERMAN: My friend Alex Calabrese, who would go on to be the judge of the Red Hook Community Justice Center, complained to me one day, "I feel like I'm handing out a life sentence to these people, but I'm doing it thirty days at a time." And that really spoke to the revolving-door nature. He was operating out of Schermerhorn Street at the point we had the conversation. Even in a busy urban courthouse, like Schermerhorn Street, he was seeing the same people over and over again. And just the futility of that.

ERVIN "EASY" HUNT: The worst part about going to jail is what we call bullpen therapy, where you go from a bullpen to another bullpen, waiting area to waiting area to waiting area, from the precinct to the courts/central booking. Central booking, or just moving to court. If you don't get released from court, you go back downstairs, and then the bus comes in.

I know a few people who copped out [pleaded guilty] because of bullpen therapy. And then, if your case was something that you decided you wanted to fight, you know, the bullpen therapy would happen every day. If you were on Rikers, you had to get up at the crack of dawn to go downstairs, eat, to wait in the bullpen for the bus to come to take you to the court, put you in a bullpen, put you in a bullpen, and put you in a bullpen, so it wasn't something I liked doing. The bullpen therapy would work on you.

NESTOR EVERSLEY, detained, various stints, 1969 to 2010s: It's 5:00 a.m., we were going to court, and I got anxiety going into the bus, and you might be the last ones and you go into a cage. You always imagine the worst things, like you're in the cage in the bus and the bus crashes, you locked up in the bus. If you have a considerate guard, he might open the gate. If you have a guard saying, "I'm going for me first," you dead.

I know it sounds crazy, but these are the things that go through your mind. You go to court and go through the whole process, cell to cell, bus and bus, sleeping and lying on the floor. By the time you get back, your suit is crumpled up and you smell like shit, and you gotta go through the same thing the next day. I feel sorry for those guys. A lot of guys cop out to things they didn't do.

SPARKLE DANIEL, detained 2014: When I went to court in 2014, I got searched, waited for the bus, and I'm in the pen area and someone is puking on the floor. And someone hasn't taken a shower in like two weeks. You never know who you are going to get cuffed next to. And I'm like, "Please God, don't let me be handcuffed next to this person." You get to the courthouse and sit in the garage for another hour waiting to get inside. They call your name and wait one by one. They put you in another bullpen and another bullpen. The toilet is nasty. They have this little bench. There's writing all over the wall. It's disgusting. You don't want to touch anything. You just want to stand. And you're literally there from seven in the morning until five in the afternoon.

Whenever I go to court, I feel embarrassed. Being a female and I'm always handcuffed. Wondering what my lawyer is thinking. Even when the bus is moving, I turn my head. I just turn away.

ROBERT GANGI: The cells were so crowded that the guys could barely move. They were all standing packed in like sardines or like cattle. And I remember Katrina vanden Heuvel, the publisher/editor of *The Nation,* was on the Correctional Association board and she came with us on that trek and she walked down the hall ahead of me. And she literally was so startled she stepped back. And when I went there to see, the men could not move. They were almost all Black men. The racism was so stark in terms of who was locked up in these facilities.

THOMAS CINQUEMANI, retired correction officer, 1983 to 2003: That's where your problems begin. If me and you committed a crime, I'm in one jail and you're in another and you're snitching on me. And the only way for me to get out is to hurt you or kill you. The best part is when I see you in the courts; it's going to be in the pens, and if nobody knows about it and we merge somehow, that's where your problem is. That's where you get cut or stabbed. So the courts are very dangerous. That's where you have your contracts. If I can't get to you, somebody else will get to you before me. There was hospital runs every day. It was just an everyday occurrence. Like driving your car every day.

EDDIE ROSARIO, detained 1990: It highlights the dehumanizing process. That's a concentrated aspect of it. The banality of evil, which is not some monster or some dramatic thing. It's an everyday thing that happens, and you normalize it. When you go to court, that's a concentrated form of banality. When you go to court, justice is a conveyor belt. When you are going to court from the outside, it's different.

While you are detained, every section of that conveyor belt that is created, that really brings home how little you mean to the world. You're treated in a subhuman way in those twenty-four hours. A lot of times, you wouldn't get back until twenty-four hours later. You're in dehumanizing conditions. If there's a toilet, it's stopped up and overflowing with feces and piss and urine. The ground was moist with that smell, and it coated the inside of your nostrils. You were treated like shit.

You waited and waited and waited, and then, when you reached the end of the conveyor belt and if you had one or two minutes with a public defender, and if you had thirty to forty seconds in front of a judge, you felt you were fortunate, and then it's back on that conveyor belt of abuse.

SADAT X, hip-hop artist, detained 2006: The court don't open basically until ten o'clock. So you just sitting in a cell with a whole bunch of other dudes waiting to go to court. It's tight in there, you understand? And it's just, man, you know, dudes is beefing about shit, and if somebody get up, you might lose your seat.

And then if you lose your seat and you can't hold it down, that's a scrap. And then, like, you might do all that and then not get called for court and they bring you back and maybe about five, six o'clock and now you miss chow. So you better hope that you got some food in your bucket or something or else you don't eat that night.

They not really rushing and trying to do shit for you. The guards work on their schedule. And if you just happened to miss dinner, then, yo, man, you missed dinner. You got to hold that. It ain't like you could get to your house and miss dinner and go tell the CO, yo, I miss dinner. They'll be like, yo, man, dinner'll come around tomorrow. You better catch that. Just like that.

HECTOR "PASTOR BENNY" CUSTODIO, Latin King leader, detained 1991 to 1994: I remember the DA bringing my pregnant wife and my mom in for a meeting, and they wanted me to inform on a whole bunch of people. They brought them inside the bullpen. I get up and walk toward the gate to speak with them and the lawyer. When I get back, my seat was gone. The guy said you have to fight for it, and I fought for my seat and I got it back.

SOFFIYAH ELIJAH, executive director, Alliance of Families for Justice: Bullpen therapy is, think of it this way, you torture people until they say exactly what you want them to say. Okay, so the experience of going to Rikers is a nightmare, right? A nightmare in real time and you don't have the power to wake up and make that nightmare go away. And your very survival day in and day out is figuring out how to navigate that nightmare, from not being harmed by other residents and not being harmed by the staff.

And so you are brought to court every six to eight weeks. And then your case gets adjourned for another six to eight weeks, and another six to eight weeks, and another six to eight weeks. Eventually, you figure it out that if you're being offered, say, a plea to time served, or even a plea if it's going to require state prison time. That means you'll get off Rikers Island and go upstate, where you kind of roll the dice to see if you get a better setting instead of a very loose area. So people will plead guilty, whether they're innocent or not, or whether or not they had a really strong defense for their case, just to get out of that absolute nightmare experience; that's bullpen therapy.

NESTOR EVERSLEY: In these bullpens, some of us was going through withdrawals. You were detoxing. I used to ball up in the corner and I would vomit and everything.

JAMES MCGOVERN, retired correction captain, 1984 to 2004: I had one slashing on my bus. We were taking these guys back one day from Queens court and it was two guys in the back. I had heard that one guy had a bad day in court, and he literally took a fucking razor and he fucking cut this other kid's face up. After an investigation was completed, they said there was really no beef. The guy had just had a bad day in court and the kid had looked at him the wrong way.

LAWRENCE HENAGIN, detained several times, 2000s: I used to hate going to court because the COs would separate you, based on what borough you're going to, but then they would have to separate the Bloods and the Crips. They would open the bullpen that had the Bloods in it. Then they would go away for a couple minutes. Then they would open the bullpen where the Crips were at and call one guy out, tell him, "Yo, go stand over there."

And when he would go over there, of course the Bloods are watching him and the door is open. As soon as the CO turns his back, they run out and jump on him and they [the COs] would let the guy get beat up and then they'd call their emergency response and break it up. And then, when everything got calmed down a half hour later, they would do the same thing to a Blood. They would open the Crips' bullpen and then open the Bloods' bullpen and pull one guy out and tell him, go stand over there, and he'd get beat up.

I think it was just rec [for the COs] and if they get hurt on the job and it's because of a fight, that's time they don't have to make up on their pension. They would sit back and watch this happen. And then, you know, after a few minutes they would pull the pin and get their response and break it up and then lock everybody down, get their porters to clean up the blood and everything, send the guy to the hospital, and I guess whatever they did when they write their report. My thing was, it can't just happen every time I go to court. So it had to be happening on other days. And how was the brass allowing that to happen? But they allowed it to happen.

JAMES MCGOVERN: I remember years ago in the Brooklyn court pens at night doing a sweep, picking up new admissions out of the court to go to Rikers. The fucking noise level was crazy. I told him we're taking new guys back to Rikers. A Spanish guy came out. I just looked at him and we were late and I don't know if he was a new admission or a court return. And I just said to him, "Stop for a minute. Take your jacket off." He takes his jacket off. "Put your hands on the wall." I frisked him. I go knock on his pants, and there's a huge metal rod and it's fucking in the back of his pants. Now we were fucking late. I know the captain didn't want to call the fucking thing in and didn't want to do the paperwork.

I said to the guy, what the fuck are you doing with this? He goes, "Oh, I found this when I was being transported." He picked it up in the yard, and they didn't search him? I'm like, oh my fuck. It was like a fucking piece of hard metal. I just took it and I fucking put it in the back of my pocket and took these guys out. Nobody else saw it. I saw the officer, and I go, "Dude, what the fuck, man, I got this guy, he had this in his pocket." And this is what you dealt with. You basically had to have an extra set of eyes at all times.

JOHN BOSTON, retired director, Legal Aid Prisoners' Rights Project: Pretrial incarceration as a way of pressuring people to take a plea seems to me is the fundamental condition of the New York City criminal justice system. That's sort of just the way things are. Lots of people have talked about pleading guilty just to bring it to an end. I don't think any prosecutor sits down and says, this guy, let's see if we can wear him down. It's just universal and pervasive.

It seemed to me that [this was] the real issue. Limiting pretrial detention limits the bargaining power of DAs. If you're out on the streets, you could wait the DA out. If you're in jail, if you're in the city jails, then really the pressure's on you and not on the DA. So, bail reform is a significant shift, all else being equal, in bargaining power from prosecution to defense to limit pretrial detention, which obviously is one reason why prosecutors are against it.

SOFFIYAH ELIJAH: Criminal defense lawyers and anyone who's been a defendant who's come through the city jail system know about it very clearly. DAs count on it. In fact, their whole plea negotiation shifts if they know that your client is waiting, awaiting disposition of their case at Rikers, as opposed to if they're out on bail and released on their own recognizance. How are they spending all the time? They play more hardball when they have a defendant who's being held because they know that someone becomes more and more desperate the longer they're held. And the likelihood that they'll take a plea to get out of that situation is increased significantly. That's why the DAs fight so hard to have people held on bail. It's easier for them to ultimately get a conviction whether the person is guilty or not.

JOHN BOSTON: I don't think anybody in the Department of Correction is purposely inflicting bullpen therapy. I'm not sure how much the court process can be streamlined other than adding fewer people. When they had twenty-two thousand people or fifteen thousand people or ten thousand people, the number of people that they were putting through a real sort of needle's eye to get out to court and back in every day and also the sheer difficulty of getting from Rikers Island to anywhere is, I think, even in the best of circumstances, oppressive and time-consuming.

MICHAEL JACOBSON, correction commissioner, 1995 to 1997: This issue drove me out of my mind. Because we were always under pressure to get people to court by nine. And then what would happen is, especially [in] those days, when it was so many more people, it's a huge effort to get people to court by nine.

A huge number of them, they'd never see a judge, and then

they'd get back at, whatever, nine o'clock at night. And New York courts were at least then, and I'm sure it's still true, incredibly slow. Back then the average number of court appearances for a felony case was something like twelve. You should never need twelve appearances to dispose of a felony case, especially since the great majority of them are your basic bread-and-butter standard. And it's especially horrible when people are in jail, right? Because you're bringing people down twelve times for the pendency of their case. And you could imagine after a couple of times, you're getting pretty fucking grouchy if you're one of the people that's happening to, and I always totally got that.

EDDIE ROSARIO: After a twenty- to twenty-four-hour experience, I used to sleep for a day or two. I had to be in a numb state. I didn't think about anything. I didn't feel anything. You felt like shit. Half the time you went to court, I wouldn't see a public defender. He or she wouldn't show up. They would say you're going back on the return, and I would have to go through all of that, the smell of shit, the sandwiches, the smell of sweaty bodies stacked together. Smell is the sense most directly connected to your brain. It leaves an indelible mark. It's almost like a hangover, like the worst you ever had in your life.

MICHAEL JACOBSON: I'm sure it was then and is still now related to some amount of violence. It's just a horrible process even to go through once. They get up that early, do all that shit, get to the court, stay there and not see anyone, sit in the holding cell, get back at nine o'clock, and then in three weeks do it again. So that's a gigantic issue. It was and still is a ludicrous process. Both the times it takes to dispose of cases, the number of appearances, and the number who aren't seen when brought down to the court. You add all three of them together and you have a system hugely in need of reform.

ERVIN "EASY" HUNT: One time, my sister asked some of the family members who was okay with me coming up for Thanksgiving. Everybody said okay except my great-niece. She said no, for me not to come up, and then she changed her mind and said, "It's okay. You can do it." I took her in my sister's den. I said, "Why did you say it wasn't okay for me to come up?" She said, "Because you always leave us, you always leave us." And I took her meaning just a step further: she meant [I was] always leaving *her.*

She was sixteen then. She's twenty-six now. And I promised her that day that I would never leave her again. And you know, she said to me, this year, she said, "You kept your promise." So those are the things that recidivism has done to me and for me.

RACE

"It's a Different Type of Plantation Mentality"

The vast majority of people held in the jails are Black or Hispanic. Correction officers are more than 50 percent Black or Hispanic, and just over half are women. But the top leadership has been mostly white. These inherent fault lines always linger just below the surface on Rikers and often erupt in plain sight.

The island itself has a tortured racial history going back 160 years. The New York City recorder Richard Riker, a relative of the family who sold the island to the city, presided over the practice of sending escaped slaves snatched on the streets of the city back to plantations in the South. Free Black people were also brutally forced into slavery in this way.

At the same time, Rikers Island was where at least two all-Black Union army regiments mustered and trained in 1864 before distinguishing themselves on Civil War battlefields; until leading Black clergy intervened, however, some of the first Black recruits were swindled and "thrust into old and worn cotton tents . . . and compelled to sleep on the bare earth," according to a Union League Club report that year.

—

HILTON WEBB, detained 1989 to 1991, 1996 [relevant to this anecdote, Webb is Black]: I had to go to court on this day. So they searched me. They said, "Okay, Webb, it's time to get on the bus. Just single cuff him, he's one of our guys." So they single cuff me. I get on the bus and they used to drive you like they were going to court, except every once in a while they take you to a garage for an additional search.

They do that with the "Ninja Turtles" [Emergency Services]. There was twenty-three of us on the bus. And you'll see why I remember the number in a minute. They strip-searched us on some blankets on the floor. They put everybody back on the bus, and I'm the last one. And one CO says, "How many people we got?" Another CO answers, "We got twenty-three pieces of shit."

The CO says, "Put them on the bus." Twenty-two guys get on the bus and I'm standing there. CO says, "Get on the fucking bus. Get the fuck on the bus." I don't move. He says, "So what's your fucking problem?" I said, "My mother didn't raise any shit." He says, "What?" I said, "My mother didn't raise any shit. My name is Hilton Webb." I recite my ID number. "And you can call me either one of those and I'll get on the bus, but I'm not a piece of shit." So the cop gets right up in my face. He's got the fucking black fatigues on, and the fucking nightstick. He says, "We will kill you." And I said, "Probably, but I still won't get on the bus."

The other cop says, "Webb, just get the fuck on the bus." I said, "Excuse me, Officer, I have to get on the bus." The guy glares at me. And he just moves out the way and I get on the bus.

I had enough intuition to know that if I showed any weakness, they were going to beat me. They are going to leave the little guys alone because they're not going to fight anyway. But a guy my size, if they decided to whip on me, they're going to whip on me for a while because they figure I can take it.

When I got back off the bus, they had set up a gauntlet. I was so scared. I covered the scared with bravado, you know? I was like, motherfucker, just take these cuffs off. We can do this shit right here. I'm sweating it. I'm scared to fucking death, but I'm not gonna lie down. Because if you accept it, they win.

In the early 1990s, Hilton Webb spent two years in Rikers, where his imposing size was a blessing and a curse.

FAT JOE, hip-hop artist: You talking to a guy with forty guys, maybe thirty-five of them got killed by the time I was twenty-one, twenty-two. It was much more normal to go to a young person's funeral than to go to an eighty-year-old person's funeral. It's simple as that. And so, everybody went to jail. Everybody went to jail. Were there good people in jail? Yes. Did they have to go to jail? Can we get them programs to really rehabilitate themselves or make them feel like they're special and they deserve and they belong? That's been the argument of people who's been trying to be peacekeepers in the community forever.

You give a kid some sort of encouragement, incentive to make it, and they'll make it. But if you on them immediately, put them in Spofford [juvenile detention], put them in Rikers Island, harass them, they're going to be a product of the environment.

There's the school-to-jail pipeline. I grew up in the projects [in the South Bronx] and in New York, it's gladiator type—prey, predator. The construction, the actual architecture of the projects, the architecture of the public school system in the inner city . . . I never got to be in Rikers, thank God, but when I used to go visit friends, the same architecture.

And so when you in there, it's a familiarity with the projects that you call home, that you grew up in. It's the same design, minus that men stay with men, females stay with females. But it's the same design. It's the same.

I can't prove that. I didn't do studies, but it's the familiarity. If you grew up in the suburbs, in a mansion, and now you gotta live in the hood, you'd be like, "What is this?" But if you grow up in the projects and the public school system and then go to Rikers Island, it almost feels like no big deal. It feels like, oh, we know this setting. I'm willing to bet that the same architect designed all three things.

AUTHORS: *Yeah, if you go out to a New York City Housing Authority development in the Rockaways where they made balconies along the hallways with the metal screens.*

FAT JOE: You can go to Webster Avenue in the Bronx for that. They got the gates. That's what I'm trying to explain. That's in every borough. It's in Newark, New Jersey. That's how Cabrini-Green was set up. I'm telling you I was *born* in Rikers Island. That's what I'm trying to tell you.

LATANYA JONES, detained 1980s, early 2000s: I still have a lawsuit with these people. I knew something was wrong, intuitively. They were searching [the dorm setting] and they'd go row by row and ruin everything. They would march you into the restroom area, and each woman would take a stall and have you stripped naked in front of like nine or twelve officers, and the ceiling is aluminum, so if you look up, you see everyone. If you look across, there are mirrors; you see everyone to your left, to your right. They'd go, "Spread!" And it was horrible, horrible, horrible.

They would deliberately make us stand there for long periods of time. I felt so vulnerable. And I felt traumatized. I felt traumatized for our people. And I'm talking about the Jewish people and the Black people. I was like, this is how it must have felt being marched into those gas chambers and being on the block, the auction block, and just standing there. I kept saying this is wrong. They'd say, "Sue us! Call your lawyer!" So I did. I made a complaint, like right before I was leaving, because I was afraid of repercussions. And it's still pending. I made sure to note with dates and names and everything because it was wrong. It was just wrong.

LAWRENCE HENAGIN, detained several times, 2000s: In December 2002, I had a car accident and I was burned over 29 percent of my body, my face, my arm, I got burns all over. Luckily, I went to Weill Cornell Burn Center and they took very good care of me. The car that I was driving, once I wrecked it, the guy called it in stolen. So I ended up being arrested while I was in a coma. They put handcuffs on me while I was in a coma. In February, when I came out of the coma, I found out I had a case for unauthorized use of a motor vehicle, a misdemeanor, but I was also on parole.

On one leg, they had just cut out a burn that wasn't healing. Where they cut the burn out, they had put metal stitches there. So for some reason when I get arrested and go to Rikers Island, they put me in the Beacon [the George R. Vierno Center], which is mostly a Blood house, one of the gang houses.

It was a pain in the ass for me because the Beacon is all metal detectors down the hallway and you have to pass through every one of them. And I have metal stitches. So every one I go through, it rings and I'm trying to tell them, I got metal stitches. I took my pants down, whatever they wanted me to do. I was actually getting harassed. And at that time I wasn't in the mood. I wasn't in any condition to actually fight with the police because my hand here still wasn't fully healed.

I was the only white guy in the block. It was Spanish and Bloods. They had control of everything. I got pushed around and the cops smacked me around because I'm trying to explain to them about going through these metal detectors. Eventually, I'm telling them, "Look, man, fuck you. I'm not going through this shit no more." I told everybody and it happened to be a female at one [metal detector]. I said, "You want me to pull my pants down and show you the cut?" And she took it as a disrespect and they were

Black. They didn't beat me up too bad, but you know, three or four of the cops got me hemmed up on a wall and smacked me around. I can't really fight. I know that if I do fight, I'm going to probably tear my stitches up. And I'm still in a lot of pain. So I just took their little punches and I got through it.

And wherever I was going, when you walk out of your house in the Beacon and you get to the main hallway, there's all these metal detectors that you gotta go through. The officer is walking with me from point A to point B. I haven't had contact with anybody. I get through the first metal detector and explain what's going on. Why do I gotta go through all the rest of them? And they say, "That's the point. That's the point." They told me that Rikers Island was a Black man's world. And they said, "Welcome to the Black man's world."

RONNY DRAYTON, musician and father of former detainee Donovan Drayton: Some of the COs, this shit that these people were doing was just unbelievable, to their own people, which is really bad. You're doing it to your own people. These are Black people, Latino people, very few white guys on deck with them. It was really interesting just to watch just how condescending you can be to your own people.

At AMKC [Anna M. Kross Center], I had been going to that jail forever [to see Donovan]. But there was a new captain on, a woman. I remember I got through all the searches, and when I got to the last search at the jail, she was standing at the thing to put your shoes through. For some reason something buzzed on my pants. It turns out I had some foreign coins in my pocket. It was German coins because I was flying in from all over the world to come see him. So she gets there and I said, well, miss, excuse me. You know, I don't want to hang up the line, but I don't understand what this is.

She's standing there. Fine. I'm gonna go through my pockets and turn my pockets out for you. Fine, sir, you do that. Make sure you do that. And I said, and this is my cocky mouth, I said, ma'am, do you have a proper way that you would like for me to do that?

She said to me, Mr. Drayton, please don't come at me with your eloquent, intelligent bullshit. I already know how smart you are.

Whoa. Where did you get that from? I take my pockets out and I reached down in the little side pocket. It was guitar picks. She said, well, what are you having guitar picks in your pocket for? And it's ironic she said that, and the CO next to her said, "Captain, the guy's famous. He's a famous guitar player from Queens. He's played with everybody in the freakin' world, Cap. He's not bringing anything in here. He knows better. I took all the money out of his pockets. It's in the tray. His watch is off. His bracelets are off. He always carries a bunch of bracelets. He's got even less bracelets on today." I only had two. Took them off. I took off all this shit on my neck, everything. The captain says, "Well, he should have been gone [kicked out]. There's a pick in here. There could be a weapon."

I said, "Cap, from me to you, here's some pictures of my last tour." She took them in her hand like they were poisoned, and then she threw them in the garbage can.

So I get through the door. Now, you go over to the desk, you sign in. They tell you if your detainee is ready to come down. And they also let you know if there's anything going on in the jail. 'Cause you know sometimes you can be sitting there 'cause there's other shit going on in the jail and in AMKC was always something going on, somebody getting cut. They tell me, "Oh, okay, Mr. Drayton, you got to put your stuff in a locker."

Okay, take my stuff, put it in the locker. The next thing I know, I got another search. I'm sick. Everybody else's got through and now I'm just standing there. I take my shoes off. She says, "Why did you take your shoes off?" So I said, well, I did want to make it easier for you because the time is getting short. There's another crew of people. "I didn't tell you to take your shoes off. Put your shoes back on." Yes, ma'am. "I didn't tell you to stand up. Go sit back down." Yes, ma'am. I put my shoes back on. Sat down. I sat there. She says, "You look mighty comfortable. Didn't I just tell you to stand up and take your shoes off?"

I said, no, ma'am, I don't recall that. She says, "Well, you need to pay attention." I got up, took my shoes off first, and stood up.

"So make sure you untie the laces too." I said, ma'am, why should I untie the laces? So I untied the laces, no problem. Sit there again. "Sir, I want you to open your pants up," do this and that, whatever. I said, here we go, here we go. So I opened my pants up. She comes down, she puts her hand around like this, but she doesn't just do that. She puts her hands down into my pants and I'm not saying anything. I have a complete poker face. I'm sitting here straight looking forward. I don't say anything and she's got like a half smile. I'm not saying anything. I'm just smiling. Another female CO says, you must really be enjoying this.

I looked at her. I said, not like I could if I was with both of you doing this at the same time. She started laughing so hard. The one that was messing with me stopped messing around with me. She said, "Get the fuck out of here." She let me go through.

EDDIE ROSARIO, detained 1990: It's really strange for me because I'm a light-skinned Puerto Rican. I never get mistaken for white by white people. You must have some kind of radar. But my own people often mistake me as white. People [in Rikers] would ask me, "What are you?" My public defender. A CO. There's this guy who sounds Puerto Rican who's light-skinned. People would say, just tell them you're white. But growing up, my father was heavily involved in my education, and we would get Puerto Rican history. So my reflex action would always be to say I'm Puerto Rican. When I would say that, then I would be treated differently.

I saw it from a different vantage point. Many of the officers are Black or Latino, and it's unfortunate because they are often worse. At Rikers, it's more of an internalized oppression. These are guys who work at Rikers who are from the same communities who were acting like a white racist would act.

RON KUBY, defense attorney: One part of the Rikers awfulness historically, and even today, is simply institutional racism. That is to say in the '80s, you still had an overwhelmingly white prison staff, corrections officers guarding an overwhelmingly Black and Latino group of people. That was true in the '70s, and even truer in the late '60s. Now some of that changed in the sense that the corrections officers increasingly came from the very communities that they were policing, but even today, even in 2020, the brass, the people who actually give the orders, remain overwhelmingly white. So that was one problem. And that problem persisted to this day.

The other problem is just inherent in the nature of a penal institution that doesn't receive any meaningful oversight. You take a group of people and you give them virtually full control over another group of people. They will do bad things. Not all of them, not all of the time, not even most of them most of the time. But if there is no real accountability, short of beating somebody to death, and sometimes not even then, the institutions, the surroundings, the culture, permit people's worst impulses to rise to the fore.

So if you tend to be a controlling and somewhat abusive person by nature, you have a perfect outlet for your controlling abuse in a penal system, especially at a place like Rikers. If you're basically a good person, but you're having a really, really, really bad day, you have the opportunity to take that out on prisoners. And Rikers permits people, the corrections officers, to be as bad as they can be without any meaningful oversight or disciplinary process, because the courts both state and federal have given so much discretion to prison authorities. And look, I don't think that there's any group of people drawn from the ranks of anywhere who will do well as a group with that type of power over other humans.

HILTON WEBB: I've had this told to me by COs that I became relatively friendly with, who said our job is to watch you, and if we can create friction, we win because if there's friction, you can't get together. So as long as we're fighting each other, and this is the mantra I used to tell [other detainees], as long as we got me hating you because you're Spanish, and you hating me because I'm Black, they win, man. And they don't care.

The people they go after are the people who can unite people, the leaders. So if they got a leader and he's in their pocket, he's going to keep his people chill. If there's a riot, they go to him. They talk. Things quiet down. But as long as they keep the Kings fighting the Ñetas, and the Ñetas fighting the whatever other fucking group there is, the Bloods and the Crips, they sow dissent.

At Rikers, they actively do things to create problems. Like you have a system where you have people with no money and they give everybody phone calls. You have these free phone calls for a day. What do you think is going to happen? So the guy with cigarettes is going to be able to talk on the phone all fucking day. The cops don't run the phones. They let the gangs run the phones. So there was a Blood phone and there was like three other phones. There was a Crip phone. They usually didn't have Bloods and Crips in the same house, but there was a Black phone, a Muslim phone, a Spanish phone. Like I said, as long as I'm fighting you because you're white and you're fighting me because I'm Black, who's in charge? The guards are in charge.

EDDIE ROSARIO: One of the things that scared me the most was this whole loss of the rule of law. When you walk into a place where your body is owned by the state and anything you do is owned by these people, when you see them acting worse than the people incarcerated, there is no law. There is just a jungle.

When I was there in the early 1990s, the COs fed into that. The COs would instigate problems between people who are incarcerated to control them better. That was the scariest thing—watching them betting on fights between incarcerated people, letting them run the telephone, and just kind of trading off on that. I helped investigate Attica and Clinton [state prisons] and I never saw the absence in the rule of law that I experienced in Rikers. It's been thirty years and I still think about it.

They had fight clubs where they would bet on who would win the fight. This is stuff you see in fucking movies. I couldn't believe that this was happening in a government-run institution. Their attitudes toward those who were incarcerated, some people who work in the field internalize the white supremacy. The dehumanizing process works on both sides. This was happening in Rikers. A CO would say, you Black like me, same neighborhood, you shouldn't have committed the crime.

There was a lot of internalized oppression. That's why I don't believe hiring would change how the system works, because you're part of the system. You could have a world with no racists, but if the system is put up in a certain way, racism will still exist.

LAWRENCE HENAGIN: I was raised in the projects in Indianapolis, and there was only like three white families in that area. So I was raised around Black guys, and I ran with them. In certain situations when I'm in jail, I carry myself a little bit different and so people know that I've been around Black guys. But because I had the accent, they don't have a clue where I'm from, but they know that I'm not from New York. So they say, "Oh, he's a fucking Klan guy." Those are usually the guys who are actually prejudiced themselves. And they try to cover it up by projecting onto somebody else. And I always get that because like I said, I'm an easy target.

Being from out of state, the first two times I was in Rikers Island, I knew very few people. After I had been there a few times, now you start seeing the same people over and over and over. But then what happens is once the Spanish guys see me, see that I'm going to fight for myself, they usually will get involved. Like, Latin Kings, they won't get involved unless whoever's supposed to be their leader will tell them to get involved. Most of the time, anytime that I've ever had a problem and I got somebody to actually come in and help me, it was always the Spanish guys. They won't do it until they actually see that you're going to fight for yourself. And sometimes they won't even, you know, actually get physical, but they'll break it up and get the guys off you. They'll say, look, you did enough damage.

JACQUELINE VELEZ, detained 1998: They would call us to go to different parts of the island to clean different spaces, 'cause some captains or whatever will have their own trailers. So they would have us go to those trailers and clean the shit out of them. But when they called [names to do this detail, it was] Figueroa, Rodriguez, Velez, Garcia—only the Spanish women. And I didn't understand that, you know what I mean? I'm like, why would they only call us? I don't know. It was just the weirdest thing. That's when I realized that Spanish people were known for that. Like, as cleaning ladies, right? In Manhattan, all these people hire Spanish cleaning ladies. Or they're working in hotels.

We were all of Spanish descent. It could have been Colombian, Brazilian, whatever, but we all share the same surnames. So thanks to Christopher Columbus.

RONNY DRAYTON: I've played all over the world, and it was, what's the best word? Demoralizing. But that's not even really what it is because as a Black man growing up in America, you're still always under the gun of this particular type of white perfection. Entitlement creates this white perfection that you need to meet a certain standard to be acceptable. So even if you're educated, even if you're successful, even if you play, you still look, on one level or another, like a nigger to them because you don't meet up to their social standard. Sometimes I used to go in there and really feel like I was nothing, just the walking dead.

The way they used to treat us sometimes was horrible. So what you played over there? Your son's a fucking murderer. Oh, you got a light-skinned kid too. He looks like he's a half-caste. Oh, you think you special 'cause you got a white woman and blah blah blah blah blah. All kinds of shit. So every chance they had to stick a dig in to reduce you, they did.

This is the shit that's really fucking crazy. Because most of the people that work in Rikers Island are all Black people. And they want to talk about all that shit about what the inmates are doing to them and all the rest. Well, maybe that has something to do with the way you are treating these people too. That you already know that they're in at a deficit. They're locked in a cage. How is the man supposed to be acting? How does an animal act coming into captivity now?

It's a different type of plantation mentality. 'Cause now Mister boss man got you working in the hot, taking everybody else through. So now you have to be more superior than the person you bringing in because that's that type of superiority where you just keep this mind dull. Malcolm used to talk to us about this all the time, about dulling the mind, thinking that a certain position of power makes you more powerful than the person who is at the deficit.

THOMAS CINQUEMANI, retired correction officer, 1983 to 2003: You'll laugh about this. Two weeks—it was a Wednesday—before my retirement [in 2003]. I'm feeling good. And I get a convict, a young kid, right? Cursing and screaming and carrying on.

And he called me his "white bitch" in front of twenty guys. Completely disrespected me.

I couldn't get to him fast enough before they went on the bus. Now I look at the books. The same twenty men are coming back with him. So here it is, two weeks later. I was very patient. I had my shirt off, my badge was off, and my sleeves were rolled up. I'm ready to go. I'm ready.

The Brooklyn bus comes in. Same guys from Brooklyn from two weeks ago. [I count off] two, four, six, eight, ten. I uncuff everybody. Officer can come back later. I know the Rikers bus is coming with the same individual from ARDC [Adolescent Reception and Detention Center].

I count two, four, six, eight, ten. Now I wait. The bus had gone. I grab the cuffs; I uncuff the guy I don't want. I say, "You, out." I said, "Mind your business." I look over at this kid. He was pale. I beat him for four hours straight. When I was done with him, the [other] convicts said, put him in here, we'll finish him off. I said, "No, that's my Black bitch." He [the detainee] was as quiet as a church mouse, and that was the end of that.

AUTHORS: *Four hours is a very long time. Are you sure it was four?*

THOMAS CINQUEMANI: Well, if you don't know what's going to happen . . . Every half an hour. And nobody came to help him. Nobody. He screamed. Nobody said two words. It was quiet, but he was screaming. I got tired. I took a break. I came back and I did it again. Remember the old James Cagney movies when you see the head in the toilet. I did that too with my Black bitch for the day.

AUTHORS: *So you put his head in the toilet?*

THOMAS CINQUEMANI: And flushed it over and over. That was my retirement gift.

AUTHORS: *And what kinds of injuries did he come away with?*

THOMAS CINQUEMANI: Nothing that could be seen. His pride was injured, and he would never do it twice. No hospital, no nothing. That was it. Nothing that could be seen.

That was my last day at the Department of Correction. I was gone that day.

AUTHORS: *Did he ask you to stop?*

THOMAS CINQUEMANI: Tell you something, he was a trouper. He was a tough kid. He was a tough kid. He was a tough kid.

AUTHORS: *And this happened in a cell?*

THOMAS CINQUEMANI: A cell ten by ten. That was it. The end of the day. That was it. That was my goodbye gift. I was leaving anyway.

I liked my job. It was me. I really enjoyed it. After twenty years, you became, like driving your car, a professional. It was easy for me. You had the look, you had the mind, you had the vocabulary, you knew what you were doing, and nobody would bother you. You had the world by your hand, even though it was a world nobody liked. I enjoyed getting up in the morning.

[We followed up with Cinquemani on this story shortly before publication and he adjusted one detail, estimating that the encounter had been spread over an hour.]

THOMAS CINQUEMANI: I flushed his head in the toilet more than once, and I hit him with enough force to let him know what he did was wrong. It went on for about an hour. He had no business saying what he said two weeks earlier. We had to teach him a lesson. You can't do that. That's in-house justice, it had to be done quietly. Back then it was seen as justifiable. I'd had the riot in 1986, which changed my whole outlook on life. You do change. You have to become part of your environment. I went from one extreme to the next. That was the job.

In the '80s and '90s, you became part of your environment. If you didn't grow into it you had to leave. If you have a problem with one inmate and you don't deal with it, you would have a problem with ten the next day. Those twenty [during the incident] who came in, knew what happened. They knew I had to do it. I did nothing wrong in my eyes, in their eyes. The punishment fit the crime.

GANGS

"Dude, That's a Latin King Tattoo on His Chest"

In the 1970s and early 1980s, gangs on Rikers were defined by borough or neighborhood identity, by colorful pulp-fiction-like names such as the Savage Skulls or the Black Spades, or by allegiance to one of the major narcotics organizations that operated throughout the city.

In the late 1980s and onward, a renegade member of the Latin Kings, which had roots in Chicago, formed a powerful offshoot in Rikers. Their power, in turn, spawned rivals like the Trinitarios, a largely Dominican gang, and then the ultimately much larger New York City version of the Bloods.

Driven by overcrowding and these new gangs, the numbers of stabbings and slashings in the jail skyrocketed—dozens of them a month. "It was wild, there was slashings and stabbings every day," said Sidney Schwartzbaum, who became a correction officer in 1979 and later led the union representing deputy and assistant deputy wardens. "They didn't make a big deal about it at the time. But the violence was out of control. It became a normal thing."

Very few of these bloody jail attacks were being prosecuted. "We had an inmate that two Latin Kings held down on the ground and they carved 'LK' into his back, and this was a Black kid," said Bernard Kerik, DOC commissioner from 1998 to 2000.

Kerik's aides told him the attackers were sent to "the Bing"—for up to ninety days. Kerik questioned why they weren't prosecuted.

"This goes back to their old motto: this is the way we've been doing it forever," Kerik said. "I said, 'They held this fucking kid down [and carved] his back. They give him a hundred stitches and they don't get charged?'"

The number of Bloods sets exploded through the 1990s well into the new century, and soon housing areas across the system were dominated by them. Their influence extended out of Rikers and into dozens of sets in neighborhoods across the city and elsewhere where they continue to be a force. A New York City version of the Crips also came on the scene.

The Correction Department struggled to control the stabbings, slashings, and broken bones these groups generated, along with other crimes like extortion, intimidation, bribery, and smuggling.

—

COLIN ABSOLAM, detained 1993 to 1996: This was 1993. I was sitting on my bed and I heard some rumbling. These guys, Ñetas, were jumping on this one guy and they were beating him up. They had a scrub brush with a long handle.

One guy had a sock with some batteries in it. He swung it at me. I sidestepped it and it hit the bed. I grabbed his arm and like the sock came out of his arm. I swung it back at him. It hit him, but the sock broke, and the batteries came out. One of the guys grabbed my legs, pulled me, I fell on the bed and kind of fell between the locker.

They were punching me. Emergency Response [Unit] came. When the ERU are running in the hallway, you hear the footsteps. They will drag the batons against the wall, or they'll hit it against the wall so people know they're coming.

They ran into the housing unit, broke it up, and took everyone that they saw that wasn't on their bed. They told us all to place our hands on the wall and just stand there. I remember I had my hands on the wall and they were walking down the lines and they was just snuffing guys, just punching guys out.

When they got to me, his arm was cocked ready to swing. I started to pretend to faint. And he said, "If you fall out, I will beat you until you wake the fuck up." They left me alone. They packed everyone up that was involved.

So they moved me into a housing unit downstairs. Word traveled. Because there are so many individuals in that gang, when something happens, it often involves them. One of the guys walked up to me and said, "Yo, what happened upstairs?"

By the time I could open my mouth to say, "What are you talking about?" he snuffed me. I fell. Then they moved me from there to another house. So I kept being moved and this was all within one night.

From that point on, from 1993 to 1996, until I made bail, every housing unit that I went into, there was a problem because word travels.

They communicate through the outside. They knew who I was, and everywhere I went, it was problems. I literally had to defend myself. It got to a point where I would walk into a housing unit and I would tell them, I'm not going in there.

The officer dragged me in there. I didn't even get a chance to put my bags down. Some of the guys rushed me. It was so many of them. And they didn't write them a misbehavior report or anything. They just took me out the house and brought me to another one. And this was going on for a few days. Eventually, I would get to a house unit door and I would see the guys. They wore beads. White beads, two red, and one black and then a cross. Ñetas. I made up my mind what I was going to do. The first one I saw, I punched him in the face. That would force them to move me. And they kept moving me and moving me. It was ongoing.

At one point, they sent me back to OBCC [Otis Bantum Correctional Center]. They surrounded me as if they were about to put some work in. A Muslim brother I called Aki stood up and told them, "Listen, we're not doing that in here." He said, "If you want to fight him one on one, you can go ahead, but we're not jumping him in here. And if y'all do that, then the Muslims are going to get involved." That's what pretty much stopped it there.

So that one incident, that's all it takes.

MARIO "MACHETE" PEREZ, detained 1970s, early 1980s: If you did time back in the '70s and '80s, it was a borough thing when I came through. There was no such thing as gangs. Brooklyn, Bronx, Queens, it was a borough thing. So once you fought, you got your name, and then comes the perks with that; you're able to go to commissary without someone coming and robbing you, sneak thieving you, because they know you're gonna fight. The Hispanics were called the Germans.

So the Black guys would call us Germans 'cause we hang out with Hispanic white people. That's where it comes from. We went from being "spics" to being Germans because a lot of us were hanging out with whites. For me, I was a renegade. White, Black, Chinese, I didn't care who you were as long as you was a man. If you rumbled, you was my man.

JAMES "SHAQUELL" FORBES, early Bloods member, detained 1990s: When I was in Rikers in 1982 [they had gangs like] the Crazy Homicides, Savage Skulls, Righteous Hell, La Familia, Savage Nomads, Unknown Bikers. I remember all of them. Back then, they didn't have uniforms in jail. So they wore outfits from the streets, motorcycle boots and leather jackets with their patches on it. On every last one, you always see "1369" with a swastika in the middle. We just started calling them the Germans. Just 'cause they got a swastika on their jackets, or a patch or a tattoo on their arm. I'm like, "Who the fuck are Germans? Have we been invaded?" "No, we just call them that 'cause they want to wear a swastika." That simple.

BARRY CAMPBELL, detained 1980s, 1990s: Back in the '80s and '90s, what they pretty much did was that they tried to separate people by boroughs because it wasn't about gangs during that time. There were a few gangs out, but they weren't as relevant as they are now. When you went into a house, people would tell you, Brooklyn's in the back, Queens in the middle, so-and-so Bronx's in the front, or whatever. And everything was set up and it pretty much was an honor system where the most violent in the house rule everything.

JAMES "SHAQUELL" FORBES: They'd beef on each other. Harlem would side with the Bronx, and Queens would side with Brooklyn, and then it would be an all-out situation, but there was nothing like the Bloods, Latin King/Ñeta war. It was a lot different.

SIDNEY SCHWARTZBAUM, retired deputy warden, union president, 1979 to 2016: You had the drug gangs when I started in '79, '80. There was the Muslims, the Five Percenters, and you would have the Savage Nomads and the Dirty Ones. They were the Hispanic gangs, and then they started to call themselves Germans. You know, they were allowed to have motorcycle boots back there, and they were wearing motorcycle jackets.

In '84, '85, there were stabbings and slashings [in the teen jail]. And when I came back in '88, it was like a war zone. When the Bloods and the Latin Kings became really big, that's when the stabbings and slashings went wild, and the crack epidemic was simultaneous to that.

The violence was out of control. We were averaging fifty, sixty slashings a month. It became routine. A guy gets slashed, we would do a search, we would transfer the guy out. Depending on the victim's case, we would make them a PC [protective custody] and the guy would go to the Bing. It became a normal thing.

MICHAEL LOVE, detained early 1980s, early 1990s: In 1992, I did about eight months. I was walking the yard, and there was a gang meeting. The officers is there acting like they don't see it. At the time, the jail belonged to the Latin Kings. They was sitting on these multi-tiered bleachers. There was a guy standing in front of them educating them, they were disciplined, they were intent. I couldn't believe that. They said some of the officers are Latin King members too. There was always a lot of conflict. It was often a Latin King house, and if a Blood or Crip went in there, there would be violence. If you neutral, what did you have to do to get on the phone? It was amazing [jail officers] let that happen.

RICK LOMBARDI, retired DOC gang investigator, 1990 to 2011: The Latin Kings started in Chicago. King Blood [Luis Felipe, now in federal prison] started his own Latin King set in New York without the authority of Chicago. It's the only set in the country that doesn't answer to Chicago. He goes to Rikers and see there's no protection and no representation. He's got the rules and bylaws and started his own set. And it went from there.

HECTOR "PASTOR BENNY" CUSTODIO, Latin King leader, detained 1991 to 1994: There was respect. The officers were getting paid. The prisoners respected that I was a leader. I called the shots. I made whatever decision needed to be made, whatever officers needed to get paid off. It was about smuggling. They would smuggle cocaine, heroin, phones, anything we needed. The officers would come up and say if you don't want an infraction we can handle this in a different way, and they would state their price. It's the code of silence. They would tell us who to contact, who are the officers on our side who are willing to work with us, who are willing to make things happen. This went on every day.

RICK LOMBARDI: I interviewed an officer who had the "Amor de Rey" on his chest. That's a Latin King tattoo. I saw him one day on the street in a tank top getting an egg sandwich. I nudged my partner Sal and I said, "Dude, that's a Latin King tattoo on his chest." Sal looks over and goes, "Yeah, that's a Latin King tattoo."

We ran into him a lot, but all we could do was make a call in. Would [the inspector general] ever do anything? Seventy-five percent of the time, no, they didn't do shit.

HECTOR "PASTOR BENNY" CUSTODIO: The Ninja Turtles came in and they would do random searches, and there was this kid. They told him to put his face against the wall, and one of the officers grabbed him by the neck and smashed his head against the wall and we retaliated. And they took the gang leaders, or the people they thought were the gang leaders, and put them in an "Apache Line." Officers lined up on the left- and right-hand side, and they had their batons out. They would put you on your knees and you had to go through on your knees. They would beat you brutally. Once they found out I was a leader of one of the gangs, I was so badly beaten. My left leg was broken in three places. I was walking around on crutches for a year and a half from that incident.

After they beat me, they threw me back in the bullpen and then took me to the medical unit on Rikers, and the nurses made up a frivolous report. They never reported what the guards did. They [the nurses] were threatened in the parking lot [by the guards] to say inmate so-and-so did this. After that, they put me in involuntary protective custody in NIC [North Infirmary Command]. That's where I began to heal, and then I was sentenced upstate.

DUPREE HARRIS, detained 1990s, 2000s: When I get to the Beacon [the George R. Vierno Center] in 1993, it's pretty much like Syria. You got your Latin Kings, you got the Ñetas, and you just had a bunch of brothers, but it was no great organization early on. We're talking about 1991, 1992. What I said we have to do is we have to establish a brotherhood in a sense. We have to look out for each other, because if we don't look out for each other, who will?

There was no label; it was just a bunch of brothers sticking together. So now when they seen that, when the administration on Rikers Island saw that we were sticking together, they started splitting guys up.

So I remember reading. One of my favorite guys that sparked

my interest was George Jackson. *Soledad Brother* [a compilation of Jackson's letters from Soledad State Prison in California]. A few of us, we were privy to George and the things that he had established within Soledad prison. And we kind of mimicked that same ideology.

Man, it was a blessing. Not only empowering the self, but what it took to bring people together for a cause. If you look at the ten-step program that Huey [Newton] and Bobby Seale did with the Panthers, they drew out a plan, right? So this is what myself with some other brothers came together to establish that we need to put a purpose behind the unity and not only to go against the opposites but to uplift and benefit each other.

One of the things that you had to do is you had to read. A lot of guys, they were ignorant. I don't care if it was the newspaper, Bible, Koran, whatever literature that was at your disposal, you had to read it. And then if you didn't know how to read it, let it be known, and one of the brothers would assist you in reading and understanding.

There was basically a unified code. There was just a set of goals that we wanted to reach. If you wanted to use the word "code," I don't want to say code, but it was a thing, like if you were going to pull together, you got to make sure you hold your brethren down. You know what I'm saying? The main thing was, we weren't going to leave no brother behind.

The brotherhood, we dubbed it Smoke. And the idea was it moved like an atom everywhere, but the average person wouldn't know the concept unless you was involved. And one of the symbols for Smoke was [an image of] a diamond. We used it to identify each other.

So in 1993, the Latin group was getting huge. It started to be like a race war pretty much. The Latins against the Blacks. They were so organized at the time that it was bad. A Black dude would go to court and they would jump him. This was a frequent situation.

We were like, "Yo, this is not going to happen." So at first the whole thing was about not allowing the police to jump on you.

Now you had the Latin Kings, and they started doing the same thing, jumping us. This had to stop.

It came to a head. There was this Black dude. When he got to the Beacon, he had his head bandaged, he had staples in his head, he had a dislocated shoulder. He must've been in the hospital for quite some time. He wasn't in no gang or nothing like that. We asked him what happened. We thinking that maybe the police jumped on him. He said, nah, it was the Latin Kings and the Ñetas that jumped him. He was like, "Yo, listen, I'm going to go the distance with a person from the Ñetas and a person from the Latin Kings. I'm willing to get some revenge." I said, I don't know if that's a good thing to do. So anyway, I said, "I respect your heart."

I said, "Yo, I know the head of the Latin Kings and the head of the Ñetas. I'm going to pull up on them and let them know your position." So I pulled up on them, two from the Kings and two from the Ñetas. So I say, "Listen, this is the deal, man. A guy just came here. He had a situation with two of your guys; they jumped him. He wants to get back. Get your best guy. He want to finish what was started. But I'm gonna tell y'all that nobody's going to jump him. It's going to be a one on one and let the best man win."

He was bandaged up, but his heart was, yo, I'm in it. They going one on one with each other. This is in the yard. They both got weapons. The guy that's bandaged up, he's getting the best of the other guy. We were sitting there, letting them go. He getting the best of the deal. They can't stand no more, so they want to go jump him. We wasn't letting them jump this guy. We all jumped in, and we went at it. Some of us got stabbed, some of them. For the most part, we was victorious. They didn't accept that. So now you have a thing between the Latins and us; it started a big thing. It resonated all over because a lot of their main guys got hurt.

RICK LOMBARDI: I actually got jumped by Smoke in the Beacon. I was a Manhattan House officer, and I was working in GRVC [George R. Vierno Center] that day. We had gotten transferred 'cause they closed one of the towers in Manhattan House and told us that we had to go to Rikers and work there.

During my time there, I get to a housing area. The institutional search had been there earlier. What they found during their search in one of the cells or on one of the Smoke members was initiation rules, regulations. You know, in order to join this gang, you got to do these things and like twenty-five different rules. So they had told this guy, what are you doing? You started your own gang here? Well, you're not going to stay in this jail. We're going to pack you up and send you [to a jail] where all the heavy hitters are.

So they packed him up. After they searched him, they put all his shit into his bedsheet. They threw it out the cell and they said, "Lock this guy in. Don't let him out until we move him." So a couple of hours go by. This guy is in his cell the whole time. I didn't think nothing of it. And then I went to meal. When I came back, unbeknownst to the officer who took my relief, there was like fifteen guys packed up.

I seen all these bags packed up. All on the top tier. So I was like, well, that looks a little odd. I remember packing up one guy, but I don't remember packing up fifteen guys. So I asked, why are fifteen guys packed up? That doesn't make any sense. I said, "I don't want to move fifteen guys, 'cause I gotta write all the names in the book. And that's kind of a pain in the ass." I said, "So you don't know anything about it?" She's like, "Nope." So I was like, "All right." And she's like, see you later; then she walked out.

At that time it was two TVs. There was one on the front, one in the back. The one on the front was for the Black inmates. And the one in the back was for the Spanish inmates. All the Spanish inmates were in the back watching TV. And they were just looking at me. All the Black inmates are packed up on the top tier looking at me. And then I noticed they just started walking toward me. I'm like, yeah, this is not going to be a good day for me.

So I backed up. I backed up as much as I could toward the aid station. The A officer was a useless female who wasn't fucking paying attention. And I start banging on the glass trying to get her attention, like they're moving toward me, you know, maybe hit your alarm or do something. And then they started running down the steps like toward me.

And I knew it was on.

So I hit the first one and just covered my face so they wouldn't be able to get me.

And the rest of them jumped on top, but there was so many and they were so stupid. They were hitting each other more than they were hitting me. I don't remember ever feeling that I got hit by anybody. They were like, "Yo, take this officer out." If we're moving our leader, we're all leaving.

The probe team came in. A couple of them got dragged out. A couple of them got locked back in. They asked me to identify the guys I thought were involved. What I thought was, it looked like the whole house was fighting me.

All I did after that was just do my paperwork and leave for the day. And it was just like another event during the day. I didn't go to the doctor. I had a very unhappy area captain that had shown up that day because it was his last day before retirement and decided to take the road of "I'm not doing any paperwork; I'm going to take care of it. Don't worry about it. It'll be taken care of. And you don't have to do anything either."

AMIN "MINISTER" KING, detained 1983 to 1987: After I get to Rikers, I'm on the line for the phone at HDM [the House of Detention for Men]. Dude [man in the house gang] says, "Yo, homey, five minutes." Five minutes? So I don't say nothing, I gets on the phone, call my numbers. "Yo, homey, you get two tries." That's when I said, "I get what?" "You get two tries." You could see the [house gang] goons, the dudes that are the enforcers, the do-rag motherfuckers, the gorillas. They doing pull-ups off the top bars. They got a little team. The police is standing up in the Bubble watching.

You looking at the police; they looking at you to see how you're going to handle it. I get on the phone. Thank God I was able to get through. My boy said, "Yo, what up, Minny?" And I go, "Who do we got here? Who the fuck do we got here?" He says, "Yo, we got Officer So-and-So. Officer So-and-So. What block are you in?" I told him what block. He said, don't worry, we got somebody there. We got a badge. She works for us.

"We got you. What cell you in?" *Boom, boom, boom.* All right, cool. Try not to fuck nobody up, and go to the box until our people get to you. That's exactly the instructions that was given to me. Try not to fuck nobody up, get jumped, or get hurt in there until our people get to you. I said, "I need one of those things." He said, "Don't worry. They going to take care of you." One of those things mean a weapon. "Yeah, we got you. You're taken care of. They going to step to you." All right, homey.

He said, who's the house gang? So I get off the phone. I said, homey, what's your name? Yo, bro, what's your name? What's your name, homey? So he says, my name is whatever, "Big Red" or some silly rabbit name. I said, "Some nigga named Big Red." All right. Got it. Yo, just chill. We got you. You need money? I tell them what I need.

Before four o'clock, the changing of the shift, my fucking cell cracks. *Boom.* I sticks out. I don't see nobody but a suicide guy and the house gang. Closed the cell. *Bang!* Because they already told me when they want to get at you, they crack the cell when everybody locked in. They got a dayroom. They get you in there and they jump you and make you shake out. Fight or just give it up.

So, when my cell cracked, I closed the gate. My cell opened again. The suicide-watch guy came down. "Yo, the officer want to see you, homey. Your name Minister, right?"

I put my shit on. My sneakers. There was a piece of a broken toilet. Back then the toilets was porcelain. I took the porcelain from the toilet as a weapon. I put it in a piece of sheet so I could hold it so I don't cut myself. Better than nothing.

These guys are sitting on the dayroom benches, the mess hall tables, this house gang. I'm sitting in this house. Yo, what's up? Where you from, big homey? They talking where you from. Queens. You name Minister? The police sent them in there to interrogate me to make sure. But he got the speaker on. Police is hearing the conversation in the fucking Bubble.

You don't know who the fuck you fucking with until sometime it might be too late. So anyway, I talked to them and I'm just telling the names I know. And they listening. "You got on the phone this morning. You made a phone call to certain persons?" Yeah. What's their name? I said, get the fuck outta here. Who the fuck you think you're talking to, kid?

I said the name, and all of a sudden I hear the intercom go off. The police knocks on the glass. Let him come through. They say, oh, police want to see you up in the Bubble, big homey. I go to the Bubble, and they look at me and it's a female and a dude that's on our payroll from Rikers Island. She said, well, how do you feel Brother Minister? We exchange names. They said, whatever you need, homey, we here for you. Well, 'cause I need me a Double-O-Seven [knife]. They say, holy shit. It's got a brown handle. You fold it, you can lock it, you can put it between the crack of your ass. You can hide it.

And I said, I need some cigarettes, but they said, you don't smoke. I said, no, I don't smoke. I'll need that to get on the phone. That was that. I said, who's running this motherfucker? That's why I needed to know. Then they gave me the house game. Who's in charge, who was in charge of the pantry. Who's in charge of the phone?

So the house gang guy came in the Bubble, where I was talking with the police. Whatever you need, we heard a lot about you. Their whole attitude changed since that fucking morning. I'm family all of a sudden. It's who the fuck you know. It's not what you know.

JAMES "SHAQUELL" FORBES: When I came to jail in 1994, I ran into a few people I knew and I was wearing a nice chain. And they said, you gotta watch out for them Bloods. They too dangerous. They run around with razors and all types of shanks. I said, "What you talking about? Like L.A. Bloods?" He said, "Nah, these are New York Bloods in New York." They got bandannas and everything. I go to court one day. I passed by a bullpen. I see it's a couple of different bandannas around their necks, and they looking at me and then one of them knew me and called my name. At this time, I'm like twenty-eight years old. I'm talking to him, and I said, "Yo, you Blood?" Yes. Correction officer was telling me to move on.

RICK LOMBARDI: I knew they weren't authorized to start a New York Bloods by the West Coast. That's why there's such a problem with East Coast and West Coast. OG Mack [Omar Portee, currently in federal prison] started that shit on his own. And then some other guys started sets on their own.

JAMES "SHAQUELL" FORBES: Some time later I'm in HDM, and a guy came through name of Kev. Boxing Kev. And he was Blood. He basically told me the ins and outs of the House about Blood and what it stood for and its standards. It was basically a group of individuals that was in C73 [George Motchan Detention Center] in 1993 in a Black and Latino house.

It was neutral. There wasn't any gang banging, but in other houses Latin Kings and Ñetas were oppressing people. Brothers inside their house with Kev felt like they needed to do something about it. We needed to unify and really straighten these guys out. These guys was disrespectfully cutting Black people and cutting Latino people that's not down with them. They're doing a whole lot of stuff to our people that we can't stand by and let that go.

So they all band together and go rise against them. Then we can get bandannas. Then we can wreak havoc among these dudes. So that's how it really started.

Guys got together, got tired of what they was seeing. It was the hate that hate produced.

So they went out there and they start cutting and stabbing the Latin Kings and Ñetas. In turn, they rised up against us and they outnumbered us.

So you know, a lot of Bloods, they just took refuge inside the Bing. They're going to Bing. Some don't come back out. Now you've got some Bloods that's cowering. They start taking their bandannas off, but a handful of us was really standing strong. We believed in it and we fought tooth and nail.

As time went on, the numbers started growing but not that much. There was only one set at the time. And with that one set you had one leader, and with that one leader you have a lot of people that might want to get down with the program but don't necessarily know him.

What happened was the main leader came down from upstate. He gave people their own individual sets that in turn made the numbers grow because now people get in a set where they feel they belong. He my boy, that's my friend, he has that set, I'm getting the next set. And people start spreading out. Before you know it, there are like ten sets.

So it's growing in astronomical ways on the inside. So the Gangster Killer Bloods was one of the sets that I founded, but it wasn't my idea. It was another brother's idea. He said, let's make our own thing, when he started hearing about all the other new sets coming about.

And we put together the name for it. We came up with the name Gangster Killer Bloods. They asked me to put together a package like a manifesto, a constitution. So I put it together and us three combined started Gangster Killer Bloods, which became one of the biggest sets on the East Coast. And now it's spread out all over.

DUPREE HARRIS: Guys from Shaquell's era, they connected and got together. That's what made it a broad thing. A lot of guys that came up with us, guys that was with Smoke, they became Blood. And that was, like, a no-no. We was good with each other, and the unity was there and everything, but we were like, nah, you don't do that. It's like, I'm with you, you get in a situation, I want to help you, but that don't mean our guys are going to join your guys. Their direction wasn't our direction. Our direction was pretty much helping, uplifting, building, not doing all this crazy, wild, ill stuff that they were doing at that time. So that's why I said the signals got a little bit crossed.

JAMES "SHAQUELL" FORBES: So we expanded. We had a good cause, fighting against oppression, but then you have people in it for the wrong reasons. They have their own personal hidden agendas. They wanted to see what personal gain they can get out of it. So a lot of them started going to the streets and they would lie. For example, a guy goes to Albany projects in Brooklyn. He wanted to start Gangster Killer Bloods right there in the projects. We up north now. Our mail is monitored. We don't get to write a lot. His [gang] already blew up before the time I write to the street. What's this Gangster Killer Bloods? We never intended for it to get to the street. It just made it to the streets. This is '96 and it started growing in numbers. All these different sets start popping up in the street. People coming home without permission and creating their own set of the same thing in the streets without going in to the person and getting approved. We never meant for it to get to the streets.

Next thing you know, in '97 somebody sent me an article. My name is in the article with Gangsters Killer Bloods. Apparently, he got ahold of my lessons [writings] from somebody in the Department of Correction. My name is all on it. So I'm like, "Wow, it's getting really bigger than what it's supposed to be." And then we start hearing about people getting cut [in the streets] because they wearing red dresses or it's part of an initiation. Why is this happening?

MARTIN HORN, correction commissioner, 2002 to 2009: There's a bullying culture. Now everybody talks about gangs and the Program and all this. It's really all about bullying on every cellblock.

There's no hierarchy of Bloods in the city or Crips in the city. There are neighborhood-based groups of adolescent men always who coalesce and identify with one group or another. And maybe when they traveled to other neighborhoods, they find other adolescents who likewise call themselves Bloods and Crips or Trinitarians or Latin Kings. But it's not like there's some citywide hierarchy. And then the jails, you go into a cellblock and there's a group of kids, young men who maybe they know each other, maybe they coalesce around some shared interest. Maybe they all call themselves the Bloods or the Crips.

And they sort of become the jailhouse bullies and they control if you go to commissary . . . they want 2 percent of your commissary. If you've got a girlfriend, they're going to lean on you to have your girlfriend smuggle in drugs. If you want drugs, they're the guys you got to get drugs from. If they want to turn you out and rape you, a group of guys come and do that. And that has been true in jails and prisons all over the country. And it's been true in Rikers Island certainly since thirty years ago.

MARTIN CREGG, retired DOC gang investigator, 1996 to 2018: I was eight months away from getting off probation [as a new hire] and I went out on meal. And in the box, they used to crack all the cells. I go to meal and I come back and they had cracked out the worst kid, "Doggy Dog." I was a little uneasy. I was sitting at the front. I walked around a little bit. At eight, they start chanting, "Blood, up! Blood, up!" They usually don't do that until eleven, when they call their roll call. And all of a sudden I get up and I see this Spanish kid come barreling toward me. I see another kid behind him. I hit the alarm. The A officer opened the cell thinking it was empty, but Doggy Dog went in and was cutting him for about forty seconds. They were chanting to cover up the kid's screams.

LAWRENCE HENAGIN, detained several times, 2000s: Bloods had the phone. This is how they used to do it. They have the phone locked down. So a guy comes back from court and the guy's got twenty-five–life as it is. He was respectful. He says, "I gotta call my people." The phone was just hanging on the hook, hanging down. They told him, you can't, that's a Blood phone. You can't use it. So he said, "Look, I just came from court. I need to call my people." They said, "Man, fuck you, you ain't callin' nobody." He went into his cell and he had made an ice pick about [six inches] long. And he came out and stabbed all five Bloods.

As soon as he pulled out the knife, the CO jumped over the table and ran out the door and ran into the Bubble. He said fuck that. And this guy was gonna kill one of the kids. He had stabbed him and the kid was on the ground [begging for his life]. This guy already has twenty-five to life. He didn't stab him again. All five of them signed statements against the guy that stabbed them. They were all Bloods, these gangsters. But as soon as they got stabbed, they signed statements against the guy. And all he did was say, "Look, I just want to use the phone."

TERRENCE SKINNER, retired deputy warden, 1983 to 2003: By 1997, they had created the Gang Intelligence Unit. Prior it was the Gang Intelligence Task Force, and they gathered info and didn't share it. They would tell me it was confidential. They started creating a database. There were two different databases, competing with each other. They reviewed the whole process, and the Gang Intelligence Unit was created. There were weekly meetings with the security captain, the ADWs [assistant deputy wardens], and deputy wardens.

What happened was, they reached a point where investigations made the arrest in the jail, not the staff. Before, you could stab another prisoner, you got an infraction, but you weren't arrested. An infraction was like a parking ticket. With the Gang Intelligence Unit, I asked the chief if we could lock inmates up [for longer stretches by adding new criminal charges]. It took negotiation, but they allowed us to arrest inmates for stabbings and slashings.

Our first big case was when we got a guy who cut someone's throat. He had a two-year sentence. We went to the Bronx DA [who has jurisdiction over Rikers], and we talked with him and they approved the arrest. The guy was being transferred upstate. I ordered my team to stop the bus, get him off the bus. He got eleven years for the throat slashing. It quickly sent a message to all of the gangs that you're going to get hit with a felony charge. That was March 1997. By 1998, the violence dropped another 50 percent because of all the arrests.

DUPREE HARRIS: After I got arrested again in 2001 and went back to Rikers, it was very difficult. I went through a hell of an experience. If you have a past, people just remember you from the things you started; it's hard to shake that away. So when I got locked up on this one, they had me pegged as the leader of the Bloods. They said I controlled everything.

I had close to three hundred to four hundred people that would listen to me on a dime. You know what I'm saying? But I never gave direction to promote violence.

I was doing things in the community. I would throw basketball tournaments, give back-to-school stuff for the kids. I would throw card games for the elders, bingo tournaments, fishing trips, crab fests, ski trips. And this don't get out most of the time, you know what I'm saying? And that's what it is.

From the day that we sat down and came up with this unified body, it was always a positive thing, but obviously negative stuff grew within it. So of course that follows and falls on me. They had me in solitary confinement for about four years. I'm talking about where I couldn't have a visit with my family. I went to solitary confinement like around January 2003. I didn't get out of solitary confinement until 2006.

The government was saying I was so strong and I had so much influence that I was sending orders from jail to the streets. When I had visits, they had to have an agent in the room. If an agent wasn't in the room, I couldn't have a visit. That's how deep it was. This was all allegations. They had an episode on *Law & Order* [which based a character on Harris].

FITZGERALD DAVID, retired correction officer, 1987 to 2014: If you put ten Bloods in a house and then you add fifteen to twenty more, and you have other regular inmates in the house, or you have five Crips in the house, there's going to be a problem. They're going to get assaulted, stabbed, cut. So the department took it upon themselves to not house inmates by their classification. They tell everyone, "Oh, we house inmates by classification." They're lying. You're not housing these inmates by classification. You're housing inmates by gang affiliation.

If you have a whole floor of Bloods, and under them you have a whole floor of Crips. Under them, you have a whole floor of Trinitarios. You're going to have a problem escorting inmates.

You're going to have a problem feeding inmates. You're going to have a problem giving inmates services and programs. You're putting officers' lives in jeopardy; regular inmates who are not gang affiliated, you're putting them in jeopardy too.

ANGEL TUEROS, former Ñetas member, detained 1994 to 1996: This was 1994. I was twenty-two years old. One of my friends pleaded guilty to a year or something, and he was leaving. He said he didn't want to leave me alone. So, he encouraged me to join one of the gangs in the facility. You had the Latin Kings, the Bloods, Ñetas, and La Familia, which eventually faded out.

And I joined the Ñetas, which is a group that originated in Puerto Rico. It was very easy at first. They didn't call themselves a gang. They called themselves an association. In Spanish: *Una Asociación pro Derechos del Confinado,* the Association for the Rights of the Confined. I was a Boy Scout growing up, and they have a set of good rules, like respect your fellow prisoners' visitors, respect the prisoners' sleep, stuff like that. So those rules appealed to me. Also, the guys who recruited me showed me articles about the founder of the movement. And I was persuaded by that.

Once I joined, I held a position of leadership. If I was going to be there, I wanted to make sure that if I go to sleep, I'd be okay. I would be able to sleep.

There were a lot of instances where someone will come into the dorm and there would be a green light on the person, meaning that the group had to jump him. That was disturbing to me. When the top leaders sent a green light against someone who came to the dorm, I became a problem because I would question it. If I was gonna do something to a person, whether it's tell the person, "No, you cannot live in this dorm," or have the group jump him. These were not the reasons why I joined the group.

I wanted to know what they did that they deserve not to live anywhere in this building or that this person needs to be jumped by a group of guys. So, I was nicknamed by one of the top leaders Tira Toalla in Spanish, which is "Towel Thrower." It's like when there is a boxing match and you throw in the towel.

Eventually, my position was taken because I would question. I wanted to know why. Sometimes we find out that there were issues like this guy will owe someone else money for drugs. And the group was not about that. That was not contemplated in the rules. So, I tried to stick to the rules, but that wasn't too good.

So I'm walking in the yard where there were like twenty guys in the yard, walking. I have the person who was supposedly the leader of the entire Rikers Island. I had basically all these guys against me and I couldn't talk, because I could get a beating. I asked to be let out of the group, but I wasn't allowed out at that instant. At that point I was concerned about my life. Luckily, a friend of mine took the position. And that basically kept me safe in that building.

At nineteen, Angel Tueros went to Rikers, where he felt obliged to join a gang to survive.

RICK LOMBARDI: I was listening to phone monitoring one time, and there was a big-shot Crip from the West Coast who had got locked up here. He had "Bloodkiller" tattooed on his face. He was an Asian guy. I didn't even know there was an Asian set of Crips. He got locked up and went into protective custody because we knew anywhere this guy goes he's a target. He had all kind of fucked-up tattoos all over him. The guy was fully tatted from his forehead down to his feet. We listened to his tapes, and I heard him tell his girlfriend in the street that the "slobs," that was his slang for the Bloods, had gotten him, they cut him.

He was putting some kind of lidocaine on it the doctor had given him because he said he fell out of his bed. Upon telling that to my boss, she said, "Go over there and see if it's true." We need to know how this guy got stabbed because he's in PC [protective custody]. How could he possibly get stabbed?

I saw he was slashed on the face and he had a defensive wound on his hand. But he wouldn't break. I never found out why or how he got stabbed.

Ten years later—I retired in 2011—I just happened to be working in a club in Times Square, and I see the guy. It was him. He's got unforgettable tattoos that are all gang affiliated. Turns out that the girl that he had been speaking to back then was a dancer at the club. I knew her as CJ. She was who I was monitoring.

I'm very good friends with her. She goes, I want to introduce you to my boyfriend. I said, I know your boyfriend very well. And then obviously, she told him. So I said, "You never told me how you got stabbed."

So he says what happened was, they were coming up for court. They were about to feed him by sticking his food tray in. The officer, he claims, was a Blood, and that officer allowed another Blood from another housing area to come in and feed him and run in with a blade, and as he went to get his tray, he reached in and cut his face.

He said the officer used to fuck with him all the time because he was a Crip, and allowed other Blood inmates to come from other areas and fuck with him and tell him, as soon as you come out, you're dead.

DUPREE HARRIS: I think it's completely out of control. Elders like myself, I can honestly say I watched it grow. I actually wrote some of the constitutions in there, but when I see the direction that it went, like, damn. It was good at first 'cause it was a unified thing, but then there was no positive coming out. It was all negative. It's disheartening, man, to see the unnecessary violence.

I respect violence. I don't disagree with violence, but I disagree with senseless violence, you understand what I'm saying? That's just like an army veteran. An army veteran understands that he's going to war, right? But it ain't going around just killing anybody. A lot of the young guys that I've talked to, that contact me and I give advice to, I always try to encourage these guys. Being affiliated is not a bad thing, but it's what you trying to get out of that. What are you trying to do? Are you trying to change the situation? You're trying to make it worse?

VIOLENCE

"I've Walked with the Razor in My Mouth"

It's like foliage, the violence on Rikers. The act of it. The thought of it. What it makes people do. Why it makes people sit up nights. It's backdrop and companion to everything that comes, and it's what follows you after you leave. It spreads across the landscape, touching the people held in the jails, officers, wardens, commissioners, their aides, relatives, medics, all the way to city hall, down through the generations, and the events remain rendered in the memory in crystalline detail years, even decades later, with all their attendant traumas and regrets.

—

BARRY CAMPBELL, detained 1980s, 1990s: I've walked with the razor in my mouth. I remember when they moved me over to the adult dorm, the first thing I did when I went in there was cut somebody because I wanted them to know that this was not a game and that I was coming to claim a certain slot time on the phone. So I took my blanket, dropped it on my bed. I looked around, looked at somebody in the dayroom, saw that the kid was on the phone, and just picked him out to be the one that I was going to make my name off of.

Barry Campbell, who spent large chunks of his youth behind bars, has been a top official at the Fortune Society, which helps people after incarceration.

MATT FREY, clinician, 2011 to 2018: We're a mental health clinic and we're next to the medical clinic. I saw slashings, broken noses, broken jaws, broken eye sockets. Some people got teeth knocked out. I witnessed a number of fights. You see everything. Some would be on stretchers. It's horrific. But at the same time, after a while you get so desensitized, it's like you don't blink anymore. It's weird to become used to that.

BARRY CAMPBELL: [Violence] was the only way that I knew. From the time that I went into foster home, I was sexually abused, not only by the woman who was in charge of the house, but also her grown kids, male and female. So from very early on I knew what violence was and what role it played in my life. I had been on the side of being a victim at a very early age, and I had made it up in my mind that I was never going to be a victim again. And the easiest way to not become a victim was to become the aggressor. And so I became the aggressor.

MATT FREY: I remember a fight where one guy punched an older guy in the face, and he shat himself and his shit hit the floor. And then another inmate came to help him clean up his mess. People just don't act like that outside on an everyday kind of level like they do in jail.

STEPHANIE SMAGLER, retired correction officer, 1989 to 2015: I was a rookie in 1989. There was an inmate when I was in GRVC [George R. Vierno Center] that got cut. They had sliced his throat. He was on the floor in the vestibule area. The probe team went inside the unit, and the captain told me to stay out and talk to him. He was lying on the floor in a puddle of blood. There was blood all around my boots. There was so much blood. He was asking, "Is it really bad? Am I going to die?" And I was saying, "It's not as bad as you think it is. You're going to be okay." But it was his throat and it was wide open on the side of his neck. I was trying to be strong for him. I had never seen a cut like that in my life. All because of [a fight over] the telephone. I was praying with him. I retired in 2015, but I'll never forget what he looked like. You never forget the traumatizing moments.

BARRY CAMPBELL: You're talking about people being stabbed left and right. I've always been about a hundred pounds soaking wet, so the way that I survived was being more brutal than anybody else in there. That was my way of ensuring that nobody would ever mess with me or try to take what was mine. Early on I understood that violence rules, and I understood that if you were willing to go further than anybody else was, then you were pretty much the one who was in charge. And so I was always the one willing to go further than everybody else because I was always smaller than everyone else. It's like the Napoleon complex. You feel you have to do so much more because everyone is bigger and stronger and physically more powerful than you are. So you tend to let weapons do the talking for you, whether it's razors or the wash bucket or just the mop itself, whatever you can lay your hands on.

DONOVAN DRAYTON, detained 2007 to 2012: Me, I adapted. I made sure Donovan survived. I never turned Blood. I never turned to no gangs. I stood on my own two feet as a man. One thing in prison that they respect, no matter what, it's a man, a person that stands on their own. Doesn't need an army behind them. People recognize and see that. No matter if you get beat up, they jump you. I fought for mines.

BARRY CAMPBELL: Other times it's just because I was in a bad mood, you know, somebody would come in the house and he would go to one person and he would take that person's phone time and I'd be like, "I don't like you, motherfucker. You ain't all that." And I just go and beat him up and take the phone time back and just give it to somebody at random because there was nothing else to do. You were bored. So, you know, violence was a change in the norm, so to speak. You did things not because somebody told you to or you just didn't like that person. There were days when you just woke up on the wrong side of the bed and somebody was gonna catch it.

NESTOR EVERSLEY, detained, various stints, 1969 to 2010s: One day, we were watching *The Michael Jackson Story,* and they were watching *Scarface.* Following day was the second part of *The Michael Jackson Story,* but the Spanish guys in the back, they didn't want to hear that. They wanted to watch *Scarface.* We had seen *Scarface* a million times. The CO was a woman and we started arguing and we almost got into a rumble right there. She said, "We're going to take a vote." We outvoted them. They was like four to five people and over here was nine to ten people.

I was sitting in the front when they were walking out, and one of them tried to knock the TV off the shelf and I was able to catch it with one hand and I popped him in the face with the other. A rumble started. Everybody started fighting and reaching for weapons and breaking boards. They called for the emergency unit. They came in. We didn't see *The Michael Jackson Story* or *Scarface* again, and we were lined up completely naked and getting yelled at. I regretted it. I should have let the TV drop.

DONOVAN DRAYTON: They're not just going to take it from me or roll over me. The real world the same way too. You can't be pushed over, from the corporate world to the streets, and let somebody take your stuff. If they think they can take it, they going to keep on taking it. You know what I'm saying?

NESTOR EVERSLEY: This kid had some glasses. This was in 1985 or 1986. They had three Blood kids in the cage. They decided to take this guy's glasses. He was a Black guy. I'm Black but I'm Hispanic. We tend to stick together. Once they did that, they turned on this one Hispanic guy and tried to take his sneakers. This guy decided he wasn't going to give up his sneakers. He was going to fight. It wasn't fair to be three on one, so I jumped in and we had the fight. The officer who came in to so-called break up the fight, he broke up the fight when things turned against the three of them. When it first started, he did nothing. I come to find out [the officer] was a member of the Bloods. We were lumped up. I remember the other guy begging, "Give me the glasses please." They didn't give a damn. They just destroyed things. They took the glasses.

SIDNEY SCHWARTZBAUM, retired deputy warden, union president, 1979 to 2016: I remember one day, it must have been like in 1982. I was working in one of the houses and a guy was getting stabbed in the yard and he was getting stabbed so bad he tried to hop over the fence. His arm got caught in the razor ribbon, and so when they escorted him through my area, his arm was hanging off. It was the most disgusting thing I've ever seen.

He was completely covered with blood. After a few years I became immune to it. I would start to develop a defense mechanism in my head to deal with seeing violence. And I remember that day when they brought him up, I said to myself, "Boy, I really created this defense mechanism. It doesn't even bother me anymore," you know?

DAVID CAMPBELL, detained 2019 to 2020: One time, I saw a blood-soaked sock in a doorway—you know, like just the evidence of it—the trauma of past violence. I saw a lot of that—guys with fishhook scars. A lot of guys with what they call "a buck-fifty," like a big facial scar—some of them very gruesome. It's a lot of stitches. You don't have to count them.

GREGORY PIERCE, detained 1983, 2015: When I was there in 1983, a guy approached me, telling me I'm going to be his bitch, and I wasn't having it. So I went inside my room, took my toothbrush, sharpened my toothbrush [on the floor], so it had a little point on it, and I came back out the room and I stabbed him three or four times.

I stabbed him here and up here [indicating chest]. I seen him upstate too. I did it straight up. He didn't say nothing. He was too busy screaming. The guards came and grabbed him. You gotta survive. Ain't nothing about me feminine. So ain't nobody doing nothing. You know? I don't know what his problem was. But I tried to solve it for him. He's lucky I didn't have something better to sharpen it with. Like a piece of metal. 'Cause, I'm being honest, I woulda killed him.

CASIMIRO TORRES, detained various stints, 1980s to 2000s: Even when you are sleeping in your cell, someone can stab you or set you on fire. It's not normal to be under that pressure all day. It takes a tremendous toll on you. If someone takes a paper clip from me it makes me really, really angry. It makes me feel victimized. That's how I felt in jail. I can be a little more aggressive at silly shit like someone is not looking you in the eye when they talk to you. It's not normal and it's not the way it should be.

GREGORY PIERCE: I got beat up by the police [correction officers] [for the stabbing]. They didn't give me no new charges or anything. No, they just beat me up, kept me locked up for about thirty-five days. Took me out and sent me over to another jail. From that, I went upstate. By that time I had already made up my mind: I wasn't taking no shit from nobody. Wasn't taking nothing from no officers, wasn't taking nothing from no convict. Once I went to Rikers, I learned that I had to shut down all emotions.

GARY HEYWARD, former correction officer and former detainee, 2000s: There was an inmate who was disrespectful to a female officer, inviting her to his private parts, said he would throw feces on her. She called us to her area, and he didn't stop with the verbal assault. We opened up his cell and tuned him up. There were no cameras inside the cell. I guess they didn't want to spend too much money. We tuned him up and we got him in line. Smacked him in the face. You hit them where it's not going to leave too many bruises. You're not going to leave marks, but he's going to know why he got his ass beat. There was a rule that if an inmate touched an officer inappropriately, he had to go to the hospital. Mandatory.

FRANK PASQUA III, former Lucchese crime family, detained 2003, 2011 to 2012: There was this young gang member, and he was trying to act like he ran the whole house. Obviously he didn't get the memo about who I was. I showed up there; I was 330 pounds. I had cops bringing me steroids. I was a monster. I could send you pictures of what I looked like in jail. And this fucking kid, you know, the Bloods had a good stronghold on the house.

I was watching this show and I was sitting where he usually sat and he said something stupid to me. And I say, "Listen, I'm not in any fucking mood for you today, because you and your idiot friend were rapping and singing songs while I was trying to sleep. So I'm not in any mood for your shit right now. Maybe you think I'm some slouch. You have no idea who you're dealing with." I said this in front of his crew.

I knew he was going to get people. It was summertime. I was hot. I was miserable. There's a big ten-gallon cooler full of ice. When it's hot, they have to give us that. So they come back in and now he's talking slick to me, punching his hands while he's talking to me. I guess he thought 'cause he had like five or six people with him I was going to be intimidated. While he was talking, I just punched him dead in his face. And this kid's face exploded, like a hand grenade went off in his mouth. He was done.

Now there's all his friends. They think, "Oh, there's a white guy in there. Oh, he's going to bitch up right away to us." There's a young Black CO looking through the window at us. Now I'm squaring off and I'm keeping my back to a wall. I'm trying to stay in a defensible position. So as they come in, I can hit them.

One of them picks up the Gatorade cooler and goes to hit me with it. And when he hits me, he grazes me with it. The full cooler of ice falls out on the floor. Now the CO looked at me and said, "Stop it, stop it."

And they were swarming me. He went to grab the phone. He looked away for maybe two or three seconds. The ice went on the floor. Since I was standing in one place, defending myself, when they advanced on me, they all slipped on the ice. They went down. He first sees me surrounded by five or six guys attacking me. He looks away for two seconds. He looks back, and just like that they're all on the ground.

He pulls the pin. I capitalized on them being down. I start hitting them while they're down. The [Ninja] Turtles come running in. One ran in with the spray bottle, the OC spray [pepper spray].

I said, don't spray me. Don't spray me. They put us all on the wall. The cop came in and this CO told the Turtles, "Listen, guys, this is the baddest motherfucker I've ever seen in my life. I never saw anything like it. I turned around to get the phone. By the time I turned back, he had them all knocked out."

But I didn't throw a punch. They all slipped on the ice or hit their heads. They were trying to get up and kept falling. But someone looking in from the outside, it looked like I turned into Bruce Lee or something. I'll never forget that. I laugh about that to this day. That was late 2012. I was about to go up top. That CO brought it up every time he used to see me.

JULIA SOLOMONS, social worker, Bronx Defenders: I've had clients who've shared that a correctional officer intentionally left their cell door open at a time when they knew they were privy to an attack and allowed it to happen. I've heard that from multiple clients. So I think there are dynamics at play between correctional officers and people in custody that are only really known and understood by people that are there experiencing them. Not enough attention is paid to that.

GREGORY PIERCE: In 2015, I seen a guy get beat up [by officers] on the stairs. I was serving food, taking it upstairs to the dorms. A guard was arguing with an inmate. And the officer told him to get against the wall, and he said, "No, I ain't getting against the fucking wall." That was it. They jumped his ass. They put him against the wall and he slid down the stairs. And that was it. They didn't actually throw him, but they helped him fall. They hit him so hard against the wall that he fell down the stairs.

COLIN ABSOLAM, detained 1993 to 1996: The segregation is encouraged, but it's also practiced by guys that are inside. So, I was sitting and this one Spanish-speaking guy walked over to this Black guy who had a chain on. Didn't say anything. He just cut him across his face and ripped the chain from around his neck. No one got up to help. No one got up to stop it. It was pretty much mind your own business because the same thing can and will probably happen to you. So I'm sitting there in shock. This is the first time I saw someone get cut, and it was blood all over the place. The officers came in the bullpen, took the guy out that got cut.

SIDNEY SCHWARTZBAUM: When I was a correction officer, I would try to stop violence in the housing area. I would see things brewing as the tour commander. I'll walk into a dayroom and see a guy sitting on three chairs, he's the boss, right? And there's other guys with no chairs, so I would always tell him, get off there, put him down, you're not running shit. And you could tell; some people would be oblivious. I would say to an officer on the side, do you see something wrong with that? Why is he sitting on three chairs? Or I'd walk around, I see a guy with two or three mattresses and somebody without a mattress. And I said, Officer, didn't you see that? Jail is all about a hierarchy.

COLIN ABSOLAM: They really didn't look for the guy that did the cutting. They just took the Black guy out and took him to the hospital. One officer, the one that actually went in and took the guy out, had to write the report. So he was upset, but they didn't take anyone out, and normally they'll take everyone else, search everyone, try to find a weapon 'cause they would need to find the individual that actually did the cutting to either charge him or write a disciplinary report. But they left us in the bullpen and I'm sitting there with the guy and I'm like, "Oh my God." Like literally begging for nothing more to happen.

GARY HEYWARD: If they slash you on the back or the arm, it's not noticeable. If they slash you on your face, that lets people know you've been into something, that you may or may not be a snitch. It shows you're battle tested. And it opens up for investigation, what's your status in the street. It could be a good thing, unless you got slashed for snitching.

MICHAEL "BIG MIKE" WILLIAMS, member, DOC Emergency Services Unit, retired 2008: We were on a search. There was a guy—his name was Faust, dreadlock guy. He had a couple of life sentences, but I don't know why he was on the island. I'm standing in front of him, talking to him. I'm saying, "Take your clothes off. Hand me this one at a time. Don't shake anything out or nothing." So he took everything off. He's standing there butt naked. He's looking me directly in my eye the whole time. And I'm saying, "I don't know. I don't like the way this guy's looking at me."

So I got my distance and they already told me, this guy is a problem. Like, he's got fucking life times two. He don't care. So this motherfucker takes everything off. He has a Casio watch on—

G-Shock. I said, "Now remove your watch and hand it to me." And he's got his hand in front of his genitals, covered. And just looking at me. I said, "Can you understand the command I'm giving you?" I turned sideways and I'm moving to him slowly. I said, "You about to have a problem, man?" He goes, "No." I said, "Take off your watch." He's looking at me.

And he starts taking his watch off, *chingalingaling*. The fucking razor falls out. He went to pick it up, I grabbed him, put my hand in his chest, pushing him back up against the wall. "Don't fucking move!" He grabbed my shit, like this. I'm a big guy. My [even bigger] partner, Bobby Lampe, big Irishman. He don't know nothing but demo. Demolition. Don't fuck with Bobby. Bobby starts to come over. I go, "Bobby, I got it. We okay. Thank you, Bobby."

And then I used my foot and I pulled a razor over. I said, you got anything to fuck us? He said, "No, yo, I don't know who you are. I never give up nothing to any of these motherfuckers, but you, for some reason, you got me today. Listen, it is what it is. I got problems in here. That's it. It's not for you. Not for any of your staff members." And all day, all I heard is, I don't know how the fuck you were able to get a razor from Faust.

RICK LOMBARDI, retired DOC gang investigator, 1990 to 2011: You could only do so much until it got quashed. I used to go to meetings, and they would say, "Tell us what you think we should do to curb the violence." I gave them a million answers. They wouldn't do anything. They did nothing. They just let it keep going on.

EVE KESSLER, director, DOC public affairs, 2014 to 2017: Some of these guys, they were like walking slashing machines. It was constant mayhem.

LAWRENCE HENAGIN, detained several times, 2000s: We had a riot in Rikers Island where it was Spanish against the Black, and it turned out to be over bananas. Out of the blue, we're in the TV room now, everybody just starts fighting and they bust the TV to get the glass and, you know, everybody's grabbing glass and trying to cut each other. They wouldn't give us bananas on our trays, and I didn't even know that we were getting bananas until then. The COs came into my cell and beat the shit out of me. But it wasn't just me. They got the Spanish guy who was supposed to be the leader, but because I'm talking to him when they come in, they come into my cell and beat me up because they see me talking to this guy. The only thing I'm trying to do is find out what the fuck was you just fighting over.

And then, you know, guys swinging canes and shit, and the CO actually runs away and goes in the Bubble and watches it. That fight went on for like ten minutes before they pulled the pin. Several people got cut. Guy got his head split open with a cane. They hit a guy with a chair. I just stayed in the corner and swung. The main guy that would lock across from me, he was one of the higher-ups in the [Latin] Kings. And so, well, immediately when he finds out from his people that they're not getting their food [bananas] and shit, that night, they just set it off.

ANNA GRISTINA, detained 2012: I went to the visitation area. There was a large Black woman screaming I was a pedophile. My friend said, "You have to stand up for yourself. Otherwise you'll have no life to live in here. You better put a gun to your head." It's like that even on the outside. I've been beat up my whole life. I will not let anyone hurt me. It was impossible for me to walk away when someone was threatening me. I had to get them to back down. I said, "Sweetheart, since you're so big and tough, take the first two hits. If I start it, I'll be locked down in the Bing."

YOLANDA CEPEDA, detained 1990s: I think it was the late 1990s. I was walking through the corridors, and a girl grabbed another girl and stabbed her with one of those plastic forks. I guess she made a knife out of it. She cut her. I remember a lot of girls getting jumped. That was my last horrible memory. I used to hate walking through the corridors 'cause it was a madhouse. It was fights all over the place. The guards, they had no control. The female inmates, they had control.

MATT FREY: I saw one inmate break someone's nose for no other reason than trying to get into safer housing. I think he was scared. He was a little person that just wanted to be separated from everybody. He was just coming into the jail and didn't want to go into the dorm housing. So when we got there, an inmate walked into the clinic, and he's a tall skinny guy. He just goes up and punches him in the nose. Totally unprovoked, never met each other in their lives.

JAMES MCGOVERN, retired correction captain, 1984 to 2004: When I worked in transportation, there was this guy from the Bronx, a good-looking Spanish guy. Really good-looking dude. This is back in the early '80s. What he was doing was he was taking young girls on dates and then raping them and murdering them and dumping their bodies all over the Bronx. They found some of the girls' hair in one of the cars that he rented.

We would take him back and forth to court. We were taking him out on the twelfth floor, and all the other inmates were lined up going back on a different bus, and he was by himself, you know, cuffed. And the other inmates were yelling, "Yo! Papi! Motherfucker!" This guy is like, "Oh, fuck you, you motherfucker. You keep on walking." Sure enough, a week or two later, I go to Rikers Island to help pick him up. The CO's like, "Oh, you didn't hear? He got cut."

Somebody put a contract on the Spanish guy, and this guy cut him with a razor for cigarettes, fucking cut him from ear to ear. Like from the back of his ear all the way down to his neck and just missed the jugular. This is what you dealt with. You know they never found that razor? I don't know what this guy did with that razor. I was standing right there.

DONOVAN DRAYTON: There'll be a fight or whatever. Then COs spray that Mace and that shit is so strong and it like caramelizes and that'll be it. And then they'll punch you in your ribs while you're handcuffed and stuff and take you to where there's no cameras at and slap you around. Once the Mace gets sprayed, it's pretty much it. Everybody is screaming in pain. And they just throw everybody in flex cuffs, and then they escort us to intake.

KAREN SESSOMS, correction officer, 1991 to 1993: I saw something pass from the kitchen to the guy that was there. The officers saw it and they pushed me back. I said it's at this table. It was a sharpened can opener. An inmate got stabbed in the head. I saw the shank passed again. And then it turned into an all-out fight. I pressed my body alarm. They had my captain in a headlock. I had officers fighting. I'm still fairly new, and I knew the worst thing you could do was show fear. The male officers pushed me back. All I did was observe. And then the squad came down and took everybody out. I had to wait until I was out of the mess hall [before I showed emotion]. One of the officers I knew came up and I was like, "Oh my goodness." The first thing that came to my mind was I was going to be raped. I was able to keep my composure. A lot happens in the mess hall. There's a lot that can happen. You have different houses coming in and out. Now they have an opportunity to settle a score.

SOLITARY

"Nobody Can Hear the Wheels Squeak Anymore"

The United Nations deems anything more than fifteen consecutive days of solitary confinement a form of torture. For years, the limits in the New York City jail system went far beyond that.

At its recent peak, there were nearly a thousand so-called Punitive Segregation cells, with some specifically dedicated for teens and people with mental illness. Research shows that twenty-three hours a day in a cell leads to serious psychological damage, especially for adolescents, whose brains are still developing. Studies also show that the punishment does little to decrease violence because those same people are later released right back into the general population.

Extreme isolation as a punishment dates at least as far back as 1831, when the French historian Alexis de Tocqueville visited the Eastern State Penitentiary in Philadelphia. Jail officials had recently begun using that new method based on Quaker teachings.

In a missive to the French government, Tocqueville wrote, "Placed alone in view of his crime [he] learns to hate it, and if his soul be not yet surfeited with crime, and thus have lost all taste for any thing better, it is in solitude, where remorse will come to assail him."

Over time, medical experts have determined the long-term damages of solitary, especially for vulnerable populations, far outweigh any positive initial result. In New York City, there are now strict limits on how long people can be isolated, and some groups are totally exempt from solitary.

Jail officials and union leaders have strenuously fought each of the changes, saying the punishment is needed to keep people who follow the rules safe.

—

HECTOR "PASTOR BENNY" CUSTODIO, former Latin King leader, detained 1991 to 1994: I first went in 1992, in the Bing. You only bathed on Mondays, Wednesdays, and Fridays. Sometimes they would spit in your food. They would put your food under your door. You had to look thoroughly through the food. They gave you a monkey suit; none of your own clothes. During the summer, you had blistering heat. Imagine spending almost four years in your bathroom, locked up, and not being able to go anywhere. That's what it was like. You were so close yet so far. I've seen guys kill themselves, lose their mind, get broken. I had to stay focused. I said, one day I'm going to be free. I'm not going to let these people overpower me. I went for a master's degree. Inside prison, you either become better or die in prison, or you fight for your freedom. I have children. I chose to fight. I wasn't going to allow the system to break me. I just couldn't be another statistic.

RON KUBY, defense attorney: Almost every one of my clients who spent any period of time in Rikers Island has spent time in solitary. It was the go-to punishment for various disciplinary infractions and including relatively minor infractions. I had one client sent to solitary for thirty days for possession of Tylenol, just over-the-counter Tylenol, and some makeup. This was at the Rose M. Singer

Center, which has women. So it was used constantly and it was abused constantly. Probably the more horrific stories are the use of solitary confinement to warehouse the severely mentally ill. I recall one case, I'm not gonna reveal her name, but she was known at Rose M. Singer Center as Shitty. And she was known for that because she was constantly using her own feces to hurl and to write on prison walls and to adorn herself.

And she was placed in solitary for months and months in this stinking, fetid, feces-covered cell. Until finally there were enough complaints about it from a variety of people that she was moved and presumably given some sort of mental health treatment. But the folks who have severe mental illness do tend, in significant part, to engage in what we would call acting out. That is, they tend to be louder and more random and spontaneous and less easy to control and less amenable to things like "Hey, just shut up!" that kind of thing. And we've all seen that with mentally ill people that we've dealt with. And on the outside world, in the free world, it's the squeaky wheel that gets the grease. In a place like Rikers, the squeaky wheel gets shut down and shut up in a cell so deep that nobody can hear the wheels squeak anymore.

HELEN TAYLOR, detained 1970s, 1980s: There was just a toilet and a bed, and you was just thrown in there, and you took a shower every other day for fifteen minutes. Your food would be ice cold, and the room was filthy. They let you clean it once a week for fifteen minutes. Everything was fifteen minutes. You had to lie there and be quiet, and if you weren't, they would come in and beat the crap out of you. There was no TV. You get an hour of rec a day.

It was like they were trying to destroy people. You had to be strong. Someone I knew for a long time committed suicide. They found her hanging in her cell. She had just lost her mother and they didn't do the paperwork in time for her to make the funeral and she hung up and she died. She didn't leave a note. That's what they said, that she didn't leave a note. She was from Brooklyn. She used to go to Lincoln High School with me.

Raised in Coney Island, Helen Taylor first went to jail in 1975. In solitary, "everything was fifteen minutes," she said.

JACQUELINE MCMICKENS, correction commissioner, 1984 to 1986: I have no problems with it at all. I think some people need to be off by themselves. That boy who decides he's going to throw chairs? Put him in a room and watch him. You don't go into Macy's and Gimbels and take whatever you want. There's a consequence. Everybody in [solitary] will go back [to the general population] eventually. Almost everyone in Rikers will be home in six to eight months. They are going to go back home. Do you want to run into him on the street if you just beat him up? This isn't a boxing match.

DR. HOMER VENTERS, correctional health services chief medical officer, 2015 to 2017: We did this analysis of about 250,000 jail admissions and came up with very compelling data that people exposed to solitary had about a seven times higher likelihood of self-harm and about a six times higher likelihood of a high-lethality self-harm. That data and that analysis was because when we gave our expert opinions, it didn't really make much of a dent. If we had gotten buy-in with our expert opinions, we wouldn't have done it.

Seeing what happens in solitary confinement, like spending time with health staff who are supposed to work around solitary confinement, really it doesn't take long to understand that solitary first of all is bad for the health of our patients. That's very clear. But also it's so obvious that solitary confinement is completely corrosive to the health staff who work in those places and that their ability to care for their patients is really compromised by solitary confinement. We have spent so much time trying to get out of the job of clearing people for solitary confinement. It's so hard to come up with a way, ethically, to care for patients. The whole box is built for punishment. It completely destroys your therapeutic alliance or your therapeutic relationship with your patients. Your patients can't look at you as having their best interest at heart when it comes to their asthma or their diabetes, when they see that you are part of putting them in, or keeping them in, a place that's harming them, dramatically and profoundly.

JOHN RAMSEY, detained late 1970s, early 1980s: One time I was in Brooklyn House of Detention, I was in the Bing. The reason why I was in the Bing, police told me, "Suck my dick." And I said, "Well, yeah, okay." Went and got some water, threw it on him, but he was on the outside. They took me down to the Bing. While I'm down there in the cell, one day they got the water hose, sprayed me down, and this was continuous; this is what they did.

It kept happening every, every few days. And the funny thing about it, [the correction officer] was from the West Indies. I go home. Who do I see? I see him coming out of a numbers place.

I got bailed out or something and he's coming out of the number hole. He playing numbers. He seen me like he seen a ghost, right on Flatbush and Newkirk Avenue. I see this guy and, you know, this is a small world.

DONOVAN DRAYTON, detained 2007 to 2012: The box is like the jail inside the jail. It's like being locked away, locked up and the key thrown away. It's like you in a little-ass cell for twenty-three hours a day, if you make rec for that one hour and it's for *x* amount of days. See, back then when I was going to the box, they used to be able to give you a year, a hundred days, four hundred.

Depending on what you're charged with, your crime, or which facility penal code you violated, you could be in a box for mad long. Now the way they changed it, because of course I don't know how they didn't see it like years and years ago. It drives a crazy person crazy in a box, man. They come out a different person. So now they have it set up to where you only [have] thirty days a pop and they take you out. They let you get it together a little bit and then come snatch you and you do a little bit more time. But the box is just brutal, man.

BARRY CAMPBELL, detained 1980s, 1990s: My first time in solitary, I thought that this is nothing. What is everybody talking about? The first time you're in there for about maybe half an hour, forty-five minutes, but this is nothing. And then you realize that you literally have no one to talk to, that you literally are alone in that cell for twenty-three hours. First I did a workout regimen until I couldn't do it anymore. And then you sing and you bang on the walls too. You can't do it anymore. And then eventually you find yourself talking to yourself and then eventually you find yourself counting the cockroaches that come through your doors, or how many times you're going to see a mouse today. And you stare out the window endlessly just looking at the grass and leaves blowing in the winds. People go crazy in there.

DONOVAN DRAYTON: I cried. At the time when I went to the box, where my cell was positioned, you could see the Triborough Bridge, and it was the greatest view and the most hurtful view at the same time because it was just like, yo, I may never, ever go across this bridge again a free man. Like the next time, they may drive my casket back to my dad's to bury me free. At the time I didn't know where my life was heading with the situation. I didn't know what was in store. That's how I was thinking. Like, damn, just looking at that view. It's like I was just driving across that bridge yesterday and to be in a box now, in a cell where I can't go nowhere . . . but my toilet is here. My bed is built into a wall. My window is a mesh screen and I can only pull the knob to open the window on a slide to crack open and I can't even open a window. I remember the first time I called my dad from the box, I cried like a baby. I don't care what nobody say. Somebody say, I ain't crying, tough or not tough, strong man, alpha male, oh, man, I was crying like a girl.

Jail already had hit me. I already knew I was in jail, but it really, really, really hit me when I went to the box the first time that I was really in jail. I adapted again. The first time I was in the box, a hundred days, a hundred days, a hundred days. I did a hundred days. The next time I was in a box for thirty days. And then, throughout the five years I was on Rikers Island, it'd be like twenty days here, thirty days here. But the longest stretch I ever did in the box was a hundred days. I did four months, almost four months.

KATHY MORSE, detained 2006: My job at Rosie's [Rose M. Singer Center] was as a grievance officer and we would receive grievances from individuals who were in solitary. And because of where they were, they couldn't come to us. We had to go to them. And it was a dungeon. I thought that the noise in the housing unit was surreal, but the noise in solitary was unbelievable. You had people banging on their walls, just screaming. It was so bad. It wasn't even like it was a human being who was screaming. It was more like an animal who was hurt, screaming for help.

I know that they changed the rules so that they can't hold adolescents in solitary confinement. But they get around that by calling it something else. And the really out-of-control adolescents they were sending up to county jail in Albany because there they can hold the adolescents in solitary.

From what I witnessed, solitary can really do horrific things to an individual. And I don't mean just physically, I mean mentally. A high number of the population in Rikers is already going in with mental health issues.

KAREN SESSOMS, correction officer, 1991 to 1993: I had the Bing, which was in OBCC [Otis Bantum Correctional Center]. When you walk in a jail, the air is totally different. There are so many smells. You have to check if someone is not moving. There are so many things you see; sometimes, when they see a woman CO on the floor, suddenly everyone has to take a piss. They all have to show their genitals, what have you. That happened twice. This happens when they know that you're new. In the Bing, they are in their cells for twenty-three hours and allowed out for one. Their meals are delivered to their cells. There's not much movement that goes in and out. As a correction officer, this is not a place where you want to just sit. You want to constantly walk around. When you are watching them, they are watching you. You can hear things being sharpened, usually weapons.

DONOVAN DRAYTON: Well, me, I ain't gonna lie to you. I'm not giving myself too much credit, but I'm really mentally tough. Everybody's not mentally tough the way I am. I feel like mental toughness is a different aspect of being strong. The box, for the not-so-strong-minded individuals, will break you. That's why people are coming out crazy [or] on medication. Never was on medication before. Now you're on medication.

ELIAS HUSAMUDEEN, president of the Correction Officers' Benevolent Association, 2016 to 2020: I worked punitive segregation. I was actually a punitive seg officer in the largest jail on Rikers Island, which is AMKC [Anna M. Kross Center]. And the one thing that I will say about punitive seg is that it works. But it doesn't work on everybody. And if you have one particularly violent [person] who just cannot seem to follow the rules, you have to be able to have something with that particular person.

Ninety-nine percent of the inmates never came back once they did their ten days, thirty days, fifty days. It pretty much helped in addressing the behavior that was unacceptable thirty years ago and now. But the 1 percent it didn't work on is where I believe we failed. The definition of insanity is to keep on doing the same thing over and over and expecting a different outcome.

Earlier in the year, I provided city hall with a list of inmates. Some of the inmates had been in and out of solitary five times, seven times, twenty times. I gave them a list of people who had been in punitive seg a minimum of five times. And I asked the question, why would we continue to put them in punitive seg when it was obvious that it wasn't working for that particular population? I can't tell you that I received an answer. The reality is we have to do something with them, but obviously punitive seg isn't working for all inmates.

And the City of New York hasn't to this day found a solution for this particular population. But they can be dealt with, but you have to be willing to do it. In my position as a union leader I've always asked the question, what do we do with this particular population? You don't want us to put them in punitive seg. It doesn't make sense to put them in punitive seg. But we have to protect the officer, the other inmates, and the civilians. I've asked this question. I even sat down with the deputy mayor. Needless to say, no one came up with any answers.

HOMER VENTERS: I'd never seen anything like this [solitary unit] in my life. I was going around with a physician's assistant who did this every day. You walk onto a unit; let's say the PA had to cover five or six units. Each of those units was like a tier of maybe forty or forty-five cells. So he walks onto the unit [and] will yell out, "Sick call!" Then he would just run down each of the tiers. If somebody had their hand up or was banging on their cell, and we would then try to make this calculus of if somebody had a complaint, do they need to come out for a sick call?

People would ask a lot of questions [like] where's my medicine or they might ask about a chronic care appointment. But he would also jot this all down on a piece of paper, and the whole process would take maybe ten minutes or less to go through all these cells, and it would be done in the morning when most of those people are asleep.

DONOVAN DRAYTON: It's hard, man. Just being in a room with yourself for so many days. It can drive you literally insane. You know what, if you're not mentally tough and mentally stable, it'll change you. You see what happened to Kalief Browder? You know, he went to jail, he was mentally stable. He came home from prison, mentally shot. Rikers Island killed that man. And many in so many ways.

He was a walking example of if you're not mentally strong, what that environment can do to you. God bless the brother because . . . when I watched his documentary, you know, and watched what he went through, I went through so many similar things. Just being mistreated by COs, fighting with different sets of people in prison that are involved in different lifestyles that you're not wanting to be a part of. So now you got to get into it with them. God willing. I knew some people in prison too, so I was all right.

He wasn't so fortunate. And he wasn't mentally straight. He came home with mental scars, and they was still bleeding and he took his life. Man couldn't deal with it no more.

When I was in the box, my dad was really bringing me all my reading material. My dad was bringing me books all the time. My dad was there, my biggest support system. Out of everybody. I had my dad. That was the main thing. That's what helped me get through the box time. Just reading.

I was going through the trying situation, so I was reading a lot of self-help books, empowerment books. I read a lot of stuff about subconscious power, the subconscious mind, speaking stuff into existence, just how the mind works, and I was getting close to God and just trying to work on my spirit. I tried to take that time when I was always isolated from everybody to try to work on my mental health as much as I can. You can't walk around and stare in that box, you can't go out and move around. So I can move around in my head.

I figured this out how to not be broken down. And that's how my dad did it for me, man. He just said, "Brother, read this." I was flying through books in a day. I started reading a book at seven o'clock in the morning, when lights go on, and I'm done by eight o'clock at night. And I would say to my dad, "I need ten more books. Send me some books." Man, I done ran through about six this week already.

BARRY CAMPBELL: For me it was everything that I can do to remain sane. And what I realized was the easiest thing for me to do was to reflect on my life at that time, everything that I had gone through with my family . . . why was it that nobody wanted me as a child? I was thinking back to the first time I met Father Harris, who's in the boys' home, thinking about what my life was like when they took me from the boys' home and put me in the group home and put me in a private Catholic school and I was going to see Broadway plays at seven, eight, nine years old. For four African American kids from the projects out of Flatbush, that was unheard of at the time. So the way that I stayed sane was reflecting on my life and reflecting on where my family was at the time, even though I was turned over to the criminal justice system at a very early age. My family was quite successful.

And I just couldn't understand that my entire family had changed their situations in terms of the lives that they were living. But I was stuck. And so I started brainwashing myself that I had the DNA for success. I just hadn't tapped into it. Why was I not tapping into it, and what did I need to do to tap into it? So then it was only logical that I could be successful if I wanted to. When I first came to this country, we were living in a one-bedroom apartment with food stamps. There were days when I ate mayonnaise sandwiches. And so remembering all of those things while you're sitting in solitary confinement helps you stay sane, whereas other people around me, you can hear the decompensation of them happening on a daily basis.

You may have started out yelling to each other, but three, four, five weeks later you're yelling to him and he's not answering, but you know he's in there. You know, the person on the other side of you originally started out banging on the walls and rapping music, and now he's in there talking to himself, having conversations. There were people that I was in there with that to this very day are either dead, serving the rest of their lives in prison, or they're walking around midtown Manhattan completely out of their minds.

MICHAEL LOVE, detained early 1980s, early 1990s: There was an [officer] who was Black, about six-six, 320 pounds. He came to extract me. I wasn't coming out. He grabbed me by my T-shirt and pulled me so hard it left a scar on my neck that I still have. He slammed me against the wall. He said, "I'm going to break your arm," and I said, "Go ahead and break the motherfucker." It's psychologically induced fatalism. You don't care about consequences. You don't care. It's in combination with elevating the confrontation. That night he took off all my clothes, threw me in my cell, and left the window open. It was cold. It was winter. It was too cold for that window to be open. That happened probably around '76 or '77. I was about eighteen.

HOMER VENTERS: The first few times I went to the Bing, I'm not sure I understood how different it was, and why people got there. I was certainly not aware of what happened when people got there. It really wasn't until two, three months into working. I went on Bing rounds 'cause I kept hearing about this thing called Bing rounds where different levels of staff, either a nurse or once in a while a PA or MD, would go cell to cell.

I couldn't understand what it was they were doing or even what the purpose of Bing rounds was. And so I went with them on these rounds, and then that really started to open my eyes to a lot of the dual-loyalty issues. I still didn't have an appreciation of how brutal or how many injuries there were in these places. But just following a health staffer, because they sprint from cell to cell to try and get off a unit as quickly as possible, was really eye-opening to me. I was starting to ask myself some questions about what's happening to our patients, and what's our health service doing in these places? How much is it helping and what else should we be doing?

DOC came to us and said, "We need more MAUI [Mental Health Assessment Unit for Infracted Inmates] beds." It's kind of an obscene thing to even say in one sentence, but it was solitary confinement for people with mental illness. It seemed like when they came to us and said, "We need more MAUI beds," what we need to do is get rid of MAUI, not get more MAUI. The reason they needed more beds is because when people go to these places, they never leave. Because it seems so self-evident in retrospect, but they decompensate and they do horribly and they get more infractions.

They wanted more beds to park more people with infractions. That happened my first week as a commissioner. And then we worked hard to put together [a responsive] memo. This memo again seems kind of naive, but basically I got all of our experts, both in the correctional health service and experts outside the correctional health service from Bellevue, from other places, to sign on to this memo that I wrote about why we not only needed to *not* expand MAUI but that we needed to eliminate it. That we needed to eliminate the practice of solitary confinement, particularly for these vulnerable groups. And then we gave this memo to everybody, and the response we got was that that may be your opinion, but it's your opinion. So give us some data.

Looking back, we should have stopped and said no. We're the experts. I had to regroup with my team and think about, okay, how would we put together an analysis that can actually show irrefutably the harm of this practice? We decided to choose physical self-harm as the variable, the health outcome that we would look at, because it's hard when you're talking about mental health exacerbations to show with data sometimes. Then we put together a regression analysis where we looked at lots of things that we thought might contribute, or be involved in, physical self-harm, including high-lethality self-harm.

TERRENCE SKINNER, retired deputy warden, 1983 to 2003: I got assigned to work in the Bing as an officer. They got one phone call for the week. This prisoner wanted to make a call, but he had already made his call. We said no. My partner was walking the tier, and the prisoner dumped a big bucket of dirty soap water on my partner. And a day or two later, when he came out of his cell, my partner and him fought. I got involved. We beat the hell out of that guy. We write that we restrained him, but we fought him until he stopped. He took a beating that day. That's the reality. About two days later, I had a different partner. The same guy wanted to make a phone call. We said no. The prisoner was pissed. I went to meal about 7:30 that night. The guy who relieved me was supposed to walk the tier and make sure everything was okay. He didn't do that. A half hour later [the] inmate wrote a letter that he didn't get a phone call and he was hanging himself. He hung himself, but because the officer didn't walk the tier, he wasn't seen. I don't know how long he was hanging. As I was coming back into the housing area from meal, they were carrying the prisoner out on a stretcher and he died. I was told the officer didn't tour. The suicide aide saw the guy hanging and yelled up front. He must have been hanging long.

He wrote that it was because of me. A few days later, the captain was telling me it was my fault. He and I had words over that. The conditions were hairy, and unfortunately the longer you stayed on the job, the more normal they became; even seeing things like that became normal. At the time, I played the macho role, and it had nothing to do with me, I didn't think. I didn't have the sympathy. I'm not blaming myself now, but I'm saying that's the way it was.

DONOVAN DRAYTON: You don't get fed like population, you know what I'm saying? You get three meals a day, and depending on what they serve, it's like you might not want that. You understand? Like unless you cool with the suicide-watch cat. Whenever the man can get some food and sneak it to you, to sneak some soups and cookies and all that stuff. If you in a box, you're not supposed to be, you're not supposed to have commissary, just straight institutional food.

BARRY CAMPBELL: [When you get out] it's like being released from jail, prison. Literally. If you went in there for something substantial, when you come out, everybody is like, "Boy, you are a crazy-ass dude." You know they gonna put you back soon. And so there's a certain reputation that follows you if you went in there for something that was violent as opposed to being caught with a pack of cigarettes. So when you come out, most of the people, if you were a violent person, most of the people know what you went in there for. They get worried when you come out. There's a level of that celebrity status that you get from coming out, and you think everything is great because you're just so happy to be able to talk to another human being again or to interact with people and you're as happy as the day that you are being released and you don't realize it at the time, but you ain't freed. But you feel freed 'cause you getting out of the box.

MENTAL HEALTH

"Cupcake Gerbil Face"

More than 40 percent of the city jail population suffers from some form of mental illness, according to jail officials. They rarely get individualized treatment beyond short visits from clinicians who are frequently overloaded with patients.

Some are so seriously sick they cover themselves in feces, refuse to shower for days, and can barely talk coherently. The fortunate ones are funneled to new specialized units where they are given added care and daily visits from medical staff. But many over the years have been tossed in solitary by frustrated jail staff ill-equipped to handle and care for them.

—

ANNE PETRARO, clinician, 2013 to 2018: I had worked in jails before. I've worked in pretty bad situations, but this was like nothing I've ever seen before. I was terrified. It's long hallways, blood on the floor. It was bad.

BARRY CAMPBELL, detained 1980s, 1990s: Mentally ill people suffered the most of any other person on Rikers Island. Back in the

'80s and '90s if you were gay and transgender and you went to Rikers Island, you suffered, but you didn't suffer as much as the mental health people, because they got it from the staff and they got it from the inmates and I'm talking some brutal shit. I watched this one dude just walk over to a [mentally ill] dude who was sitting in the corner, take out his dick, and start peeing on that motherfucker, when the dude is just sitting there and I'm like, "Yo, what the fuck is you doing?" That shit makes no sense to me. He wasn't bothering anybody. He may have been playing with a roach or some shit.

And then in terms of the staff "on the count" [when officers count the detainees]. Mental health motherfucker don't know the difference between on the count and off the count, they don't know. But because the count was held up because he chose to stand in the bathroom shitting on the toilet as opposed to wiping his ass and running out there for the count, you now put him on the list of be fucked and you not only fuck with him; you pass word to all your friends that are on staff, "When you see him, fuck with him." That's bad. People would literally go over there and just start fucking that boy up for no reason whatsoever other than some staff members heard to. It's sad and breaks my heart. It almost makes me want to cry sometimes what I've seen some of those dudes go through.

TAHANEE DUNN, lawyer, Bronx Defenders: I remember going into Rikers after a family member of a client had called and said that he was having a really hard time mentally. He was mentally decompensating. And as soon as I got into the holding room, he was hysterical and this is not a young man who shows emotion ever. He's pretty stoic. He was just sobbing. And I just remember putting my hands through the little tiny slot, because they put him in solitary confinement as a result of his mental decompensation because he was acting out. So rather than giving him mental health care, they just threw him in the box. So it was noncontact, but there was a little teeny slot. And I remember like pulling out my arms after a three-hour visit and my arms and hands were numb because the whole time I had just been holding his head in one hand and his hand in the other while he cried.

We talked about reality and trying to just take things hour by hour for three hours. I had massive imprints under my arms from where my arms have basically been sitting on, like, the grate of the little slot that I could sort of put my hands in and hold him. I was sore for like a week after that.

He is a young man from the Bronx. He's given me permission to speak about his situation in Rikers, not so much about his case, but his experience. He grew up in the Bronx, one of like nine brothers and sisters, single mom, and he started to get in trouble around like thirteen, fourteen, just hanging out with his friends. I think the turning point for him was when one of his best friends was shot and killed in front of him. And he basically held him while he died. That was the pivotal point for him. There was a lot of gang violence, so carrying a gun was just par for the course. Like that's just sort of what one did for protection, not because you had an intention of using it on anybody or initiating violence against anybody, but certainly for protection.

He had been in and out of jail on some pretty hard-core charges from like seventeen years old until when he was incarcerated on this case now. Now he's been incarcerated for just over three years pretrial. His charges hold a life sentence if he's convicted. He went in when he was twenty-one and he's twenty-four now. He's had an incredibly hard time. There are multiple co-defendants in this case. So he has a lot of separation orders, which means that there's not many facilities in DOC that he can go to, which means that he often finds himself in restrictive housing, just because DOC has nowhere to put him.

So all of these things were sort of coming to light and, yeah, one night he just sort of lost it and acknowledged the first time that he was feeling very depressed. And he was having anxiety and insomnia, which could also be a lasting effect of COVID that was untreated. He had COVID back in March, lost sense of smell, taste, all those things, the cloudy thinking. And yeah, he reached out and said, "I finally need help. I want to see a psychologist. I want to go see a neurologist." [That] was a big deal for a young man of color, particularly given the stigma of mental health in the community and certainly in jails. DOC's response was to put him in solitary confinement. He's been in restrictive housing, where he's shackled to desks.

Every time he leaves a cell, he's shackled from head to toe, from feet to around the waist in the back, which is actually a violation as well because of his medical conditions. He's not supposed to be shackled in the back. He's supposed to be side cuffed or in the front with one hand free. And they also put him in mitts when he's out of his cell. And that's been going on for four months now, despite the fact that I have hounded DOC, testified on the record at Board of Correction hearings, shamed the chief of staff and general counsel and the commissioner. They're just a rogue agency, so that's still where he is. That was the very beginning of us seeing that he was completely unraveling.

DAVID CAMPBELL, detained 2019 to 2020: You heard of the Brad H. [legal] case? They use that in there to say, if you get a Brad H. letter, you're a "Brad H.," or you can also use it to say like a dude's crazy. Like, "That motherfucker's Brad H.!" Like pretty funny. Or "MO" [mental observation] or "730" [mental evaluation] you can also say. Brad H. is pretty funny and the most common one.

FITZGERALD DAVID, correction officer, 1987 to 2014: I watched inmates do some things that I've never seen in my life. I watched an inmate who should've never been on Rikers Island, should've never been locked up. He should have been in a mental institution. He was in a holding cell to be seen by medical, and I watched this individual do a headfirst swan dive into the bars, knock hisself out, he was out for quite a while. Then he got up and started eating the feces and drinking the piss out of the toilet bowl. It was incredible.

Then I watched another guy, an Indian guy who should have never been on Rikers Island, break the fluorescent lightbulb and actually cut his penis, slit his penis in half. That was unbelievable. All the staff, even other inmates in the intake area, screamed. It was unbelievable. Totally unbelievable. He didn't say anything. He was just losing his mind. We tried to help him as best we could, get him to the clinic.

ANNE PETRARO: There was an inmate who would slash himself, blood everywhere, like blood flying. It was crazy and he would just be like, "Okay, now can I go to the mental observation unit?" Obviously he belonged in MO.

It was hard. There was a guy that used to call all the staff "Cupcake Gerbil Face." He was huge and used to mutilate himself so bad that he would end up in the hospital. Rikers medical couldn't help him. He would have to be transported. And for some reason, I was the only person who could get through to him, so they'd be like, "Before you cut, can Ms. P. come?" And he'd be like, "Only if she comes." And I would go there and he would still be bleeding. He's like, "I won't finish cutting myself." I saw his bone. That's how bad it was.

And when you actually talk to him he was such a teddy bear. But he had this tough exterior because he was in that environment for his entire life. I wouldn't react. I'd just be there for him.

That's self-mutilation, self-harm, goal-directed behavior, but then there's the people who are so emotionally harmed that they do it to feel pain so they don't feel the inside pain. That's how they explain it. And they know they're not killing themselves; they just want to hurt themselves. And then there's the people who are really seriously trying to kill themselves. You just want to be careful, because these people could really hurt themselves and they're so hurting that they hurt other people. Hurt people hurt people. Is that the phrase?

FITZGERALD DAVID: I watched an inmate get on the phone, speak to his girlfriend. And his girlfriend either was seeing another guy, or she wanted to leave him. And the guy went and ripped his underwear off and wrapped his underwear around his neck and tried to kill hisself. He hung the underwear on the bars, tied in on the bars, hung hisself, and we had to actually cut him down. We got him in time because the other inmates were yelling, "Hey, Mr. D., Mr. D., this guy's trying to hang up."

Certain inmates should not be on Rikers Island. Certain inmates that have been arrested have mental issues. You know he's not a real threat to the public, but he's a real threat to himself. That person should be in a hospital.

I watched several inmates that would draw these demonic signs on the wall in their cell and actually sit there and talk to themselves and have conversations. You know this man doesn't belong there. But you also have another problem on the island, which is that you have a lot of mental health doctors who really don't do anything for these individuals. You can't just keep giving people pills. That's insane. You only see maybe four or five inmates a day. You're there for eight hours. That's ridiculous. But you can hold staff accountable for when these inmates flip out? No, you can't.

The department back in the '80s had lightbulbs, before the fluorescent lightbulbs. I saw an inmate in the pen actually break the lightbulb out and gouge his own eye out. That's insane. These people don't belong there.

EDDIE ROSARIO, detained 1990: Rikers is one of the largest penal colonies in the world, and is also the city's de facto mental health facility. Fifty to 60 percent of the incarcerated are diagnosed at some point in their lives. If you have someone hearing voices, it's going to be disruptive, and they are going to get flack from the guards and from the people who are incarcerated or detained. What happens is that those mental health needs overwhelm the jailers. I saw abuse from guards who didn't have the skill set to deal with someone hearing voices. There's friction from those trying to sleep and the guards on post.

They would get caught in this intersection of abuse from both sides of the cage. You would hear things like "If you don't get this guy out of here, we're going to blow him up," meaning hurt him. Some guys were clueless. Other guys were trying to tell him, "You need to calm down." There's a lot of frustration to begin with in jail. Shit is going down. Any little thing that upsets that precarious balance means that shit can just blow up. It could be on a hot day just 'cause it's a hot day. We were caught in a framework that treated us as animals. Sometimes our only recourse was to behave in kind.

MARTHA GRIECO, lawyer, Bronx Defenders: It's like, you did something bad, so we have to punish you. We don't understand how mental illness works. The vast majority of people with diagnoses like schizophrenic disorder do nothing to harm anybody. But there's just always this thread of people in the criminal justice system who just have blinders on about accountability; that somehow if you know what you're doing, if you're not actually under the illusion that there are green men telling you what to do—that's the only kind of crazy where they're like, oh yeah, you can't control what's happening and you think green men are attacking you and you're just attacking them back.

So if you know where you are, if you know who you're with, if you know the situation, but yet you can't control yourself or you don't have the physical tools to manage certain emotions, because of trauma, because of abuse, or because of a genetic disorder in your brain, that's not something that's understood. And it makes sense because you can't step into somebody else's shoes if you're not mentally ill. And unfortunately, because those who are mentally ill are so marginalized that they never become prosecutors and judges. There's lots of mental illness among prosecutors and judges, but not this type, where the diagnosis is schizophrenia, schizoaffective-type diagnoses.

And they all want to rely on Rikers. It makes no sense to me. Rikers triggers people with mental illness. It makes it worse. It makes everybody worse. If you weren't the type of person to do something before you went into Rikers, Rikers will turn you into that type of person, like no other—I'm sorry, now I'm on my soapbox—no other institution gets so many passes for failure as the criminal justice system.

If you're a judge and you sentence somebody to something, you never have to check in with them again to see if they never committed a crime. That was the whole point of sentencing in the prisons—teaching them a lesson. You're going to send them to prison for five years, but you don't check up on that person. You don't know if what you did was right. Can you imagine if a scientist was like, "I'm just going to make this cocktail and put it in people for years and years and years. And I'm never going to follow up with these patients to see if it actually cured them"? Ridiculous.

ANNA GRISTINA, detained 2012: I got the best treatment Rikers could give anyone. [A woman named] Candace, she was in protective custody, too. She was suing Rikers. When she was in gen pop, she picked a fight with an inmate for no reason. Then they wouldn't let her out. She decided she was going to climb out through her food slot and got stuck. They went and got grease and got her out. She started flipping out and threw bleach on the guard. They put her back in PC. She was now locked in a room and she wanted out. She took all her clothes off, shoved them in the toilet, and overflowed the entire floor. She kept flushing it until there was water an inch and a half in the floor. She deserved everything she got. She started shit with me nonstop. There's no winning or losing with someone who is mentally not there. We signed a petition to get her out. You know what it's like to walk on eggshells with someone like that?

All I could hear in PC was the howling and screaming of the mentally ill. It would carry through the night from the outside; you had to plug your ears with toilet tissue to drown out the sound. They were screaming that someone in the room was trying to have sex with them. There is not the mental health treatment that some of these people desperately need. Even if they had something, there was no medication in Rikers. The mantra was "You're in Rikers, deal with it."

EDWARD GAVIN, retired deputy warden, 1982 to 2001: I was always looking to make overtime. And one of my fellow tour commanders—I was assistant deputy warden then—she asked me to take her shift. I said yeah. So I walk in. I hold roll call. An hour later into the shift, I get a call into the mental observation area. And it's two tiers. So, apparently this one inmate came in on a drug charge, it was sad, she's probably like early forties. She didn't get her methadone; the inmates call it the green biscuits. She didn't get her green biscuits. She was kicking. The doctor didn't feel she needed it. So sometimes, when they don't get their green biscuits, sometimes they start eating sugar packets.

There is supposed to be an officer on each tier, and there is a desk on each tier right at the top. The officer is supposed to walk by there every fifteen minutes on the mental observation area. But two officers were downstairs watching TV with the inmates. This inmate, she was just wandering up the stairs. There's a bar and she tied a sheet and hung [it] around her neck and she jumped off the tier.

And so when you walked up the stairs, you just see her hanging. We cut her down. She pooped herself and pissed herself. You could see it. It was gross. She lost her life. Maybe had the officer been doing their job, maybe she wouldn't have bought it that particular time? I don't know. Maybe the medical staff should have done a better job screening her. Maybe she needed more than we were able to give her. Maybe they just didn't give a damn. I don't know. It was the summer of 1997.

Dealing with the mentally ill is a huge part of the job. People don't understand. And we're not RNs or LPNs or physician's as- sistants. We're not doctors and we have to deal with all these peo- ple. There's a clinic. You send them there. There's just too much to manage, even for the medical people. It's like managing a monster, you know?

You could go into a cell, get a sheet, tie it around your neck, affix it to a railing, and then jump. You're gonna micromanage that? It's not like you're holding a baby. These are people. They're mobile. It doesn't happen that often. It can happen. They are in- carcerated. They don't have their drugs. They are missing their loved ones. Whatever else is going on in their world. Their world is coming to a standstill, and some people opt to kill themselves.

EVE KESSLER, director, DOC public affairs, 2014 to 2017: I would estimate that probably half the people in the jails really shouldn't have been there and they should have been in a drug program or a mental health facility somewhere. But that's what jail has become. [The former commissioner Joseph] Ponte said publicly many times that Rikers was the largest mental hospital on the East Coast. That's not about the jails. That's about our society that's relegating so many people with so many problems that we don't have the right kind of help for the jails.

A lot of the jail staff thought that there were people who just preferred jail accommodations to the streets or the shelters. I mean, certainly they would get better medical care in the jails. There were people who, when they show up to jail, it's the first time they've ever seen a dentist in their lives or gotten their vision checked. I mean it's a sad and terrible comment on our society. So from that point of view, it's like everyone's talking about the jails are so brutal . . . it's society that's brutal. It's the society that works that way.

KANDRA CLARK, detained 2010: I've grown up around people with serious mental illness my whole life, and I suffer from mania and anxiety. I'm always a mover and shaker. I can't just sit at the same space all the time. I need to be moving. I need to have a lot of positive affirmation. I can get depressed if I don't really stay positive and stay focused. I think what I saw the most inside is that there were so many of us that had those exact feelings, whether it was either mental illness or serious mental illness. However you wanted to distinguish between the two. There was no support. I cannot tell you how many times I would request to be seen by a nurse or speak to somebody, and not once did I ever meet with a therapist.

They brought me down one time to speak with some counselor who did absolutely nothing. It was not an actual psychotherapist. Nobody ever put me on medication. I had no talk therapy inside. I think us women tend to band together more and really form families and look out for each other. So there was one woman specifically who had a severe mental illness that reminded me, actually, a lot of my mother, and there were other females that would pick on her sometimes. So I would try to do my best to stick up for her and just support her.

I'd sit and actually talk to her, have a conversation with her. I think that's what most people want: is just to be heard and be listened to. And so we would try to kind of sit down and work together on that.

Kandra Clark is the vice president of policy and strategy at Exodus Transitional Community, which helps people who spent time in jail get back on their feet.

MATT FREY, clinician, 2011 to 2018: Some people were so out of their minds they just totally didn't belong and it took them months to get to a psych hospital for a 730 mental health evaluation. And then they ended up staying there for like a very long time 'cause they're so sick. Those people should never be in jail. Also people developmentally disabled definitely did not belong there. They were just preyed upon. And they didn't oftentimes know what they did wrong to end up in jail because they're on the spectrum.

Some people just come in and haven't showered in God knows

how long. They can't hold a conversation. They're babbling. They'd be in a much better place if there could be somewhere where they could go, somewhere where they can mandate medication to actually get them to a level where they can communicate. I would have to do a mental health intake on somebody completely incoherent.

BARRY CAMPBELL: You got mental health people on Rikers Island who can't comply. Officer gets upset, he woke up on the wrong side of the bed, and he sends his goons after him. And this dude don't even know that he offended you in any shape, form, or fashion, because it wasn't intentional. He has a mental health problem or the dude has HIV/AIDS or the dude is transgender. For whatever reason you don't like him. You don't like his lifestyle. You're going to send people to hurt them. You're a piece of shit. Sorry, but that's the way I looked at you.

JULIA SOLOMONS, social worker, Bronx Defenders: Something like 40 percent of people in custody have a diagnosed mental health issue. But the amount of specialized units that exist for people with mental health needs is significantly less than that.

So a lot of our clients fall into a category where they're not acutely ill enough to be receiving those specialized services and in one of those units because of how limited resources are. So they end up in a general population unit. And the difference between the sort of care that they get in those two units is very stark. I think even the folks that are in the specialized units could be doing better in a hospital or receiving care in the community.

And that population is not being released with the same frequency as people who do not have that Brad H. mental health designation. Recently, you can see that trend in the data. People are not getting the support that they need in jail. And that translates to the court after viewing them as not being in a place to released, and it also reduces our ability to advocate for them when they're not receiving services in the jail.

For example, if a client is trying to access treatment as part

a plea or as a condition of release of some kind, if we can point to services that they've been receiving in the jail and how they've been doing with those, which is much easier to do when they're in one of those specialized units and have that specialized attention, we're more likely to be able to convince a judge or a prosecutor that they would be able to be successful in treatment or in the community.

But if we don't have anything to point to because they're not getting care in the jail, it's harder to do that. And it's harder to make the case that they need those services if they haven't been designated as needing them within the jail setting.

GABRIEL KRETZMER SEED, chaplain: There was actually a case when I was assaulted at one of my Jewish services at AMKC [Anna M. Kross Center]. It turned out it was someone who I knew well who was having a mental health crisis, and was probably hallucinating and seemed to think I was someone who I wasn't.

It was Friday morning. What I've been doing every Friday morning before COVID is sing some zemiroth [songs] for Shabbat and then teach a little bit about Shabbat for twenty minutes at the end. We had finished singing and I'd started teaching and he would sit in the front and there may be six or seven individuals in the pews. And this person had been sitting toward the front, and he got up and punched me in the face.

He was a pretty strong person, but I only ended up with a bloody lip. He might have been mumbling something, but I don't remember what he said specifically. I was quite shocked. Everything happened so quickly. I was totally in shock because I had known him for a while and he was the last person I thought would hurt me.

It obviously was scary. But the other detainees at the time came to my defense, the staff rushed me to the clinic, everyone from the wardens to the tour commander to my supervisor, my colleagues showed up to check in on me.

And, amazingly, I was able to work with the mental health staff a couple months later and revived my pastoral relationship with

that individual, and I still have a good relationship with him. He's still in custody, and I still have a good relationship with him. And it's good that I was able to continue to be there for him. And once we determined that he was comfortable with it, and to work with the staff to deal with that therapeutically.

There used to be more mental health care in the community. So people didn't end up in our facilities. I feel much more strongly about that than I did before I started working here.

DONOVAN DRAYTON, detained 2007 to 2012: I was in the house one time and they had this old man in the house and he barely could move around. Like you could tell he could barely move. He was peeing on himself. No disrespect to the brother. He was an older cat. He needed to be in a medical ward, something like that. You know what I'm saying? He can barely move back and forth to the mess hall, let alone fully use the bathroom and get up in the middle of the night and pee. The guy needed a bucket on the side of his bed to pee.

That same guy, he had a seizure and busted his head on one of the beds and almost bled to death after we was telling them. We was telling the warden, we was telling the dep, we was telling the captain, "Yo, man, take this old man out this house, bro. Why y'all got him here with us?" He needs to be in a medical ward. He has to have like a nurse on hand or medical or something on hand; like this old cat, you know, he can't function properly.

If I'm not mistaken, he was locked up for some before case from like 1980, [for] some old crime that he supposedly committed and they just caught up with him years down the line. It just goes to show he shouldn't be in the house, man. His head never would have got busted open if they would've just put him in a proper housing unit he was supposed to be in. It's not that hard to do—a little paperwork, stroke of a pen, and voilà, but no, they lazy, man.

JERRY DEAN, detained 1987, 2003: When I went back as an adult, it was a different experience for me, because from being a young kid who was a boxer, who was good with his hands, now I had been dealing with mental illness. So I went to the mental observation unit. These were the worst dormitories on Rikers Island because you had all these kids and gang members and Bloods and all in solitary confinement.

And they would fake suicide attempts to get into the mental observation units. And then they would love it. They would be vicious. These men, these people with mental illness, want to get food and a bed. You want to get cereal in the morning, anything; the gang members were the ones giving out the food for the correction officers, which was totally insane. It was a big mental hospital. That was 2003.

JACQUELINE MCMICKENS, correction commissioner, 1984 to 1986: There are some inmates who won't cooperate with you under any circumstances. They're crazy or they're such losers. So what you do is that you isolate them and you train officers to handle them. And yes, it may be brutal, because if you want to fight, we have a bigger fight. You can do what I ask you to do and we won't touch you. But you may not sit nude in the middle of the floor. We're going to remove you from the middle of the floor and we're going to put a blanket on you because you're ugly and I'm not going to hurt you doing that. But that's what's happening now. And it happened when I was a correction officer before I could have anything to do with it. I watched that kind of stuff.

I went into a jail once and there was blood on the wall. Now, I know that was not correction officer blood. What he'd done is that they [correction officers] had mopped that inmate up and off the wall several times. But you [the detainee] will never do that again on my watch. If there's any blood on the wall, you better get it down before I see it, one, and two, it better not ever happen again. They used to have inmates do a thing that was called thumb cuffs. I didn't ever see it, but I heard about it. They would pull the inmate out of a cell and make him stand on his tiptoes. I mean, that kind of stuff, they thought it was funny. But that's a culture.

Some people are just crazy. And so you give them the kind of environment that they deserve, which may be no sheets 'cause you'll hang up and no mattress because you'll smother yourself and no chair because you hit me. And you say, "Oh, that's cruel." Well, wait a minute, I'm going to give him a chair so he can hit the officers? We're trying to feed him. I'm going to give him bedsheets so he can hang up? What's cool about that? I'm not gonna put you in any straitjacket. A man who floods his toilet? I'm going to turn the water off in your toilet and that's going to stink. And guess what? Eventually, we all get sane. I have to help him not be bad and not throw feces on the hallway where my officers need to walk and carry my food. People think that's cruel. What's cruel about that? What about walking in feces?

ELIZABETH GLAZER, director, Mayor's Office of Criminal Justice, 2014 to 2020: There's been a big focus on trying to address the mentally ill. Obviously, violence is complicated, but I would be very hesitant to say the reason why there's so much violence is because there are more people who suffer from behavioral health issues.

RON KUBY, defense lawyer: This becomes much more of a policy discussion. When there was a decision made, and this was primarily during the Giuliani era, and to a lesser extent in the Bloomberg era, the decision was made that something needed to be done about homeless people who were mentally ill. And there were a lot of things that we could have done, but the easiest, and the one for which there was an apparatus already created, was to arrest them, charge them, put a bail on them that they could not make, and send them to Rikers Island for the duration of their case, whether it was a month or six months or even a year, they were off the streets.

So Rikers Island by default or by policy reasons became one of the city's largest shelters for people who were mentally ill, in some cases severely mentally ill, and they were not equipped to deal with that. Corrections officers are not trained therapists. They're not social workers. They're not nurse practitioners or psychologists or psychiatrists. Corrections officers know just two things, obedience, which they demand, and defiance, which they repress. I mean, that's kind of their job. And that's not a criticism of them individually. Many of them are capable of kindness and decency and compassion like everybody else, but their job is to maintain what they considered to be order in a penal context.

MEDICAL CARE

"Factory of Despair"

Medical care for people behind bars has shifted from private hospitals to a for-profit corporation to the current city-run public care system. The results have largely remained the same: long waits for routine care with some catastrophic, and fatal, endings.

Some of the worst cases occurred during Corizon Health Inc.'s fifteen-year tenure in charge dating back to the Giuliani administration. In one case, a state oversight commission found the lack of care "to shock the conscience" while a seriously sick detainee was untreated by staff during fifty-seven visits.

For some less severe cases, just getting an appointment to go to the clinic can be a challenge.

—

LLOYD HAYNES, detained 2019, 2020: A CO would come inside your housing unit and yell "Sick call!" At times inmates would not hear and they'd miss it. So you'd have to sign up again. If you miss the CO yelling "Sick call!" you can't see the doctor until the following day. There were times where a week or two would go by [where] they wouldn't even call sick call. A lot of it is based on what is going on in the building at the time. There could be a lot of alarms. It's almost as if they are punishing you for that. People acting up. Security measures. They like to play that role a lot of the times due to security.

I missed, what, ten, eleven, or twelve specialized hospital visits. And sometimes I didn't even know. There were times they never even brought me to medical but they produced me to court. Or they'd say they couldn't bring me to medical because I had court that day. Medical is supposed to supersede court.

Lloyd Haynes is struggling to stay healthy following a 2019 stint in Rikers.

DR. HOMER VENTERS, correctional health services chief medical officer, 2015 to 2017: Sick call has always been a problem. One of the quickest ways to understand the culture of the correctional health service is to kind of dig into sick call, into what works and what doesn't. I would hear often from patients that an officer might literally whisper or say very quietly, "Sick call." If you're standing within five feet of that person, you might hear, and everybody else might not.

And that might not necessarily reflect maliciousness by the officer. It's that in the facilities where you have escorted movement only, that officer only had time to take five people or six people, and they were only going to do it once. So there literally would be some sort of quota that only a handful of people could go to sick call from that housing area, which doesn't tend to the reality that more people needed sick call that day. And so then people would have to decide for themselves, how much are they going to try and compete with other people to get sick call.

And they have to deal with officers. Just advocating for yourself to say "I need to go sick call" could put you in pretty hot water with the housing area officers if it's going to mean that they need to do another trip, or that they need to make extra calls to get more escort officers, things like that.

So sick call is an area of great, great difficulty. It always has been at Rikers. And a lot of it really, I would say, flowed from the idea that this problem wasn't taken seriously. If you ask people who work in jails and prisons about sick call, a common refrain is, "Some people need it, but a lot of people abuse it, and a lot of people use it to just hang out in the waiting area or just to go to clinic." And what this framing reveals is that there's a kind of dismissiveness toward the important sick call.

I think if you pushed people, they would say, "I can't tell when I look at a piece of paper which of those people has a life-threatening problem or which has an urgent problem and which is going to be coming for something that I don't think is legitimate."

That's the cultural component of dismissiveness of sick call. When I investigated jail-attributable deaths, there's the notion that because some people access sick call in a way that the providers don't like, or the correctional officers don't like, that allows the culture of that dismissiveness to seep in. And that dismissiveness really is involved in a fair amount of deaths. Preventable deaths.

KAREN SESSOMS, correction officer, 1991 to 1993: I was in the Rose M. Singer Center. I was relieving someone, and soon after I got there, an inmate keeled over on her bed. I asked her if she was okay. She looked older, maybe in her forties. She had come to me a couple of times before that, saying she had been waiting since the last tour for a hospital run. What had happened was she had miscarried and her body was in the process of expelling the fetus. It was becoming toxic.

It had been a while and nobody else had done anything. I spoke to the captain and they got her out. She had been sitting there eight hours, and then the second shift came and still nobody did anything. It must have been about ten hours total. She was curled up in a fetal position on her bed. When she came over to me, she could barely walk.

There's a back end to the story. One day, my car wasn't working. I had to take the bus. I happened to bump into her. She was going to Rikers to pick up her property. She was with her husband, and she saw me and recognized me, and she said, "This is the officer who helped me." Her husband said, "Thank you so much. God bless you. She told me about you." I said, "Stay out of trouble." Even though I wasn't there a long time [working on Rikers], and even if it was only to save one person, it meant a lot. People in jail are often judged for their actions, but where is the rehabilitation in that? You have to be part of that rehabilitation.

LLOYD HAYNES: It was a thing, I wasn't making it to the hospital. I would go see the doctor. And they would say, "Okay, Lloyd, we want you to go to Bellevue." But then there would be transportations issues, intake issues. And all of this would be due to the fact that medical would be put on the back burner. It would be all "Okay, well, well, we scheduled you to go to Bellevue, but we didn't have a bus to take you to the hospital," or "We don't have no escorts at the time." A couple of times they sent me to Bellevue, late, and by the time I got [there] they would call upstairs, and then they would say, "Well, the doctor left for the day." And turn me right back around.

HOMER VENTERS: [Hospital care] depends on if you were going on what was called a three-hour run, which is you're going in a Department of Correction van versus going out in an ambulance. If somebody is waiting to go on one of these three-hour runs, you want to make sure if they're under medical observation that somebody's keeping an eye on them, and they're not going to sit in an intake pen and then wait a long period of time in that intake pen without anybody medically keeping an eye on them.

LLOYD HAYNES: I was born with Hirschsprung disease [a condition that affects the large intestine] and neuronal dysplasia, which is basically missing ganglion cells, and nerves in my colon that are just dormant, they don't work. So I really don't have, I would say, push power. Every six months to a year or every two years, I would have to get disimpacted, which is just like a water irrigation system that would clean out my rectum.

When I got incarcerated, they thought, "Okay, you have a colostomy bag." I explained I have a rare disease and I gotta get cleaned out and I wear these special supplies that are honestly very hard to get. I even explained where he [the guard] could get them. But he must have thought that the supplies that I get are one size fits all. But I have two holes in my stomach, [one] bigger than normal.

I've been dealing with this all my life since I was a baby. So I really know the ins and outs of my body. I know the seriousness of my ailment. I understand it fully, but explaining it in a system that really doesn't cater to complex care, that was the problem. It's good when you have standardized sickness: cold, diabetes, high blood pressure, things that are common. But when you have complex care, it's either not built for it, or the people that work for these institutions are just not equipped. They don't have experience.

ANNA GRISTINA, detained 2012: I was in the bullpen, waiting at the processing area. There was a woman. These girls were going, "She needs to get to the doctor. She's shaking on the floor." A couple minutes later, everyone is screaming. The guards, they are having their lunch. This sergeant with braids, she says, "Shut the fuck up! Mind your own business!"

We were looking and we saw this woman from across the pen, froth coming out of her mouth. She's having a seizure. She's vomiting foam. The guard says, "Mind your business. You're in enough trouble. Keep your mouth shut." We came back from a lawyer visit, and they had taken her out on a gurney, dead. The guards had denied her medical, and she died. I don't know her name or her age.

She [the woman who died] had covers over her body when they took her out. She had been screaming for hours for help. She had been half the day in the holding pen with no water, no nothing, having seizures. I'll never forget the feeling of telling my lawyers a woman died in there and they shrugged their shoulders.

ROBERT GANGI, director, Correctional Association, 1982 to 2011: There was a woman who could barely stand up. I remember she was slender. She was a Black woman, and she was holding onto the cells to stand up. And the other detainees were saying she needs help. And it turned out, she told me she was seven months pregnant and she was getting no assistance from anybody, from the correction officers or anybody. We told the correction officers, you gotta call EMS and get this woman to a hospital.

DAVID CAMPBELL, detained 2019 to 2020: I saw an older guy die and it was totally avoidable. He was a tiny little old Puerto Rican guy. They just called him Viejo. He was like eight months into a sixteen-month bid. He had some terrible chronic lung condition where at night he would often be really heaving to breathe, and he would sit up in bed on the side of his bed all night. He told me when he got out in a couple of months, he was gonna go right back to using heroin and smoking cigarettes. And he had no place to live. He was going to go to a shelter if they'd take him.

He really should have had a respirator and an oxygen tank. But they weren't going to give them that. I don't think he would have lasted long on the outside anyway, but the DOC knew about his condition. He kept going to the clinic for it. The night before the night he died, they called the captain down to escort him to the clinic in an emergency.

I woke up and he was sitting up, but he was really heaving to breathe, and guys were trying to get him to come to. One guy was just kind of like patting him, not slapping him, but just kind of patting him on the cheek. He had inhalers that they were trying to use, but they couldn't even get it up to his lips. He had foam on his lips; he looked kind of mottled. And people were trying to open up the windows and press his face by the window. They're going to one of the Bubbles [where an officer is stationed] saying, "Yo, he needs to go to the clinic now, call them again."

They were saying, "Call, call the clinic again." And the CO said, "They're saying they don't have anyone." He really looks bad. This one guy, Bats, said, "Fuck no! We ain't doing that!" And he picked the guy up. He was a big dude, Bats. Viejo was tiny. He picked the dude up and starts carrying him like a bride.

Now, to get from our dorm to the clinic—even if you show up with a guy who looks like he's on death's doorstep—means you have to go out of the dorm. You have to go get them to open the buzzer door, go up a flight of stairs, get them to buzz another door, get into the buzzer gate, walk down a hallway that's like two city blocks long, getting them to buzz two or three more gates.

I worked as a funeral director for years, and I know that when someone is not putting any ounce of effort into you carrying them, they can be way heavier than they look. So I knew Viejo was 110 pounds. Bats, a big dude, is not going to make it that distance without setting him down once. And once you set somebody who can't get up down on the floor, it is mad hard to pick them up.

I throw [on] my flip-flops. Bats was already out the door with Viejo in his arms. I said, "Look, man, there's no way you're gonna make it." And he said, "Okay," and dumped him in my arms. So now I have this guy and I gotta tell you, as soon as you put him in my arms, I was like, this guy feels like a body. Fingernails turned blue. His skin, splotchy. I could barely feel him breathing. The bunk right by the door was wide open. There's nobody on it. I put him in there. There was an extra book there. I put it under his head. Somebody gave him a blanket. Somebody gave him a pillow, trying to keep him warm. It was really nice. I mean, guys, trying to take care of this guy. They were really banging on the Bubble, telling him to get somebody to come.

People were saying, "Yo, stay with me," people holding his hands. People were putting a hand on his forehead. Like, "Yo, we're gonna take care of you, Viejo." Somebody threw an extra blanket over him. Somebody threw a pillow under his head, which is not nothing. I mean, these are probably extras. Like, this guy had two pillows, this guy had six blankets, whatever. But, still, to give something away to a guy who looks like he's in pretty rough shape, it's nice. You know, I mean, you don't really think of jail as being a sharing environment.

Guards weren't doing anything. Clinic workers came and did CPR for about twenty minutes. And then he just didn't respond. I pulled the sheet over his head.

All I know is that they didn't take it seriously. I mean, they took it seriously once he died. Then they had three captains, two deps [deputy wardens], a watch commander swarming around the bed after he died. And we went and waited in the gym for like five hours until the ME [medical examiner] could come pick his body up. And they had staff psychologists come in and take statements. The guy didn't need to die.

HOMER VENTERS: When we find a higher level of acuity, and we try and address it with a special housing area, or special resources, we often think in a very linear fashion, and we don't think about the whole person or the whole patient. And unfortunately the health risks of incarceration are not spread out evenly. And so when we look at jail-attributable deaths, what we often find is that a person had one set of problems that we recognize, and then there's a whole other set of problems that we either didn't recognize or we didn't address.

DONNA HYLTON, detained 1985 to 1986: It [the clinic] was in the open. You sat at a desk. You had the officer right there. It was just an open area, and they were asking all these questions and it couldn't possibly be private. You didn't believe you had rights. They would ask you a question, and you would have to yell it out. It's thirty-five years later for me and I'm still talking about the same thing and the same issues.

JOHN BOSTON, retired director, Legal Aid Prisoners' Rights Project: One lawsuit [we filed] was about the so-called Rikers Island hospital. It was to a hospital as military music is to music. That's not an original observation; that's borrowed from the title of a book about military justice. But it was a very nasty place, not a good place to keep sick people. Later, when I took an engineer to look at it, he said, "I don't really want to be in this building any longer than we have to." It was that decrepit. That lawsuit involved complaints about the physical conditions which were mitigated before the case was resolved because they moved that function to a different location.

And the other was a case that was filed about the prison wards and in the city hospitals—Bellevue, Elmhurst, Kings County. So at that point, this office had litigation about every location where detainees were held in the city jails.

DONNA HYLTON: They did start processing me, they said she's got to go with the adolescents. I didn't know what that was. They took my clothes, gave me a smock, a green plastic cup, and a wool, scratchy blanket. They took me to a housing unit. It was basically involuntary protective custody. They kept me there for six months. There were some who were nice and a lot that were not. I was having nightmares, and I hadn't spoken to anyone, family. When I told the officer, whoever was making rounds, he said, do you want to see someone? I said, I guess so. Maybe two days later, I was taken to the medical area.

I saw a nurse and told them the issue. I don't remember the response, because I was so sleep-deprived. Later, an officer came with medication and told me I had to take it. I said, what medication? I've never taken medication. He said basically I had to take it or I would be in trouble. It was 150 milligrams of Sinequan. I started swelling up from it. I couldn't get off it. I didn't know nothing about throwing it away. I just did what I was told. I was told that I had to go to court for the courts to take me off the medication. So I did.

The court, the attorney said, "Who put you on it?" I said they said I had to take it for nightmares and [because] I couldn't sleep. There was a battle back and forth. Eventually, I was on it for six months. Sinequan is a very strong psychotropic. It made you feel crazy and also throw up from it. I thought I had to take it.

It wasn't so much withdrawals; it was that it made me sick. One time, I had to leave court. My tongue was swollen. I would get sick from it. It was a zombielike feeling.

MICHAEL JACOBSON, correction commissioner, 1995 to 1997: When I was there was when they started to really up their game. Montefiore Hospital was to help provide and they were iconic and I loved them. They knew what they were doing. They were very expensive, so they were always taking shit for how much money they cost, but they cared about this stuff. They would want to start to develop these medical mental health units and started to think about solitary confinement in different ways, especially for people with mental illness.

When I left Corrections, nothing to do with me, Montefiore got into a big fight with city hall and gave it up. That was a bad thing for the system. I think St. Barnabas Hospital replaced them. They were a disaster. And then for years it was that private [company]. They were bad. Montefiore was the shining example of what health care could be.

DR. ROBERT COHEN, director of the Montefiore Rikers Island Health Services in the 1980s: It was Giuliani. He and Montefiore were feuding, which shouldn't affect the care at all, but it did. And the group that was put in from St. Barnabas shifted [and] was given a risk contract, meaning that whatever they didn't spend, they got to keep, and they didn't spend a lot, because they did not send people to the hospital, which they were supposed to do. They let them rot and die on Rikers Island.

And they didn't staff positions, and they made money every time. [To not] do something was a national phenomenon and still is to some extent, less so because this is understood by some cities and certainly by class-action lawyers. But the care was really terrible. There were lots of deaths in the infirmary, which shouldn't have happened. The quality of the care went down quite rapidly. And they were essentially thrown out in a clinical scandal. And then PHS came in after that, Prison Health Services, which later merged with another organization to become Corizon.

DR. SUSI VASSALLO, toxicologist, expert on heat-related illness, consulted on Rikers conditions: Well, when the medical care is a private company [Corizon], the more you send patients out for care, the less their profit is, right? Because every time we call an ambulance, it cuts into the private company's earnings. So everybody arriving in Bellevue was near death because we knew that they [Corizon] didn't want to get specialist care and didn't want to transfer the patient, 'cause it costs the company money to do that.

EDDIE ROSARIO, detained 1990: [When I went back as a counselor] I remember talking with this female captain. She wore a fur coat. Sometimes I was waiting for a bus, and she had a Cadillac and wore a fur coat. I thought she must be making good money. One day she gave me a ride. I was talking with her in the women's facility, and this woman comes up to her and tells the guard right next to the captain that she needs a sanitary napkin and the captain turned around and says, "Excuse me, can't you see we're talking here? You wait."

The woman has her legs pressed together. She's bleeding. She's flowing. The captain is talking, completely ignoring this woman, who is now bleeding you could see. She is going through the humiliation of having to beg, but she won't get that. And this captain is a Black woman. How do you compartmentalize that? The banality of evil could be run by Blacks and Hispanics because it's built on dehumanizing people. You could put Mother Teresa there, and in a month she'll be shanking people. It was very different but equally horrific.

YOLANDA CEPEDA, detained 1990s: I had an addiction with an addiction. They had no programs. If you had to be detoxed from heroin, you had to wait 'til the following day. I remember girls dying because they were going through withdrawals on the bus, 'cause they wouldn't medicate you in the morning before you went to court. They would medicate you afterward. I remember a girl died on the bus, handcuffed, from withdrawal. She died. That was in '89. If you go there now, you get medicated right away, because of the deaths. Girls would go through agony. Girls throwing up all over the place. It's just horrible. Medical was terrible.

NESTOR EVERSLEY, detained various stints, 1969 to 2010s: When I went back to Rikers in 2016, we had [Narcotics Anonymous] groups and stuff like that, and so the people there were in the program. This guy came off the street, and instead of sending him to a detox, they sent him to [jail]. This guy was kicking heroin. He was fucked up. He shouldn't have been there.

When they call medication in the afternoon, everybody and their mother gets up to try and get high. Every time they call medication, you get it. If you going upstate, they cut you off and bring you down. They detox you. You have to suffer.

Detoxing was bad. You can't sleep. You uncomfortable. You in pain. You throwing up. It was bad. So, I noticed when they said detox, that guy didn't move. I like to help out if I see you are weak, so I went over and asked him if I needed to make a phone call for him. The guy didn't talk. I said, "Oh, fuck you then." I didn't know his condition or his problem. I told the officers about him because

I was in charge of the floor. That night, some of the guys was high and they were up all night.

This guy tried to get up and go to the bathroom. He couldn't make it and he dropped right there. He died right there.

[One of] the officers got fired. He failed to recognize the man was in dire need of help. The tape showed he [the officer] was sleeping. The other one got moved because he didn't do anything. That man was on that bed for eight hours or more. They evacuated all of us and put us in the dayroom. I could see his bed. I saw when the doctor came and tried to revive him. She looked like a witch doctor. She came up and put the electric stuff on him, but he didn't come back. After a while of trying that, they declared him dead.

The medical thing in Rikers: they are very lax in kindness and in caring. He died from withdrawal. He was in the wrong place. They should have sent him to the clinic. They shouldn't have sent him to a program. That was 2016. I wish I could remember his name because I would have called family and I would have put a lawsuit in.

There was a year that I was working in the clinic, and since I knew a lot of officers, I was able to get the best jobs. I was in the clinic and this guy came in. The clinic is a hangout. It's where you sell your stuff because they have one bullpen and they have where the sick people come in. The new people don't want to buy drugs or they got drugs in. It would be like a market in the clinic.

This guy who came, and he was one of the regulars, but the officer doesn't have the right to tell someone they can't come in. He came in claiming chest pains. She told him to leave. He took six steps and he dropped dead. I didn't know the guy's name, so no one could know the truth. They probably told his family he just had a heart attack. They aren't going to tell the full story. Chest pain is one thing where they have to see you and clear that up. What are they going to do—wait until you dropped dead?

Those are some of the things that happened. Back in my days, you had to detox on your own. You had to curl yourself in the corner and throw up until you can't throw up no more; then they take your blood and they take your temperature before you get a bed. Before you get a bed, you're halfway dead.

SOFFIYAH ELIJAH, executive director, Alliance of Families for Justice: I remember very clearly being at Manhattan court on Centre Street and I was making my way around the courthouse, going to different courtrooms doing my cases. And this is back in the age of pagers. I remember my pager going off; I was in court. As soon as I could finish up the case I was doing, I went out to the hallway to check the message. I saw there were several calls from my office.

So I called the office wondering what is the emergency. And as I found out that one of my clients had a heart attack at Rikers Island, and the people in the area being detained were pleading with the guards to take him to medical to do something to try to save his life. And they didn't touch him. They didn't do anything. And he died on the floor.

And I remember just standing numb in the hallway of the court building, saying, "This is absolutely horrific. This whole system is horrific." The man was in his fifties. I remember during the arraignment saying to the court, he has a medical condition, that he had a heart condition, and the judge said, "I'll mark his papers that he should have medical attention." I don't know if that was done or not. But I know I never saw my client again.

At the time that my client had a heart attack, the medical care on Rikers Island was probably some of the worst in the country. A lot has changed since that time. There's still room for more improvement. The people who are in charge of medical care on the island are trying to do a better job, but there's still a lot that needs to be done. And the reality is people who have behavioral health needs cannot be adequately cared for in a jail setting. It's a nontherapeutic setting.

MATT FREY, clinician, 2011 to 2018: As quickly as we can see patients, it's on to the next one. One referral comes in, then another one, then another one. You're always being rushed to finish up so you can see the next person because they've been waiting for three or four hours. And I know I hate waiting ten minutes to see a doctor. So I can't imagine what they're going through. Everyone there is in despair.

It's a factory of despair.

PREGNANCY

"The House of Pregnant Girls"

In 1998, Hazel Figueroa was in her mid-twenties when she was arrested in a drug case in the Bronx and shipped to Rikers, where she learned she was pregnant—thus joining a sorority of women who experienced a pregnancy while incarcerated there. Celeste Ricciardi found herself in the same situation in 2010.

—

HAZEL FIGUEROA, detained 1998: I was born in Chicago and moved to New York, where I had a relationship and then things didn't go well, so I tried to look for a job. I worked at McDonald's. Then after McDonald's, I stopped working and I started doing wrong things, you know, to get that money, and I ended up being arrested in the Bronx. It's not something that I'm proud of. It was a learning experience. I learned; I grew out of it. It was a hard time.

I was twenty-five, twenty-six, and I was in Rikers for almost a year. That was my last time. How can I say this? I was there because I made the wrong decision. It was me because my family taught me good values, principles, morals. I always had them in the past, but I think it was more my stubbornness and my disobedience that got me there. And the soul-searching, I got into my little girl and had a conversation with her like, come on, girl, this is not you. This is not your life. This is not your world. What are you doing?

At the beginning, when I didn't know that I was pregnant, I was going through withdrawals. I requested to be drug tested, and that's when I learned I was expecting. I also found out because my period didn't show up. I requested [medically supervised detox], but it was denied. Once that was taken care of, I wanted them to be reducing the doses of methadone until I was clean. It's just that I need something to feel better. It's not that I want to stay on it.

Then this is what I never agreed with: even when I learned that I was pregnant, they continued with methadone at the same level. I asked to be given lower doses, little by little, so I didn't have a baby that was addicted to something. I requested to lower the doses and let's see how my body and my baby react, so when she or he is born, they won't be going through withdrawal, 'cause babies also go through that. But they never did it. They stay with the same doses until you give birth. They justify it by saying they don't want to put the baby and you in danger because you are in [Rikers]. They don't want to experience any lawsuits for the loss of a baby.

I wanted to be out of the substance. Which I did on my own. I used no program. No, no substance, no medication. I went straight to God and I went through the withdrawal and I never looked back.

At the beginning I was in regular population. I don't take jokes from no one. I mean, how can I say this? It's not that I'm a bad girl, but it's just my mom taught me never allow anybody to disrespect you or humiliate you. You will stand up for yourself. If I'm not around, she said, you guys do it for yourself. So that lesson was well taught. I was always a loner, but always with one or two or three girls, we were Puerto Rican, we stick together. No one would mess with us.

So I was in regular population until I was almost six or seven months. They don't really care. I requested to be in the house of pregnant girls. You go to the library and write this request and put it in a box. It goes to the captain. There's procedures and a chain of command. It was never taken under consideration. You fight, you fight, you fight, and it's like . . . There was never a reply back. They didn't move me until I was almost eight months.

They put me in, not in the ward, but in a regular unit where half of the women are not pregnant, like ones going upstate, and five rooms to take the pregnant girls, top tier and bottom tier. Like six of us were never in the pregnancy ward. Never. Half of the unit was pregnant, and the other half were waiting to go upstate. I was in the top tier. When I think about it today, I think, how could I have handled all that? Oh my God. But I thank God it's over.

It was like fifty-fifty [with women who were pregnant and those who were not]. I'm gonna explain: You have girls that are not pregnant dealing with issues. You have pregnant girls dealing with hormones and going crazy, arguing, fighting. So you're put in danger between the two groups. If a fight starts, you're put in danger, two humans, the unborn child and the mother. Because if a fight breaks out, you're putting, you know, the rest of our girls who were pregnant at the time, risking our lives. So you should have special units for pregnant girls and keep them safe from the rest of the other girls who are dealing with the emotional roller coaster, up and down, of going upstate.

I fought another pregnant girl. She tried to, like, hit my belly, and I punched her right in her face. I protected my belly, but trust me and believe me, I'm not happy about it, but I punched her and I protected myself. You trying to violate me when I'm pregnant? No, no, no, no. It was something very silly: I had said something, and she didn't like it. I had lived with her in another unit. My way of being, I'm always solo. I don't like to be around a lot of people. I don't recall what the fight was about. I know she tried to come out at me and I didn't allow it. It was not nice. I'm not proud of it. I was trying to protect me. And I end up punished. They put me in solitary.

I tried to look for something helpful and be positive. There was nothing else to do. Read the dictionary. You try to analyze yourself, evaluate yourself, what got me here, what was the reason why I reacted like that? If this is gonna be thirty days, what are we gonna do every day? So let's make a routine. Look for something helpful, positive.

Don't get me wrong. There were times that you would just sit and just think, read, there was nothing else to do, you know, write poetry, read the dictionary, or read a book, but they take everything. So you don't have nothing there. So it's just the Bible, you, and that's it.

I grew up in the Roman Catholic Church. My mom always ensured that we know morals and principles of religion and the love of God over all. When you are younger, you don't dwell on it as much as when you grow older or when you go through an experience, and then you look back and you just analyze and say, if I would've just listened or thought before I acted, or made the right decisions instead of just acting and then thinking. I began to read the Bible more. I got closer [to religion], I can say that.

I would read. I learned . . . I became very literate because I learned to read the dictionary, all the words.

They put me in for thirty days. Their justification was their rules: there's no physical contact, no physical fights. Then I wrote the warden and she took me out after fifteen.

AUTHORS: *Did they have a nurse come and check on you while you were in solitary?*

HAZEL FIGUEROA: No. No, no, no.

I get out of solitary and I'm about eight and a half months. They moved me out of the regular population to a dorm with regular people. Here we go again. With regular girls, not a pregnancy ward. And from that dorm, I went to give birth.

I knew the baby was coming because I was just in a lot of pain. So they take you to the infirmary and they check. They took me to Elmhurst [Hospital in Queens]. I was handcuffed and shackled. Wrists and in front around the waist and shackles around my ankles . . . All around.

It was lonely. Just praying that your baby and everything will go well. It's like, you're not even thinking that you're incarcerated at this time. All you want is just for your baby to be born safe and healthy. The sad part is when you have to depart from her. That's the hard part, because remember I requested to be in the ward with my baby afterward until I go home. I continued to ask and request it. It was never approved or denied. They just never responded back. It was just hard times.

Because they never replied back, that was out of the question. There was no way I would go back [to Rikers] with my child. I would go alone, so I had to call family to come pick up the baby. They have that special unit or the space with the bed with the little crib, and unless they have everything written down, you won't go back with your kid. It has to be approved. It was frustrating.

I saw her only one time for about five minutes on the first day she was born, and they sent me back to Rikers. That gets me mad.

So I had to call family, her father, to go pick her up. Her father and his aunt to go pick her up. They brought her in to me for only five minutes, and then they [family] came and got her and went home. Thank God.

Imagine a person that doesn't have no one outside. What would happen to that child? That child would go through the system, to a foster house or a friend's. And I don't know where the baby would end up.

I was in Rikers for another thirty days or so before I came home to her. I was very anxious, very emotional, all these mixed feelings: once I hold her again, would she remember my voice, would she know my smell, would she know who I am? A whole bunch of questions.

There's no words to describe how a parent feels when they meet his or her child for the first time. It's all joy, happiness, tears of joy, nervous, anxious, all the feelings mixed all together.

She was in good health, but she did exhibit symptoms of withdrawal. It was very hard. It was very hard. She cried a lot because her body was uncomfortable and we gave her warm water and we massaged her muscles; she would cry, cry, cry, and cry. The body needed to . . . It was a month or two months, maybe three months that it was hurting the baby. She would sleep small naps but not the whole night, cry because she was not feeling well.

She's now twenty-one and in college in Florida. She doesn't know exactly what she wants to be. I was just like, go do your first year with the basics and just think and decide what is the major that you want to continue to take. What is your path? What is the major that you want?

I'm fifty-two now. I work and live in Puerto Rico. I graduated with my master's. It's been almost twenty years clean and sober.

So that means something.

Hazel Figueroa, photographed in San Juan, Puerto Rico, found out she was pregnant in Rikers in 1998 and had her daughter while in jail.

—

CELESTE RICCIARDI, detained 2009: When I first got there [after being charged in a series of robberies in Manhattan], I was put into the pregnant unit. Building seven. So that was better conditions, obviously the cleaner rooms, and there were considerably less fights because women are a little calmer when they are pregnant.

And sadly, you start seeing how some people live. Like this one woman in particular was pregnant with, like, her eighth kid, and I know because the next year I saw her, thin as a fucking rail, because that's what she does. She comes back to Rikers to have her kid. Some people do that. It forces them to eat and be clean and take care of the kid. She's not the only one, sadly.

It was better conditions there and again a little bit more food, and it was always, like, fresh fruit available. And milk was available and box cereals and closer to medical.

So they took me to Bellevue for the abortion because I was so far along. I had to be put under. It was so uncomfortable. I didn't want to have a kid in a friggin' prison. I never had a kid. This was not the time or place to do it.

I was chained to the bed the whole time. I think during the entire surgery. It was fucking horrifying. I'm not going to lie. There are parts of that experience where you're among normal human beings in the hospital. But there's no confusion that you're an inmate. Cops are surrounding you.

Apparently, that also means you're not privy to the same amount of decency or care. If I had gone in clothes instead of an orange jumpsuit, I would have gotten a lot better care in clothes. They don't say, "How are ya?" They don't treat you like a human being. You are just like a vessel to be worked on and moved on.

I was crazy. I was so fortunate because their transport officer who took me was a woman. She told me not to be alarmed but when I woke up they warned me I was going to cry. She had it down. And I have never cried before, but I totally did. I don't even know why. You know what I'm saying? Like, I had kept myself so cold and detached to the entire process to not get emotional about it, you know what I mean? And so I was kind of shocked that I did it anyway.

It was really shocking actually that the officer who took me was so human and so calm and, like, rubbing my leg and she's like, "You okay?" She was really, really sweet, and then cut to maybe like a month later, I ended up moving to that building, that housing unit where she was the main officer. And as I'm checking in, she asked if I remembered her. I didn't. She was like, "I was the one with you." I didn't remember her at first. "Oh my God! That's right! Thank you!"

There were a few officers who were fucking amazing, and I just don't know her name anymore. She was really amazing. It was a really human moment. But to most of these officers, you are not human. There's no compassion. There's a separation of church and state.

I'll never forget the ride back from the hospital. I'm still kinda out of it and I'm bleeding profusely. I was put in the bus in the front cage filled with twenty guys coming back from court. The entire ride back I'm being harassed, saying the nastiest shit. I was still emotionally traumatized from the day.

When I came back, they thought I was suicidal because I came back crying after being in the hospital twenty-four hours and then stuck in intake all those hours. It's basically eighteen hours of transportation and I was totally exhausted and felt like shit being everywhere. And they took that [as] she's gonna kill herself. So honest to God it was the most insulting, demeaning punishment to put me in a fucking dirty-ass dorm that houses people who are mentally fucking crazy. So clearly no one's cleaning in there because they are fucking crazy.

So it was the worst place to put someone like me that was profusely bleeding after having an abortion at six fucking months. Not the place to put anybody, especially someone with a serious medical issue.

FOOD

"That's When I Became a Vegetarian"

On December 24, 1959, a one-paragraph item headlined "City Prison Food Fells 100" in *The New York Times* reported that the unfortunates took ill from eating boiled tongue served up on Rikers. Forty were sick enough to be sent to the prison hospital.

There were often strange things on the menu in the city jails, such as the boiled pigtails and beans that Sandi Sutton was served in 1971 at the old Women's House of Detention in Greenwich Village.

There were shortages, delivery problems, cooking issues, and vermin in the kitchens over the decades. The quality of the food was one part of a sprawling fifty-two-page consent decree signed by the Koch administration in 1979 that largely went unresolved.

The most monumental political battle over Rikers food started in about 1990 over a plan to introduce a system called "cook/chill" in which the food was cooked at a central kitchen, chilled, then reheated in the individual facilities.

As the retired Legal Aid lawyer John Boston recounts below, in the end the outcome hung on the question of whether the food service division should be moved out of Queens to a new central

DONOVAN DRAYTON, detained 2007 to 2012: Yo, they serve this red Kool-Aid on Rikers Island, and they said it makes you infertile, and if you drink that, it's like you might've sniffed a bag of dope. It'll put you to sleep. It's like NyQuil. You spill it on the floor, it stains the floor for weeks. I never drank it.

GREGORY PIERCE, detained 1983, 2015: Oh yeah, nah, he wasn't lying [referring to Donovan]. They had all kinds of punches, but the red punch, I never drank that, because someone told me they put saltpeter in there. Whatever was in that punch, they said saltpeter, so I said, nah, I'm not drinking that shit.

EDDIE ROSARIO, detained 1990: The red punch. That's what they served every day. There was this tuna salad thing they used to make; they added celery. It was very bitter. To this day I can't eat tuna salad. It would be on the menu at least twice a week. Rikers was different. What you got at commissary was not sustainable. Now they sell noodles, but back then it was candy and coffee. I can still make "Jailhouse Cappuccino." You take grains of instant coffee, crush it down with a tablespoon, and add a couple of drops of hot water and a lot of sugar and with the spoon beat it and beat it until it becomes a paste. If it got enough air into the mixture, and then hot water, it would create a froth. We drank a lot of coffee because it would take your appetite away.

DONOVAN DRAYTON: On Thursdays and Sundays, they served chicken, and served fish on Fridays. Still might be pretty universal around the world, around the United States, "Fish Friday" in prison. But they served a lot of [stuff] I used to hate. They used to have this stuff called beef stroganoff. Terrible, man. It was like snot and noodles, and then sometimes they give you the noodles with all the water in it still. So now your meat got water in it. Like, you got to tilt the tray to the side to drain it, you know what I'm saying? They used to give tuna fish and stuff, but they put this, I don't like celery, in my tuna fish. Like, celery, man? Tuna fish with celery?

kitchen in the upstate Rockland Psychiatric Center immortalized by the poet Allen Ginsberg in his most famous work, "Howl."

—

YUSEF SALAAM, detained 1989 to 1994, Central Park 5 case: There's a scene in *The Matrix* where Neo, after his awakening, goes and gets some food and it looks like slop. That's what the food looked like. It looked that disgusting. That terrible. The spice of the food was revolting. And you think about that, especially now, in the age of COVID-19, a lot of people were coming in with health issues because they've been in communities where people have only had fast food, and that is exacerbated with the fact that in prison you have even worse food. Not that you have fried chicken and french fries and all of that fried stuff, you just don't have nutrition in the way that you would have nutrition.

SANDI SUTTON, detained 1971: One of the meals I remember was pigtails and beans. And the pigtails had fur on them, had hair on them. It was absolutely the worst meal I've ever had in my life. And they had it every week. And people ate it. How do you eat a tail? How do you ingest that? They didn't even cut the hair off. It was horrible. And beans. I would eat the beans. Most of the time, I didn't eat. That's when I became a vegetarian.

EDDIE ROSARIO, detained 1990: The bullpen food, you were lucky if you got a peanut butter and jelly. I used to try to trade the baloney for cigarettes. One time, I had maggots in my oatmeal. I didn't eat it. I complained about it, and the guard said, "Oh, stop complaining about the food." He said, "You don't know what else we're putting in the food." After that, I got very hungry. Most people don't know what hunger is. I'm not talking about missing a meal; I'm talking about being so hungry that your entire being is consumed with thinking about food. You could be so hungry that that baloney sandwich is the best thing you ever had. But no one ate that crap, man.

SANDI SUTTON: When I first got commissary, I put my commissary—candy bars and potato chips and stuff—under my pillow, but that was the wrong thing to do, because at night I had rats all over my face trying to get under my pillow. It was the worst experience I've ever had in my life.

We used to go to sleep, and as soon as the lights went down, the rats would start running around. I mean, they were *rats*. They weren't little mice. No. They were big-ass rats.

I jumped up in horror. I got out of bed and my celly was like, what happened? She told me not to put the candy underneath my pillow or in my bed or anywhere. She said there was a shelf, which is above your head on the wall with no stand. It's just a shelf that comes out of the wall. You have to put it up there. She said it's hard for them to get up there. But they do get up there. There's no stairs, but they figured out how to jump or climb up the wall.

WILLIAM VANDEN HEUVEL, director, Board of Correction, 1970 to 1973: One thing I did was I went to the food critic of *The New York Times* to come out and have supper with me at the Brooklyn House of Detention. At the time, I said, "Well, [would] you sell what food was being served?" It didn't have to be done that way. It was not nutritious. It was heavy, heavy food. So we changed it, the menus, and it made a difference. At the same price you could provide a much better diet. That's what we did. It didn't cost more. Just had people who worked with food. You could undertake a health objective. All these people are going back into their communities. If you're really working for the City of New York, you want them to be less of a threat when they return to their community than when they came in.

HILTON WEBB, detained 1989 to 1991, 1996: There were days where the meal was pretty good. You know, I remember one Christmas Eve, I went to the mess hall. It must have been Christmas Eve in '90. That was the only time I was there for Christmas. And I went to the mess hall and they had spaghetti and meatballs. I'll never

forget. And the guy fills my plate with this mound of spaghetti. I'm like, wow. And then he puts this dark red sauce on. I was like, "Oh shit, they actually cooked it." Usually it's just warmed up. So if you got, like, this bright red sauce, you knew it wasn't cooked. And then the guy asked me if I want fucking cheese on my fucking spaghetti.

And I just dropped the plate and I said, "You motherfuckers can cook!" I yelled it. I said, "These motherfuckers can cook! Look at this. It looks like a regular fucking meal in a restaurant. You guys even offering me fucking cheese!"

ERVIN "EASY" HUNT, detained various stints, 1970s to 2010s: As long as I was on the serving line, I'll tell you one thing I loved about being in the kitchen on Rikers was every Thursday was chicken day. And I loved when the chicken skin would get stuck on the cooking sheet. That's where all the seasoning was. Oh my goodness. I can still see that there, so that when they would take the chicken off the cooking sheet, they would say, "Easy, want this pan?" Yeah, leave it there. I could eat chicken skin all day long. I used to get some of the whippings of my life at home when I would skin my mother's baked chickens.

JAMES MCGOVERN, retired correction captain, 1984 to 2004: Some of the COs were bringing in seafood for these wiseguys from Little Italy. Eddie [Gavin] one day went into the pen and saw pieces of shrimp on the floor.

EDWARD GAVIN, retired deputy warden, 1982 to 2001: I found shrimp tails in the court pens once. All these wiseguys were in the Manhattan court pens. It was a big Mob trial, and the cops had to shut down the whole area outside the courthouse. After we found the shrimp tails, we wound up transferring all of them to other facilities. This happened in 1992 or 1993. My theory is they were so nervous when I was searching, the tails fell to the floor. They knew I was onto them. This happened during the San Gennaro Festival. Uniformed staff had to have brought it in to them.

BARRY CAMPBELL, detained 1980s, 1990s: The food in commissary wasn't any better. I still suffer from rotten teeth today, and I'm afraid of the dentist because of jail [and] prison. It's one of those unwritten rules. You never go to the dentist while you're locked up, because the only thing they gonna tell you is that it has to come out and they gonna pull your teeth. And so I never went to the dentist, but I was always eating candy [and] junk food, everything. And so today my teeth suffer from that.

JACQUELINE MCMICKENS, correction commissioner, 1984 to 1986: We used to have problems with food. Why would we run out of food? Because we had inmates who were hoarders. Because they had lived in a situation where they didn't get enough food so they hoarded it. We had to teach them there would be more beans for them. The officers ate the same things the inmates ate. There's always some food in the jail. If you run out of food, you give them a cheese sandwich until you can make some more beans.

But some correction officers wouldn't do that. Some people just have a mean nature. Or you'd find an inmate that was a hoarder and tell them to put back some of the beans. It's a human experience. It's not a concentration camp. These people lived in your community. They are somebody's cousin. Somebody's brother. Somebody's mother. But you also have to train correction officers to believe that. And if you don't believe that, you are in the wrong place.

JOHN BOSTON, retired director, Legal Aid Prisoners' Rights Project: The problem was that as with most other things, they had no system. They theoretically had menus, but the food they actually served didn't necessarily conform with the menus. They had a storehouse, a central storehouse, but the whole business of making sure that they got enough at the central storehouse of the right things to get it to the individual jails, in the appropriate quantities at the appropriate time, was all screwed up.

They were constantly running out of food, so they would wind up substituting whatever they had lying around, if anything, and so the meals never conformed to the menus. Their equipment for food storage was unsanitary [and] dilapidated. They served food often that was, if not spoiled, close enough to it so you didn't want to be standing there.

The people who were doing the work to a great extent, you know, had no particular qualifications and no supervision. And of course there were sanitation and environmental health problems rampant. One of my tours of the food service operation—this would've been in about 1983 or '84—the day's entertainment while we were there, a rat ran out and the inmate workers all started running after the rat, chasing after it with whatever implements they had to have, and finally, you know, they cornered the rat and they beat it to death with broomsticks. It didn't happen every day, but it was far, far from a unique kind of thing.

BERNARD KERIK, correction commissioner, 1998 to 2000: You had to make the food hot, palatable, [and] crunchy. That's why I remember those words. It's got to be there within so many minutes. And a new kitchen was the one big thing when we took over. I remember my first meeting, they say, yeah, that is gonna cost $50 million or $500, I forget what the number was. [It was up to $300 million.] It's going to cost some crazy amount of money for a new kitchen.

And I said, what's wrong with the kitchen that's there? Why can't we put the food in the heating units and move it? Well, it's better if you do the kitchen. Why? I don't know. You don't know. I don't know. So who came up with that number? You know what I mean? That's the kind of stuff we were dealing with. Like just craziness.

JOHN BOSTON: One of the provisions to the original consent decrees said that food had to be maintained at the proper temperature. People like to make fun—"Oh, the inmates are complaining that their food is cold"—but if you talk to a food service professional, the third thing out of their mouth will be that keeping hot food hot and cold food cold is the single most important thing in avoiding foodborne illness. So it's essential. After various incidents of failure to do that, we instituted a regime in this process, which [the Office of Compliance Consultants, which monitored jail conditions] would go around and take the temperature of the food. And if the food was not at the proper temperature at the point of service, the Department of Correction would have to pay fines to the prisoners.

Now, this galvanized the Department of Correction in a way that we had never seen before. But I mean, paying money to the court is one thing, but the idea of having to pay it to the inmates was such degradation to them, such lèse-majesté, that they couldn't tolerate it. In any case, we had a regime of enforcement of things like maintaining the food at proper temperatures over a period of time, and prodded by the fine regime, it did get better. First in the existing facility and then they got into their nice new facilities. And they had more qualified staffing. So, that was one of the more successful gargantuan enterprises within the jail conditions litigation.

The experts all recommended introducing a system called "cook/chill." Essentially, cook the food and then chill it. And it's almost ready to go. And then you take it chilled to the point of service and you heat it up and either you're just reheating it or you're maybe completing the very last stage of cooking, the point being that you can do most of the work centrally and have a core of people that know what they're doing, as well as central control over supplies and facilities and so forth.

And all the people have to do at the facilities is reheat it according to simple directions and then take it around and serve it. This was a widely praised system and everybody agreed we should do it. What happened, though, is that this requires a much smaller cadre of people to do it. So, there would be some people with jobs on Rikers Island who would no longer have jobs on Rikers Island.

Further, they were planning to contract the food, making everything up to the final step to the kitchen at the Rockland Psychiatric Center. Did you ever read "Howl" by Allen Ginsberg? Remember "I'm with you in Rockland [where you're madder than I am]"?

Anyway, these folks went and their union went to some local politicians about the fact that some number of dozens of jobs, at least, were going to be shipped out of Queens and into [Rockland] County.

And so this became a big brouhaha in the state legislature, which started getting seriously agitated and threatening to legislate against it, setting up a potential constitutional confrontation of the first magnitude, which was the last thing anybody wanted. While this was going on, those of us who were working on this from Legal Aid were bit by bit losing our confidence in the cook/chill system, which, while in some respects was a less complicated system, in other respects was a more complicated system because it required a large amount of coordination and timing.

The first thing that happened was that the city basically said to the federal court, "Screw you. We're not doing this and state law forbids us to do it." And we moved for contempt and Judge [Morris] Lasker appropriately held them in contempt, and he then entered an order they were supposed to go forward. What the city then did was it proposed that we just take another tack because they could not be in the position of violating state law. Nobody really wanted to have King Kong versus Godzilla.

ERVIN "EASY" HUNT: There was always what you had access to because in the kitchen you worked with civilians. And so with that, you saw exchanges of stuff. You saw exchanges of cigarettes. Sometimes some relationships—some inmates would have relationships with some of the women who worked in the kitchen. Like I said, it was always a place to get something and have something to eat. And so a lot of times you don't have to worry about commissary, because you always had something to eat. My thing was Frosted Flakes, the little mini Frosted Flakes box. I was always into that, always. There was always the bread. They bake the bread right there.

HECTOR "PASTOR BENNY" CUSTODIO, Latin King leader, detained 1991 to 1994: If you didn't have a connect with the guys in the mess hall, you would have to eat the slop they served. The only people who ate good were the Muslims and the Jews. We had to deal with whatever slop they gave us. If you didn't have a guy who would hook you up with decent food, and you had to—they would make their own meals and sell them for a pack or two packs of smokes, and that was their hustle. They would make steak and cheese sandwiches.

TAMI LEE, retired correction officer, 1989 to 2020: We had one Hasidic rabbi that they used to bring it from, they used to bring the truck every day, and the assistant deputy had to keep their food in their refrigerator and deliver it to the inmates personally to make sure they got them. Kosher food, like fish . . . 'Cause they get kosher meals, blessed over and all that. The assistant deputy would go get it, put it in the refrigerator, and go take it, heat it up in the microwave or whatever, go take it to them personally. And they would come for every meal. The truck would come for every meal three times a day . . . We had a lot of rabbis, so they would always bring their food. That was a regular.

DIMITRI ANTONOV, detained 2020: One thing that people usually try to do is get to the kitchen. 'Cause half the stuff that was supposed to be on the menu, especially, like, the good stuff, like snacks or whatever, never actually goes out, never gets served. Just, like, whoever's in the kitchen would just bag it and give it out to whoever they wanted. They have these PB&Js and honey buns, snacks. [It's] like, kind of like an additional course, especially the cupcakes; they would always be kind of, like, pocketed and distributed to people.

MICHAEL "BIG MIKE" WILLIAMS, member, DOC Emergency Services Unit, retired 2008: I remember we had an inmate that every time he came to jail, he cooked food for the warden. No inmates are allowed past those gates. I remember saying to myself, that motherfucker will be coming out the mess hall with that tray with the fucking silver shit like you in a hotel. And even then, an officer be with him and he says, "Gates, please." I tell him I'm not going to open the gates. "Gates, please." And I'm like, "Yo, where the inmate going?" "Yo, he cooks for the warden, open the gates, let him through." What the fuck?

Fuck no, I don't think so. Inmate's name was fucking Minnehaha. Yes, the fuck it was. That's what the inmate went by. He was a gay inmate. Minnehaha cooked for the warden when I came on the job.

He got escorted by an officer and they dropped off the food, and then they would come back to get the empty trays and shit. Every time he came to jail, the warden gave Minnehaha a job back in the kitchen. That motherfucker had the lay of the land. He was kind of untouchable in jail.

BARRY CAMPBELL: Being from foster boys' homes, jail, and prison, I didn't have anybody on the outside sending me money. So everything that I had, I took from other people. And even to this day, I'm a very picky eater, so I wasn't eating in the mess hall very much. So between taking other people's stuff and intimidating the people that worked in the kitchen to bring me stuff like raw eggs or cheese or stuff that you can get from them. Fruit, apples, and bread and stuff like that. So you intimidated the people that worked in the mess hall or in the KK, which was the officers' mess hall.

FRANK PASQUA III, former Lucchese crime family associate, detained 2003, 2011 to 2012: There's something in Rikers Island called the KK. It's the officers' mess. They pay like $3 or $4 and get a meal cooked for them from a preset menu made of the stuff that we were getting that day, only they would cherry-pick all the best stuff. If it was beef stew, we'd get, like, a little bit of fat and gristle. They would get all the beef. And they would have chefs and they would have seasonings and things would be prepared correctly.

And in the morning they had eggs, stuff like that. So, now all the officers had the option to go to the KK or bring their own food. Most of them would bring their own food. If they weren't bringing something specifically for me, they would either give me some of their lunch or go to the officers' [mess] on their break, get a big tray of whatever the officers' food was, and bring me that.

They would go to the mess and get me basically a dressed-up, much better version of what we were supposed to eat that day. So this way I don't have to eat the garbage—just a lump of rice that's hard, that breaks your teeth, and some, like, some watery soup on top of it. This was the way that I ate better. And then on top of that, if I had a regular that was working with me, which I usually did maybe once a week, I'd give him an order. I'd say, "Hey, get me a gabagool sandwich with fresh mozzarella and roast peppers and bring it for lunch." And then I'd eat it in my cell.

BARRY CAMPBELL: If you came to me and you said, give me a pack of noodles, I'd give you a pack of noodles, but you have to return two to me. And there were certain instances and certain people that you didn't like and you charge them double. So you come to me, I'm charging two for one, you come to me, you paid three for one 'cause I don't like you, motherfucker. And if somebody took something from me and didn't pay for it in a timely fashion or didn't want to pay it all, then it was a reason for me to handle it.

DAVID CAMPBELL, detained 2019 to 2020: This guy who would gamble a lot asked me to lend him something until commissary. I didn't really know him. I felt okay saying no, but I also was like, okay, well, I'll test it out and see if he gets it back to me. It was a pack of ramen noodles. He was like, "Can I get, like, a pack of basic ramen or something until tomorrow when commissary comes on and I'll get you back for it?"

I gave it to him and then commissary came and he didn't get it back to me. I came back from work, and there was something else that was half the value sitting on my bed. And I was just like, yo, is this you? And now this guy, he's a Crip. And he's kind of a tough guy, like a street guy. He was like, "They didn't have what you want. So I just give you that." I didn't know how else to say it, because I know people are listening. They don't know who I am. And I was like, "I don't want this shit. Give me what I gave to you."

And he's like, "Well, commissary doesn't have it, it's not my fault." I was like, it's your fault for banking on commissary when you know they don't have shit all the time. So give me what I gave you or give me something of equal value or else it's a fucking problem. He was going home in a couple days. This is one of the reasons I felt comfortable saying it—he's going home [in] two days. So I knew he wasn't going to fuck me up, you know? That helped a lot actually.

ANNA GRISTINA, detained 2012: Rikers was almost like being inside a surreal TV show. It's like you're the filmmaker. These women, coloring their hair: they would fake injury by rubbing themselves to get hydrogen peroxide and save up the tiny bottles and dye their hair, or they would take red or blue Kool-Aid and then you got hair color. They were ingenious. They would make "Inmate Sushi." You get packets of rice in tinfoil and tuna in a packet, save up crackers, and crush it. It wasn't that bad. It was so inventive.

DAVID CAMPBELL: When I first went to commissary in EMTC [Eric M. Taylor Center], this would have been about three months into my bid, they had stopped the practice of tipping commissary employees. There's an inmate on the other side of the Plexiglas, and to be nicer, [you say,] "Get yourself a pack of cookies or whatever." I had never heard of that. I've never been in jail.

I come to a new place and the guy on the other side of the glass, after he fills my bucket, picks up a pack of fish, and he's nodding at me, waving it in the air. I'm like, sure, I'll take an extra pack of fish [mackerel]. I didn't know what he was saying. It became clear to me that he wanted that as a tip. He hadn't asked anybody around me. I'm the only white guy. I have glasses. So he came out to the waiting area where you wait with your bag of commissary stuff to pick up the tip. And I was like, I don't have that for you, man. I didn't understand what you were doing. I've never heard of that before.

And he kind of went crazy on me and I was just like, yo, fuck you. I don't know you; you're not asking anybody else if they wanted to tip you. So, get the fuck out of my face. And people were like, oh, Campbell, you're so crazy. It was the right choice, even though I kind of lost my temper. It was a risk. I would rather not have done it that way, but it actually worked out.

FRANK PASQUA III: Here's a typical meal that we would make. It would be kind of like a seafood paella, with rice, ramen, smoked oysters, regular clams, tuna fish, every seafood item on the commissary all mixed up. We'd make enough of it for like ten people. Everyone would go in on that. And then we'd get a big bowl of that. It was difficult to even get bowls. You would have to use the TV dinner trays that they would give for the Jewish meals. That was your bowl and you'd clean it. So I would throw in on a meal like that with the guys, usually with the Latin Kings or Rat Hunters, and say here, I'd give them say $15, $20. And I would get two big bowls of that when they cooked on that night.

JACQUELINE VELEZ, detained 1998: We would make rice and fish and each make a different part of the meal. I worked in the bakery, so I might bring something baked that I snuck out that we can share. Have a little piece of bread with our meal.

One of the women worked in the kitchen. And we used to eat out of bags, like Jack Mack out of a bag, like, you know how you eat tuna fish out of a can, they would sell fish in a bag. You rip the thing off and you break up the fish like you did tuna fish and we would put onions and peppers and salt, black pepper. And she would steal these things from the kitchen, bring them to the house.

And seasoning. We used a lot of the seasonings from the ramen noodles. We used that to season the rice. We didn't have adobo, none of that. But she would bring us onions and peppers and stuff.

I would bring the bread and she brought the onions and peppers and my friend brought the two bags of Jack Mack. Somebody else would bring the seasoning from the ramen noodles and somebody else would bring the rice.

And then one day, when they come to check everybody's stuff, to see if you have any contraband, and they just yell, "On the count," and you got to stand straight with your hands on your sides while they rummage through your shit and throw everything all over the place and they don't fix it obviously. They also search you. They searched this woman and she had a crack pipe in her vagina. I'm like, wow. I'm thinking in my head, I've seen crack pipes before. And it was glass. Ow! How the fuck does this woman have a crack pipe in her vagina?

Obviously, she got the pipe from a visit. So when she got caught over the crack pipe, I'm like, "Fuck! My fucking dinner's done!"

Jacqueline Velez, here near city hall, landed in Rikers as a teen and later as a young mom. She's now a community activist in Massachusetts.

CONTRABAND

"People Made Weapons Out of Bones"

In October 1964, a plasterer named Baldassare Magro, aged thirty-five, of Queens Village, stepped off a ferry arriving at Rikers and found himself in handcuffs. Inside his lunch pail, detectives discovered ten cans of Mace, an aromatic spice from the membrane that surrounds the nutmeg seed. The Bronx prosecutor David Blatt said at the time detainees were using it to get "high and excited." Magro, thus, became an early name in a very long list of people caught smuggling contraband into Rikers.

Crack, heroin, K2, food, the unsmoked ends of cigarette butts, and even an obscure spice used in a good masala. The underground economy in Rikers has always been like the weather or the tide: an elemental force that resists all attempts to prevent it. New rules became growth opportunities. When the city banned smoking in the jails in 1996, and then tobacco in 2003, a lucrative black market blossomed almost overnight. A $2 pouch of loose tobacco bought at a bodega became a $200 commodity on the tiers.

Jail officials often blamed the smuggling of contraband on visitors to the jails, and went to extraordinary and controversial lengths to ban visitors caught with contraband.

But there was also a river of illicit stuff coming in through the correction staff, as one indictment after another has demonstrated. It wasn't until November 2014, after an undercover investigator posing as an officer smuggled drugs and a razor blade into six different jails, that department officials agreed to order hard searches of staff entering the system.

But even then, it didn't stop. In May 2021, *seven* correction officers, a counselor, and an exterminator were busted for taking tens of thousands of dollars in bribes to bring scalpels, razor blades, K2, marijuana, tobacco, alcohol, and cell phones into Rikers jails.

The underground economy brought items like factory-made razor blades or store-bought knives and sometimes guns, but more commonly detainees make do with what's around them—shivs fashioned from light fixtures, toothbrushes, a broken piece of a broom, a jagged fragment of metal ripped off a radiator and wrapped in a scrap of torn bedsheet.

"They fashion weapons out of the institution itself," the correction commissioner, Richard Koehler, told *Newsday*'s Joseph W. Queen in 1988.

—

COLIN ABSOLAM, detained 1993 to 1996: They'll make weapons out of anything. I've seen an individual take the piece of Plexiglas that covers the light of a long fluorescent lightbulb. Then he took that, took toilet paper, and made a wick. If you unroll the toilet paper and then roll it back up, tuck it in, and light it, it burns like fire, like a wood fire. Then he put the Plexiglas over it and burned it until it melted. And then he broke it off and he sharpened it and filed it down and made an ice pick about twelve inches long. [He] just wrap a piece of a sheet around one end so he could grip it. I was surprised at his creativity. But I feel sorry for somebody to get stabbed with that.

BERNARD KERIK, correction commissioner, 1998 to 2000: I remember they physically brought an inmate downtown to 60 Hudson

[DOC HQ at the time] to show me two things: how they were transporting the weapons and the razor blades. And this guy sitting in front of me in my office actually pulled out a piece of dental floss he had tied to his tooth. He had six fucking razor blades he had swallowed and he pulled them out, all tied to fucking [dental floss]. He had just swallowed them. And he pulled them out, and then he had all the razors he wanted.

Early on, we were finding shivs, makeshift knives out of Plexiglas. And they brought another inmate down to see me, because I had seen some of these things and said, they're being done in the fucking workshop—somebody is cutting them there, on a machine. But they did it with a piece of dental floss. Somehow they would chip the Plexiglas, heat it up, and the guy would stick it between his legs and saw the Plexiglas with the fucking dental floss and I mean, perfect, like, *perfect*. He'd draw a line, he wanted to make a knife, wanted it this big. He would draw it all out and then he would cut this fucking thing and then sharpen it on the ground. And it was like a blade.

NESTOR EVERSLEY, detained various stints, 1969 to 2010s: I had a toothbrush. You file it down to where it becomes a weapon. You get some tape and put it on one end. You in jail, you make do. Back in the day, they used to give us real forks. After a lot of stabbings and a lot of deaths, they went to plastic spoons, but that really didn't stop a lot of stuff. People made weapons out of bones. They take the bones from the mess hall. They might get a piece of meat that was bony. You have to add tape to it. You might find something as you walk into the building.

Rikers was falling down. There's holes, there's leaks. When it rains and you walk down the hallway, it's full of buckets catching water. Even the handle from the bucket, if you can break it off, it becomes a deadly weapon. The handle is metal, so it becomes an ice pick. You might be working in the paint shop or in a place where you have to use pliers, screwdrivers, the shop class, and if they aren't on top of it, you can sneak it out. They have tricks for passing metal detectors. They pass it on the food wagon. The food has to ring because it has metal pots as it goes through the metal detectors. Some carts are so big, they don't fit through the metal detectors. It's up to the officer to check, but sometimes you have officers who let you go by. Some are lazy and some are thieves. You can also fashion weapons out of springs.

GARY HEYWARD, former correction officer and former detainee, 2000s: The most amazing weapon is if you line up about six to seven cigarette butts and mash them for a long period of time. The cigarette butt is fiberglass, and it creates a sharp enough edge. You put it under the bed frame and sit on it, and mash them together, and it can cut somebody. During the searches we would find those. They would put it in plastic and put it in their behind. The fiberglass isn't metal so you can't detect it.

ROBERT CRIPPS, retired warden, 1983 to 2013: At one point on Rikers when I was in SOD [Special Operations Division], they were using a cocaine oil and you would never think it was cocaine. It was, like, oily brown stuff, and they would smuggle that in, like, cream lotion and stuff. Even looking at it, it would look legitimate. But it was actually liquid cocaine. Then I went on the internet and I found out that this is a new method.

We had to change our search methods to check this cream. It's amazing. They think of any which way they can to get [drugs] in, but we did a lot of good things to stop it. We set up a trailer. Dogs came in and we put all packages on the floor. The dogs run past them and we find them right away. So we did eliminate a lot of that stuff, but you're never gonna eliminate all of it.

STANLEY RICHARDS, detained 1986 to 1988: So for me, when they talk about predator or prey, I was involved in it from the predator's side. I was the one who was doing all the deals. I was the one with the cigarettes and selling all of the swag, the food. I had access to all of that stuff like that. I was part of a group of people that smuggled stuff into the facility. I could tell you many ways. We used to

bring it in a watch. You set the time about the time you think you are going to a visit. The stretchy ones. We'd take off the back and stuff it with as much coke, dope, or crack as you can fit in there. And you and your girl are hugging and it goes off. It comes off her wrist and goes on yours. That quick. The one thing you were allowed to bring on a visit was a watch. Now they don't let you do that.

The other thing we used to do is shirts. You take the collar and the stitching around the collar and you stuff it with dope. Thinly bagged dope all around. And you send it in as a package. When they search it, nothing. All they'd do is shake the shirt. They wouldn't feel it.

The other thing you should do is *Playboy* magazines or *GQ* magazines. The paper is really thin. We'd take a page and take dope and fold it into a page and combine the pages. And you take a little bit of toothpaste to seal it. When they search, they flip through the pages and never notice. "Enjoy your magazine!" That's what we used to do.

Stanley Richards spent time on Rikers in the mid-eighties. He was photographed in his office, where he is senior vice president of the Fortune Society.

And then I had access to movement. So if a package came into Six Lower and it needed to go out to the Five Mod, they'd wait until I come around with the food. We had those canned groceries. I'd come around with the canned groceries. I'd pick up the package and it had to be delivered to Three Upper. And how [I] got paid [was] through cigarettes, or people put cash in someone's account.

FRANK PASQUA III, former Lucchese crime family, detained 2003, 2011 to 2012: I didn't do my time like I should. People would come to my cell and think it was someone's living room. I'd have wall-to-wall carpet with the Muslim prayer rugs. I had curtains. I had two or three radios. I would take a file folder and fold it into a cone, tape it up, attach it. That would make a speaker. So I would have three radios with the cones all set to the same station. So I didn't have to keep the earbuds in. I could just listen to the ambient music. I lived very good there.

I was in there with Joey Meldish, who was a hit man for the Genovese, for any family who wanted. He was freelance. I was there for about ten months of that with Joey. We were in the same house. He was very influential in the jail. Everyone knew who he was—high-profile double homicide. Hit-man case. The cops did anything he wanted. He had cops coming in every day, giving him a pack of cigarettes for free just 'cause they liked him. And they wanted to be around a hit man like him. When I was there with him, the doors got thrown open. He's like a third cousin of mine.

And so he introduced me to everyone as his nephew. He would go and tell people that this kid's going to be a wiseguy soon. His dad's a made guy. His whole family's made guys. He's going to be a made guy. So he would explain this to the officers ahead of time. And they knew if he's in the Mob, they'd never have to worry about me informing on them. And he would also tell all the gang members; everybody in the jail knew that I was basically royalty. That was the best stretch I ever did on Rikers.

At this time, there were still passes. If you had to go to medical,

they give you a pass, and you walk from the house to the medical. Me and Joey were both Mob cases. Our movements were supposed to be completely controlled. But they wouldn't enforce it. The guys who were writing the logs would just . . . Every twenty minutes, three times an hour, they have to write down what you're doing. They would just write down sleeping for the whole day. Meanwhile, me and Joey would get passes. We would go all over the building. But we were also in something that's called administrative segregation, ad seg. Because we were connected and we had cases like that.

For ten months, I'm in admin seg moving around. If I needed to go somewhere, I would go. There was this building that were dorms called the West Facility. West Facility had air-conditioning. If you had a medical condition, you got there. So, we would get officers that were on the security team—I'm not talking about regular officers. Guys that had clout. We'd tell them the day before, like, this one guy, I'll say his name as "Rockwell." I go, "Rock, tomorrow, like twelve, one o'clock, you can take me over to West Facility?" He was like, all right, write it down. The cops are not supposed to carry their phones, but they do. And that's how I would FaceTime with my family sometimes.

I told Rockwell, put it in your phone or you're going to forget. I make him put an alarm on his phone for 12:30 as a reminder to come get me. And he would walk me all the way to the other side of the building, then out the door of the building, to the other building to go see other people. I would go have lunch with friends. I would go deliver drugs to people that way.

Anyway, he was from East New York, Brooklyn, and he had seen me. I didn't remember him, but he told me he remembered me. He used to go to Howard Beach, a pizzeria there, New Park Pizza. And he remembered me from being there. He knew that we would bump into each other in the street. He wanted to be around someone like me. Other guys tried to look out, and when I offered them money, they took it. When I used to offer him money, he'd say no. Maybe, maybe $1,000 the whole time.

AUTHORS: *There were a lot of searches. How did you get around the searches?*

FRANK PASQUA III: I would usually have a holster. I would have somebody that would basically . . . I always picked an older guy and I'd have maybe two. If business was good, I have three holsters. And these guys, during the day, I would spot-check them. I'd grab them and say, "Hey, where is it? Where is it?" And if they didn't tell me that it was up their ass, I would cut them off. First of all, for my own personal use—tobacco, drugs—I would always keep a couple of fingers. Most of the time, when I was out of my cell, it was inside me. And if you follow a strict protocol of anytime you're out of your cell, the contraband is boofed. You keep it inside you. Otherwise, you're going to catch a new charge.

DONOVAN DRAYTON, detained 2007 to 2012: I've seen people do a lot of creative stuff in prison, hide stuff in peanut butter jars, all types of stuff, foods, [and] seal stuff back with toothpaste. So it looked like it never was open. You have the most craftiest minds in prison, man. If there's a will, there's a way.

CELESTE RICCIARDI, detained 2009: I actually went in wearing contact lenses. And I always used mine way more than I should. Every two weeks. I wore mine for like a month. Every time I needed a new contact, I'd be like [to my partner before his visit], "I need my left one today." He'd come to visit with the contact on his tongue, you know what I mean? And so I could get it during the visits. When he met me, I'd take it and put it in my eye. And I'd just say I was putting a contact in my eye [if officers asked what I was doing]. They give you contact solution, but they wouldn't give me more contacts. They do give people glasses.

DAVID CAMPBELL, detained 2019 to 2020: K2 is fucking crazy in there. They call it "plain" or "deuce." A lot of the guys who were smoking were guys who were addicted to heroin and crack on the outside, and they just want some escapism. People send it in. It's like an open secret, just because it's so undetectable. It's odorless, soaked in paper. They just use a spray bottle, soak it on a piece of paper, like a letter that you've written, and send it in. Every once in a while, the mail ladies take a letter out of an envelope and hold up to the light and go, it looks like it's soaked in drugs. But then she would just fold it up and give it to you anyway. [Security] rarely was an issue.

Once you get it, you just smoke the paper. An eight-and-a-half-by-eleven sheet is like a thousand dollars retail value in jail. You sell it in stamps, like a postage-stamp-size piece of paper. You tear that off. You sell that [stamp] for fifty bucks. And once you buy that, you tear it up into tiny little flecks and you sprinkle your flecks on a page from whatever book, like a pocket-size combination Psalms and New Testament.

You roll that up and smoke it. Those guys get really high. They'd joke about getting epileptic seizures. They call it "catching an epi" or "getting stuck."

BARRY CAMPBELL, detained 1980s, 1990s: Most of the times it [drugs] was brought in either by civilians, officers, or through other inmates on the visit. So if you got the hookup, like say if you're connected with one of the cooks in the kitchen, he'll just walk in and you'll just go see him whenever you can see him. Or if you work with him in the kitchen, we'll pass it to you and then it's on you to get it back to your house, however you choose to do that. There were some relationships that I have with officers that would never search me.

There were other relationships that I had with officers, whenever they seen me, they wanted to search me. And so you get to know who's working what shift, who's working what hallway, who's working what gate. It was kind of like a quid pro quo. So if somebody was giving the officer a hard time, he pointed him out to me and I go dust his ass off real quick. It wasn't about me paying him. It's about me taking care of something for him and he taking care of something for me.

NESTOR EVERSLEY: On the Rock, because I knew the whole jail, I was able to make money. I went in with $10 and I came out with $1,200. You couldn't smoke, but people smoked anyway. I worked in all those areas where no one else could go. The officers smoked in there. I would go into the male and the female locker rooms, and I would find cigarette butts. I accumulated forty butts and broke them open and remade them. A Newport is like $10 for one. I used to break them down and sell them by the finger. A finger is $30 or $50, the price depends. They would say I need a finger, they would put the money in my account, and they would get their fingers. You have to survive one way or another.

BARRY CAMPBELL: Now, in terms of the civilians it was about the money. A civilian may look at you, and you may say to the civilian, if you bring me a carton of Newports, I'm going to give you $200.

JERRY DEAN, detained 1987, 2003: I went back to Rikers in 2003 and they sent me to a unit, and when I walked in, there was a guy; he was waxing the floor and he had on like fifteen gold chains and a velour sweat suit. They're like, that's Trinny, he runs the dorm.

It was vicious because this guy Trinny, he had like six or seven guys who worked for him. He fed them cigarettes, and anytime somebody would get out of line, Trinny would beat the fuck out of them. And the guards would look the other way.

They would put them in the dayroom, and then they fuck them up in the dayroom, *boom, boom, boom.* And the guard would just look the other way. It was totally insane. And Trinny would just sell the cigarettes. And then I come to find out that the guy who was giving them the cigarettes was a counselor who ran the dorm. He was giving the cigarettes to Trinny to sell, and in return Trinny would keep the place in order.

The guards were supplying him with tobacco. He had a shank he used to walk around with. When the guards would tell him they were going to do a shakedown, he would hand the shank to the guard. And the guard would put it in his desk and then give it back to him when the searchers were gone.

BARRY CAMPBELL: One of the gentlemen I did time with was Rastafari, and he tied it all up in his head. His girl would bring it in in a cavity, she would take it out. And he would either make one or two choices. He would either put it in one of his own cavities, or he would wrap it up in his head. I really didn't care how you did it. As long as you got my shit to me.

FITZGERALD DAVID, retired correction officer, 1987 to 2014: You had inmates there that was so smooth they could talk to you and gain your confidence and have you bring in something for them. You cannot share any of your personal business, personal life. You have to keep it straight, narrow, and professional at all times.

When you're book smart, you think you know everything, you're dumb. So you come in the job thinking, oh, I can talk to these inmates. And now you given these inmates your business. Now they got you. So now I know all about Officer So-and-So. I know what she likes. I know what she doesn't like. Now I start talking to her in a whole different way. "Oh, yo, you look nice." You know, to draw you in. Now I've snared you. Now, for a male officer, "Yo, what's up, bro? Yo, I know so-and-so and so-and-so." "I know him too." "Yo. That's my man."

That's the game. Now I got you ensnared in a conversation. Now you know a person that I know. So of course it's going to intrigue you to go talk to that person. Now you just fucked your whole career up.

GARY HEYWARD, former correction officer and former detainee: Being from the neighborhood and knowing a lot of people, that's how I got into bringing it inside. Cigarettes was allowed. That opened up a market. Even though the inmates couldn't smoke. The officers were allowed to smoke. It comes in through the visit floor, the girlfriends. The second way is a corrupt officer that brings it in. I don't see no other way.

It's hard to check each other's bags. I'm not going to be that asshole officer that runs all their stuff through the scanner. We're drinking buddies. Why would I do it to you? If you bringing liquor inside, you going to let me know. An inmate approached me that knew me and that I felt comfortable with. I brought him a pack of cigarettes that his sister sent to him. I found out that there was weed in it. I was upset at first, but I knew his whole family. I never did it again after that. My wages was getting garnished, my car was getting repo'd, I had to move in with my mother, that happens to a lot of officers.

At any given time, officers are propositioned. You can't whip an inmate's ass every time they ask you to bring something in from the street. At the time, Top's tobacco was $2 for a pouch. I would take one pouch and the inmate paid $250. He's going to make as many mini cigarettes as he can for $20 each. He's going to make more money than me, but all I spent was $2.

MICHAEL "BIG MIKE" WILLIAMS, member, DOC Emergency Services Unit, retired 2008: More than once, there's been shootings. Inmates shooting other inmates. How does a fucking inmate get a gun on Rikers Island? When I was in ESU, I responded to two. That's scary. Coming into a dormitory, you see fifty beds, like a military base. Lockers welded to the beds. It's fifty guys in there. You don't know who the fuck got the gun.

In one, somebody welched on a fucking Super Bowl bet. Didn't pay the guy. It was over commissary, but they take this shit like it's in the streets. He bet on whoever was the team that lost, and when it was time to pay up, he didn't have it. They had a gun stashed in there, and they shot him. We found the gun. Twenty-five automatic. Something they could boof up their ass. Like a Raven. That's the most low-level fucking gun they got.

So we go in with the submachine guns—MP5s at the time. You gotta go in dynamic, you gotta stack. One hand on the shoulder. Team break to the right, team to the left. Last one on the bullhorn yelling commands. Don't move, you'll get shot. And we don't know who's got it, where it's at. The fucking guy's still lain out on the floor, bleeding and shit. The officers that was working in the area when it happened got out of there. How the fuck did a gun get in here, man? Not knowing that one or more of these assholes would pop up and start shooting us—even though we had on vests and shit, you could catch one to the face, the head, whatever. That was the hairiest moment.

Then you gotta cuff one inmate at a time. You pass them out and then you take them out to an isolated area. And then we had to do the GSR, the gunshot residue, on everybody's fingers. They didn't think we would be that advanced, but we had been in school for all of that stuff. We got who it was, but the fact that an inmate shot another inmate in jail . . . that shit is crazy.

TAMI LEE, retired correction officer, 1989 to 2020: A couple of years ago, at the Brooklyn House, they were sending a fishing line through a hole in a window from the ninth floor down to the street. There was this big influx of drugs into the facility and cell phones. Everybody was high. They had K2. Crack. Marijuana. People rolling around on the floors. We could not understand how.

What the inmates were doing was they took the string they give out for hanging laundry—it's heavy, almost like rope—and they were lowering it onto the Smith Street side and pulling up the drugs from people on the street.

They always get high, but I'm talking about you going into the housing area, you like, "Whew!" because the marijuana smell is so strong. Officers were like, "Open the windows!" The marijuana smell was so strong, and you know that K2 makes them go crazy. They had inmates going to the hospital every day from that K2.

They also found a lot of crack on searches. I didn't even know people still smoke crack, but they had like a lot of crack. All inmates was walking around high. All of them, they was sitting in the dayroom all day, like nodding off. And it came in on the ninth floor, but you know, they spread it throughout the building.

We didn't know how long it was since they started. Once they put it out, it don't take nothing to pull it up. Like five minutes, they pulling it back up so they could have been doing it all night for a month. And plus, those cameras outside . . . nobody watching them.

One night, a captain was coming to work on the midnight tour, and she actually saw the string out there. She saw the people outside and everything. After that, they took all the inmates out of that house until they could fix those windows, and it didn't happen again. But those same inmates moved from Brooklyn House to Manhattan House and they did it there, too.

MARTIN CREGG, retired DOC gang investigator, 1996 to 2018: A finger of weed was $25, but the girls who were doing the smuggling would never know what they were actually getting. They would say, "I just want the misdemeanor. I don't want to fuck with the felony stuff." So she would boof a misdemeanor but not know what was actually inside her. After we got it, we'd be like, "Babe, there's two Suboxones in there. That's heroin. That's a felony. You're going to get charged now." She's like, "No, it was supposed to be a misdemeanor!"

RICK LOMBARDI, retired DOC gang investigator, 1990 to 2011: We bring this high-ranking Latin King down for drug testing, and he comes up positive for heroin. As part of the Latin King rules, you can't do heavy drugs. You can only do weed. I said, "If we put you in the hole for coming up positive, then all the Latin Kings will know." He's begging us, "You can't violate me because of heroin. Just say it's weed." I said, "No, dude, it's heroin and it's a felony." He's a big guy, six foot six, and he's begging me, "You gotta help me! You gotta help me!"

I said, "Just give me the blade that's in your asshole, because I know you're carrying a blade in your asshole." This guy drops his pants, puts his fingers up his ass, pulls out a razor blade, and throws it on the floor. So I kick it toward [my partner] and yell, "Razor blade." [My partner] grabs it but it's covered with shit. So it's all over his fingers. [He] drops it on the floor and says, "Are you serious, dude? He fucking got shit on a blade and now I touched it?"

So after all this is said and done, [my partner] is fucking fuming. He says to the Latin King, "Go back to wherever you came from and bring me ten fucking clean razors blades or we're fucking violating you." So the guy goes, "How am I going to get ten blades to you?" I said, "Asshole, the same way you got this blade. Whatever you gotta do, bring me ten razor blades and they gotta be clean." About forty minutes later, he comes walking back to us and hands us ten razor blades with the cardboard still around the blades like they just came out of the box.

ROBERT CRIPPS: In many cases I would deal with the head gang leader and I would say, listen, whatever you guys are doing, we all know. If you attack someone and you're breaking his jaw, you're stabbing him, you can bring so much attention to yourself. You're going to be locked down.

I'd have to talk to them in inmate lingo, and they listened to me. When I was the warden of AMKC [Anna M. Kross Center], I had this discussion with an inmate. I said, "You know, this is not acceptable." I said, "You guys are going to be killing yourselves 'cause I'm gonna lock every one of youse down."

That night the inmate approaches a captain. He says, can you give a package to the warden? Captain goes, "What do you got?" He goes, "Well, I have this bag. Can you make sure the warden gets it?" The captain looks in the bag and it's got freaking twenty-five weapons—razor blades, everything. He collected the weapons from all his members and gave it to me. I came in the next morning and I had a bag of weapons. I didn't charge anybody, 'cause he did that voluntarily. And you know what? All of a sudden, in AMKC, the stabbing stopped, the broken jaws were reduced. You could look at the records.

RICK LOMBARDI: I had a really good CI [confidential informant]. He had given me a Trinitarian leader named Omar for holding, according to him, upwards of a pound of weed and all kinds of shit in his cell. Omar was like the King of Washington Heights, selling "purple haze" [marijuana] back in the day. And I think he had gotten forty-five or fifty years just for selling marijuana.

He was one of those guys who came down on a bullshit paternity suit because he knew that he could come back to Rikers, get contraband, sell it to everybody, make a lot of money, and go back upstate and be rich again. That was his thing.

So I tell my boss we're going to do a cell search. We close it down and every single officer is searching. We send in the dogs. We find nothing. I'm kind of embarrassed. The warden is like, see, I told you. Gang intel doesn't know what they are talking about. You guys are always causing all kinds of troubles in my jail. Now I look like the biggest dick in the world. My boss is telling me I fucked up.

So I grab my CI and I say, "You better fucking figure it out. You just made me look like the biggest jerkoff in the world. I called all this overtime and all these officers, like I just cost the department probably a hundred grand in overtime. Where the fuck is this shit?" He's like, dude, he has it. I'm telling you, he has it. We searched the cell with dogs and everything. We must have had 150 to 200 officers there. He's like, "Dude, it's in the wall."

I said, "It can't be in the wall. We had dogs in there. There's no way it's in the fucking wall. Don't make me look like a dick. I already look like the biggest asshole." He goes, "Dude, it's in the wall. It's in the windowsill. You gotta take the window out." I'm like, what? How could it be inside the window? You need a special screwdriver. He's like, he's got a tool, bro. I said, "How am I going to take the window out?" You need special tools and everything.

So we took out the window and we found it. It was over a pound of weed. I was like, you've got to be fucking kidding me. Inside the windowsill. He had two or three razor blades, $1,500 in cash in a money belt, he also had all kinds of Trinitarian leader status paperwork, and when we found it, they said, here's the deal: you can rearrest him. And Omar laughed in my face and told me the same thing. He goes, "You can rearrest me for that pound of weed because I'm an upstate prisoner to begin with and I would love to stay down here on an open case for a pound of weed because I can guarantee I'll have a pound of weed tomorrow."

FRANK PASQUA III: I had money in jail. I would use it to set up businesses in jail. I had an officer and I would consistently send Western Union to his girlfriend. And he would bring me pouches of tobacco or anything I wanted, and I would sell it in there for profit. So I did business in jail.

I would begin a small casual acquaintanceship with officers, and then I would see where I could take it. If within a month I'm eating his lunch when he comes in, I know I got him in my pocket. Later in life, I had amassed a big rap sheet. So the officers are able to go and check that rap sheet and they could see, "Oh, look, he gets arrested, he never tells on anyone." So they'll approach me sometimes.

A pouch of tobacco, I was always buying like ten of them at a time. So I would get them for fifty bucks apiece, five hundred bucks. I'd get ten pounds of tobacco. In jail, you usually make $250 on a pouch. You make fingers and sell the fingers for $25, like fingers of a glove. Up to the first knuckle is like $25. The whole finger will be $50. Some places, $100.

In the [jail I was in] tobacco was cheap, because that's where the people from upstate that are fighting their cases on appeal are placed. In the state prison system you're allowed to have tobacco. Guys are always coming from the facilities in the state with their whole asshole full of tobacco. So there, you would get a whole finger for thirty bucks. But if you're in [another] building, that same finger might cost you seventy bucks because we don't have state inmates coming there.

So say you get a bundle of dope, right? When I had a cop who was working with me, I would give him a flat salary every week, and I would have friends meet him and give him what I wanted. I very quickly switched over to Suboxone because Suboxone is pharmaceutically stabilized. It lasts forever. You could have the same Suboxone strip in a finger up your ass for ten years. Take it out and it still works. So I would have him bringing in Suboxone.

I never had issues with people owing me money. As long as it was a reasonable number, if it was like two hundred bucks, three hundred bucks, I tell him, "Hey, listen, you know what, you're burned. Try to send me a little something every week." Until you paid the debt you can't do business with me or anyone who works with me. And then I would let the other dealers know, don't let him buy from you. Number one, he's not good credit. Number two, it's a disrespect to me. And then that person would get cut off and they would end up wanting to pay the money back.

If it was, like, a bigger number, say $1,000, I would just have somebody go either beat him up or cut him. I'm not going to say I never did it myself.

Occasionally if I saw an opportunity, like I was walking in the hallway, I would jump him on the line. If it was given to me on a silver platter, I would handle it myself. But I didn't want to bring heat to my operation and fuck up my lifestyle.

JOHN ALITE, former Gambino crime family associate: In the early '80s, I'm moving coke into Rikers with a guard's family. Angelo Ruggiero was [John] Gotti's right-hand man. He was involved in heroin trafficking. I'm already moving coke. I was a big coke dealer. And I say I never moved heroin before, but yeah, I can move it. Let me see. Give me some.

So I go, "Hey, [guard], you know anybody that can move this heroin? Now, I knew he fucked around a little bit with heroin. So I asked him, is this any good? He goes, yeah, it's all right. They're stepping on it too much, though. I go, all right. So I say [to a Gotti associate], give me what you got. He gave me an eighth of a key [kilo], which was a lot, especially in those days. Keys of heroin went for a couple of hundred thousand. Coke went for $40,000 a key. Big difference. I said [to the guard Pete], can you move it? He goes, "If you give me something better, yeah, I can move it."

So we made a deal. And he started moving it and every couple of days he was coming back to me. He had inmates in there that he would give it to, and the inmates would move it. He also gave it to some of his friends that were guards that were in different sections that were moving it. You have to remember all these guys are our neighborhood guys. This is the biggest mistake prisons make.

His brothers grew up with me. They were my partners in drugs. So it's not like some big maneuver where I'm dealing with people I don't know. I would go to his house. He would come to my house. We're doing business every day together. He got the money back to me. For the most part, I went through his brother to give me the money back.

There's a thin line between police and gangsters. I've always said it. And they tiptoe over that line all the time. That's why they do what they do for a living because they're kinda on the edge. It's just part of that world. These guys are just as bad as us that are in there. And obviously that's why they're doing what they're doing.

MINISTER

"We Get Our Gun In"

As a teen, Amin "Minister" King, born Larry Frazier, joined the Fruit of Islam, the security arm of the Nation of Islam, learning self-defense and self-empowerment. After a split in the movement following the 1975 death of its leader, Elijah Muhammad, he left the group. He became an enforcer in the ultraviolent Lorenzo "Fat Cat" Nichols/Howard "Pappy" Mason organization that dominated the Queens and Brooklyn drug trade in the 1980s.

—

AMIN "MINISTER" KING: Back in the mid-'80s, I did something that, in the history of Rikers Island, had never been done before.

This was 1987. I had like three, almost four years in. By that time, I had a network going. The police was on the payroll. I couldn't do it myself. I had to pay. They could have cash, however they wanted it. They wanted cash. I had cash. Get on the phone, "Yo, I need five solid." Solid means cash.

"You'll have it tonight when they come in." "All right, good looking out, big homey." Whoever come in, it'll be in an envelope.

brush, and the antenna goes into the groove of the brush. You tape it, lock it down. Take some cardboard and take the nail and bend it like a hook and put the rubber band and *boom,* it hits the back and the bullet comes out.

So I made two zip guns. For the rest of the crew, they had the gun itself.

The plan was to have somebody call in, use my name, and say, "Tell Minister we can get to him anytime we want." 'Cause I'm trying to get out. If I can get a lawsuit that I got shot by an officer, in my sick mind, I thought they weren't going to send my Black ass upstate if I got shot at Rikers Island.

We make two zip guns, and we have the real gun. The agreement was that in each block, we bang off, shoot somebody. Somebody was supposed to have shot me, somebody else, he supposed to have got shot, and the guys in the block that had the gun was supposed to shoot each other's hands.

The tiers are the length of a football stadium. Long. The hallway is like that too. In the middle, there's slop sinks because it's too big to be running a bucket all the way down a mile to a half a mile to get water to clean. So they had a slop sink in the center. The agreement was when you finished shooting, take the gun, wipe it down, and throw it in the slop sink.

So the stupid motherfucker threw it in the slop sink, but the gun was wrapped in the towel and it clogged up.

Water! *Shhhhh!* [Mimics the sound of flooding water.]

It was supposed to be done at a certain time. Everybody was supposed to got shot ten minutes after nine, quarter after nine, because they shut us down at ten o'clock. We were supposed to do it ten minutes before they said, "On the lock-in!" That's when they ring the bell. *Ding-ding-ding!* When they ring the bell, you can bang. *Bang, bang, bang, bang.* Everybody said, we got it.

I'm on the phone, and then you see the SWAT team come in, [shouting], "Shut it down!" What? "Somebody just got shot in three block!" "Yo, four motherfuckers just got shot." Get the fuck outta here. "Yo, gotta go." They cut off the phone.

But it was not supposed to happen, not tonight. It was supposed to happen the next Friday night. These motherfuckers did the thing on a Wednesday or a Thursday. [The incident happened on April 1, 1987, a Wednesday.] And not only that, but somebody got trigger happy and did the fucking thing before the lock-in.

The Orange Crush comes. These motherfuckers come. They brought in the FBI. They brought in IG, the attorney general, the inspector general, because this never happened before. They got us locked down. They tearing the cells up.

Guess what I get busted with? Double-O-Seven [knife], 'cause I keep my knives. I got busted with the Double-O-Seven and the guillotine wire. They said, "You, Minister, step out the cell." So they got three of these orange guys around me. "Put your hands behind your back." "What I do?" Big motherfuckers. I got slippers on. My drawers and slippers.

They handcuff me. And they got these two big fucking orange guys. I'm facing the wall. They say, "No, turn him around." Turn me around. I probably should have thrown the shit out, 'cause motherfuckers start talking. "You see that motherfucker with his hands up?" "Minny, Minny did that." "You see the other guy that got stabbed?" "Yo, Minny did that." So they got me. I think I'm going to the box.

They put me into the "Why Me" pen. The whole jail is shut down. I'm in the Why Me pen, standing there ten hours, thirteen hours? They got a guy with a shotgun in front of the Why Me pen with a trench coat on, like one of them James Bond trench coats. We found out that he was the feds, 'cause he wouldn't say anything. After like seventeen hours, the feds come question me.

I said, "Look, what's going on?"

They said, "You might want to tell us what's going on."

"I don't know."

"You heard about the guys that got shot?"

"That wasn't my block."

"We figured that. Bring his ass out of there." They handcuff me again, took me down to the interrogating room. A long table with folders filled with pictures. I know everybody on the folders. Guess who told? Two people in my crew.

Not the house gang. My other crew, the ones we brought the guns in with. The house gang didn't know anything about that. This was a little too advanced for them.

I thought these guys were leaders and two of them, well-known guys, told. They said that I orchestrated it. They gave the officer name and everything, said I paid the guys. They went and got the officer, and he told. They had him under pressure, and they put him in a drug program. So he got a drug program and fired. And I think he got five years' probation, but he told. He said, "All I know is his name was Minister."

It wasn't my real name. My real name was Larry Frazier. I changed my name when I got to Attica.

They interrogated me for like nine, ten hours. They were telling me you outdid yourself this time. He said, "These guys are kids compared to you. They're fucking kids." And he says, "This never happened at Rikers. What about the gun?" I said, "I don't know what you talking about." "You're not going to tell us what happened?" "I don't know." "Your name is implicated all over." So they isolated me and they banned me from HDM. I can never go back on Rikers Island ever again. I got banned by the government.

Man, that was thirty-something years ago.

[Six weeks after the gun incident, Minister started a twenty-three-year sentence in state prison. He was released in 2010.]

RIOTS

"All Pandemonium Broke Loose"

To deal with the exploding population, new jails on Rikers opened in 1964, 1971, 1972, 1978, 1985, 1988, and 1991. Still, the overcrowding was so bad that the city bought a series of jail barges to house the overflow and even used an old navy brig in Brooklyn.

Richard Koehler, the correction commissioner from 1986 to 1989, saw the red flags himself. "Right after I became correction commissioner, there was a riot," he said. "A lot of the inmates were beaten up. They were being transferred. It was packed. There were about eighteen thousand inmates."

In 1986, the temporary jail at the Brooklyn Navy Yard exploded in violence. And two months later, Rikers itself was racked with ten days of rioting blamed on serious overcrowding. The unrest began with a large brawl in the ARDC (Adolescent Reception and Detention Center) law library and spread to the Correctional Institute for Men (CIFM), where roughly 150 men threw up barricades demanding better treatment. And then the correction staff refused to take their posts. A few days later, there was a second major standoff at CIFM. Officers with batons formed a gauntlet and forced inmates to run through it. Investigators found the command structure collapsed and a range of examples of extreme excessive force.

Major riots followed in 1987, 1988, and 1989. In 1990, detainees beat correction officer Steven Narby and stole his jewelry. When the detainees were charged only with assault, instead of attempted murder, the correction officers' union blocked that "Bridge of Hope" for two days.

That led to another riot in the Otis Bantum Correctional Center. Dozens of inmates and correction officers were injured. Once again, probers found that excessive force was used by staff.

The riots were a result of larger problems: overcrowding, inhumane conditions, and the rough hand of correction staff.

—

THOMAS CINQUEMANI, retired correction officer, 1983 to 2003: It happened in the jail they put in the Brooklyn Navy Yard. August 8 of '86. It was on the third floor, dorms A, B, C, and D. The dorms were all Black and Spanish, and they had a rival gang issue. I was one of four correction officers on the afternoon tour, but the four that we were relieving didn't tell us about all the problems that they had that morning. So they just went home and left us blind.

The issues in the morning, I found out later, were the sparks for the riot. It was all gang related. The Blacks didn't like the Spanish; the Spanish didn't like the Blacks.

The officers we were relieving just wanted to go home and figured we could handle it. Well, we couldn't handle it. It was only four of us. And you had 120 men, or boys, between thirteen and eighteen.

Around 6:00 p.m., all the dorms were escorted down to the mess hall. It was a very narrow path. The corridor wasn't even eight feet wide, I don't think. Two dorms, A and B, came out in the corridor. I was with C and D, and when they were coming out, it exploded right there.

There was nothing to stop it. You can't stop a fire.

When C and D came out to go forward, instead of going forward, they turned. And we were the four trapped right there. It was approximately 120 inmates against the four of us. The two rookies, with A and B dorm, ran away. They were just out of the academy. They were terminated on the spot for cowardice.

But it left me and my partner, Darrel Harris, to fight for our lives. Darrel saved my life. I was being pummeled in the head with soaps in socks. Soap in a sock is worse than a piece of steel. That state soap they make in New York State [prisons] is just like concrete. I can knock you out with it.

We had no way out. There was no way out. They wanted each other, but we were there and they took their anger out on us also.

I was fighting two men—two boys. And you could only do so much when you're getting hit from behind. What I was told was that Darrel basically covered me as a shield and took the blows while I was down.

From the tapes I saw after the fact, it was a bloodbath. The correction officers came up and pulled me out.

I went to Long Island College [Hospital] and I was out for a year. I had neck and spine injuries. My head was a coconut, twice the size that it is normally.

[Harris was convicted in 1998 of shooting three people to death in a Brooklyn nightclub called Club Happiness. Cinquemani testified on Harris's behalf at his sentencing and told the story of the riot twelve years earlier.]

He's doing time. I moved on with my life and that was it.

In 1986, before the riot, my boss, a captain, always told me, "Use your mind, use your words, you don't have to fight nobody." And he was trying to give me his experiences. Well, the riot happened. When he came to the hospital, I looked him in the face and said, "I will never use my words again." And I never did, never did. I used my brain. I used my hands. And that's how it was.

KENNY GILMORE, detained 1971: Conditions got so bad in '71 that we started, for lack of a better word, *revoking.*

At that time there were no contact visits. We were all waiting to go out for our visits, but out of the forty booths only ten of them have working phones. So the thirty other visits have to scream. You can imagine thirty different people screaming through thick glass trying to communicate. So nothing is audible to nobody except for the few of us that have access to the phones.

You come to the island [for a visit] hypothetically 8:00 a.m. to maybe get a visit at 3:00 p.m. for one hour. So the frustration building up on both sides, "Oh, I'm not coming back out here; you're losing your girl, your family." "Oh, you can't even get a good phone." And administration is creating this atmosphere. They're creating it because they know these phones need to be in a working condition. But no.

We would do is get soapy water, throw it all on the floor. So when they come in, they have no grip, and they slip. We was prepared to fight. We got our broomsticks, we got everything, and they'd be saying, "Oh shit, these motherfuckers is crazy." But we had to make a statement. In seven block, they kidnapped a captain and held him up on the third tier and said if we don't get this, that, or the other, we're throwing his ass off the tier. So they lined up bulldozers outside in the yard prepared to come in if they didn't resolve it in a peaceful manner. The feeling was the same up and down the blocks. Everybody's frustrated.

We got busy with the police. They came in. There wasn't turtles then. They'd just get the extra police out of each block and tell them, "Yo, go down to so-and-so block." So we fought. Our block was called "homicide block." They knew it was a special event with us. There was some things we were prepared to do and ways in which we could get our frustration off on them. But it also took that anger away from each other. We wanted to have a common cause and a common enemy.

We fought. They busted our heads; we busted their heads. Everybody respected us. And we would do it as often as we had to do it to get our point across. So they was more inclined to give our block things that they wasn't giving the other blocks.

RICK LOMBARDI, retired DOC gang investigator, 1990 to 2011: I walked into a hostage situation in GRVC [George R. Vierno Center]. I told the warden, I think you should send ESU [Emergency Services Unit] in. I don't think the officer is coming out. The fucking door is barricaded. They're all wearing pillowcases over their faces with the eyes cut out. It don't look too good. So he ran down there. This went on for hours.

JAMES MCGOVERN, retired correction captain, 1984 to 2004: I was there for the riot in 1987. I remember there was no type of supervision. It was just mayhem. I remember going into this housing area and they had the whole area barricaded and some of the guys had wet the floors down with soapy water. They were taking [injured] people out of these housing areas one by one. I remember [a commander] coming into the facility and saying, "What are you guys doing?" And there was a fucking puddle of fucking blood on the floor. They were just taking these guys out, bringing them down to the intake area unsupervised all the way down. I remember them using chemical agents. They use chemical agents to quash this whole thing. I remember coming home that night, my fucking anger burning. There was really no accountability back then.

EDDIE ROSARIO, detained 1990: During my first stay at Rikers, there was a work slowdown [by the staff]. It was the middle of a heat wave. The first day there was no breakfast; the second day there was no breakfast and no lunch. By the third day, it was still hot, there was no food, and the COs had blocked the bridge so nothing was coming through.

People who were supposed to be let out were not. People weren't going to their court dates. Put all that together and it just exploded. You could hear the house next door blowing up. You could see it blowing up, and people in my unit started blowing up.

People were burning the shit they bought from commissary. They tried to smash the window of the Bubble. In some places they did. Those bunk bed frames are made out of steel. Some guys used it as a battering ram. Guards just ran. We took over. I was in a corner. The Ninja Turtles came and the SWAT team came, and they hit us with gas, which is not like on TV, where you hit the floor and crawl. That shit just inflames you. You shit and piss on yourself. It incapacitates you. That took the fight out of everybody.

They put us in a gym and left us kneeling with our hands on our heads for a long time. The guards walked around and hit you with a stick if you didn't sit up straight. After hours of this, the guards made two lines, and you had to run through the guards who were swinging sticks, and as you ran, they hit you. When it was my turn, they said, "This guy's too skinny." But if you were a big guy, they were cracking heads left and right. Once you get your head cracked, you're never the same again. That was my first time at Rikers. It was probably my scariest time in prison. I've been to state prisons. Rikers is up there with Sing Sing especially in the late '80s and early '90s. There was no rule of law. We became animals.

HILTON WEBB, detained 1989 to 1991: It was 1990. I was watching this show called *Thirtysomething*. I was in the dayroom by myself. I mean, you have to picture this view. The gallery is really long— it's twenty cells—and then a big gap and then twenty more cells. That's how long it is. And it's concrete. It's wide. This huge space has got maybe two rows of tables and places where you could eat or just hang out and party. Nobody wanted to watch this show. It was about a bunch of white folks. Like *Friends* and fucking *Seinfeld*. I was interested in the zeitgeist. So I'm just watching my show and I hear this scuffle. Then suddenly it's a war. I look up and this Rasta dude is up on the second tier. He yells out, "Rastafari!" and jumps off the fucking tier with two knives. He's got a knife in each fucking hand. I'm like, "Holy fucking shit." And when he lands, before he really even lands, he stabs one of the Muslim dudes.

I also had my knife on me 'cause you carry a knife. You have to.

That guy, Tuff is his nickname, was the leader of the Rastafarians. He had had a confab with the Muslim leader, and I thought they had come to an agreement, but obviously it was a setup. I looked to the right and Tuff is lying there on the floor with blood gushing out of his temple. Somebody had stabbed him in the temple, and every time his heart beat, a stream of blood came out of him.

We have these white towels; that's what they were handing out. One of his boys was holding the towel, and the fucking towel is turning red in his hand. That's how much blood Tuff was losing. It was just a melee. It was everybody. There was just knives everywhere. And they had metal garbage cans that I found out were made by Corcraft [the prison work division]. I ended up working at Corcraft in Attica. So I grabbed the garbage can top like it was a fucking shield and pulled out my knife and just stood there, saying, "We're not doing this in here. We're not doing this in here." You know, I'm standing there. "You guys want a war? War the fuck out there." There was a line of Spanish dudes across the gallery, and they were saying, "You're not bringing that shit back here." It seemed like ten, fifteen minutes, but it couldn't have been more than five to six minutes. There was blood everywhere.

People were getting stabbed left and right. It wasn't like razor slices. It was stabbings. Finally, the squad came in. When I heard the gates opening, I just backed up, dropped the fucking garbage can top back on it, broke the shank, threw it in the garbage, and went back and sat in front of the TV. After about four or five minutes, one of the guards says, "Yo, what the fuck is you doing? Come here!" "What, what, I'm watching TV. What's the fucking problem?"

I played it off like I didn't know what the fuck was going on because you can't speak; you can't say you saw anything. They locked everybody in their cell. And then they came down the gallery, which is really stupid. You're going to stand in front of a guy's cell and say, "Did you see anything?" "No, I didn't see a motherfucking thing. I was watching *Thirtysomething*." He says, "That's a white boy show." So I says, "Well, I'm not a white boy, but I was watching a show. Is that okay?"

[The next passage refers to an incident that happened on September 17, 1990, during the presentencing interview of a man named Mauricio Espinal, who was convicted of raping a nun in an East Harlem convent. During the interview in a courthouse holding area, he took Probation Officer Maureen Trenk hostage using a shiv made from a metal mop bucket handle. He demanded to speak with John Cardinal O'Connor, archbishop of New York. The ensuing standoff lasted seven hours.]

EDWARD GAVIN, retired deputy warden, 1982 to 2001: From where the gate was, there were three wooden tables about twenty-five feet from where he had her hostage. He had her in the corner of this very large holding pen. He's got one arm around her body, his left arm. And he's got his right arm with the shank at her neck.

Cardinal O'Connor came. They had him on standby.

I was there with Pete Mahon, a deputy warden. I was a captain at the time. Pete and I, we had just gotten off work and we hadn't gotten that far when we were beeped. I went back with him. Pete was the ranking officer on the scene. Ex-marine, two tours of Vietnam. I'd follow this guy into hell.

He told me, "Eddie, listen, I don't know what's going to happen here. Just go downstairs and get a gun." So I went downstairs. I got my personal gun, a Colt Detective Special, and I gave it to Pete. Pete was seriously considering shooting this guy. You know what I mean? We weren't sure what was going to happen.

But then once Emergency Services showed up, Pete decided against taking a shot. So he gave me the gun back, and I put it back downstairs.

Emergency Services brought this thing to the scene called an ISPRA [Israeli-made antiriot tear-gas gun]. What it does is, it shoots tear-gas canisters. But it's not meant for indoor use. It's *explicitly* not meant for indoor use.

One of the guys from ESU brought it up anyway, maybe as a show of force. So we hold this guy at bay. We're just watching him and the gate was cracked. It was closed, but not locked. So all we had to do, if we were going to go in, is just open it, and we could kind of go in there and bum-rush him. And we waited and we waited.

She [Trenk] was calm as a cucumber. He had the shank to her neck the whole time. She just didn't move.

NYPD ESU had snaked this camera in, and they were able to actually see this guy really close up, what his eyes were doing. And that was fed to a TV screen.

Then all of a sudden the command was given to go in because we saw him looking like he was falling asleep. These large tables blocked the officers from getting to her, but these guys were all in riot gear. Big, big Emergency Services guys. They went flying over these tables. They were able to get to him and take the weapon from him and free her from him.

Right at that point, in all the commotion, one of the officers from ESU inadvertently hit the trigger to the ISPRA and Pete Mahon was standing right there. The gun wasn't pointed at anybody. It was just pointed upward. When he hit the trigger, the canister went right in front of Pete's face, and it literally burned the skin off his eyes. Because the primer, the agent that fires this thing, it's hot. It hit Pete right in the face.

[The DOC spokeswoman Ruby Ryles told the press at the time the firing of the tear gas canister helped subdue Espinal.]

So he was all fucked up. I had to take him to the hospital. I think he went to the burn center. We went by ambulance to the burn center and nobody showed up. The commissioner didn't show up. There's nobody there. It was just me and Pete.

Nowadays, an officer gets poison ivy, he goes to the hospital with [the former Correction Officers' Benevolent Association president] Norman Seabrook, you know what I mean? In those days, nobody came. Fortunately, they treated him with some different treatments that they had. He had no loss of vision, but his eyes were still burning and he really couldn't see that well.

So they told him that he needed to get air on his eyes. So I wound up driving him home in his Buick. He lived in Woodside.

I'm driving the car and he's got his head out the window the whole ride. He's in the passenger seat with his face blowing in the wind so that the wind would soothe the pain. It was a September night. The wind was doing him good. We went across the 59th Street Bridge.

He had to take like a week or two off work because the skin also came off, like the skin over the eyes, like your eyelids, your nose. He looked like a raccoon. A raccoon has that stripe. Think of a stripe, but only raw skin. That's what it looked like. It was horrible actually, but he made a full recovery.

They wanted to keep him for observation. Pete was a marine. He wasn't staying overnight. He came back to work a week later.

[Trenk] came to work the next day, like nothing happened. She never talked about it. She wasn't afraid. She didn't call in sick. And she was probably one of the bravest people I've ever known. It didn't even faze her. It was like she wasn't even a hostage.

[Espinal] wound up with a broken rib or something. Between the tables and the guys going in there, charging him.

We didn't get home 'til like five. The sun was coming up.

EROBOS ABZU LAMASHTU, detained 1990: When I first went to jail— the Brooklyn House of Detention in 1990—something happened on Rikers Island. The way it started was this: CO got robbed for his jewelry [on Rikers]. 'Cause you know he, I guess he thought he was at a fashion show or he was making a rap video or something.

So he got robbed and I think maybe stabbed for his jewelry, and that created a set of events that just went through the entire system. Many of us in Brooklyn House didn't want to go to Rikers Island. It escalated because the guards attacked, I think, an inmate imam over there, and I think they busted his head as a form of retaliation. And that just turned into an entire shit show through-out the entire island. People were attacking the guards, guards were attacking the people. It got so bad.

The COs were coming with riot gear in random houses and just beating the shit out of everybody there just for retaliation. And once that word started getting out, they eventually shut down the phones so you couldn't call out or anything.

But people had their ways of communicating with each other, whether it was yelling from building to building or passing messages from the guys handing out the food, and then they cut that out too. So, it was just the COs handing out the food. You could imagine if you got bread, sometimes you were lucky, the way they would violate the food—spit in it or whatever or just give you juice and some cookies. And that was the meal. This went on for fucking weeks.

A crew of us decided to refuse to leave Brooklyn House. They wanted to swap people to break them up. The whole idea was split you up between the four borough houses, sort of break up the organized cause.

So nine of us refused to go there, and for days we were in the bullpen. They got smart after a few days and said, okay, we're going to take you out one by one and put you back upstairs. They loaded us on the bus and took us to Rikers anyway. When we got out there, we refused to leave that bullpen. We was like, listen, we're not part of whatever the fuck is going on out here; we want nothing to do with fighting COs or fighting anybody. And we want to go back to Brooklyn House. So we were in the bullpen for some more days.

It stinks and they feed you horrible sandwiches that are days old. Maybe you might get a little cup of, well, they stopped giving the coffee because some guys were so pissed off, they was pouring the coffee on the COs. So they'd give you a box of juice, something like that, or not even that. Just give you one of those green cups and tell you just drink water out of the sink—if there was any water in the cell to begin with.

Then the captains would call and we'd tell them the same shit. We want to go back to Brooklyn House. We don't want to be part of this fucking zoo that's going on out here. So that went on for some more days. And then they would move us from one cell to the other, and we wound up at the rotunda at HDM [the House of Detention for Men]. It reeked of piss. And that was a psychological way to make us give up.

Days are going by, and you don't have access to a shower, clean clothes, or anything. You wearing the same shit you basically got arrested in in some cases and you just been wearing whatever you left Brooklyn House with and we already been in the cell for days. At one point, it got so bad we refused to get off the bus. So they got to turn us around. It was interesting because they'd send out the captains and lieutenants, and sometimes a deputy superintendent would come and talk to us, and we'd be like, listen, we're not trying to get into a fight with nobody.

They never had any intention of sending us back. And then you get tired of being in the bullpens 'cause you can't take a shower or nothing. You just fucking stinking. By process of attrition, you get demoralized and grinded down enough where you just get tired and say, well, fuck it. I'm out here. I'm still doing my time. Everybody knows that we're not there to start no fight or no problem. So eventually we got put into different cells and they break us up where they put us in different blocks in HDM.

ALFONSO "JUDAH" WASHINGTON, detained 1999, 2002 to 2004, 2011: In 2011, I was on Rikers Island on a parole violation during the [NCAA championship], and we literally had a riot in the dayroom. I remember I was moving to the dorm and I wanted to watch the game, but the dorm had rules. Every dorm you go to, they're going to have their rules of how the TV works. And what the TV schedule is. Generally in most jails, sports supersede no matter what the program is. With that being the case, the Spanish guys, they had the TV from, I think, nine o'clock to lock-in at ten o'clock. So that means no matter what's planned at nine o'clock, the Spanish guys coming to the TV that are watching Spanish programs until lock-in.

However, during the 2011 NCAA championship, when UConn with [the future NBA star] Kemba Walker beat Butler, they had already negotiated with the Spanish guys that when the finals come on, we're going to watch the finals. You can take another slot or whatever, basically. And for those that don't know the rules, when coming into a jail, they somewhat fall under the umbrella of someone or an organizational group that's going to protect them. So most Spanish guys, they come in, they stick with other Spanish guys. And for some reason it's somewhat of a rite of passage to seem tougher than you may be.

The day of the finals, we were in the dayroom and we all sitting around waiting for the game to come on and a young Spanish guy comes in—all he knows is he's young, he's Spanish, and 9:00 is Spanish time—and turns it to the Spanish channel. The house exploded immediately. All pandemonium broke loose. I mean, chairs thrown. People getting stabbed. An old guy hit the young Spanish guy, and I'm trying to break it up because all I want to do is watch the game. If there's a fight, they're going to shut everything down. The squad's gonna come in and lock everybody in. So I'm trying to stop the thing. I break up the initial fight, but it was too big. It was the whole house. Literally the whole house. All thirty-six bodies were involved.

I mean, it was just pandemonium, chaos.

ESCAPES

"Ron, You Couldn't Pick a Better Name Than John Hancock?"

In the lore of Rikers, there are apocryphal stories of the few who were lucky enough to make it to freedom. The guy who snuck out in a garbage truck. The detainee who pretended to be her sister. The drug addict who fashioned his own ID to actually sneak *into* Rikers. Surrounded by water, save for that skinny bridge, you can't really swim out even if you did make it to the water's edge, because the East River currents are too strong. And then there was Ronald Tackmann, a thief and card-carrying member of Mensa whom retired jailers still speak of in awe even after his death in 2020.

—

RONALD TACKMANN, detained 1980s: In 1985, I was in Rikers Island and I saw these Spanish guys carve these little statues out of soap. I said, "Wait a minute, didn't John Dillinger make the gun out of [wood]?" So I started carving one out of soap. 'Cause I could carve statues, anything. I'm an artist and they look pretty good. And then I said, "Am I out of my fucking mind?" I broke it up, took it away, and then I started thinking about it more. This could actually work. So I carved another one out.

MARK CRANSTON, acting correction commissioner, 2014: I remember hearing about the soap gun. I came on in 1987. There was always talk about people fashioning weapons and different stuff out of soap. There was one person who re-created a Folger Adam jail key. The big skeleton keys, made by Folger Adam. There are some crafty people who can be very creative when they sit in their cell and think of things.

RONALD TACKMANN: I put little screws in. Chrome plated the whole thing. The chrome was from cigarette paper. The trigger guard was from glasses. And it looked real. I used a family-size bar of Ivory. And when I asked my mom to bring up a big bar [of] soap and a gun magazine too, first thing out of her mouth, she said, "Oh no, you ain't gonna make a gun out of soap." I said, "No, no, no. I'm not doing that." But it was funny that she picked it up immediately. John Dillinger, they just auctioned his gun for $20,000. It was made out of wood in the shape of a gun. That's all. But his reputation, when he put that gun behind the guy, they were scared to death. After I make it, then I gotta get this thing on a bus. So I get it on the bus. I never told anybody how. But I got it on the bus. I knew there was another van following us.

MARK CRANSTON: There's always safety training around transporting inmates around anywhere. Usually anyone going out to transport is searched by officers. They are strip-searched to make sure they don't have any contraband on them. That's done by the transportation officer, and then they are put directly on the bus so there's no gap.

RONALD TACKMANN: We had to lose them. We were going from Rikers Island to Downstate prison. It's like a holdover where they give you tests and all sorts of crazy stuff. Everybody goes there. Halfway up I took the handcuffs off. I had a plastic key. It was easy getting that. I tap on the metal screen with the gun. It had a little metal barrel. And for sure you could hear metal against metal, and I said, "Don't move. I got a gun, turn around and look, I got a gun back here." So he turns around, looks, and he says, "Joe, he's got a gun back there." I said, "Get into your left lane. Take your guns out. Throw them out at the next sign. You'll pick them up later. Nobody's gonna die." Once they throw the guns out, at least I know I'm not going to get shot. I may just get beat up.

So then I say, "Get into your right lane. Make a left. Make a left. Stop the bus and I want you, driver, to cut the engine and get out and open the side door of the van." I said, "Don't do anything stupid or I'll shoot your partner." I had to go to Manhattan because that's where I had money in a safe-deposit box. So he gets out, opens up the side door. They thought I was just going to run away. I say, "Okay, get in the back." I tell his partner, "Leave your jacket and hat and get in the back." When we do that, I lock the door, I drive the bus back to Manhattan and I put the [uniform] hat and jacket on. And it's all Black inmates [in the back] and two Black COs. And I'm driving, get to Manhattan, and I hear they're looking for the van.

MARK CRANSTON: Escape risks would be moved by the department's Emergency Services Unit. Gang leaders. They call them central monitoring cases. There could be a chase vehicle or some undercover units if it's a really high-profile person. Anyone involved in a cop killing.

RONALD TACKMANN: By the time I got to Manhattan, a couple of the inmates say, "We want to go too!" But I don't know what's going on in the back of the van. The inmates are passing notes to the COs, saying, listen, we're going to tell them we are going to go and then we are going to jump him. The COs are saying, no, forget about that. We are not going to do that. So I go to open the side door, and one of them tries to hit me. I go, "Yo! Back up!" And I pulled the gun out.

He's swinging and I'm blocking with one hand. Then the other inmate saw that since I didn't shoot him, he's gonna get brave, and he came out. So now I got two Black guys I'm trying to fight. I need both hands. I throw the gun down and I'm trying to knock these two out. The minute I threw the gun down, the two COs come out. So now I'm fighting with four guys in Manhattan and one of the COs grabs my legs and I fall. People are passing by and I'm going, "Yo, put these guys back in the van! Help! Help!" I'm hoping that a stickup kid will come by or something.

But I'm not thinking. I'm the only white guy. These guys are all Black and we're in Harlem. Nobody's gonna help me. Finally they handcuff me and put me back in. The CO picks up the gun, scratches it, and says, "Oh shit, this is soap!" He shows it to his friend. He puts it in his pocket, and then they press the button on a walkie-talkie and they call six New York City police.

When they get there, they say, "What happened?" They say, "He made a gun out of soap and took over the van and had us throw our guns out." They burst out laughing, like, *you idiots*. They said, "Oh yeah?" He pulled the gun out of his pocket. He said, "What do you think of that?" They all shut up. That's how real it looked. They said, "That's soap? Damn."

MARK CRANSTON: I found in almost every facility I worked in there'd be one or two inmates who would create different things out of soap. More sort of ornament things like a chess piece or a figure that they'd do as a hobby, and some would do it as a business to sell it to the other inmates or for an inmate to dress up their cell. Typically you know the inmates you are handling, and no one would ever throw those things away unless it had a sharp edge or looked like a weapon. You always have to be careful of a ruse where it looks like it's harmless. It would typically be an older or younger person where you could tell it's more of a hobby than a threat. It's soothing for that person as a hobby to pass the time and be creative.

RONALD TACKMANN: I get back to the Bronx House. I'm in a bull-pen and five IGs come over and say, "Tack, we only got one question for you. How come you didn't take one of the real ones?" I said, "Listen, my gun was working fine until those two inmates jumped me." They burst out laughing.

MARK CRANSTON: I don't doubt that he could do that. When you perform a strip search, it's not an exact thing. Obviously, people have totally smuggled things hidden in their body cavity. A metal detector doesn't catch that. I'd imagine he figured out how to do that. And sometimes it's complacency on staff. Typically you are supposed to remove your underwear and squat down. He was a pretty crafty individual.

RONALD TACKMANN: I never said this to anybody, the way I got the soap onto the bus. I had double underwear sewed together. I made, like, a pocket. You just pull your pants down when they check you before getting on the van. So they didn't see anything. In my cell on Rikers, I made a cardboard thing under the toilet and put it there. Like a little pocket under the toilet. That was easy. I made it when I was in the cell by myself. I had my own cell. I worked in a barbershop because I cut hair. I used my ID card for carving. And some other stuff. I forgot. It was a long time ago. It took me less than a week.

RICK LOMBARDI, retired DOC gang investigator, 1990 to 2011: [Tackmann's] the only guy who has escaped from Rikers like three times and upstate twice. He's brilliant. He's a member of that group for smart people, Mensa. He's slick. And you wouldn't think nothing of him. He looks like a little old man.

HILTON WEBB, detained 1989 to 1991, 1996: Around my trial time, so it had to be December of '90, I come back from court. I was really pissed, and there was basically a bulletin board, but they would never use it for a bulletin board. It was just a piece of plywood with metal strapping behind it. So I came back and they had tossed my cell. I looked at my cell; my legal work was everywhere. It was like they went out of their way to fuck with me. And I just got so mad. I punched the fucking thing and I broke a bone in my hand, a boxer's fracture, I guess.

They couldn't do anything at the clinic. So they took me to Bellevue and they said, this guy obviously needs a great hand surgeon. And the doctor said, well, listen, we're going to see if we can reduce the fracture. He had me in the back room, in the back of the emergency department, and my finger in this wire mesh thing. And he says, just hold your hand like this, and take the cuff off. They take the cuff off. Now, mind you, I had been sitting in Rikers Island, and in those days you had street clothes.

MARK CRANSTON: When I got on correction in 1987, one thing took me by surprise was everyone was walking around in regular clothes. Jeans, jackets, and boots. If they weren't wearing their IDs on the outside, you couldn't tell who was who at times. In the 1990s, the department had to petition the Board of Correction to put everyone in uniforms. That's when we also got the ability to monitor phone calls. We made the case that this was bad for inmates. They used to get stabbed over sneakers and jackets. It was just absurd. We were one of the only jurisdictions that allowed it. From an escape level, it made a huge difference. When someone goes on trial, they change clothes so they can be seen in front of a jury without the uniform.

HILTON WEBB: So, I'm in my jeans, a vest on, and T-shirt, and I'm like this with my finger *[he raises his hand]*. And the cop in the seat, he falls asleep. I say, hey, Officer. The other guy's gone. Fuck this. I took my finger out. My main goal was to smoke a cigarette, but . . . I walked out. A door was open and there was a breeze and I walked out and I'm standing on the street underneath the fucking overhang. I had friends who lived at Tudor City. So if you know where Bellevue is and you know where Tudor City is, it's not that long a walk. It's like twelve blocks. And I'm standing there and I'm going, well, I could leave, man. Wait until Monday. It was a Thursday night. And I had told them I was Muslim. So I got Fridays off from court.

So I smoked some cigarettes, I smoked like three, four cigarettes. And I started weighing, where would I go? How would I get to the money I had in the bank? My safety-deposit box. Where would I go? Would they look for me? Would they care? Ah, they wouldn't care.

RICK LOMBARDI: Any escapes, gang intel was dispatched to go find them. A lot of times they were erroneous. It was like missed paperwork, or they released them a little early. But we did like one a month at least. There were stories that the jails would go out and get their own guys when they realized they fucked up. They would have their own people try to quash shit before we knew about it. They wanted to make sure we didn't get the full story out. They wanted to go with the watered-down version to make it look good for everybody.

HILTON WEBB: And then I kept thinking, if you run, it's gonna look like you're guilty. *If you run, it's gonna look like you're guilty.* There's no way they could convict you for a crime you didn't commit. And I actually believed that at my core. I didn't believe that in America, the greatest nation in the world, you could be convicted for a crime you didn't commit. So I walked back to the room, I wake up the cops, yo, what's up? Man, it's cold outside.

What do you mean it's fucking cold outside? I said, I was just outside. He says, you what? What the fuck? I don't believe you. You're fucking pulling my chain. I said, come here. I'll show you. So we walk outside and I said, those are my cigarettes. I was smoking right there. He says, why didn't you run? I said, I didn't fucking do it. I've been telling you people that for two fucking years now. I didn't do it. Why would I run? I want my trial and I want my court; I want to stay put.

He says, wow, man, thank you. Thank you for what? He says, you could have run. You could have cost me my job. I said, they wouldn't fire you. He said, hell yeah, they would fire me. And his partner comes back and they started talking. He says, yo, dude, man, thanks a lot. He said, you want this sandwich? I have a nice roast beef sandwich and a bottle of soda. And they brought me back and I guess whatever they told the other cops, when we got back a couple of days later after I had surgery, they treated me a whole lot better in jail afterward, which made it easier to do time, I guess. They actually stopped searching me at HDM [the House of Detention for Men] after that.

JAMES MCGOVERN, retired correction captain, 1984 to 2004: This one guy was going into stores on Madison Avenue and he was raping girls in these stores [five rapes circa 1984]. So make a long story short, the guy's upstairs, he got caught. He's upstairs on the twelfth floor. He throws the holding cell open, and he walks down the fucking stairs and right out the door. The correction officers only realize it like an hour or two later. This fucking guy disappeared. The transportation officer, really, really nice guy, showed up to bring these guys back. So let's say he brings back twenty bodies, picks [up] the phone, says, I got twenty bodies. I've got twenty coming back to Rikers Island.

MARK CRANSTON: The counts are very effective if done properly. You need to make sure they are all okay, alive, and there. You assume the responsibility for all the people. The counts are done three times a day. And during each shift, you have to be very OCD to keep track of where people are and if they left. At any given time you should be able to rattle off where everyone is. If someone is in the clinic or law library. When I was a supervisor, the first thing I'd ask people is, what's your count? If you don't know that basic stuff, you're not in control. The counts are of the utmost importance. Do they prevent escapes? No. They detect escapes.

JAMES MCGOVERN: So as he's on the phone, they take this guy's paperwork. They just shoved in his paperwork. When he gets to Rikers, he reports this. He said, listen, I got the paperwork. I never picked this guy up. They suspended him. They said, he must have escaped on you. When you come out into the Manhattan courtyard, there's two sally ports. Years ago, inmates slipped their cuffs, and they went under the bus and hid and waited. They're saying that's what happened.

And he's like, this guy was very sharp. He was like, no fucking way. I know I had twenty bodies. I counted them; my partner counted them. It's on my sheet. And they suspended both of them anyway. P.S. the guy gets caught jumping a turnstile. They bring him in and they question him and they always tell the truth later. "Bus, what bus?" he said. "I escaped from a couple of these motherfuckers upstairs." The guys always told me, beware, count your fucking card when you leave that courtroom.

RONALD TACKMANN: After I did the first one, in 1985, every time I got on the bus they'd joke around with me saying, "Tack, next time you better fire a shot through the windshield, otherwise nobody is going to believe you." I thought about that and said, "That's a great idea." I'll build a black gunpowder pistol, get it on the bus, fire a shot through the windshield, and then they are definitely going to let me off. So I made black gunpowder with sulfur and charcoal. You can make a barrel out of anything.

Just like fireworks. So I used a soda can, cut it this way, and rolled it up, taped it up. Bent it back. Put a pinhole there. Put the powder, then a tissue, then a lead ball that I made and a piece of tape over the hole and a match on top of that. It fires. No fuse, and I got three shots. So on the Brooklyn Bridge, I fired a shot through the windshield, saying, "This time it works. I'm canceling my appointment with Judge Crane." They said, "We ain't dropping shit!" Now I'm thinking to myself, I'm dead. So we are having a Mexican standoff.

They are telling me to drop my gun. I'm telling them to drop your gun because you are getting suspended anyway. Finally, after about twenty minutes, I give up. I throw the gun up in the air. They call ahead. "Tackmann just tried to take the bus again!" When they call, the head of IG [inspector general] was in Manhattan at the time. When we pulled into the bay, the whole place is filled with COs. They want to fuck me up.

The head of IG gets on the bus, puts his arm around me, whispers in my ear, "Tack, you all right?" I said, "So far I'm all right, but I think they're going to beat the shit out of both of us." He said, "Don't worry about it. Nobody is going to fuck with us." So we get inside, he says, "Tack, listen, when you get out, if you want a job in security, I'd hire you in a minute." It was funny as hell.

The funny thing is there was a Puerto Rican CO. One day I got on his bus and he said, "Listen, Tack, I know you are going to do something again. Please don't do it on my bus. I've got a wife and kids, and I can't afford to get laid off." So I look at him and say, "You know what? You got that. I won't do it on your bus if I do anything." When I did the second thing, he came to the Brooklyn House and came right up to me and shook my hand and said, "Thanks, Tack."

EDWARD GAVIN, retired deputy warden, 1982 to 2001: When I was a correction captain in the Manhattan court division in 1993, we had a CMC, a centrally monitored case [meaning a detainee designated dangerous]. He came to court and then took ill, and they had to transport him to Bellevue Hospital. When he left the court division, he went with three correction officers, but it should have been a captain and two correction officers because he was CMC. But we didn't have a captain to go. So the earlier tour sent three correction officers. I wanted to get there.

He was a really bad guy—homicide charges, a gangbanger. I fly up there. I got to the emergency room, and the doctor tells me there was a captain on duty, [but] he never came to check on the inmate. There were three correction officers with this guy, and they weren't the sharpest. I'm just walking in the door, and the doctor's telling the correction officers to uncuff him. This guy said that he swallowed a razor blade or a pill, but he had feigned an illness to get to the hospital. He's got the leg irons, and he's got the one handcuff on the gurney. You don't take that fucking thing off. That's what was holding him to the gurney in the first place. I just know in this stupid fucking city, you never . . . The doctor was an idiot. You don't take that handcuff off.

He's got one free arm, but they gave him two. The doctor was a fucking twit. I walk in there. I've got my .38 on my side. They uncuff him and he goes fucking crazy. He started running and trying to get away. He goes to the end of the fucking wall. It was fucked up. Nurses and staff were running around. When he jumped up, he knocked over a cabinet all full of medical supplies and gauze. He tried to run, but thank God, there was nowhere to go. He went the wrong way, and it was a dead-end corridor.

I pull my gun. I say, get on the fucking ground. And he's still got his leg irons on. I say, this is it. So I go back up. I keep telling him to get down. They call for backup. My fellow captain came down with a baton. And just as this is going on, a cop got shot and [the then police commissioner] Ray Kelly is coming through. This guy [the police officer] was shot in Alphabet City, a Spanish guy. He's on life support.

Ray Kelly and the whole fucking Police Department are coming in. Kelly was there just as the ambulance pulled up. I didn't want to get near him. I didn't want to shoot and kill him. He's a felon. He's been convicted or charged with murder. I'm trying to maintain everything. We're calling for help because we didn't want to shoot the guy, and he knew that I was ready to fucking shoot him.

So then, this captain, who was no joke, came and his crew just bum-rushed him, and he got on the ground and he wasn't injured and that was that. The captain later died of colon cancer. Ray Kelly never knew. No one knew and we handled it and that was that. It never hit the papers. This stupid fucking city.

RICK LOMBARDI: There was an escape, and during the investigation they asked how the guy escaped, and we learned he knew that one officer sleeps through his shift. He had already popped his window out the night before, but he didn't have enough rope. The second day he actually got out. Someone saw him on the bridge. He said the only reason he did it was because he knew there was this one officer who slept on duty.

JAMES MCGOVERN: There were these two officers, a female and a guy. They both had time on the job. They were transporting an inmate out of the Brooklyn House, several of them actually. It was Sunday very early in the morning; they were in the bus. They were probably doing a six-to-two. They back the bus out of the Brooklyn House, heading to Rikers on the highway, and just as they made the turn onto Rikers, this fucking inmate—a skinny white guy, very small, very thin—got out the window and jumped out of the bus.

The male officer was the driver. I don't know how many stops they had, but I remember this guy was a detox inmate. There's a streetlight right there where you make the turn. That's where he jumped out. When they got to Rikers, they realized, "Fuck, we have a securing order without a body." They are saying, what do we do? They go into 95 and slap the paperwork on the shelf [as if nothing happened].

The commander was pissed off. They fucking realized they were in trouble. The female officer came forward and said, listen, this is what happened: the fucking inmate escaped on us and we tried to cover it up, and she gave up the male officer. What do they say? First one to the table gets the deal? She went to the table first. The male got suspended. She was put on modified assignment and fired.

RICK LOMBARDI: One time, they took this guy into the security trailer. There are four pens that you keep detainees in. You put your bodies in those. There's a fingerprint machine. They were warned that this guy's a runner. They were told, you should cuff him, he told us he was going to run. [A tenured gang intelligence officer processing an arrest] says, "I got it, I got it, don't worry about it." This guy ran right past him out of the trailer. No shoes on. He ran straight down the road and into the ocean. You know how far the run is to the ocean? Maybe more than a mile. Who knows how many officers saw him running with no shoes on and he jumped right in the ocean.

MARTIN CREGG, retired DOC gang investigator, 1996 to 2018: He went into the water and then he was on the rocks.

RICK LOMBARDI: Everybody fell off the cliff trying to get him.

MARTIN CREGG: Everybody put in for three-quarters [a tax-free disability pension] just because of that. Nine guys got three-quarters out of that. The funny part was then they went back and searched his cell, and they found he was working on the window. He was [already] trying to get out.

RICK LOMBARDI: I think the charge they were arresting him in the first place was for attempted escape, so they had to have known he was trying to work the window. And one of the officers was like, "Don't worry. I got it. Where's he going to go?" And then he ran right past him and like three other officers who were standing there.

MARTIN CREGG: He just went poof out of that trailer. One of our guys couldn't get out of his chair or said he couldn't run.

RICK LOMBARDI: Another idiot that was there, instead of chasing him, he ran back inside to get a flashlight. It was only about 4:00 p.m. He was this big weight-lifter guy and he realized he couldn't chase him, so instead his story was he needed a flashlight. At 4:00 p.m.

And Fat Guy Frank, a big white guy, just sat there. He was at the front. He didn't even attempt to get up. He might have been eating his little bullshit lunch that he brought from home all the time. Or he was googling shit on the computer and he said, "You know what? It ain't my bag. I'm not working right now," because it wasn't his tour yet.

MARTIN CREGG: So [the then DOC commissioner] Dora Schriro came and was like, get him out [of the water].

RICK LOMBARDI: They had to fish him out of the water. We used to have a harbor unit, but not then. They had to call the Port Authority to send out a boat from the airport to make sure he didn't try to swim away.

MARTIN CREGG: So they brought him in the back door because Dora loved inmates and we didn't want her to see his face, because it was kind of . . .

RICK LOMBARDI: His face was definitely rearranged.

MARTIN CREGG: And when these two guys from IID [Internal Investigations Division] saw what was going on, they took off.

MARK CRANSTON: There were a handful of times we had to call on the harbor unit when the staff caught someone at the shoreline or in the water. The officers would go in and grab the guy. It's pretty hard to jump in there and swim to somewhere else. There was one time someone swam to the runway to LaGuardia and was picked up there. We had a red alert that someone got past the perimeter fence. A red alert triggers a perimeter search around the whole grounds. They call it beating the bushes. You're down on the shorelines and see if anyone is around. We used the Port Authority police. They found the person by the runway.

TERRENCE SKINNER, retired deputy warden, 1983 to 2003: In GMDC [George Motchan Detention Center], in the back section of the woman's house, in the jail, a male officer was roommates with another male officer and he stole the guy's shield and went into work. He gave it to a female prisoner and walked out the front gate with her. They had been involved and they wanted to run away together. They have to take a bus. When you get off the bus, there's a turnstile and an officer is supposed to check to make sure the officer is who they say they are. She tried to go through with just a badge and no ID card. Fortunately, the guy was doing his job. He saw that she didn't have an ID. It happened many times, where they didn't check.

JAMES MCGOVERN: In, I want to say 1987, three guys escaped from the Queens House. When you're going to Kennedy Airport, you get on the Van Wyck and you see the Queens House—those three windows on the side and a police booth.

I remember early on a Sunday morning, I heard over the radio, "One-85 Able over to base. We have an escape. We have an escape, we have an escape from the Queens House." The cop that was in the booth was probably sleeping, and he later looked up and he sees this big thick fire hose hanging down the side of the building. They basically rappelled down the side of the building. They had gotten some plumber's keys, gotten the hose, and they all went up to the roof and came down. But they end up getting caught. One guy made it all the way to Indiana. Very few escapes work. A lot of times, they have a red alert, and within twenty-four to forty-eight hours they find the guy still on Rikers Island.

RONALD TACKMANN: In 1985 on my other bid, I couldn't believe it when I got busted. I watched the lawyers go in and out, and most of them didn't even show ID. So I figured this is easy. I thought about World War II. Those guys were making IDs and just had a pencil. They didn't have nothing fancy. I got all sorts of stuff. So I made up an ID. I had a photo sent from upstate so I could cut it out. I pasted a suit over it. Just the face with the suit and I put everything behind the plastic. I got the suit photo out of a magazine.

When you go to Manhattan court, you have your suit and everything. The only thing is you have Patakis on. Those are the [black or orange] sneakers. They call them Patakis [after Governor George Pataki, who insisted all detainees wear them]. I took my socks and pulled them over them so it looked like I had suede shoes on. Then, when you get to Manhattan court, they tell you to walk around, go into the bullpen. If you are the last person [in line], you can't make this move. You have to be the first one. There are ten people. I was first. I walked around and stayed outside the bullpen and was talking to one of the inmates in the bullpen. I checked the door to the court.

The door's open. I go back and I'm talking to the inmate. Finally the correction officer comes and says, "Counselor, you can't be in here. It's too early in the morning." So I said, "Okay. I'll leave." I knock on the door. He said go out through the court. The court officer answers. I saw he was the same age as me. I said, "Listen, my mother's in Bellevue; I need to get there fast. Just had a heart attack. Can you tell me how to get there the fastest way?" So as we're walking out, he's telling me. And I had money on me. I had $20 on me, so I was going to take a cab, but then I said, nah, I'll take the subway to my house. A cab would take too long. It was the morning. I got $7,000 [from the house] and went out looking for my son. First thing I did was I bought ten cell phones. The throwaways.

Then I went looking for everybody that knew him. I gave $100 to them and say, listen, when you see him, call me up, there's another hundred. I got to talk to him. I figured I could talk him into turning himself in. Anyway, couple of days go by. One of his friends calls up. He said, yeah, he's hanging out up here. Go up there and it's in Harlem. All of a sudden one guy comes behind me, another guy in front of me. They said, "Don't move!" I'm thinking to myself, "Isn't this is a bitch? I'm in Harlem. I'm getting fucking robbed." And then they told me, "Up against the wall!"

Now I know they are cops, so he says, "You got any ID?" I said, "Yes, my back pocket." So he pulls out my passport that I made and he looks at it and he comes over to me, to my ear. And he says, "Ron, you couldn't pick a better name than John Hancock?" I burst out laughing.

[The interview excerpted in this book was Tackmann's last before he passed away of cancer at age sixty-six in 2020.]

"When the Music Stops, You Better Have a Seat"

Nearly eight thousand city correction officers are charged with keeping the peace every day on Rikers Island and the city's other borough-based jails. For many, the job is not their first choice as a career. It's a paycheck with good benefits and the ability to retire after twenty years.

Pop culture portrays them as caricatures of evil who beat up detainees at every opportunity that arises. In reality, many are single mothers just trying to pay for the basics or men looking for a no-frills public service career.

They all hate the term "guard" and insist on being called officers like their law enforcement counterparts in the Police Department. But unlike cops, who have their own recently built billion-dollar training complex, the Correction Department uses a small storefront by a strip mall in Queens to teach its new recruits. For years rookies were sent right into jails and taught by hand-picked mentors.

On the job, the lucky ones find ways to get transferred out of housing units to work in areas like transportation or perimeter security, checking for escapees. The unfortunate ones rarely find peace and are constantly moved around to different facilities where they are on the hook to cover random shifts. Most who don't get promoted get out the first chance they have after their full pension kicks in.

—

TAMI LEE, retired correction officer, 1989 to 2020: I never smiled for thirty years. I never smiled at that job one time. Sometimes I'd have to think about it—like, *"Smile."* I didn't want to smile so they could think I was playing with them because I was *not* playing with them.

CHRISTINE WEST, retired correction officer, 1991 to 2004: My kids were preteens. I wanted to be home with them. I was a single mom on the wheel [a type of assignment where officers don't have regular hours or regular days off]. You have to depend on other people to raise your children. When you're not at work, you are sleeping. You miss quality time out of your life.

If you worked 9:00 to 5:00 with weekends and holidays off, you had normalcy with the same amount of money. But if you were on the wheel, you didn't have a normal life. That was difficult. I woke up one night, scared to death thinking I fell asleep at work, but I was at home.

I couldn't get comfortable even when I was off work. When I was off work, I was preparing to return to work. It was a never-ending cycle. I was able to give my children wonderful Christmas gifts, great parties, none of which I was there for. They had everything they wanted, but they didn't have me. You get to a point where you realize that the money isn't everything.

I was broken when my daughter had a function at school and she had won an award and she was dressed up and so pretty, but I couldn't go. She cried. How come you can never go with me? I explained I have to work to give you these things. That sounded like something good to say, but she wanted me there.

As an adult, she reminded me of the basketball games that I missed and those little things that meant so much to her. That's why I'm clinging on to this one [her younger daughter]. You can't get those moments back. And they remind you when they get older. When I was running out the door, I was hoping I wasn't late for roll call.

When she brought me back to that moment, I realized I failed as a mother. I filled in the gaps with gifts. She's a manager for a company. She's doing well. She reminds me of those tough times. It hurts me that I hurt her. She told me the money wasn't everything. So even though I don't have a lot of money now, I have peace, serenity, and happiness and that's life to me.

SIDNEY SCHWARTZBAUM, retired deputy warden, union president, 1979 to 2016: I grew up on East Fifty-eighth between Avenues K and L [in Flatlands, Brooklyn]. I was a kid who was very good in the ninth and tenth grade and then in eleventh and twelfth grade, I started to cut out. My last six months in Tilden High School [in East Flatbush], I had to go an extra six months to do five classes of gym. Believe it or not, I cut out of gym.

[When I became a CO] we had more of an older, more military thing. A lot of ex-military guys when I started. A lot of Vietnam veterans, a lot of ex-cops who became COs after the layoffs in '75. I took the test in 1974. I scored well on the test. I didn't get hired until '79 'cause they had the '75 layoffs. So they didn't start hiring until the end of '78, '79. And then they hired thousands.

I was twenty-five. I was a street kid, though. So I was sent to ARDC [Adolescent Reception and Detention Center] at the time, which is RNDC [Robert N. Davoren Center] now. What I learned in the academy was to be fair, tough, and consistent.

They stressed to the rookies: you're an army of one. I was in good shape as a young man. I could run up twenty-five flights. I had like eighteen-inch arms. So physically, I knew I could handle myself. I got into street fights as a kid, and I knew that I was a wild kid and that I could have gotten in trouble, so I felt compassion for some of the kids in Rikers. I know some of them didn't have a father like mine, who used to chase me all around and make sure I tripped, but I didn't fall on my face, you know?

JACQUELINE MCMICKENS, correction commissioner, 1984 to 1986: I met this young man who I played cards with every Friday night. I'm chatty and asked what he did. He said he was a correction officer. I had never heard that word in my life. I'm from Birmingham, Alabama, and had been in New York for all of three or four years at that time. He told me what it was. It sounded interesting. He said they were giving an exam, and he put in an application for me. I got a notice in the mail that I had to take a test. And I took the test and I passed.

I got called and was assigned to the women's house, of course. When I worked for six or seven months, I was hired provisionally. I saw that they had hired [a young man] who was lower on the hiring list. So I had to bring an action against the city. I hired an attorney, and he then worked it out. I was then appointed retroactively. I got back my seniority. This young man later killed himself. And so when I hear of these policemen killing themselves, and the job of dealing with other human beings, being in control of them, can be daunting.

When I was younger, I was quitting every day. I was not going to do it again. Correction is not easy unless of course you understand that everybody is a human being. Not everybody understands that. My motto was that I'd be able to meet any inmate in an elevator alone and they would not want to hurt me. Because I'd treat them with courtesy and respect. I'm doing my job. These are the rules, and as long as they are followed, they will get their toilet paper and soap and food.

They used to call me Crazy Micky because that's exactly how I treated them. I was not going to fight them. I was never more than 115 pounds. I didn't like it when correction officers would aggravate inmates and cause them to want to fight. I worked with a correction officer one time and I told her to go watch television and don't talk to inmates. I don't think I had three fights in twenty years. And the three that I was involved in, I was invited. I didn't start them. Jail is not easy. Every time a person is in jail, that means they failed. No one wants to be reminded that they failed by not treating them with respect.

Jacqueline McMickens was the correction commissioner from 1984 to 1986. She's now a lawyer representing officers.

EDWARD GAVIN, retired deputy warden, 1982 to 2001: We graduated from Rikers Island. It was 1982. My father was a New York City fireman, and I told him where I was graduating from. He said, "Where's the graduation ceremony?" It was not like it was at John Jay College, and I told him it was going to be at a jail, so my father says, "That's a sewer job." After the ceremony was over, I had my white gloves on. And I was being assigned to C-74, which at the time was probably the most violent jail in the United States.

SIDNEY SCHWARTZBAUM: There was a suicide aide. I helped him get a high school diploma. And he saved me one day. He told me an inmate was trying to escape. We had no alarms. We had no razor ribbon at the time. It was 1979 or 1980. And he comes to me and he says twenty cell is going out the window.

I went to the cell and the window is out. And the other inmate was ready to go. I grabbed him. I called the tour commander. They didn't even consider it a use of force back then to grab the guy, as long as you didn't punch him in the face. And I just wrote a little report. I think it was downplayed a little bit. I didn't put it in the report where I heard it from [the suicide aide]. I didn't want to get him in trouble.

I'll never forget the tour commander. He's actually on my hall of fame list: Vito Carbonaro. And he said, "Good job, Schwartzbaum." And he said, "I'm gonna tell you something that I want to stay in your head for the rest of your career. It's good you caught this. Correction is like musical chairs. When the music stops, you better have a seat." And I've repeated that story to correction officers over the years.

TERRENCE SKINNER, retired deputy warden, 1983 to 2003: While on "on the job" training out of the academy, I was assigned to HDM [the House of Detention for Men] with veteran COs to train me further. We were told not to get involved in anything. If something happens, don't respond. Stand by.

We were in the Bing. One day, prisoners were being escorted to the law library. They had two officers escorting ten inmates. We were in the main corridor. If you're new, your uniform is in a different color, and so the inmates knew we were cadets. They got past us by about fifteen feet in what they called the rotunda. The ten prisoners then jumped the two officers and started beating the hell out of them. I left the group and started fighting with the prisoners.

The captain and the officers hit the alarm. Receiving room staff came, and others. It was a full-on extended fight. It must have gone on for two minutes, but it felt a lot longer. Help came, and then the entire group of officers were pulled up to the conference room.

The training officer said to us [new officers], "Weren't you told you're not supposed to get involved?" We said, "Yes." He replied, "Good. Never listen to the shit they teach you in the academy, because the shit ain't real."

JACQUELINE MCMICKENS: The best job I ever had in corrections was being able to start the academy. Before [then], you got your shield and went to work. You got assigned to somebody who you'd work with for a few days or months depending on how quickly you'd learn or how much they liked you. You were lucky if you got somebody who would teach you something.

The academy started under Ben Malcolm [correction commissioner from 1972 to 1977]. I had to laugh because the rule book was maybe twenty-nine pages. When I left, it was a hundred or something. I'm sure they hated me for that too. I really am sorry that I didn't keep my first rule book. There weren't a lot of rules, because the inmates did what they were supposed to do and the officers did what they were told to do. And then there was a period of unrest in the city and the Black Panthers and that whole era and there was a need to generate a whole different type of jail system.

MICHAEL "BIG MIKE" WILLIAMS, member, DOC Emergency Services Unit, retired 2008: I remember one guy, he came in with me, this fucking guy. He was in my class. He was a little older than me. We get into the jail, and it must've did something to his soul, because he went and got a Mr. T mohawk. He thought that shit was going to do something. He looked like a clown. The inmates was like, what the fuck is you doing? I said, you all right? He ended up getting fired. The job wasn't for him. It's not for everyone. This job is obviously not for everyone.

SIDNEY SCHWARTZBAUM: My third month on the job I was walking down the hallway with a senior officer, and they jumped him. A couple of the inmates in the hallway and instinctively I came to his aid and I was fighting two or three inmates. One guy was punching me from the side, and one of them hit me over the head with a chair he had picked up in the hallway.

So I had a big concussion.

I remember the warden came to the clinic and he said to me, "I want you to take a few days off." I was told in the academy, if you take off when you're on probation, if you go on sick, they can fire you for that. Don't come late; don't get sick. So I told them I'm on probation: "Warden, I want to come in." And he says, "Listen to me, I don't think you're understanding me. I'm the warden and what you did was good. You came to his aid. You prevented him from getting hurt."

He says, "I'll tell you what, you passed probation. I'm Warden Delia, you have three months on the job. I give you my word. You passed probation. I want you to take a few days off. I don't want the inmates to see you with a hematoma like that." I said, "Okay, Warden, if you say so." I never asked him for it in writing. I never forgot that. He actually cared how I was.

TAMI LEE: They used to hear ghosts on the midnights. A few people committed suicide there [in North Infirmary Command] while we worked there. They would always say those people were coming back to get us. The other people that worked steady midnights, they would always say, oh, they couldn't even sleep, because they would hear noises, like the cells opening.

MARTIN CREGG, retired DOC gang investigator, 1996 to 2018: One day I got there on the midnight. I go in there, I'm looking around, and there's like twenty ambulances lined up outside OBCC [Otis Bantum Correctional Center]. I'm like, "Oh fuck. What's wrong?" I go inside and look at the schedule, and I'm actually 5:00 to 1:00. So I said, "Okay, I'm 5:00 to 1:00, let me get the fuck out of here."

But the captain sees me and says, "Cregg, what are you doing here?" I said, "I just came to get something out of my locker." He goes, "No you didn't. You fucked up, rookie. You thought you were midnights, but you're actually 5:00 to 1:00. Guess what. You're on midnights now." I said, "But . . . but . . ." He said, "No, put your fucking uniform on. Get those guys out of their cells." What had happened was, they'd set the floor on fire. Each inmate had set a fire in their cells.

MICHAEL "BIG MIKE" WILLIAMS: The inmates work out all day long. These motherfuckers, if they don't go to the yard to work out, they make shit in the dorm. Two-liter soda bottles. And they fill them up with water when they empty. Yeah. And they take fucking sheets and rip them up, tie sheets to the neck of this one, and tie sheets to the neck of that one. And they'll get the mop handle and put it in the middle. And that's their fucking weights.

They doing push-ups all day. They doing sit-ups all day. I've seen guys come in as crackheads, and in about four months they're crazy strong. I'm like, yo, you cleaned yourself up well. It's like they just put on a fucking suit with muscles. They've been doing this all their life. They outnumbered us that way, and they also outnumbered by way of the ratio. Normally, fifty inmates to a dorm. There's only one officer in there. That one person in there with those fifty inmates, you got to hold on until help gets there, man.

So I've never liked that. When I was a rookie, we had the new admissions dorm. It had like fucking 110 [detainees] and one of us in there and you'd have to call, listen, I need a third officer. So then they put two [officers] for the 110, which still . . . *come on.* And by the end, when something does go down, it still takes about five minutes. It's a mental thing. You gotta build up. I remember when we first came in, man, you know, they prepped us in the academy and they told guys, listen, you know, if you got some comedy shit in you, you gotta get serious.

RICHARD KOEHLER, correction commissioner, 1986 to 1989: They always blame correction officers. They still do. Everybody blames the correction officers. I don't care if it's the Legal Aid Society. It's always the correction officer. That's the problem.

MARTIN CREGG: The warden comes in, and he is in one of the cells in the back with two inmates talking to them. So I'm waiting by the elevators, and the warden comes up and says, "Cregg, you know I just want to get through to these guys." I said, "You realize you're on the ninth floor in Manhattan House with twenty of the biggest jerkoffs. They would cut your throat and have a baloney sandwich afterward." And he says, "But you know I just want to get through to them." I said, "Listen, I'm here about money. I'm not here to get through to anybody. I'm here for my daughter's college fund. That's what I'm thinking about."

MICHAEL "BIG MIKE" WILLIAMS: Trust me, whatever the jail officers couldn't handle, an alarm went off, and we went over there gladiator-style, whatever needed to be done. We're going to get this back in order. Whether it was a borough facility, whether it was a court facility, no matter what. So we had so much shit to handle and we handled it.

Escapes, every fucking thing. But yet, you know, sometimes within our own ranks, you know, the fucking so-called upper echelon, they treated us fucked up equipment-wise and we were mostly minorities, but we were the fucking monsters out of the whole department. Some of the inmates even know us. They've grown up with us, our family members. So that's how we could defuse shit. But the upper echelon didn't want that. Fuck that. Kick their ass. Fuck that. Send the gas in. Fuck that. Send the dogs in. But then when IG [inspector general] comes to us and our job's on the line, y'all don't know nothing. You don't know nothin', meaning, I never told you guys to go in and do that.

And it was usually from above, chiefs that gave these orders to the wardens and then tour wardens gave it to our commanding officer. This is just what they're saying at the top. Fuck the top. I was a defiant motherfucker. I was not insubordinate. Never. But come on. I got common sense. I grew up in the streets of New York. You understand? So yeah. We had that among ourselves. Just say, listen, we in this shit together. We like a family. Fuck what they say. We're going to do what we're going to do. But there's somebody standing way over there while we're in here with the fucking inmates, they're looking through fucking lots of Bubbles and shit, while we were in there, toe to toe with these guys.

JACQUELINE MCMICKENS: There's no room for error. If a man is throwing water at me and I'm walking by with my cup of coffee, it would take a lot of restraint for me not to throw my cup of coffee at him. If I'm in the mood, I might do that. I might not because I have an ethics in me that says I'll just go and change my clothes, or better yet I will just keep my clothes and with all my coffee staying on it and I won't take no chances on giving you any more coffee to throw on me. This is real people here.

I will tell you that for twenty years I never had a problem with inmates. And if they did throw coffee at me once, it was the last time. I don't remember anyone doing that on me. And I didn't bring an inmate a candy bar, and I never smoked, so I never brought an inmate a cigarette. Why would an inmate throw water? Somebody did something. Every officer who gets into a fight has to ask themselves why it happened.

SIDNEY SCHWARTZBAUM: People were appreciative of having a city job, of having health care, of having steady work. I remember the COs surrounded another CO in the locker room once and told him, you're a little too fucking friendly with these cons. They fucking start to manhandle the guy. They say, if we catch you fucking being corrupt, we're gonna kill you in this fucking locker room. The CO was scared to death. Back in my day as an officer, we were more afraid of our peers than we were of IG.

MARTIN CREGG: There was a Chinese kid in Manhattan House, there for a slashing. They're all smoking weed. The dep's there. The officers are there. So I start laughing, and the Chinese kid goes, "Fuck you, you fat cracker." So I said, "Listen, I will beat the fucking living duck sauce out of you. The fried rice is going to come pouring out of your ears. I took a shit that weighed more than you this morning."

Later, the chief says this kid's not coming out [of his cell]. I said, I'm not going to fight with him. So the Chinese kid goes, "I'll come out if you get me a haircut." So he comes out and we get him a haircut. I go to the civilian barber and I said, "Fuck his hair up real good." And the kid is talking like he's from the hood. I said, "I want you to *zeke* his head. I want you to make him look like a fucking retard." We put him back in the cell. He calmed down.

FITZGERALD DAVID, retired correction officer, 1987 to 2014: There were a lot of officers who had a lot of issues going on with alcohol and drugs because of the circumstances that they would be thrust in. A lot of people don't realize that. Working in that hostile environment with upper management who were very abusive. They were retaliatory. People were working triple tours. You would do your eight hours, do another eight hours. And then you would go three or four hours into another tour. So these people were frustrated and had nowhere to turn.

GARY HEYWARD, former correction officer and former detainee, 2000s: A couple of officers committed suicide. Correction officers are people with normal problems. It definitely puts a strain on your marriage. There's depression. Your wife leaves you or you find out she's messing around. There's child support. A lot of people are driven to drink to try to cope. The job itself, you have to be cut out for it. If you can stomach people getting beat up, it's good. Some people are too compassionate. They aren't aggressive people. That wears on you. [Kalief] Browder is just one story out of many.

MARTIN CREGG: I'm sitting on the post and this guy, his nickname was Murder, comes out of the shower and says to me, "When I get dressed, I'm going beat you, cracker." A female correction officer goes, "Yo, Murder, don't worry, I can handle this." I say, "No way. I can fucking take care of him." So she calls the captain. Earlier in the tour, someone called and said a search was coming, and she says, "Yo, Murder, just so you know, the search is coming, hide your shit." So, I go, "What did you just do?" Murder's like, "Good looking out," and she says, "I love you, snowflake." And I'm like, "What the fuck just happened?" She then tells the captain I'm the problem. I say, "Cap, I'm not getting into it with these guys. I'm not a fucking troublemaker."

RICK LOMBARDI, retired DOC gang investigator, 1990 to 2011: We used to search him [Murder] twice a day, and every time he had contraband on him obviously being brought in by staff. He had all kinds of shit. You name it. Recorders, DVD players, weed, watches he was able to dial phone numbers on. Whatever you could think of, he had.

MARTIN CREGG: Another time, I see this Spanish guy, he's a Latin King. I pull him outside, and I fucking search him, and he's got a fucking ice pick. I said, "Ghetto, what's going on? You're sitting in the corner alone. And there's twenty Black guys and you in the corner by yourself. None of your bros are here. You got nothing." He goes, "It's so bad. They got Spanish guys serving the Black guys in their cell like waitresses." I said, "Why didn't you go to Miss So-and-So, the steady officer, and say something?" And he goes, "Well, she's in on it."

I said, "I'll work with you, but if I find out that what you're telling me about Miss So-and-So is a fucking lie, I'm going to fuck you." I come to find out that she was banging this guy "Hood." She was bringing him Chinese food three to four times a week. And she might have been a union delegate. She was the A officer, but she would go into his cell and bang him. I called it in and nothing happened.

TAMI LEE: This one officer, she used to have a locker next to me. I noticed she had a very distinctive tattoo on her arm. I remember it was a name. And some flowers. Then she also had a name. I think it was her kid's name.

And there was an inmate [she was involved with]. Everybody was saying, "Oh, y'all better do something. Y'all better do something because she's taking him in the pantry, staying for hours, this, that, whatever, do something about this."

I worked in security, so the dep was like, "Look, everybody's going on the search today, including you, Lee." He said, "You go to that inmate's cell and look at his pictures or whatever." He said, "Make a diversion so you could take him downstairs so y'all can look through his stuff, right." So we go up there, an officer says something to him, and he starts acting crazy.

So he takes him to the intake, and I go into his bucket, and I look through his pictures. So I see a picture of a female with her head cropped out, but I could see the tattoo. So I take the picture back. I said, it's the officer that [has a locker] right next to me. It's the same tattoo. I see that tattoo every day. I know it's her. So then they tap her phone. They call IG and come to find out she really is messing with this inmate.

They suspended her right away when they found out, 'cause they were listening to the phone calls. He was calling [her] from the jail phone and everything. She was an older lady. She was like forty-something years old. He was like twenty, twenty-five. She quit.

She had been sending him naked pictures without her face. You could see her body and you could see the tattoo. How many tattoos like that do you see? I seen it for years. We've been right next to each other talking to each other while we were getting dressed.

He had the pictures in his cell. And then after the IG got to him, he told. He said, "Yeah, it's her." Like, you did all of that. Now you don't have a job. And this [detainee], he told on you. Dumb-dumb.

TERRENCE SKINNER: So, we're getting off work, and a female correction officer says, "So where are you going?" I said the name of a place. She said, "Oh, let's go together." It was on Astoria Boulevard, a local place. I don't know if it's there now, but it was by like Eightieth Street or something. Right near Rikers.

So we went over and she went to take a drink and she slapped herself on the thigh and said, "What are you gonna do for me if I give you some of this?"

And it was a shock and I was like, "I'm not going to do anything. It's got nothing to do with the job." She said, "Another dep told me he'll give me 10:00 to 6:00 [daily schedule]." And I said, "Well, sleep with him." And then two weeks later, she got 10:00 to 6:00.

FITZGERALD DAVID: The main thing was a gate one pass, [which] means you can drive across the bridge and park in front of your jail. You'll sell your soul for that. I've seen females that come on

the job. They look regular. They work for a little bit. Now they getting their hair done, wearing makeup, and this, that, and the other. Now all of a sudden you're fucking this captain or you're fucking that ADW [assistant deputy warden] or that warden. And now you're living the high life.

CHRISTINE WEST: Some of them made their careers by dating supervisory staff that put them in positions that didn't have them working with inmates. The worst position was in the dorms. There were so many other jobs, support positions that didn't require inmate contact, and you still make the same amount of money or more. There were report writers, control room staff. You could move out of the jails entirely or work downtown in the office or in the hospital where officers come. There were so many other positions that did not include jail or inmates. One woman dated the commissioner. She was a driver for different people. You just drive people from meeting to meeting; you're just sitting around. You still made $80,000. Who wouldn't want that? Women would fight you for those positions.

TERRENCE SKINNER: In the academy you're taught there's no relationships with other staff. It's against the rules. I think they called it undue familiarity. But then you get assigned and everybody's dating each other. Captains, deps, wardens, and you're like, what's going on here? And it's not just that they're dating; they're married and messing around. I think that's common in most places—people who work together end up dating.

I remember going to a—I think it was an Emerald Society dinner—and [a] chief was on the dais being celebrated with his wife, his son who was an officer, and his [the chief's] girlfriend, who was a captain. They were all sitting together and I was like, does she know? Or does she not know? So initially that was weird to me. By the time I left, that was totally normal. Totally okay.

CHRISTINE WEST: I was attacked by a female officer over a guy she liked. Women would attack other women and fight at work or in

the parking lot. I was 120 pounds soaking wet. It was the morning shift. I was coming from the bus to go to the locker room to put on my uniform. My locker was in a corner. Only one way in or out. She was huge and she blocked the exit and she started saying things like we were in high school—"Oh, you think you're cute."

She started coming toward me. She and her friend blocked me in. The closer she got, the more hateful the words. I had to fight my way out of that corner and then fight my way out of the locker room. The male officers heard the commotion. They came in and separated us. I was fighting her off me. I knew that we would get fired because we were on probation. I was angry that I had to fight because I did not want her boyfriend.

It was ludicrous. Here we had this opportunity to make great money and not even work hard, and she wanted to blow it over a man that didn't want her anyway. I was raising my twelve-year-old brother; my mother had just died. I had all the reasons to need the job. They didn't care I was defending myself. They put me into a whole nuther jail where I had to start over. At the time I had a steady tour and a steady post, and they transferred me out. It changed my understanding of justice and fairness.

She was ashamed. Everyone teased her for her black eyes. They used to call me Tyson after that. She didn't think I could fight because I was so little and mousy. When I would see her, she would never even give me eye contact. We both had to go downtown to face disciplinary charges. Mine got dropped. I don't know what happened to hers, but she stayed on the job.

TERRENCE SKINNER: When I was a captain, I was in ARDC [the jail for teens]. It was crazy, totally violent. The prisoners were in the mess hall and we ran out of ice cream. They were refusing to leave the mess hall and go back to their cells. The response was usually pretty simple: we suit up and force them back to the cells. Usually a small number will fight, and the rest will go back to their cells once they see it's serious.

But in this case, the tour commander said, we're not beating them up over ice cream. I said, that's not safe. He had someone

call around to see if other jails had extra ice cream. BCF [Brooklyn Correctional Facility, once the old Navy Yard brig, now long closed] had ice cream. The tour commander sent a guy in his car to get ice cream and brought it to Rikers.

The majority of staff and supervisors all said that guy [the tour commander] was a pussy. The other side was we didn't need to use force. At that time, I didn't think it was a good idea to get them the ice cream. Today, the fact he didn't have to use force, it worked, and I wouldn't criticize it at all.

Later, when I was a deputy warden for security, we had a group of prisoners in the mess hall and they didn't have their dessert. They said they wanted to speak to the warden. The ADW decided you're not speaking to anyone. I heard a radio transmission say they were hitting the alarm and everyone was suiting up. I said, I'm going in. He begged me not to go in, saying, "You're going to make me look weak." I said, "I'm going in to talk to them." I went into the mess hall. I told them, "Right now I don't give a fuck. This isn't how you make complaints. You have a [detainee] council member. I'll deal with him. But right now you are going back to your cells or we'll kick your ass." They all got up and went back.

If I had been a captain years earlier, I probably would have said, "All right go ahead, kick their ass." But just because you're allowed to do it doesn't mean you should. When you're in that macho mindset, a lot gets blown aside. It took me a long time to see that they were human beings just like us.

At some point after that I went on a cursillo, which was a Catholic retreat where you go away and you all talk and confess your sins to the entire group. You're praying and asking for help. This was 1987 and I was a captain in ARDC. It made me see that we're all human and we all screw up in different ways. The majority were alcoholics, mostly police, correction, and FDNY. Everyone talked about their secrets and problems. That was the biggest thing that woke me up to everybody being a person. It still took a few more years to fully kick in.

When I came back from the retreat, one day there were prisoners coming out of the mess hall. Now, usually we would yell, "Quiet down and deuce it up!" But this time, I said, "Gentlemen, please give me two lines." You know, polite. They were like, fuck you. Here I'm trying to be nice, and they are telling me to fuck off. The other captains were laughing at me. After a day and a half of them telling me to fuck myself, I snapped and yelled, "Get in two fucking lines or I'll kick your ass." One of the guys in the cursillo later said, just because you're trying to change doesn't mean they can hear you when you talk nice and calm. They are used to getting the hell beat out of them.

So where do you find the in-between? It's a hard thing to find.

TEENS

"They Used to Call It Vietnam or Gladiator School"

On August 12, 1969, a seventeen-year-old detainee named Rodney Brown hanged himself in the teen jail. The Brooklyn youth had been arrested for robbery. He snaked a belt around his neck and tied it to a light fixture in a housing block with 379 detainees staffed by two officers. In detailing Brown's death, the state senator John Dunne noted he was being held only because his family couldn't afford bail. "I think the mayor [John Lindsay] should show a little concern for them," Dunne said.

Four months later, six NYU graduate students in social work sent a letter to the media, as well as President Nixon and Governor Nelson Rockefeller, decrying the use of Rikers to house teen detainees. "The Rikers Island reformatory is a dumping ground," one student told *The New York Times*. "The boys there are making a last cry for help and nobody's listening."

In response, the city correction commissioner, George McGrath, described the students as "immature young people . . . making faulty judgments."

In 1972, the city opened a new jail on Rikers for teen males dubbed the Adolescent Reception and Detention Center (ARDC), but little really changed.

By 2008, ARDC had been renamed the Robert N. Davoren Center (RNDC), at that point a thirty-six-year-old relic in poor condition and riven with violence. The beating death of eighteen-year-old Christopher Robinson by gang members essentially deputized by correction officers there in October of that year became a seminal moment. And the city paid out $2 million to settle a lawsuit filed by Robinson's family.

The case exposed something called "the Program," where gang members controlled housing units with the ignorance or tacit approval of staff. The practice predictably led to pages of broken bones and slashed faces. DOC officials often shrugged and said that teens were simply the most violent of detainees.

Once again, little changed, until the case of Kalief Browder, arrested for stealing a backpack and held for three years in RNDC from age seventeen to twenty. After the charges were dropped, Browder hanged himself at age twenty-two in 2015. His loss crystallized much that was wrong with Rikers and fueled the Close Rikers movement.

—

JACQUELINE VELEZ, detained 1998: I wouldn't say that my upbringing prepared me for Rikers; I would say it led me there. I grew up in Bushwick, Brooklyn. I grew up very poor. While you're eating a bowl of cereal, you see two antennas sticking out the box, like, "Oh my God, I just ate something that roaches were all over." As I became a teenager, there were always mice. My mom fed us out of cans, Spam and corned beef. And those were treats sometimes.

By the time I was sixteen, I was a high school dropout, but I had never even been to high school. I was just registered. I would go to "Hooky Jams," hooky parties in the daytime, when someone's mother was working. I was definitely not going to school.

I had one cousin I hung out with and he had a whole bunch of guy friends and they were looking for their girl gang. He tells his president of this gang, "Yo, I think these are our girls." Me and my friends. And it was over from there on out. We literally carried on like we were a gang. It was like, don't fuck with those girls. There was a lot of fighting, and it even involved men.

One of those fights led to me cutting a girl. A hundred and ninety-six stitches on her face and her neck. I put my initial on her face. And I'm not very proud of that, but I did do that.

My anger just boiled over.

I went to Rikers. I was scared to death. I'm seventeen. I'm trying to act tough, but I'm really not. And here I was in the jail with other adolescents that committed armed robbery, all kinds of shit. You can't wrap your brain around that because they're all under eighteen.

They had a juvie section in Rosie's [Rose M. Singer Center]. I remember that we played like little girls. We played truth or dare. People would take the dare because they didn't want to tell the truth about anything. The dare would be something crazy that would bring attention to you. Like, run down the corridor to the Bubble, tag it, and then run back. Or lower your pants and moon us.

We were literally little girls. We just trying to be adults and trying to make sense of it. All the girls were hurt or abused in some way. That all came out and we all bonded over that time that we were there.

CASIMIRO TORRES, detained 1986: I was seventeen, and I went to Rikers on a one-year bid. I was put in a dorm with a hundred other kids. The best way to describe that dorm would be violent. It was extremely violent. They used to call it Vietnam or Gladiator School. There was rape or people setting people's feet on fire. They'd wrap people's feet in toilet paper, soak them in baby oil, and then light them on fire. They'd do it most of the time because they were bored. When the lights went out, that's when the shit happened. They used to sell Magic shave, a shaving cream. If you left that on someone's head, it would burn them.

Some people used to use that on people's heads when they were sleeping. Most of the time they'd look out for people who were afraid and picked on them. If you weren't ready to fight, they'd pick on you. And there ain't no protection. They wouldn't send you to protective custody. There was no safe place.

PRAKASH CHURAMAN, detained 2019 to 2021: I first entered Rikers Island [when] I had just turned seventeen. I do have a lot of PTSD and experience a lot of depression, anxiety. Just a mixture of emotions and feelings. It really is hard going through that, man. Just to be raised by the New York City criminal injustice system is sick. I know how it feels. I experienced it firsthand. Being property of the city.

Prakash Churaman, arrested at age fifteen, was held almost six years pre-trial, then released to home detention while he was waiting for a new trial. In June 2022, the Queens District Attorney dropped the felony murder charge against him.

RICK LOMBARDI, retired DOC gang investigator, 1990 to 2011: Here's the deal with the Program. Every housing area in RNDC had obviously different gangs. So, it wasn't necessarily Bloods or Crips. It was really the strongest kids in the housing area. And sometimes they would be Young Gunners or Young Bloods.

When you walk in a housing area at lunchtime and you see there are, out of fifty kids, fourteen of them sitting on the floor, eating their food, and there's empty seats and tables, and you ask them, why are you not sitting down?

And they say, "Because we can't." Then obviously, you know there's a program. And when you go in there and you see the same kid on the telephone for six hours when you know everybody else is supposed to make phone calls as well and nobody else is making phone calls, then you know there's something wrong.

PRAKASH CHURAMAN: You either get down with the Program or you continue with "the World Tour." That's terminology on Rikers Island, meaning you are moved along to other units within the jail. At any given time. It's survival of the fittest. You gotta basically prepare yourself mentally. You have to adjust your mental state to adapt to that type of environment and the culture of Rikers Island.

I got into fights over the phone. Fights over plain disrespect is one thing. One thing is you can't show any sign of weakness. It's like wolves. You're in an environment around wolves. And once they see a prey, someone weak, they take full advantage of that. People like to test people. Nine times out of ten it ends in violence.

RICK LOMBARDI: The Program led to violence because they had to fight. I'm in there investigating fights every single day. He's fighting because he doesn't want to sit on the floor anymore. They would label one of the tables the "Dick" table. That was the step up from the floor. However, you're still not on the real table. If you're at the "Dick" table, to get off, you'd have to fight a second time. So you'd have to fight two or three times. If it's the same kid fighting three times, obviously I know he's trying to work his way up the chain. There was maybe ten to twelve fights a day in RNDC. That's not normal. I'm an outsider and I'm coming in and I see it. So how do you [correction officers] not see it if you're there all day? I guess complacency, lack of caring. Maybe it made their day easier, closing their eyes.

MATTHEW BROCKINGTON, detained 2014, 2015: I won't tell it all, but it was "Gladiator School." I was eighteen [in 2014]. I was in the three building. I got sentenced to four months. We were kids. We just went in wild. I did ninety days.

People fight over the littlest things, but I didn't have to defend myself, because we in New York City. I already know everybody. *[Laughs.]* I'm from Manhattan. So, there's people I knew in there, they already know me. Rival gangs. When you first come, you're upset, but then it's "You gonna be here." That's the main thing in your mind. I'm gonna be here, so I gotta deal with it. You get there and you see the boys and it's regular like that. The dayroom, playing cards, playing games, watching TV, eating, and then you got the "team," the top five in the dorm. So you see who's running the dorm, right?

This one boy got punched off the phone. He was using it when he shouldn't have been. That was by somebody else, a punch dummy, a pop-off dummy [sort of a lesser enforcer for the "team"].

They should just give everybody their own phone. There's a lot of fights over the phone. The main thing is the phones, gambling, and gangs. That was weird.

DEVONTE HERNANDEZ, detained 2015: I [had imagined] myself graduating college, possibly going to the NFL or doing sports medicine. I was a defensive end at Evander Childs High School [in the Bronx]. It wasn't really an A1 team, but for a person who was skilled, it was a good opportunity to just get more of the spotlight. I didn't get that far because I got locked up my sophomore year.

My first day there, they had me in intake and it had been what, three days since I heard from my family. So, I'd been asking for a call to call my family and they just kept telling me, no, you do it when you get to the housing area. Another guard came in an hour later, and he asked me if I wanted to use the phone, and I jumped at the opportunity because the whole situation is new to me and it would just make me feel better if I heard from my family.

You have so many Bloods that nine times out of ten the house gang will be Bloods. I wouldn't say I was scared, but I was just a bit shocked and nervous, just trying to soak everything in all at once. I just kept my mind focused on my life outside, just to keep me distracted from what was going on inside the jail. [I focused on] my friends, my lifestyle, my family, and everything that I was enjoying before I got incarcerated and just looking forward to doing it when I got out again.

It used to startle me at first, the [sound of the] cell doors opening up and closing and just that jail smell. It's kind of stale, almost like dry food, almost like a dry apple.

CASIMIRO TORRES: When I was a kid, I saw a kid sodomized by a mop stick by a group of kids in the back section at night. As much as I would have loved to help, I knew better. They were using it as an excuse. They hurt him pretty good. I know they took him to the hospital afterward. They were probably bored. I don't think the kid was a snitch. He was just soft. They just try to find things to pass the time. I was in the section across. I knew something was coming. I didn't know what they had planned. They had a pillow over his face. He was crying and he was bleeding. They just let him go and he staggered away. He went to the Bubble, and the CO came and brought him out.

It's something I don't want to remember. Something may trigger that memory, and I just push it back down. You cannot relax. You have to be on point twenty-four hours a day. Anyone who tells you they went into prison and came out the same way is sadly mistaken. You can't go through that and not change.

RICK LOMBARDI: I had gotten a tip from the Board of Correction about a teen inmate named Kadeem John. [John was eighteen in June 2010 and in Rikers for jumping a turnstile.] He had been rushed to Elmhurst Hospital the night before. If I came across a pretty bad injury, I would want to find out what happened. I can't go in there and investigate twenty-seven fights. They couldn't get any information from the jail.

So I took a car, drove out to Elmhurst. He's got water on the brain, a cracked skull. He's got all kinds of really serious injuries. And I'm like, what the fuck? What happened to this kid?

What had happened was, it was part of the Program. He was a kid that wasn't down with what they wanted to do. He wasn't standing where they wanted him to stand in line. He had words with another inmate. And when they got back to the housing area, he gets to the top step and they kicked him down. He flies down the steps, which is a good twenty steps, gets to the bottom, and every single kid in the housing area took a kick in this kid's face as they walked into the housing area. Then they just left him there. You don't ever see the officer.

AUTHORS: *The video didn't show the correction officer's response?*

RICK LOMBARDI: No, not until the end. Once he was already completely out. He was in Elmhurst for quite some time.

[The other teens] would all come up with the same story, whether or not it was true. It'd be like, no, he was the guy in charge of the housing area and he was abusing us. So we just gave it back to him, which was nonsense. This kid definitely was not running the housing area. He was a little frail kid, had no friends. He wasn't gang affiliated. This kid was a nobody. But that was the story they would always give. A kid who's the assaulter, he would always claim he was the victim. They aren't stupid. Ninety percent of the time it's bullshit.

His family sued the department and they wound up winning a lot of money. [John received an $850,000 settlement from the city.]

MATTHEW BROCKINGTON: The first time I saw a person get cut in the face, we was in the yard. They was playing basketball. I'm standing on the line waiting for the pull-up bar. I see these two guys whispering, talking. One of the guys in front starts doing his pull-ups. One of them behind, the one talking to the other guy, came right behind him. *Bop!* So the guy jumped down and he touched his face. First, it looked like, what did he do? Then his face bust open. I said, "What happened?" Yo, he just cut him with a scalpel. They tell me, "Oh, you can get it from this person, pay for this and pay for that."

[It was] something about gangs. I don't know what he did. I know they was in gangs. I know Bloods. I know Crips. I don't do none of that stuff. I came out of my mother by myself. My thing is a neighborhood thing.

When I came home, I was eighteen turning nineteen. I went to this school. Co-op Tech. They was a trade school, but it was supposed to give us a stipend, which they wasn't. We didn't get the stipend. I stopped going and started working at Foot Locker. So in between that time, I was just working. And then in 2015 I got caught with a gun.

RICK LOMBARDI: They have gangs just like adults do. They get promoted to the big gangs like the major leagues. It's like high school with no girls. It's bedlam. Out of fifty-six kids, you're not going to find forty-six good ones. It's bad for everyone—the kids, teachers, the nurses, the staff, the doctors. The kids are bad. It could be just because they're teens. They haven't matured enough to know what's right and wrong. They just do what they think is funny. They do what their friends tell them to do.

DEVONTE HERNANDEZ: The funniest thing I saw was a dude had a beef with the guy in the cell next to him. They were arguing all night. One of them somehow popped open his cell door. Then he took a shit in a cup. Then he had popped the other guy's cell and he just started throwing shit at him. And then they started fighting. So then the dude runs out the cell and the other dude's still throwing shit while he's running away from him. The guard didn't really notice, because they were all in the Bubble, just conversing, laughing, and joking around until he seen two dudes running in the hallway throwing shit everywhere.

ROBERT GANGI, director, Correctional Association, 1982 to 2011:
There was a period where I participated in a Principal for the Day program. I picked the high school on Rikers. I think it was telling that they didn't know there was a high school on Rikers.

I remember one student [talking about] the system, and his articulating of it was fairly sophisticated: I'm just a number. There's a certain amount of money that they're gonna spend to house me. There's a certain amount of money—maybe they'll get it in their budgets, because they need funding in order to run these facilities. Nobody really cares about me and the rest of us.

Often when I was in a class, observing, some of the students would just fall asleep. Put their head on the desk and go to sleep. And the teachers never interceded. Just let that happen. You think, maybe they don't really care, but part of it was recognizing that a lot of the kids were housed in dormitories that were very noisy, that were threatening places, and they often didn't get a good night's sleep.

RON KUBY, defense attorney: [Rikers] is not the place where anybody should spend their formative years of their adolescence. The lessons that are taught by virtue of the way Rikers has worked are not lessons that are constructive in the real world. Those lessons are that you can do whatever you want, as long as you're bigger and tougher and have more allies, [and] that force and brutality are the go-to measures in order to demonstrate that you are somebody worthy of respect and make sure somebody is watching your back at all times. I mean that's a horrific way to grow up.

I have a current client who was arrested when he was fifteen years old and he is now twenty-one. He's currently pending trial after his conviction was reversed. Hasn't seen a fair trial in six years. He spent all of his formative years on Rikers Island. Not what you want. It doesn't produce people who can shift to normal society. It doesn't teach any of the things that we want people to learn to reintegrate. And the worst thing is we, as a society, don't care. We have never cared. And I don't know if we ever will. I mean all of these folks wear the label "criminal," whether they're convicted or not. And we just want them away from us. Liberal New York City—we want these people, who are "these people," not *our* friends and neighbors, put away from us. The "good" people.

RICK LOMBARDI: The adolescents were just totally housed inappropriately. They screwed that whole age group up. The city does it all the time. They should be housed separately. They shouldn't be around state prisoners.

These are guys who are already doing time upstate. They are only coming down on family court matters, usually paternity and divorce. But they housed them with adolescents. You are bringing the leader back to school the kids on how to become gang members or how to become better gang members. It makes absolutely no sense.

The state prisoners manipulate the system because they want to be downstate. It breaks up the monotony of being upstate, and when they're in the city, they get a lot of drugs and a lot of weapons and a lot of visits.

The teens are vulnerable. You put them in dorm settings, which I think is really bad. They have to be in cells.

DERRICK HAYNES, former counselor, Spofford Juvenile Detention Center and Horizon Juvenile Center: I was coaching basketball at Rice High School, and I started in 1992 to work as a counselor at Spofford.

Coaching kids at Rice, the last thought they have is fighting, because they're going to be suspended. Most of the kids were looking to go on to college. When I started working with this population, I found the total opposite. They're gang members. And they've lost all the support that they need at home. So my mentality had to adjust.

What was going on at Rikers Island was the same thing going on at Spofford, where guys was getting 150 stitches across the face. And that was being done by the Bloods because they had decided to mark people. We're going to mark individuals that we got a problem with, so if you see a guy with a mark on his face, he had a problem with the Bloods. When they came to you and said, you're going to join, and you said you didn't want to join, then you got a "buck-fifty" across your face. That was going on consistently both on Rikers Island and at Spofford.

DORIS OSEI, DEVONTE HERNANDEZ'S GRANDMOTHER: That is not a place for these young kids. They need to be in a different environment. An environment of encouragement. It's the worst place for any young teenager. If not for our support, he might have committed suicide. This is not a place for them. He had us for support. Many young families don't have that opportunity; young boys don't have that opportunity. They need to be in a setting where they are going to get help to change their lives.

JERRY DEAN, detained 1987, 2003: It was so violent. The kids were getting sliced every day, and I remember that the kids used to sneak razor blades in their shoes into the dorm, and they would cut each other up and it was just really vicious. There was one correction officer that said, "Yeah, you're in the house gang." The house gang did the work for the correction officers.

They kept the other kids in line and smacked the shit out of them if they got out of line. They would steal their sneakers; they would steal their clothes. I mean, it was crazy. And then if you were like the bottom of the barrel, like you couldn't fight, you'd have to actually wash other kids' underwear and shit. Boy, you were a "Hoover," the shit stain remover.

DERRICK HAYNES: My first real experience of a riot happened in the chapel. We were in the process of praying; a kid got up and sliced a guy with a razor across his nose. And when it hit his nose, it hit right on the edge where the nose connects with the skin in the face. So when the kid sat up, his nose was dangling. His nose was *dangling*. Meanwhile, the other kids were fighting, so they hit the panic button and that's when security and supervision and other staff members, who were on lunch break, responded. I think I had been on the job maybe two, three weeks.

Once one altercation starts, that is the command for the other altercations to start. So once I pop off, now you gotta pop off. Everybody's gotta pop off on somebody from the other side. So it's not like an altercation happens and everybody sits there. Once the one thing happens, everybody's gotta pop off on somebody else.

If you didn't, as soon as you get back to the hall, they going to be like, "Yo, you didn't fight. You didn't jump in."

Now they going to get you.

JERRY DEAN: They [guards] used to bet on fights. They'd have people come in and say, "Listen, you want to fight, Jerry?" Put a pack of cigarettes on it. We got five packs of cigarettes and I would fight. If I win, I get the cigarettes. It's crazy. It would happen in the back of the dorm.

ROBERT GANGI: Young people were coming out of Rikers and they would tell us "the Program" was going on, and my guess is they were talking to a number of people. What we were hearing from the young people was not the only way we were getting a sense of what was going on.

We reported it. The sense we had is they were not surprised, but I never got the sense that they took it as seriously as they should have. And it might've been a function of they didn't really want to believe it. It might've been a function of, they didn't know what to do to stop it, or to change it. But we didn't feel that we made much headway in getting them to take it on.

My judgment is once you know that's going on, heads have to roll. I mean, there's correction officers who are encouraging or even arranging for the kind of things we were hearing about. You have to fire them, and that clearly was not going to happen.

DEVONTE HERNANDEZ: Say you just a guy that's just trying to fit in with everything and trying to get into everybody's business. They prey on that because now you're showing them that you're vulnerable and that you don't know how to mind your own business. So, eventually, they start pushing the boundaries, see when you going to break, seeing what you're going to take and what you're not. And once they know, they keep doing it.

[They] insult you. Or they'll ask you for commissary once. And then, if they feel like they can keep going back to you for commissary, they'll keep doing it. And when you try to say no the next time they ask you, they will always want to fight because all the other million times you said yes to them and now they feel entitled.

DONOVAN DRAYTON, detained 2007 to 2012: They just teenagers in they minds, you know what I'm saying? We see ourselves as teenagers in our minds. Some of them are gangbanging. It's just impossible for it not to happen. Fighting in prison over stuff like chairs, for instance, it ain't the chair. It's the principle. It ain't about the shit. It's about these are my chairs, don't touch my shit.

I had one of my friends that got murdered. I had just got off the phone talking to my dad about it. Before I had got on the phone, I had some chairs in the dayroom, and how they used to do it was you used to put your ID or your cup in the chair to mark it. That meant these chairs are occupied, right?

So after I got the bad news, came off the phone, and I was tearing up and you could tell I was hurt. So I went back to the dayroom, where they had the TV set up. And this guy was sitting on my chairs. So I'm like, excuse me, man, can I get my chairs back? He was like, "What? You not shit." I said, "Yo, man, I put my ID in the chairs, brother, like, you know how this goes."

He got in my face, and I just punched him. We had a fight. The COs came and took us to intake. After the smoke cleared, it finally dawned on me, "Wow, bro. I really was fighting over some stink-ass chairs." I would never have fought nobody over no chairs out in the free world.

DERRICK HAYNES: At the time the policy was, once a kid left the facility, you couldn't help them. But when kids left in particular both Spofford and later Horizon, because they didn't have the support at home, they would come back and hang out in front of the facility and wait for particular staff.

If you was a good kid and it was payday, staff would give you sandwich money or cigarette money or juice money. Because we knew these kids didn't have the proper parents or the proper foster parents, we knew that they needed some type of help. So we would take them across the street and get them a sandwich, get them a pack of cigarettes, or whatever the case would be. And this happened so many times, but the agency never addressed it.

Even when staff would come in to roll call, and in roll call we would say, well, so-and-so kid was outside, just so the other staff would know in case there was a problem. You know, the kids would just say, "Hey, listen, man, yo, hey, I didn't eat last night." You know? "I didn't eat breakfast today." And I'm like, "Well, hey, man, take $10, man. Get you a sandwich and some milk, all that."

I was totally upset.

[After the 2011 murder of the high school basketball star Tayshana Murphy in Harlem, cops swept up two dozen teenage gang members not directly involved. Haynes pleaded with his bosses to get city assistance for the wayward teens.]

I grew up in Harlem, the Manhattanville Houses. I knew all of those kids. I was begging them like, yo, bring any one of those programs to Grant [Houses], to Manhattanville. These kids, they need it. And the job just totally ignored me.

So I made a decision to leave. My allegiance was no longer to the job and making money. My allegiance was to helping the youth in my community. The point is, in twenty years nothing had changed. I made the decision to go back into the community and make the change myself. It's like what they say, be the change that you want to see.

DEVONTE HERNANDEZ: I started seeing a lot of guys that I knew from the streets, and it caused a problem for me. It was a lot of tension. When dudes see a face once, they never forget it because you had done something wrong to them. So, whenever guys see each other, your heart is racing. Your adrenaline is pumping. You just trying to anticipate what's going to happen next.

[At a certain point, Hernandez encountered a member of the rival gang his gang had been clashing with.]

DEVONTE HERNANDEZ: He didn't really know that until we started talking, and then we both started putting two and two together. It didn't really go beyond verbal words. But it was just the fact that he just wanted to know why it all happened.

We were just talking about all the situations going on between us, in our groups. He'd be like, yo, like the guy you killed, he was a good dude. And I would tell my side of the story and I would just tell him, listen, it really had nothing to do with me. You know the issue between you guys. I was just doing my duties, being a part of the gang. So it was nothing personal. It's not like I intended to do it, but I was just doing my duty as a gang member. And he understood that.

Once we interacted with each other for the first time, we're talking [and] the first two things that a person wants to know is, where are you from and if you're gang affiliated and everything else, as far as the name, that's like secondary.

I was from Gun Hill Road, but you know, the people I was with, they were from Kingsbridge. He was from the other side of Kingsbridge by the armory.

After we spoke what we spoke, we just went our separate ways— just knowing the other person's side of the story and it was just enough to be like, all right, now I know what really happened, so it's really no need to go beyond it.

DORIS OSEI: There were two to three occasions where gang members tried to get to him. The captain knew he had to be transferred, and as soon as I told them, they did something. The last incident happened the same weekend they moved him. Prior to that he was placed like in protective custody. I was very upset. That's what I told the captain. I was very upset about it.

DEVONTE HERNANDEZ: It was in the middle of the day. I was in my cell, and then my cell door just opened up. And I just seen a lot of officers with gloves on. And they handcuffed me and they packed all my stuff and they brought me to intake and I stood there until a van came and transported me to Valhalla [a jail in Westchester County where city detainees are sometimes sent for security reasons]. I didn't ask too many questions. I just wanted to try to contact my family and just to let them know that I was being moved.

They said it was a safer environment and it would be convenient for my family to come up even more than to just be going to Rikers Island, through all the hassle.

DORIS OSEI: He was in Valhalla for a year and a half. It was a whole different environment. How can one jail be one way and another completely different? I don't know why Rikers Island is so dirty. Valhalla was clean, nicely lit; you would go across an open room. The walls have color. It's a place you can go and talk to your loved one. It was a completely different approach to how families are treated.

CELEBRITIES

"Yo, Could You Listen to This for Me?"

The well known, along with the unknown, have cycled through Rikers over the years. Among them, Tupac Shakur, Lil Wayne, Ja Rule, Shyne, Foxy Brown, and the Jets defensive end Mark Gastineau. The list goes on. Most were put in isolated areas away from the general population. Jail officials faced constant challenges from within and without in handling the attention they would receive.

—

TAMI LEE, retired correction officer, 1989 to 2020: Tupac was there and they put him in the medical dorm. They put him in there by himself. He could not get any sleep, because the gate was right there for the regular inmates in that dorm. They would be there all day rapping to him. "Yo, could you listen to this for me?" He would be in his cell all day listening, like, "Sigh, all right, all right." He's in cell number one, so they could see him. After he was there a few months, he asked, "Can I move to this cell over here?" They moved him so that the inmates couldn't see him. That was funny. But after that, they used to just write the rhymes down and send them to him.

Until 2020, Tami Lee worked as a correction officer at Rikers, where she did her best not to smile. She was assigned to the North Infirmary Command, where jailed celebrities often ended up.

FITZGERALD DAVID, retired correction officer, 1987 to 2014: Celebrities were treated differently than other inmates. They were placed in different holding pens by themselves. We would get calls from the chief of the department. The commissioner would call the chief. The chief would call the warden. The warden would call me or my captain, and they'd have to be placed in a separate area. No one was treated the same.

Tupac was treated differently by upper management. Upper management would go to his cell and sit in there with him for a while. It was ridiculous.

The superiors were starstruck. Wardens and captains that used to go to Tupac's cell did the same shit with Lil Wayne.

FAT JOE, hip-hop artist: I went to visit Lil Wayne in jail, who's *harmless.* They had him chained up, chained by the feet, chained by the hands. Almost like Hannibal Lecter. He was hopping [just to get into the room]. That killed me. That destroyed me. They brought him to the visit like that. Like Hannibal Lecter. Lil Wayne. He was the biggest rapper on earth at the time, *hopping.* When it was time to leave, they did the same shit. They threw the shit around him, and I was just like, wow.

SADAT X, hip-hop artist, detained 2006: I read as much as I could. I ain't really do too much writing, because I ain't really have nothing to write about. A lot of dudes say, "Why didn't you write in there?" And I was like, "It was nothing for me to write about. I couldn't see the outside world." I ain't want to write about it. Only so many songs you can make about being locked up with a whole bunch of dudes. That's not what people want to hear. So I didn't really write too much. I did a lot of exercise, basically read, slept, watched TV when I could watch TV, wrote letters, stuff like that.

MICHAEL "BIG MIKE" WILLIAMS, member, DOC Emergency Services Unit, retired 2008: Lil Wayne got arrested one night with one of my other old [security business] clients, Ja Rule. I get the call wanting guidance on what we should do. How do we handle this and that? They were actually supposed to make a deal together. They got the same lawyer, Murray "Don't Worry" Richman. They were setting up a deal for them to do one year on the fucking gun charge. They would have done it together on Rikers Island. Ja Rule fucked around and fought the case, and then the deal was off the table. But Lil Wayne took the deal.

When he went in, I had people in my old facility, and that's where he was serving [his] time. I said, "Just make sure he's all right." I never asked anybody to do anything outside the scope of their job. Just make sure he's okay. Talk to him. Let him know that there's people who care about him. I was retired with all this shit going on, man, and people still called me. Every time he got in trouble in there, I would get a call. "Mike, you better have somebody talk to that boy." He wasn't doing nothing crazy. He just had so many people that was willing to do shit for him.

They found a fucking phone watch in his cell one day. And then, you know, two cells over, they found the fucking charger for it and all the contraband. And you know, Wayne had unlimited money at the time, so people were willing to do whatever for Wayne. They would always say, "You asking me to keep an eye on him, but you gotta tell him to relax." We actually had officers get in trouble. They had to put a memo out that if you don't work over there, do not get caught over there. You had so many women getting caught over there. One lady CO, she actually got suspended. They tried to fire her for that. What the fuck are you doing? Starstruck!

TAMI LEE: Lil Wayne was in the medical dorm. An officer got in trouble for bringing him something while he was in dorm four. It was a male captain. He was bringing him food and he got in trouble. He's retired now. I think Lil Wayne promised him something. They suspended the captain, and then the captain just retired.

But then, after that, they moved Wayne from NIC [North Infirmary Command]. I don't remember what jail he went to, but they moved him and he didn't come back.

MICHAEL "BIG MIKE" WILLIAMS: I got a call one night from a correction officer who was doing a lot of security on the outside too. He said, "Hey, Mike, listen, I just got the call: facilitate Wayne's release." I said, "Count me in." Again, I was retired. He said, "But we need to know what time they let him go and all that." So I still had connections inside. I made the call and they told me; they said, "Listen, it's too crazy over there. News set up everywhere on the other side of the bridge. What do you think?" I said, "I don't know." And they said, "We're thinking Queens House of Detention, a private vehicle, get him off the island and just let these people know quietly." 'Cause they had a tour bus. Rolls-Royces. All kinds of shit.

So that's what they did. They snuck him off the island and took him to Queens House, and that's where they released him. I helped facilitate that as well. He actually had his family waiting. I think they was at the fucking Trump Plaza. He didn't want to hang out. Everybody was thinking they wanted to hang out, go to a club. Lil Wayne said no. Rikers Island, Wayne will tell you, fucked him up. Fuck all that bad-boy shit. Jail, he said, he don't never want to go back to Rikers Island. So he got the therapy. Meanwhile, fucking Ja Rule ends up getting convicted and goes upstate and does a couple of years.

TAMI LEE: When Shyne [Moses Barrow, the hip-hop artist and now politician in Belize] was there, he brought Alicia Keys in and they had a concert—Alicia Keys, Fat Joe, and him had a concert in NIC. Those inmates went crazy. Oh my goodness. They were so happy. The officers and the inmates were happy. That was nice.

FAT JOE: I did two performances at Rikers Island. I did one with the late great Big Pun. That was in the middle of the yard. I don't know who asked us to do that. And so we did that to uplift the morale of the inmates and make them feel good. Then I did one for Shyne. He's a good friend of mine. I hated to see him in jail, but he asked me to come perform for the inmates.

That one day they treated me nice. That one day the correction officers were nice. Everybody was nice. They had food for the inmates there. I felt bad because I knew Shyne since he first became a rapper. And I knew he was about to go do ten years in jail. That it wasn't a joke. It was sad to see him in there like that.

Visiting jail has one moment that's always the same for everybody. And that moment is leaving. The hardest part is leaving your loved one or your friend that you love and looking back, knowing that they're going back in there and you're going back to do whatever you want to do. That's the one moment, the one emotion that nobody can escape.

MICHAEL "BIG MIKE" WILLIAMS: When Shyne was there, I started talking to him every time I saw him. I said, "What are you doing while you're here? While you're sitting here, make your time count. You signed to Def Jam. Jay-Z is there. Have you spoke to him?" He says, "Nah." He says, "You have access to him?" I said, "Yeah, I know Jay-Z's driver. I've known him thirty years. Want me to reach out to him?" He said, "Nah, I'll reach out to Jay." I said, "You talk to Jay and let me know that you did that, and then I'll speak to Jay-Z's driver."

A few days later, he said, yeah, I called him. He's coming up here. So I called the driver, said, "What's up, man? You know anything about Jay going to visit Shyne?" He said, "He mentioned it to me." I said, "Well, I'll help facilitate it. Let me know what vehicle you're going to bring up. Sweep that shit, make sure nothing's in there."

Someone had just come up to see some other celebrity recently before that. And they kind of disrespected them by making them park on the Queens side of the bridge. They wouldn't give him clearance to come all the way over the bridge. I said, "Fuck that. I'm getting a clearance to come straight to the front of the jail." And I did, through gate one and straight to NIC. Parked right in the front there with the Maybach. That's a $450,000 Mercedes. I was on the phone the whole time. It was my day off, talking to my people in there to make sure everything was going good. They had a good visit. I seen Shyne afterward; he said he had a great visit, great conversation. It was just Jay-Z and the driver.

The warden at NIC was actually one of my supervisors years ago. He was horrible to the troops. He moved up the ladder eventually and he was the [NIC] warden at the time. They told me, "Hey, Mike, the warden is telling us to not let Jay leave the building without bringing him to his office." I said, "Fuck that. Listen, tell that officer in there with Jay-Z and Shyne to whisper to Shyne to tell Jay-Z to not fuck with that warden. He don't care about none of us."

Shyne acknowledged it. He must have whispered to Jay-Z because when Jay-Z is ready to leave, the other officers said, "Excuse me, sir, the warden would like to see you before you leave." Jay-Z said, "Oh, I can't. I got a plane on the runway waiting for me. Tell him on the next visit, I'll definitely stop in to see him." They had already been told, fuck that warden. He was a clown. He always wanted to take the fucking photos with all the celebrities that come up. That felt good, getting him back.

JERRY DEAN, detained 1987, 2003: You know, it's funny. I was an actor and I had been in some movies. They had two movies I was in on VHS: *Bullet,* with Mickey Rourke and Tupac; and *Gloria,* with Sharon Stone. So they would watch them and would be like, "Yo, man, you fell from grace man. You in here now with us; you had it all and you here with us."

One day this mentally ill inmate grabbed my ass. I was taking a shit or sitting on the bowl, and he reached over and pinched my ass. And I flipped out and I started hitting him. I broke my hand on his head. But people were joking because in the movie *Gloria,* Sharon Stone makes me take my clothes off, and I have on a leopard-skin thong, and now they're watching this on Rikers and one of the guys says, "That's what you get. You want to pull your fucking pants down on TV, now you get motherfuckers trying to grab your ass."

SADAT X: One guard in there knew about Brand Nubian. And I was cool with her. She would bring me McDonald's every now and then. She would call me to come and act like I got to do a job with her or something. Then she'd say, you got five minutes to eat this, and I'd have to eat like a whole meal real fast. Another one of the officers was cool and let me come downstairs and into his office and watch basketball. I started working with him at night. So at night all I would do was just clean a couple of garbage cans and then go in his office and watch TV for the rest of the night. We was cool.

RICK LOMBARDI, retired DOC gang investigator, 1990 to 2011: I was a huge Mark Gastineau fan. I saw him play six times. From 1990, he might have been locked up five times. Actually one officer was infatuated with the Jets. He snuck in a fucking Mark Gastineau jersey and had him autograph it during the search. He's like, "Mark, do me a favor and just sign this jersey," while we're tossing his stuff.

MARTIN CREGG, retired DOC gang investigator, 1996 to 2018: I'm setting up an inmate, going to take him down to court. I put the cuffs on. He comes out of the back and says, "Officer, may I borrow a pen?" So I look straight at his chest. He's gigantic. And it's Mark Gastineau. I look up and go, "Oh shit, it's Mark Gastineau."

SADAT X: This kind of sticks with me. One day, we wanted to go to rec outside and we couldn't go. So dudes was like, we going to complain to the captain. So the captain came one day for whatever he had to do. That's the white shirt. And we explained like, "Yo, captain man, we supposed to get our hour recreation regardless of what happens, you know." The captain was like, you know, they are right, and he wrote up the CO for that. The CO held that. One day was super cold outside, and he was like, who's going out for rec?

We was like, cool, we going out for rec. We usually stay outside for an hour. So the hour came, and dudes was ready to go because it was cold. We say, "Yo, CO, we good, man. We ready to come in." He was like, "Nah, y'all wanted to beef to the captain about staying outside. Well, now y'all stay outside." We was outside for two hours. My hands and feet was throbbing, and in my mind I was like, "Yo, man, look how they treat me—like an animal." They just control. Dudes were so cold that all you could do was just sit there and try to thaw out and think about the situation that you was in. That said it all. Like, look at this: I'm outside in the freezing cold looking at New York City.

EDWARD GAVIN, retired deputy warden, 1982 to 2001: We had Héctor "Macho" Camacho in the jail. He was a young kid, and he was talking on the line. Summer 1982. You weren't supposed to talk. So this tough-guy CO goes, "Shut the fuck up. I told you to shut the fuck up," and he bitch-slaps Héctor "Macho" Camacho. It's 5:00 a.m.; we're getting him ready to go to court. Héctor was cool.

I said, "You just hit Héctor 'Macho' Camacho," and he turned white.

ROBERT CRIPPS, retired warden, 1983 to 2013: Foxy Brown was being released from the Rose M. Singer Center [RMSC]. I had a plan to release her so it wasn't a big deal, but I was overruled by the chief of the department and by the chief of security. The chief of security says, "I'm handling this situation, and we're not gonna use Warden Cripps's plan; we're gonna use my plan." I said, "All right, in the event that goes wrong, it's on you, right?" He goes, "All right, it's on me if it goes wrong." They ended up releasing Foxy Brown at eight o'clock in the morning instead of with the other inmates. So she made up this whole scam that she had to get a certain medication and she knew they didn't have the medication until eight o'clock.

He ends up calling me and says, "I don't know what's going on. She's still not out of there. Warden Cripps, go to Rose M. Singer Center and see what's going on with her." So, I walk in there. She's getting her medication. I said, "What's the holdup? She's good to go, right?" "Yeah." She had all these Hefty bags filled with clothes and stuff. They were difficult for her to carry. She turns to me and says, "Oh, Warden, can you do me a favor and grab my bags?" I said, "Are you out of your mind? You think I'm going to carry your bags out of this facility? Whatever you can't carry, we'll mail to you. How about that?" So she reaches back, hands cuffed, picks up the bags, walks out, and I release her.

Then I'm watching her walk into the control building. She goes, "Warden, can I use the officers' bathroom because I have to change." First of all, what the hell does she have to change for? Just get in your damn car and go. What she apparently did was put something on a website about her release so she could have fans waiting outside Rikers. So unbeknownst to me at the time, all these people were showing up, looking for her to be released as she was going to make a video of it. On the other side of the bridge, a limousine is driving in.

It was a big scene. The media was all across the street.

There's two ESU [Emergency Services Unit] officers there, and the limo driver has to make a U-turn. So they let him go into the parking lot to make a U-turn. The chief of security went ballistic and said, "How is that limo in our parking lot?" First of all, it's not our parking lot. It's a public parking lot. And he was in the parking lot for about ten seconds, drove around, and made a U-turn. The two officers that were in the parking lot are both ESU officers with twenty years or more on the job. Walsh calls me up screaming: "How did that limousine get in the parking lot?" Blah, blah, blah, blah.

I said, listen, let me look into it. I talked to the two officers. They said, "Warden, we had to let them make a U-turn." That was it. We have a video of the limo coming in and leaving and it was a matter of maybe twenty seconds. I would have had her out at 4:30 in the morning. I would have dropped her at Queens Plaza, and no one would have known.

So then the chief of security and the chief of department want these two officers written up and they want days taken. And I'm like, I don't think that's necessary, boss, because these guys got twenty years or more on the job. All they did was let a car make a U-turn. We're going to hit them over the head for that? Come on. He wanted them hit. So I wrote command disciplines for both of them. Called them both in my office, looked at their records, they had perfect records. And I said, what I'm going to do is you're going to sign for a reprimand. It's going to be a written reprimand, but after one year the record comes out of your folder. But I'm not taking days. I couldn't bring myself to take that vacation.

The chief of the department heard that I didn't take any days. They moved me to the Vernon C. Bain Center [a jail on a boat on the East River] because I didn't take the correctional officers' vacation. He kept me up there for two and a half years. Siberia. All because I didn't penalize two officers for allowing the car to make a U-turn. They even tried to charge me with some bogus charges. They tried to ruin my career over that.

MICHAEL "BIG MIKE" WILLIAMS: I was in the locker room getting dressed and the door swings open and it's one of the supervisors, the captain. He looks around and says, "Suit up. Bring all your heavy shit. We're going tactical." We got to go pick up John Gotti's hit man [Joseph "Joe the German" Watts].

He said we're going to Staten Island, we're going to get him, and we're bringing him to Brooklyn. He said it's going to be a shit show, so have your shit together. Commissioner's going to be out there, commanding officer. So, we go to Staten Island. It's quiet as a fucking mouse, man.

We walked to the back. Fucking dapper gentleman, silver-white hair, fucking $10,000 suit on, silk socks, is just sitting in the pen by himself. He sees us; he goes, "Oh, hey, guys, how you doing? How you doing, sir?" "We're here to move you, pick you up." And he goes, "Okay, no problem. Just let me know what you want me to do." I'm saying, "What the fuck? This guy's what? They found body bags in his soda shop in Staten Island? That nice fucking guy?"

The officers that work there, they hand us the fucking keys. They're supposed to come with us and open that shit up, but they're scared. So it was just me and my partner back there. Well, I felt comfortable. We said, "Listen to our instructions. We're gonna strip you down. Do you have anything that you think may be contraband before we get started? Let us know." He was a fucking gentleman, man. Stripped him down, one thing at a time. He listened to everything. Gave him his stuff, treated him with respect. "Okay. You can get dressed." Now put the handcuffs on him. Put the leg irons on him. Got the waist chains on him.

Fucking NYPD was out there. Lights and sirens from Staten Island to Brooklyn. I see the fucking commissioner.

The funny thing is, I seen him several times after that, in the facilities, and he fucking remembered me. Hey, Mr. Williams. Oh, Mr. Watts, how you doing? Everything all right? Fucking shelf of legal paperwork, stacked up high and neat. Fucking like ten pair of brand-new white Capezios. He had cassette tapes. I didn't even know inmates could have cassette tapes. He's preparing for his trial.

I think he spent ten months on Rikers Island dealing with that case, and he beat the fucking thing and went back to the feds to finish his fed time. Maybe a month or two later, I pick up the Sunday *Daily News* and it's him. While he sat on Rikers Island, he and John Gotti Jr. made almost a million dollars in a phone card scam. I said to myself, "What the fuck? I'm doing something wrong here."

SADAT X: [The day I left] I was thinking first of all, I'm never going back again. I need to get back on my music. That's what I wanted to do and keep my shows going. And just try to forget this shit, man. I don't wanna have too many memories of this. I don't wanna have too many friends coming out of this. I just want to leave this where it was.

LGBTQ

"They Had What They Called Homosexual Housing"

G ay and bisexual men and women in the United States are far more likely to be sexually assaulted while locked up, according to a 2013 study by the Williams Institute at UCLA. In February 1979, New York City opened a separate jail unit for gay men and transgender women on Rikers, the first of its kind in the country. Most other lockups housed that population in either solitary confinement or dingy secluded housing units without basic services found in general areas.

The specialized unit on Rikers was extremely popular.

"Their behavior's beautiful. They're the easiest inmates in this institution to deal with. As far as I'm concerned, I'll take a whole prison full of homosexuals any day," Deputy Warden Henry Bernsen told the *Philadelphia Gay News* reporter Jack Veasey.

The success did not last. Detainees lied about being gay to get into the unit, and violence began to spike in the area. In 2005, the city closed it and vowed to create a better system to screen people coming in. But like much else in the Correction Department, jail officials are still struggling to properly identify gay and transgender detainees for the unit.

Meanwhile, on June 27, 2019, a twenty-seven-year-old transgender woman, Layleen Xtravaganza Cubilette-Polanco, died alone in a solitary confinement cell in the woman's jail on Rikers after an epileptic seizure. She was being held on $500 bail.

Her death highlighted a series of systemic failures and spurred calls from people like the U.S. senators Bernie Sanders and Elizabeth Warren to end solitary entirely.

—

MARCUS GRICE, detained multiple stints, 1994 to 2017: My first time incarcerated in Rikers Island, I was fifteen. I was not supposed to hit Rikers Island, but they sort of finagled it, so I didn't go to juvenile. I spent a year there. And it was very traumatic, first of all, being in prison. Period. And second of all, I found out then and there that I was HIV positive.

I found out from a test that I was required to get in Rikers. It was November 1995, chilly and cold. This woman gave me the test, and you had to wait a week to get the results. That was the most awful week you can imagine. They gave you a number so it was anonymous. Before we had been laughing and talking about things, but when I came back for the results, she just looked at me and I knew. She was surprised because I didn't look sick. She looked at it and looked at me and I knew. She was sad.

But there was no emotional support to help me deal with the trauma of finding out that I had a disease that at the time we believed was going to kill us all.

The other teens were crushing pills, doing anything to numb the pain, to get away from what was going on. There were people dying all the time. They put us in "categories" to keep us separate. They used to have sayings to tell you someone died [from HIV-related illnesses]. It was the "monster." He died from the "monster." "Miss Honey got the package." "She got the kitty. Why the kitty? 'Cause the bitch kept scratching."

I had blond hair and I was scared to death. I was fifteen years old, and through the processing, which was extremely long, I eventually worked my way to the Tombs. As I was getting processed, the question came up, am I gay, or am I a homosexual? It was pretty obvious.

At that time, they had the adolescent "homo house," as they called it, and they put me there, which was safe. Safe-ish.

I remember filing through the four building and seeing all these different bullpens for the first time and dudes screaming at me, young guys screaming at me, and giving me such a lashing for being there: "Fucking faggot, homo, this, that, look at this motherfucker." All this horrible treatment that I was getting from other inmates who could not reach me.

I was shocked. I was still in shock of what was going on with me. I was still numb. You understand? Sure. This had just happened to me. I made a bad decision. I was hungry. I was homeless. I was in the Village, and I made a very bad decision. I was a kid.

Marcus Grice first went to Rikers at age fifteen and was shuttled in and out many times. He says he survived on his wits and an ability to read palms.

MELANIA BROWN, sister of Layleen Polanco: She was a magical person. Layleen held no grudges. She was very forgiving. She'd take the last dollar in her pocket and give it to a stranger. She taught me kindness. It first started with animals; she'd bring animals to the house, heal them, and send them back on their way. And then animals started turning into humans. They'd stay with us. She was a great sister. To know her was to truly love her. She was my church. She had dreams and hopes of being a vet one day.

DAVID SHANIES, attorney for Layleen Polanco's family: Layleen Polanco had a really sparkling personality. She was always described as a bright light by everyone who knew her. And she became a symbol for the mistreatment and abuse of transgender women of color in our criminal justice system, in our jails and prisons, and her case brought a lot of attention to a lot of issues that were just coming into the conversation. But it pushed that conversation forward in a lot of ways because of who she was and how tragic her case was.

Layleen Polanco was a twenty-seven-year-old woman from Yonkers, where she lived with her mother. She was a transgender woman. She was a member of the House of Xtravaganza, which is one of the most if not the most prominent houses in ballroom theme, which has gotten a lot of fame and notoriety, through shows like *Pose*.

Layleen had been arrested in May 2019 on misdemeanor charges. She had bail of $500 set on her, and she did not have the money to make that bail.

MELANIA BROWN: Although my sister made it look easy, I know life was hard for her. Being that she was a transgender woman of color, they always denied her employment. To be able to take care of herself, she turned to sex work because that was the only job she was able to get. I know how hard it was for her.

DAVID SHANIES: She was stuck on Rikers Island in the Rose M. Singer Center, also called Rosie's, and she, in June, was put into punitive segregation, which is one of the names that they use for solitary confinement, put in isolation, for disciplinary reasons. And she was left there.

She had numerous medical conditions, including epilepsy,

which ultimately was the cause of her death. But she had other medical conditions that should have disqualified her for being placed in punitive segregation. At the time there was a lot of pressure to create bed space and to put people in the punitive segregation who may not be the best candidate for it. And in particular with transgender inmates, there was a lot of pressure to find beds for them in spaces that were not in a medical observation unit, even when that was warranted.

So in June 2019, Layleen was in her cell, just after lunchtime, and was left unsupervised. Inmates in punitive segregation are supposed to be visually checked on every fifteen minutes to confirm that they are alive and well. Officers didn't do that. And Layleen had a seizure and died.

MELANIA BROWN: She was just amazing. She was just remarkable. She was flawless with her pureness. My sister taught me to see the world through her eyes. I'm the older sister. I'm supposed to be teaching her. I couldn't cry in front of her, because if I cried in front of her she'd flip the whole house and ask who did it. I will do everything in my power to make sure the world does not forget about her. I'll do everything in my power for those correctional officers who watched her die to remember what they did. To remember her face. I told her that they will have nightmares of what they did to her. My sister truly did not deserve what happened.

DAVID SHANIES: Her case really ignited a lot of emotion in the community. It came during Pride Month. And it came as a confluence of issues really showed themselves. In Layleen's case, one was bail reform. The state legislature had just passed a law that basically said, we shouldn't be locking people up for misdemeanor offenses. And they've actually passed the bail reform law, which, if it were followed, would have meant that Layleen would not have been in custody.

There was a lot of talk about the use of solitary confinement, and all the damage that has been shown to cause and a big push to reform or eliminate its use altogether. But also issues about policing in the transgender community. The so-called walking while trans ban—Layleen was originally picked up on a prostitution-related charge—which was repealed. And when that law existed, it was a very common problem in the transgender community, especially among transgender women of color. It essentially said that if you're walking on the street and a trans woman, you risk getting arrested for loitering for the purposes of prostitution.

Layleen was frequently stereotyped, and judged, based on who she was and how she looked. It also highlighted the major issue of how we treat transgender inmates, and how we treat disabled inmates in jails and prisons. So all of these issues kind of came together in Layleen's case. And combined with the sort of garden-variety reckless disregard of inmates' health and safety caused the death of this young, vibrant, beloved person.

PARADISE MONTANEZ, detained 2007, 2008: Girls in their teens are not nice in any situation, and then when you lock us up in a corridor and you keep us together 24/7, it's never fun. Ironically, there were a lot of, I don't know how you would label them, I'm a little old-school, so I call us a bunch of dykes. You always had one girl that was like, "Oh, I'm not gay. Stay away from me. Don't give me your gay!" And you always had to explain to her that that's not how it works.

I dated this girl who was in prison for murdering her mother. But she was a really nice person. She's still in upstate prison. I used to write to her. But I had to let that go.

MARCUS GRICE: When I got to the six building, it was no longer homosexual housing. It was general population for adolescents, and I was told years later, when I got to be adult, that I was the first gay person that ever stayed and made it through their sentence. I said, "What? Why didn't y'all tell me?" They said, "'Cause we would've terrified you." Most of 'em didn't make it. Usually, soon as they got there, them boys beat them up and packed them up and sent them back. Back to the four building. If I would've known it was a choice, I would've went back to the four building myself. But I didn't know it was a choice.

The thing that carried me throughout a lot of my bids: I could read people's palms—legitimately. And that's why a lot of these COs used to come to me. Can you believe that? They would come and pull this little boy out of his cell and say, what do you see? I had officers, captains, deps, pulling me and saying, what do you see? And no inmates was beating my ass.

GRACE DETREVARAH, transgender former detainee, 1980s: Nineteen eighty-three was my very first time going to Rikers. It was horrific back then. But they had what they called homosexual housing. The police did it by your appearance. They did not really have a procedure or directive. And if you were a criminal, you knew that if you went into custody, if you asked for homosexual housing back then, they would give it to you. And it was just special housing for those of the LGBT community.

In 2007, the Department of Correction started having another gang problem. The Crips couldn't live anywhere else on the island, and once they found out about homosexual housing, they signed into it. That was the beginning of the end of that special housing because the Crips took it over and it became a hiding spot. It wasn't being used for what corrections created it for.

MARCUS GRICE: I've been arrested over seventy-five times in New York City. Rikers is not there to help you. But I remember reading an officer's palm in Rikers and told her, "Listen, you going to get a house, and then you going to buy a house." She's like, "I don't know." I say, "I have to tell you what the spirit telling me to tell you."

On one of my later bids, she came over and said, "Marcus, Marcus, I wanna talk to you. I went to buy my house, like you told me." I'm like, trying to remember what I told her. Then she said, "And then, during that process, my mom died and I got her house." I said, "I'm so sorry." She said, "No, my mother was suffering. This was peace for her. And she went in such a peaceful way. Thank you. I was prepared. I was prepared."

BIANY GARCIA, trans former detainee, 2009: I used to have my own cell. It was the loneliest place in the world. Imagine losing your freedom just for being trans. I try not to remember. I know that I went to jail. But I don't want to remember. I try not to remember when the light went out at night. It's part of my life and I'm here to share it with the world what it's like when you're trans and in prison.

Being a trans person of color, immigrant, a person who doesn't speak the language, was hard. Not only my gender, but also not having the opportunity to talk to the COs about what you need. If you're having pain, you can't have that conversation with people when you don't speak the language. There's a lot of violence against transgender people or gay people in Rikers.

MARCUS GRICE: Did Rikers ever change as far as us? It got much worse. It got unbelievably worse. We had homosexual housing. I was in the homosexual housing as an adolescent before I was sentenced. Adolescent housing was much better than being in general population. Even homosexual housing for adults was better than being in general population.

But I've literally been thrown in dorms where they told me, "You're not staying in here or we going to hurt you bad," all because of my lifestyle. The worst thing that ever, ever, ever could have happened is for them to stop homosexual housing. You understand what I'm saying? It was inhumane. They have housing for, I believe, transgender people. It's not fair. It's not right, because you have this tiny little bitty thing who can't defend himself, but doesn't identify as or look trans, so you're gonna feed him to the wolves?

AUTHORS: Do you remember a specific experience that illustrates that? The thing where you get to a unit and they go, "You're not staying here?"

MARCUS GRICE: Which time? Come on now, there's hundreds of times that's happened. It is a very, very broken system that is constantly changing, and it doesn't make any sense why they change so many things—because a few people over here say something isn't working, or a few lawsuits over there. It's just because you have different people that come into power and they think a part of showing that they're doing their job is changing things instead of actually doing research.

Have I ever got beat because I was gay? A couple of times. And, it was a time or two where they let it, as they call it, "build up." But the real reason is, "I hate that fucking faggot." So they make up a reason to keep fucking with me or keep harassing me until something happens, until I fight back. You gotta push back. Ain't no such thing as you gonna let them keep harassing you. If you are in a dorm with sixty-seven motherfuckers, you gonna let sixty-six people harass you night and day every day? Are you gonna do that? No, you can't do that.

I've seen people who push back get jumped on by five other people. And because of our lifestyle, us trying to get away, they went and told the CO and told the captains and whatever, so they got labeled a snitch. And when they went somewhere else, they got it worse. Ten times worse.

You know how many kids in there or grown men, grown people, that have gotten beat to death because of standing up for what was right or just being just completely and utterly tired of being oppressed physically and emotionally?

In Rikers you got to see people with their masks down.

BIANY GARCIA: One of my big challenges was to find hormones inside Rikers. Because when I was outside, I was with the hormones. And then, when I went to Rikers, I didn't take my medication for like almost a year.

I asked for hormones the first time when I was arrested, and they told me no. At that time, my English was not good, which made me shy. But after ten months being in Rikers, I decided to go back to the clinic and ask for hormones because that was my treatment. The doctor started giving me hormones in three weeks.

They moved me straight to the men's facility. I never imagined being with forty men in a cell. In a sleeping area. It was crazy because I didn't have the chance to go to the bathroom, because we have to share the bathroom with men. There are three or four places to take a shower, and sometimes they don't give you a chance to take one by yourself. And you're always afraid of being raped or something else. I got beat up one time. The Latinos and the Black community started fighting and one of them punched me in the face. I started bleeding and they took me to the doctor.

MARCUS GRICE: I'm gonna be honest with you. A lot of them officers was not fucking bad. They wasn't. Now, if you present yourself as an asshole, they'll turn it up on you. But there were captains that were bad. You know, when it came to putting me in a situation that could actually get me killed.

This is one of the typical ways that they do to the homosexuals. They'll leave us in the cell all day long and start housing people, and you be like, where are you gonna send me? They were playing a waiting game. And you'll know that whatever house they sending you to, you [aren't going to be able to] stay there.

But there was a female officer who told the captain, "Yo, oh, he's part of the LGBT lifestyle." She was very respectful. And she told the captain, "He can't stay here. We just had one here." They had just pulled somebody out of that house that was gay because her hair was all ripped out and she got fucked up. They had to drag her out.

Why would you send poor me there? Little poor me. You know what the captain told me? "You're housed." "You're housed. I don't care. I'm going home." I said, "Are you really going to do this to a human being?" They turn around and walk away. What is that saying to you? "I don't care if you live or die, right? You are on the next shift. You have been housed. You are no longer a part of my problem." No one deserves that.

The captain left and the female guard did something slick. She's not gonna endanger her job, but she had a heart. She opened up my cell. She knew that if I walk out and say, "I'm not going back in there," they can't put me back in there. She opened my cell and her excuse was, oh, to let you out to get some air for a second.

She know what she doing. She was trying to help me get out of there in a peaceful way.

She opened the cell 'cause the other inmates had already heard that a homosexual was coming to the unit. 'Cause you can hear everything. It's nothing but bars. So they were already starting to plot. So my cell opens and I just went out and she said, "So you're telling me that you're not going back in there?" *[Nodding, imitating the officer.]* I said, "No, I'm not." She said, okay. And then she turned around and closed and locked the gate. And I stood out there until they came and got me and moved me to somewhere else. That was about five years ago.

AUTHORS: *That's not too long ago, in a society that's supposed to be more enlightened than it was thirty years ago.*

MARCUS GRICE: It's not about society. It's not about that. It's about dealing with an entity within an entity. This is something that's living inside something. They have their own reality behind those walls. It's sad. It's sad. They have their own reality behind those walls.

BIANY GARCIA: I still remember the first day when I went to the [Vernon C. Bain Center] boat [jail] in the Bronx. It was a cold day. I was wearing shorts and they bring me a jumper or something. I put it on, and officers forced me to take off my female clothing, everything. And they forced me to use men's boxers. It's just not okay to do that. After being in that cell for like eight hours, they bring me to another cell that had like forty-five men in it. They just keep looking at me. And I did my bed and then I fell asleep, you know? Because I really don't want to talk to no one. I take no shower for fifteen days because there were a lot of men walking by. And that was scarier.

There was a pretty cool inmate. He asked me, "Do you want to take a shower?" I was like, yeah. He says, "Okay, go to the shower at 10:00 a.m." He told me he's going to be at the door and no one was going to bother me. I didn't see that from a CO.

MARCUS GRICE: There were so many times where I contemplated suicide between Rikers and the state. At one point, I was physically assaulted. When I tell you that, this guy had my eye hanging out my head because he thought I stole something from him and I didn't. And they was not gonna move me. They was not going to move me away from this guy. When I found out how well connected this guy was, it made me want to kill myself because I knew how the rest of my bid could go, how the situation could end up.

There was other times where I wanted to kill myself. When I had a robbery charge, grand larceny rather, and I knew I was looking at so much time. I was so drug addicted. I couldn't get off that shit. And I made a stupid decision by going inside a boutique on the East Side and I ran out with some woman's handbags and got caught. Lord have mercy. What was going through my mind when they put those handcuffs on me? And the arresting officer said that he had someone who committed suicide on him. And I seen why. Because all you see is this time that you're gonna have to do.

AUTHORS: *How'd you find your way through it?*

MARCUS GRICE: One slow step at a time. One slow, slow, slow, slow step at a time. One horrible, slow step at a time. Jesus Christ. One horrific, tiny, slow step at a time. That's it.

CONDITIONS

"Er, Uh, Uh, We Need a Plan.
We'll Be Submitting a Plan"

On July 22, 2011, the Legal Aid lawyer Dale Wilker sent a note to the leaders of the city jails inquiring about the effects of an excessive heat wave that summer on inmates in the Central Punitive Segregation Unit (CPSU), known as the Bing.

"We are very concerned about the effect of the current heatwave on inmates confined in CPSU cells," Wilker wrote. "Obviously, we are experiencing the hottest temperatures in nearly a decade. Would the department please advise us what has been done?"

A curt response came—seven days later. "Please know there's not much we can do about the hot weather," a jail official wrote. "We do not monitor the interior temperatures in the CPSU."

It was just one small exchange in the long battle to improve the deplorable conditions in the city jails. The struggle had raged since the 1970s, when, as Michael Mushlin, another former Legal Aid lawyer, recalled, the Department of Correction's position was simply to fight every improvement effort.

"It was an attempt to do everything they could to defeat it by resisting, full blast, indicating no willingness to discuss settlement, forcing trials at every stage, and going up on appeal whenever they could," said Mushlin, now a Pace University law professor. "And they were losing constantly. And it was beginning to generate some negative attention to the city."

In 1979, though, Mayor Ed Koch agreed to a fifty-two-page consent decree aimed at improving the conditions. The effort largely floundered and the litigation raged on through the 1980s, through the overcrowding crisis and the jail-building boom into the 1990s. Mayor Rudy Giuliani, who took office in 1994, chafed at the consent decrees. And then, in 1996, Congress passed the Prison Litigation Reform Act (PLRA), a law designed to undermine consent decrees and discourage lawsuits. Giuliani and his correction commissioner Bernard Kerik attacked the decrees with relish and got a number of them overturned.

"There were consent decrees on everything from food service to washing the windows for inmates," said Kerik, now a law enforcement consultant. "And these were federally ordered consent decrees, but some were completely ludicrous, and they were all financially absurd."

Still, basic conditions in the new jails, and the old ones, coupled with the Correction Department's stubborn resistance to outside involvement and even outright subterfuge, continued to raise disturbing issues in critical systems like fire safety, ventilation, heating, plumbing, cleanliness, lighting, and housing quality.

"You ever see that old painting *The Raft of the Medusa*?" he said, referring to the 1819 work by the French painter Théodore Géricault showing shipwreck survivors adrift and starving on a raft.

"Well, it was sort of the modern equivalent," the retired Legal Aid lawyer John Boston said.

—

JOHN BOSTON, retired director, Legal Aid Prisoners' Rights Project: Back in the mid-'90s when we were doing our fire safety inspections, one of the things that we did was go to a housing area with the fire safety experts and look around at the fire extinguishers and so forth. And then you go to the fire exits and say, "Can you open these fire exits so we can go out of it?"

They say, "We've got to get the key." "Okay," we say, "get the key. Can we get the key and can we get the key today as opposed to next week?" Anyway, they get the key and we go out the fire escape. And one of the fire escapes was so choked with rubble, apparently from some construction thing, that it was a safety hazard just to get down it.

There were fifty people per housing area, and either two or three floors' worth of people would have come down that fire escape. So it would've been either one hundred to one hundred fifty [people] or two hundred to three hundred, depending on whether two sides of an area came to the same escape.

We got down the internal fire escape to the door, stepped outside, and walked down the shorter set of stairs to the bottom of the fire escape. And there's a tree growing at the bottom. If you were running away from a fire, the tree would be right there in your way.

Now, it wasn't a big tree. It was one of these ailanthus trees, I think, the ones that are always popping up in the corners of parking lots. The real tall thin gray ones. And it was like four and a half, five feet tall.

Known both for his relentless manner and wry rejoinders, John Boston is the former director of the Legal Aid Society's Prisoners' Rights Project.

But the point is, fire safety is supposed to be inspected pr
often. How long had it been since somebody paid any attention
that fire escape that there was a four-and-a-half-foot tree at t
bottom of it blocking the people from escaping? It was sort of en
blematic of the whole experience of dealing with the Departmen
of Correction.

SADAT X, hip-hop artist, detained 2006: I remember they had us
cleaning out this building called HDM [the House of Detention
for Men]. That was an old building that closed down. We was moving old shit out of there, like lockers and insulation and stuff like
that. And I was like, "Y'all, I don't think we supposed to be touching this stuff like that." But we was doing that. They had us cleaning walls and doing all types of stuff where I come to find out
you're supposed to have a hazmat suit on, or some type of licens-
ing. Inmates were not supposed to be doing that.

And that's where I think my recurrence of asthma really came
from. 'Cause when I came back, a little while afterward, I had
asthma and I know that was the buildup of doing that. 'Cause we
ain't really have no masks like that on. We had to rip up T-shirts
and make our own masks.

And you know with that insulation, it get on you. It's like prickly
stuff, man. And, we breathin' in this shit, man. Nobody ain't really
know what the ramifications was behind that. I quit that job. I was
like, yo, man, I'm not going to keep doing this, man. We worked
that job for like two, three months. We'd be in there for like five
hours. Without masks.

**FRANK PASQUA III, former Lucchese crime family, detained 2003,
2011 to 2012:** And you know what, they would fight to get that job.
Guys would fight to get that job 'cause you eat better and you get
more time on the visit floor. They would ask for that job, even
though they knew asbestos was there.

**DR. ROBERT POWITZ, environmental health expert, investigated Ri-
kers conditions:** Here's the problem. Rikers is old. The modular

[temporary trailer] units, which are originally designed for eight years of service, and at that point were already thirty years old, something like that. So what we found: they were pretty well gone, structurally. They're still going. They patch them up.

HELEN TAYLOR, detained 1970s, 1980s: I first went to jail in about 1975 at the old women's house [in Chelsea]. That was awful. We had cells infested with mice and roaches and water bugs. Rats and spiders. That's what you slept in. No matter how hard you tried to clean it, the water bugs were there.

At one point I got bit in the eye by a spider and my whole face [was] disfigured. I looked like the guy in *Face/Off*. I had stuff coming out of my face. They said there wasn't nothing they could do. When I woke up, I could barely see. They were doing a search. When I got to the door, a female officer screamed, "We gotta get her to the clinic."

A male officer picked me up and ran me to the clinic for three days, and then they rushed me out to the hospital, Elmhurst. I was there for seven days on antibiotics for a spider bite right next to my eye. They said it laid some type of eggs. I didn't think my face would ever come back to normal. I had to take a strong, strong antibiotic.

JOHN BOSTON: What they did because of the overcrowding in the '80s was started a building spree and a real estate spree. They were opening up all of this new space without having that much idea how it was that they were going to operate it.

HELEN TAYLOR: I was one of the second groups they put in Rosie's [Rose M. Singer Center, opened 1988]. The concrete was still wet. The building wasn't ready to put us in there, but they did. There was no medical staff. Thank God we didn't get really sick for the first four months. If you did, they had to rush you out, and they would take you back to the old women's house to see a doctor.

JOHN BOSTON: [After the city won court decisions discontinuing consent decrees following the passage of the PLRA], we reviewed what was in the consent decrees to see what there was that, on its face, was not supportable as a matter of constitutional law in 1999, which was considerable.

And we started to develop evidence on the things that we had a pretty good idea were not entirely constitutional. One of the things that we did was we retained an expert in environmental health. And so we started inspections. I will never forget the first day that we got out there. It was November 30, 1999. It was bitterly cold. We went into the George Motchan Detention Center with our sanitarian to look around. I have never been so surprised by anything in all my years of doing that work.

ROBERT POWITZ: We walked into a few cells in the infirmary. There was ice on the wall and the inmates were basically bundled; all they had was their eyes and their nose out. Very little heat. And this was an infirmary setting.

JOHN BOSTON: We went into the infirmary, the temperature was in the fifties. It had been my expectation that since they had known for years that there was a high likelihood that this was the way it was going to shake down, they were going to have to have some proceedings about the conditions, that they would be in there taking care of business before we got there to inspect. And that we'd go through and look around and just come out with a punch list: "Take care of this stuff and we're out of here, it's been fun." But it was a disaster, and the place was overrun with cockroaches and mice.

There was filth and disorganization everywhere. It's like somehow there was no communication from anybody who had an idea that there was a potential legal proceeding here.

We went through the jails finding appalling conditions. And it was sort of funny because we would go to housing areas and Dr. Powitz would want to look at the laundry soap. They didn't have any laundry soap—laundry soap, laundry soap, wonder where it is. "It's around here somewhere. I guess we ran out." The usual "dog ate my homework" stuff. But as we proceeded through the jails, they started having more and more laundry soap. Clearly they were looking for laundry soap.

JACQUELINE VELEZ, detained 1998: I worked at the tailor shop, where we did the sheets, towels, and stuff like that. From working in there, I caught this very bad acne. It was horrific. I've always suffered from acne since I was a kid. But having acne all over your face at the same time, I've never experienced. I don't know where it came from, whether it came from that or from the other materials that they give you like soap. It was so horrible that I would wear my hair down to cover my face. I would just be itching and itching, and I'd want to rip my face open.

ROBERT POWITZ: If an inmate sent their clothing or their sheets in, there was no guarantee that they would get it back. So what happened is they started laundering themselves and they took basically buckets of these square pans that we use in the kitchen. And did their laundry in the bathroom, normally in the showers, where they could draw water, and then hung those things out in the dorms or in their cell or someplace.

When we first got there, they were using their body soap that they got either from commissary or was jail issue. You can't use body soap, because it has aloe and different emollients. And they had hand soap. The interesting thing about the soap is laundry soap has a melting point. And the melting point of most laundry soap that's cheap is 140 degrees Fahrenheit.

You can't have water over 120 degrees Fahrenheit in a [jail] living area, because it causes scalding. So here you had soap that wouldn't melt. And there was this pushback from the city: well, we gave them soap. So most of the guys and women, they did their own laundry. And that causes a couple of things. One, I think the biggest issue here from the inmates' standpoint is it causes dermatitis. If you have soap left on your clothing, you're going to get itchy. And it's going to bother you.

Laundry soap is a high-pH soap, which was lye. Skin irritation. Surprisingly or not surprisingly, African Americans are most susceptible to that, just the nature of their skin. Secondly, their laundry was constantly wet. And if it's constantly wet, you now have biofilm, which is basically soap scum, water, and a lot of bacteria. You have mold growth, and you have, because of constant wetness, spalling of tile, peeling of paint. And that makes conditions you can't clean.

JACQUELINE VELEZ: When I got a job in the officer's Bubble [a glass-enclosed booth where an officer sits to observe the unit], that was a privileged job. I didn't know that. So the girl that used to do it was a Black girl. I don't know why she picked me to take over her job. And she basically trained me. The job was to keep the Bubble clean, but also to supply the women with the supplies they needed, like Kotex, tampons, tissue, like all kind of shit.

That soap would bleach your fucking clothes. A bar of soap would bleach white clothes. So we would wash our clothes with the bar of soap they gave us, not bathe with it.

It would burn stuff. Like if this shit is taking stains off white shirts and bras, would you want that on your skin? You still putting it on your skin if you think about it. So I don't know if the soap was the reason for that breakout, but it was bad.

JOHN BOSTON: [In the mid-2000s] basically the judge found that the ventilation was in an unconstitutional condition and about 40 percent of the ventilation in the jails was not functioning. Period. Just completely defunct. At RNDC [the teen jail], the ventilation ducts in a good part of the jail were blocked off with sheet metal. Why? Nobody knew. They had been rendered nonfunctional. Not just lack of maintenance, they were affirmatively blocked. So what they were supposed to do under Judge [Harold] Baer's order was bring the ventilation systems into working order.

At the same time that this was going on, the Office of Compliance Consultants [OCC] was continuing to make observations and write reports. And it just so happened that, in maybe 2005, 2006, they had their ventilation person go out and make observations, within a few days of the date that the city certified the ventilation systems as being in working order. We got the report from OCC, and it basically said that things were in a hell of a mess out there. So, after stewing in my office for a while, I wrote a letter to Judge Baer.

[I wrote,] we would like the department to explain how it is that three days before or after these observations were made, they're certifying that their ventilation systems are in working order. The judge endorsed that letter with an order that said, "Yeah, I'd like to know that too, please explain. It is so ordered." So the city wrote to the court, and the executive summary of their letter was, "Er, uh, uh, we need a plan. We'll be submitting a plan." There was never, ever really any explanation for what the hell they thought they were doing. One hopes that the people who were sending in those reports either didn't know or didn't care that they were a pack of lies, but we didn't pursue those questions.

We were interested solely in getting the job done. So they said, we're going to submit a plan. We basically said, yeah, you better, and withheld any further action. And so we got that plan, and behold, it was good. So we drafted up a proposed order that essentially took all the things that were in their plan and turned them into a court order for the judge to sign. And their response was, again, an executive summary, "But, uh, but, uh." Judge Baer signed the order. They appealed.

So we wrote a brief to the Second Circuit that recounted the history, and the lawyer for the city got up and said, "What happened here, Your Honor, is," quote, "we lied. And we got caught." End quote. The most honest piece of lawyering I have ever seen.

Fire safety has been sort of a protracted train wreck for decades. The consent decree said, maintain a safe and healthful environment, and not burning to death or dying of smoke inhalation was part of that. Nobody really argued with that. We had the beginnings of a fire safety work plan process going on about the time Giuliani came in, and like everything else cooperative, it pretty much shut down as the Giuliani ethic began to take over.

[In roughly 1998], one of the things that we discovered was that there was a whole new fire alarm system installed in the Brooklyn House of Detention. There was only one problem with it. Nobody hooked it up. It wasn't working. We discovered that, and we were taking depositions before going into this hearing about fire safety, and the person in charge of assets management did not know that this whole new system that they had spent millions of dollars on and installed wasn't operating.

[Circa 2010, DOC admitted it was submitting inaccurate fire safety status reports.]

JOHN BOSTON: In 2010, they were supposed to be making reports to the courts on various things that they were doing or failing to do. A guy named Lewis Finkelman became general counsel and discovered that they were submitting fire safety reports that were not accurate; they reported things as working when they were not. And he said another "We lied and we got caught," except they didn't get caught. They turned themselves in.

I should just say that Finkelman was one of the good guys in this process. He was one of these guys who was straight about everything. We didn't look at why were these people lying and who was lying and how far up did it go? We were interested in the results. Part of the problem was, at that point Bloomberg was not interested in the jails. I think the basic municipal policy about the jails was, we don't want to hear about them and just, you know, keep the lid on.

ANNA GRISTINA, detained 2012: It is in such disrepair. They make you walk on cardboard boxes through water through metal detectors. I refused to do it. I'm not walking on water through electric. They said, "Gristina, you'll walk." They wouldn't let me walk around the water. I was one of the few people who was bright enough to know that eventually the water and the electric would connect.

FRANK PASQUA III: There's holes in the cells. I've seen guys get new charges because the heating radiator had a hole in the wall, so the pipe could come through from the other cell. And they'll come to do a search, and they'll shake us down and lock us in our cells. This one guy took like fifteen grams of heroin and stuffed it through the hole into the other guy's cell. The other guy got the charge.

ROBERT POWITZ: We went into some mental health unit. This was one of the structural units that was designed for mental health. It was built with cells on either side and a walkway in the middle. The cells toward the main building, they looked out onto the yard, and in a corner there was a generator. They had to run the generator apparently because they needed the power. They didn't have adequate power on the island. And there was an inmate in the cell that was mentally ill. I measured the sound level from the generator at about 110, 120 decibels. It was going constantly. And the temperature in the cell was 110 degrees.

So we stopped. We had the attorneys with us and everybody else. And there was the deputy commissioner. Anything over 85 degrees, if you're on psychotropic medication, there's a hazard. We know this. There was this unbelievable indifference. "Oh, well, we'll take care of it." Well, it hadn't been taken care of, and sooner or later somebody was found dead. And the temperature of that cell, I think, was in excess of 120.

I remember that headline [Jerome Murdough, a mentally ill inmate, died in 2014 of complications of heat exposure. The city settled with his family for $2.25 million]. So this was something that we saw. We mentioned it. I couldn't do anything about it. I'm the plaintiff's expert. John [Boston] would argue and there was another guy, [Dale] Wilker. He would argue on anything. They did a stellar job, but it fell on deaf ears, just fell on deaf ears, or this indifference, this haughty indifference.

It bothered us. When we left, we all said, this is not going to bode well. And it didn't, but here again, this was a failure of maintenance. They needed the power. So the generator was running right under the guy's window. [It was as if they were saying,] "He's crazier than hell. He won't mind." And here's this generator running so loud, you couldn't hear yourself. That level of sound is almost like the ass end of a jet, right? And it was hot. You throw somebody in there with mental illness, with that constant din, hot but they can't get out of that heat, no matter what they do . . . that is indifference to me.

DR. SUSI VASSALLO, toxicologist, expert on heat-related illness, consulted on Rikers conditions: In 2004, Legal Aid and DOC agreed that I would be a good expert. I had done this work on heat and prisons in Mississippi and subsequently in many other different places . . . What really surprised me about Rikers is, here we are in the middle of New York City, a city that we think is one of the most progressive in the world, and that people were held in conditions of absolute dangerous temperature.

You fly into LaGuardia and you see the island right there, and the conditions are just as severe as any of the work prisons I've been in. Now, I've been in many, many prisons, including ICE detention centers, 'cause I worked as a medical expert for Homeland Security for a while. That was the most striking thing. In New York City, we think that we are a little bit more progressive or we have something less racist or less something. What really struck me is that is so much not the case.

[During the inspection,] first of all, they prepared our [visit] and all of the cell doors were open. So of course that's not the normal way. They had opened all the cell doors. We had thermometers and they had thermometers. We would insist that the cell doors be closed to measure these temperatures. And at that time, some of the temperatures were in the nineties.

I was saying to Judge Baer, we came to the idea that above a temperature of 86 degrees was absolutely dangerous.

The outside temperatures—and if you remember, some of those years, we had temperatures of a hundred degrees. And I then knew that the temperature in the cells were also a hundred degrees. In some circumstances they're kept there twenty-four hours a day. And then the idea that fans would somehow lessen the risk by moving hot air across somebody who's incarcerated? We know that's not helpful. We know that it can increase our sense of comfort, but it does not increase our safety. The other thing is, we would put a piece of paper up against the ventilation, and there would be no ventilation at all.

You go to the roof, and what struck me is that the ventilation system is on the roof in the hot New York City sunshine. And that's the hot air that's coming in and being pumped through. And even though they knew we were coming, many of the ventilation [panels] didn't open normally. They wouldn't work normally. They had a lot of warning. And actually it was intolerable even to us, as a group, to close those and stand in those cells. It was very hot. People were sweating and they didn't like the job.

What's so striking about Rikers is that we would never allow New Yorkers [to be without heat in winter] and even the [jail] officials would never think of not heating in the cold of winter. But for some reason we've gotten the idea that air-conditioning is something that shouldn't be expected for prisoners.

MARTHA GRIECO, lawyer, Bronx Defenders: The heat crisis is so predictable, which is what makes it even crueler. Every year. And every year, they say that they actually measure the heat in certain cells, and they'll just report nonchalantly the temperature is 85 degrees in this cell, it's 92 degrees in that cell. At the beginning of the summer, they're like, okay, showers, we're going to produce people for more showers, but then you can't control the temperature on the showers.

[During the heat litigation, internal emails showed DOC staff was manipulating the "heat sensitive" classification by removing detainees from the list when the temperature dropped to an 86-degree court-ordered threshold.]

SUSI VASSALLO: What they did, and I have the emails that show this, is they declassified people. So if the judge said, if you have certain conditions, then you must be moved to air-conditioning at 86 degrees. Well, they had a list of people who are heat sensitive based on their mental health and their medications or their conditions. And as soon as it got to 86 degrees, they [DOC] declassified them so nobody was heat sensitive. So if you can't move all those people, you can just say they're not heat sensitive. That was one of the most shocking things that happened there.

I was shocked by it because, first of all, a federal judge orders that people with these conditions are heat-sensitive individuals. And clearly their condition hasn't changed, nor has their medication changed. And if they do take a patient off the mental health medications, first of all, it's dangerous.

When the law is involved and a federal judge orders something, it's not really just unethical, it's . . . what is the step beyond unethical: immoral?

I don't know that morality and ethics should be their standard when it comes to the Constitution and the Eighth Amendment. I think it should be illegal. And I think it is illegal. Now we know it's illegal or it is unconstitutional to hold people at these temperatures. It's been so ruled many times now. The Fifth Circuit has said so and every other circuit [court] that's entertained this issue. As a matter of fact, it goes way back, way before I started this work—that excessive heat in a prison was seen as an Eighth Amendment violation.

I think what was shocking to me is that someone would so flagrantly take action to undermine, to violate what's already been ruled at the level of the Supreme Court.

So you're heat sensitive. You're on mental health medications, which your mental health condition as well as the medication makes you three or four times more likely to die from. And they move you there on a Friday. But they don't classify you [right away]. So you spend the whole weekend, which is plenty of time to suffer heatstroke in a place where a federal judge has clearly said that is unconstitutional and a danger to their health. Clearly, they know when they put them in there, it's just sleight of hand.

FRANK PASQUA III: Absolute infestation. I had a mouse that lived in my cell. They give us Rubbermaid bins to keep our stuff in. I would always make sure, even if I had to pay for it, that I would get the best Rubbermaid bins that actually clicked closed. I basically made a deal with the mouse. I leave some food all the way in the corner, opposite corner of the cell, and you leave my food alone. And every night that mouse would come in and there'd be a half of a Slim Jim and maybe some potato chips in this little spot on the floor. And when I woke up, the food would be gone and there'd be little mouse droppings right in that little corner. And he kept the deal with me. He stayed in his corner, my food stayed in mine, and never the two met. *Infested.*

ROBERT POWITZ: The City of New York pushed back on everything. I've been to worse facilities. Don't get me wrong. But at least there was some conciliatory or some cooperative discussion, somewhere along the line. Hell, I'm a high-priced pro coming in there. My doctorate is in institutional environmental health. So I know what the hell I'm doing. So ask me, and we have the answers. No. You aren't allowed, and we were summarily told no.

Everything was no.

VISITATION

"A Humiliation Process"

In 1979, Archibald Murray, the head of the Legal Aid Society, noted in a hearing before the city Board of Correction that detainees housed out on Rikers Island got half of the visits that detainees received in the Tombs, which is located right next to the courthouses in lower Manhattan.

"An imaginative sadist," he said, "would be hard pressed to find a place within our city's borders that is as isolated from our courts, that is as difficult to reach by public transportation, and that is as far removed from the families of most of this city's defendants as is Rikers Island."

Indeed, as anyone who has visited Rikers in the past forty years will tell you, the visit ordeal stands as yet another penalty exacted on the vastly Black and Hispanic population obligated to make the journey just to see a loved one.

The city, though, just kept building jails on Rikers, and nothing really changed.

—

EDDIE ROSARIO, detained 1990: I had been living with my aunt, and she was in her mid-eighties. I told my cousin not to let her come see me. One day, the officers say, "On the visit." None of my girlfriends would visit me because I was a real dick. My cousin was there and she goes, "Don't get mad." And in comes my aunt. They gave my cousin a hard time. She has big breasts. The officers were being lecherous. It just fucked me up. They are fucking with my cousin, and my aunt was telling me, "I needed to see you because I don't know if I'll be alive when you get out."

LASHARN HARRIS, wife of former detainee Dupree Harris: When Dupree was in Rikers, I was raising my daughter by myself and working as a bank teller for Chase. We weren't together then, but I would go and see him because we were friends. I never turned my back on him.

I would take the train into Queens to meet the bus. I would have to stand in line to get on the bus to take you to the bridge. That was the Q101. When you get to the bridge, you still have to wait for an extreme amount of time for another bus to get you to the island. It was just very aggravating. The bus drivers weren't nice.

I lived in Brooklyn. I would have to leave home at 7:00 a.m. for a visit that was at 9:00 a.m. I would take the G into Queens and then switch to the Q101 and then wait for the bus to cross the bridge. I wouldn't get home until 4:00 p.m. If it was a later visit, I wouldn't get home until seven, eight o'clock.

When you cross the bridge, you couldn't bring your phone. If you didn't have a car, you had to leave your phone at home or leave it in a store across from the Rikers parking lot where you had to pay $5 for them to keep it for you.

[Dupree Harris, now forty-seven, was held on Rikers several times in the 1990s and the early 2000s. In 2006, he was convicted of involvement in a drug conspiracy and sentenced to state prison. He remains incarcerated there at this writing. A parole hearing was slated for July 2022.]

SADAT X, hip-hop artist, detained 2006: I had a lot of visitors at the beginning. I had a girlfriend at the time, and she would come every week. I had a couple of other friends come. My moms came one time, but toward the end I told them to stop coming because it becomes such a process. And then you gotta get searched. And you know, like my moms is old, she didn't need to be coming to that.

LaSharn Harris often rode the bus to Rikers to visit her friend Dupree Harris before he was sent upstate. They later married.

LASHARN HARRIS: It wasn't until you got to the actual facility that you would find out whether the attire you were wearing was okay to wear into the facility. And if they said it wasn't, then you have nowhere else to go because there's no stores near there, so you would have to go all the way home and go back another day.

This is when I was at my wit's end. You would go in. The process is long. You would wait an hour, two hours, for them to process you. Then you get processed and then wait for another bus to take you to that section. It was a hot bus. They would assign you seats. Once the bus is full with the visitors going over to that section, you would go.

You still had to go inside, and there was another process after that. You still had to wait for the COs to open the door, and they were always rude. I always kept quiet. Sometimes, they would say to other people, "I don't know where you think you going; you can't wear that."

It was always changing, what you could and couldn't wear. I would try to remember what I wore before so I wouldn't have to go through that. One time I had my hair in a ponytail, and they told me I had to remove the rubber band. I couldn't understand why. You couldn't wear bobby pins. You needed a quarter for the locker. If you wanted to leave money for commissary, you had to stand and wait in another line.

SHANIEKA DESCARTES, mother of Devonte Hernandez: One night, I forgot 8:00 p.m. is the cutoff time, and they had just implemented that you couldn't have ripped jeans. I get there and they say you can't wear that no more. So, I had to run back to my car, wait for another bus. I grabbed some sweats and got back and I was one minute late and they would not let me into the building.

My son waited for me and waited for me. They had no sympathy. They said good night. Never mind how far I come, how long it takes you, they don't care. They have no compassion. I used to say be careful because one day it could be your loved one. Be careful how you treat and talk to people because you don't know who's who. They can't put everybody in one basket.

If a parent is being treated like that, imagine how the son is being treated. My husband couldn't go no more. He just couldn't bring himself to go. He said, "I can't do this." They are very disrespectful. There's a lack of respect for the family members.

DEVONTE HERNANDEZ: It kind of pissed me off because everybody knew her there and I never gave any guards trouble. So when that happened, it kind of got me mad because I was looking forward to seeing my family. But I took it as accept that, and it's a catalyst for growth, just to remind myself that I will never put myself back in this situation to experience that again.

YUSEF SALAAM, detained 1989 to 1994, Central Park 5 case: Visits were scary because on the visits people got assaulted. Sometimes people's family. To be labeled as rapists is one thing. But to be labeled as the Central Park rapists meant we already came in with high notoriety of being the scum of the earth. I really don't like to say this, but for lack of a better description, the only crime that trumps rape is child molestation, and inmates have their own way of dealing with that kind of atrocity. You go in knowing that they will try to stab you, kill you, make your life a living hell. And so if you ever get out of that, you end up wanting to kill your own self.

CELESTE RICCIARDI, detained 2009: Visits are the most horrifying experience. I went there to visit [my boyfriend] all the time. Just to go and have a one-hour visit with him would take me six to eight hours to get there and back. The entire day. It was fucking miserable. It's horrifying. I'm not kidding. There's a whole big bus ride to get out there. You sit and you wait forever. The second you get to the island, when you [are] first checked, it looks like Hitler loading up the Jews. People are shoveled into [buses] with no water and wheeled over to the jails.

LASHARN HARRIS: Before you get off the bus, they would bring in the dogs. They would put a number on the seat. Everybody would get off and have to wait for the dogs to come in and sniff the seats. A lot of times the dogs will then come and sniff you. You couldn't go in until that was done. If they found someone with something on them, you had to wait until they dealt with that person. It degrades people a whole lot.

SHANIEKA DESCARTES: We had an issue with the dogs. My daughter is allergic, and they would sniff her. I told them she was allergic, and they said, "If you don't like it, get off the island." They had no compassion. They were just too aggressive. Their faces were always screwed up. The thing is you have to support the families because that support is very important for them to reform. They have to know they have outside support.

JULIA SOLOMONS, social worker, Bronx Defenders: Dogs are always a very shocking thing. I remember being shocked by that even though I was told it would be there. When you drive there, you do not get sniffed by the dogs. But if you come on the public bus, you do, regardless of whether you have a secure pass or not, which I think is an interesting thing.

To me that seems like a very obvious sort of like class differential that is not actually based on your credentials, but on the mode of transportation through which you arrive at the jail.

LASHARN HARRIS: Then, in the facility, they search you again. Sometimes they would search women three at a time, and you have to remove your bra or lift your bra. I think that was the most degrading thing. I had already been searched three times. And it was just the way that they spoke to you. It was never anything inviting. It was do that, do this, talking to grown people as if they were children.

If you go through a metal detector and it rang, they would make you go through like a hundred times. Or if it rang, maybe on a button or something, you would have to convince them you don't know why it's ringing. It's always the fault of the visitor no matter what happens.

And then you go through all that and the visit is only one hour. Sometimes, I would have to wait for him to come down. They had to wear these jumpsuits. Since he was a large guy, they didn't always have one that fit him. So he would have to wait. I don't think they washed them. They just traded the jumpsuits.

I remember there was a person visiting and I believe she had a toddler still in diapers. The toddler kept crying. They came to remove her to check the child. In the past, I guess, someone had tried to smuggle drugs in their baby's clothes. I found that to be appalling. It was both things—that they would search a toddler and that someone would hide drugs in a baby's clothes.

DUPREE HARRIS, detained 1990s, first decade of the twenty-first century: I was coming from a visit [with LaSharn], and back then they would let some guys, like a favor, say, no, we're not stripping them. And I had this chip on my shoulder already. So, the officer that was in there, he was a Spanish dude. He let the Spanish dudes go, and when he come to me, now he's stopping me and telling me I gotta strip.

I'm saying, what's going on here? I felt like I was being profiled. I said I'm not doing that. I said you let a couple of these guys go without having to be subjected to that. He says, "You ain't going to go nowhere." So I said, "Yes I am." He said, "Nah, you not going nowhere." They beat the mess out of me. They beat me pretty bad, man.

It was in the back of the visiting area, where they strip-search you. Everybody's locked in a cage, and it's just you and a whole bunch of other officers. So they get in there, they stomp me, they beat me up pretty bad. Then they wanted to kick me out the jail after that. It was bad. They was favoring the Latin guys.

FITZGERALD DAVID, retired correction officer, 1987 to 2014: Listen, I've seen on videos where you have inmates in different jails on the visit floor, having sex with their visitor, their visitors are bringing in balls of drugs that they've secreted in their vaginas or their anuses. You also have mothers that bring up their children to see these inmates, and they secrete contraband, drugs, weapons, all types of stuff in the baby's diaper. How do you do that?

But then they want to say, oh, the Department of Correction searched me wrong? Are you serious? Just think about this: Imagine somebody in there facing major time and a gun gets actually secreted into the building due to us not searching. An inmate gets that gun and kills an inmate that was going to testify against him. Who's to blame for that? Correction officers, of course, because you didn't do your job.

You have a lot of these females, visitors that are straight lying. They come in, they get off the bus. There's an amnesty box right there. They tell you to drop all contraband in there. And it is what it is, that's your amnesty time.

ROBERT CRIPPS, retired warden, 1983 to 2013: What I initiated [in a jail he commanded] was if you test positive for drugs, then you are confined to a booth visit. And it was pretty good because most of the drugs were coming in through the visit. They would kiss, swallow a balloon, go back to the housing area, it would come out in their excrement. They would open it up and have the drugs or whatever. So it was working very well. And all the inmates that were high on drugs were in a booth visit, no more contact visits. It became very difficult to get drugs in there.

Everyone fought us on it, Board of Correction, prisoners' rights, and they ended up going to court, and the judge ruled that unless we physically catch them passing the drugs on the visit floor, we can't put them in a booth visit. And I was like, "Why not?" How could you run a facility where people are high on drugs and you can't impose any penalty other than you could put them in lockdown?

Every time you try and implement a policy, you had Board of Correction, prisoners' rights, sometimes the court. And the city never fought back against whatever policy they wanted to change. That was a prime example. I mean, how bad is it that the inmate doesn't have contact with a visitor but could still talk to them in a booth? Is that really that bad of a punishment?

MIK KINKEAD, lawyer, Legal Aid Society: My first legal visit, I remember I had to work with someone on a case and papers needed to be notarized. I had my notary stamp, and I remember having an argument with the guard at the front gate about whether or not I could bring in a notary stamp to my meeting with my client. And their thought process was that I couldn't because notaries are available in the law library. And I thought, this is rubber and plastic. I will be holding it. If you're letting them in the law library, you should let them into the visiting room. There's no reason not to do this. And the notary isn't always available. So this is better that my client has all the paperwork to finish today.

The legal purpose for which I was visiting couldn't be accomplished. And that's very individual. That's one CO making a decision that another CO would make completely differently. It's very hard to challenge these decisions, because the general point of view is that you don't contradict or embarrass your colleagues. So if one CO has said, a notary stamp isn't allowed in, even the supervisor will find it challenging to correct them.

JULIA SOLOMONS: All the counsel visit areas look different depending on the facilities. I remember that my first visit was at RNDC [Robert N. Davoren Center] with an older client of mine. Actually we saw two people that day. It was an older client and a younger client who were both being housed there. And the visit booths there had sort of like this mesh metal barrier between the attorney or the advocate and the client.

And it was very much like there's a barrier between us and them to the point where we really couldn't see facial expressions. I don't know if our client could see our facial expressions, and it was my first time meeting one of those clients. I felt so strange that even though we were in person, we still couldn't really see each other. It's not like that at every facility, some of the facilities you are in an open booth with a client.

SHANIEKA DESCARTES: On the searches, they would take you in the back and touch you up. They would check in between the bras. I just started wearing the same bras, the same pants, and the same shirt so I wouldn't have to go through that stuff. I had family members who would not go back.

DEVONTE HERNANDEZ: I got a lot of words of encouragement, *just keep going*. It gave me a tad bit more strength.

DORIS OSEI, Devonte Hernandez's grandmother: This was an experience we have never experienced in my family. I'm fifty-eight years old. I came to the country at age sixteen. I went to high school, college; I got married, had three kids. All my kids went to college.

I've been thirty-two years as a registered nurse in the Bronx. That's why Devonte surprised us so much.

The first time we spoke to him after his arrest was at Rikers. He was only sixteen at the time, but they would not let us see him at the precinct. We finally got to visit him at Rikers. It was the first time I had ever been there. I had no idea. I had never even thought of visiting a jail or anything.

It was an eye-opener for me. He didn't have any idea what he was getting himself into. When I saw the changes in him, I spoke to him about gangs. I let him know that people influence you, but you have to know we are your family. We will stand for you. No one else will do that for you. It's the saddest thing, what happened.

HECTOR "PASTOR BENNY" CUSTODIO, Latin King leader, detained 1991 to 1994: They would have people wait seven to eight hours. It was like a humiliation process. People would have to endure it. It's just so disgusting to see my mom and daughter and ex-wife come in and say they had been stripped of their clothing and had to show their bras. It was humiliating. They'd spend five to seven hours to get through the process to spend forty-five minutes to an hour to see us. That's what hurt me the most. I endured officers telling my wife, "He's never coming home." One officer gave his number to my wife, saying, "He's a loser, he's not coming home, why don't you get with me?" I was so angry.

LASHARN HARRIS: They don't see you as an individual. They put all African Americans in one box, and they view us all the same. They put all the prison population in one box. If people saw stories about Dupree, they would look at me the same way.

The thing is I raised a daughter who graduated from college by myself. I'm about to get my master's degree. They don't see that. They only see the negative. It's like we're convicted of a crime that we didn't commit. Not only is the person convicted doing the time, we're doing the same time. We're not behind the walls, but we get treated the same when we go for a visit.

HECTOR "PASTOR BENNY" CUSTODIO: Once my mom bought some underwear and soap and stuff. They had her go through the rigorous process. Once she got to the visiting room, they told her to get out. They scanned the money and found some kind of residue on it. They had her sit all that time, and just when I'm about to see her, they canceled the visit. She had come from the Bronx. She didn't speak English. She was a humble woman. To do that to her, I was so angry.

SPARKLE DANIEL, detained in early 2000s and currently in state prison: Before you go on a visit you get searched. You put on a jumper, go into a little room, and are sitting across from your family with a little barricade. They'd ask how I'm doing. I'd say I'm fine. I just didn't want to burden them.

JACQUELINE VELEZ, detained 1998: One of the jobs I had was cleaning after the visit. The floors, the tables, wipe everything down, put everything in order. I didn't want my family to come. I know what you go through. I didn't want them to go through that. And I also didn't want my daughter to see me in that jumpsuit. My daughter used to cry every day for me. She never was away from me that long. She knew I was in jail. So they were saying, you should let her come see you. And my family was trying to convince me to let her come see me. They said, maybe if she sees you, she'll see that you're okay, and be better. She was crying every day, sometimes multiple times a day.

So I agreed. They bring her. I could see while she was coming into that visit room they were checking her extra because she's a kid. I guess people have tried to smuggle, you know, whatever with a kid. But when she got past the magnetometer, she ran into my arms. I couldn't put her down. She didn't let me put her down. She didn't detach from me, stood in my lap, and she was just holding on and smelling, like her face was snuggled into my neck the whole visit. Visits on Rikers are only one hour. But the officer that I worked for that supervised me regularly was on the floor. When it was time to leave, and they say, all right, five minutes, my daughter started crying. All I could feel was wet tears on my neck and my chest.

She was not making it easy. I had to not cry. I had to not let her see me cry. When I looked at the officer—I don't know if something pulled on her heartstrings in my eyes—she was like, "You don't have to leave." She waved us off, don't worry about it. She let me have a three-hour visit. But I know I only got that because I worked for her. She knew I would bust my ass to clean that room. And she just gave me that little perk because of it.

RONNY DRAYTON, musician and father of Donovan Drayton: After Donovan got arrested, I remember we went up to "the Barge" [Vernon C. Bain Center] to go see him, and I remember just being highly anxious at that point. Scared, anxious, not really knowing what to do, really bad anxiety. I never had anxiety attacks, and I walk on stages all over the world and perform, but this really had me freaked out.

We get in and he's got the prison clothes on. He's got these long braids. He's looking at me, I'm looking at him, and he's scared to death, bro. He's like, "Dad, what the fuck?" I'm mad. I want to smack the shit outta him because he should've went to school that day. "I told you all the time, just go into school that day and you wouldn't have this problem." So we are talking to each other, and now I'm thinking to myself, how am I going to raise money to get a lawyer?

He's going like, "Dad, they got me in here for, for manslaughter. They're saying I was part of a murder plot to kill someone." He looks at me and says, "Dad, please don't give up on me." I turned around and said, "You're going to find out just what kind of a father I really am, Donovan."

DONOVAN DRAYTON, detained 2007 to 2012: It was scary when I got on the [barge]. What kept me afloat was just my hope, my faith to get back out. That's what kept me like just grounded. Just coming back to my fam and getting back to my dad, getting back to my loved ones, because you know when you're in such a dark environment around so much corrupt stuff going on, it's hard to stay positive. It's hard to stay light.

RONNY DRAYTON: The next thing I know Donny's like, "Dad, can you get me socks? Can you give me this? Can you send me commissary? Can you do this?" I said, "This is the fucking weirdest sleepaway camp I ever heard of in my life." This was not camp. We in jail now and it really didn't dawn on me how serious the jail shit was until I had to fucking go over to Rikers Island the first time.

At that time there was a van where this old Jamaican man used to cart people across. He's dead now. And I remember getting in the van and the guy said to me, "What's your name, sir?"

I said, "Ronny." He said, "Your son in here?" I said, "Yeah." "What's he in here for?" I said, "Why are you asking me these questions?" He says, "Don't worry about me asking questions. You're going to be asked a lot of questions, 'cause you got the murder look on your face." Whoa.

All of a sudden everybody's chiming in telling me about their cases, and these people never seen me from nowhere. I'm sitting there and then the first checkpoint, that little gate first, and then across that bridge, and I'm thinking of the movie *The Bridge on the River Kwai.*

DONOVAN DRAYTON: For the person coming to be seen, it ain't really that long for us, but for y'all to come and see us, it's superlong. They don't call the inmate down until you're actually down on the floor or you're about to come out. So they'll call us and like you've been waiting five hours.

The other side of the process is you come downstairs, you changed from your regular clothes, institutional clothes, gray jumper, and they seat you. They have assigned seating, and they direct you where to sit. Once you get down onto the visiting floor, you got an hour. If you're cool with some of the COs, they may give you a little extra time or whatever like that, give or take how they day is going.

I used to love visits, how you live vicariously? People that come to see you keeps you alive a little bit.

DEATH

"There Were Some Rosaries and Beads"

In the Grant Houses, on 125th Street and Amsterdam Avenue in Harlem, Ronald Spear, an itinerant actor and doting uncle with a mane of salt-and-pepper dreads, was picked up for trespassing in a Rite Aid. Spear became another number in the NYPD's low-level arrest campaign, a path that often led to Rikers.

Matthew Velez, a reed-thin seventeen-year-old, grew up a short city bus ride east in the Senator Robert F. Wagner Houses in East Harlem. Wagner's son, Mayor Robert F. Wagner Jr., had created in 1957 the first Board of Correction, a watchdog agency that was supposed to set standards of care in the jails and investigate any matter it wanted. The job was unpaid.

Velez found himself in the Rikers jail for teenagers after a police raid in a friend's apartment turned up a gun and some drugs.

Neither made it out of Rikers alive.

Both were beaten to death—Velez, by Bloods gang members in the Robert N. Davoren Center on January 31, 2000, in what was an atmosphere of correction officers letting gang members run the house and brutalize fellow detainees.

Three of Velez's attackers went to prison for short bids. Two rookie officers were disciplined, but no supervisors. In 2008, eighteen-year-old Christopher Robinson was murdered in RNDC under almost exactly the same circumstances.

Correction officials had learned nothing.

Spear, at fifty-two already afflicted with ill health, died from an extreme beating in the North Infirmary Command on December 19, 2012, by an unhinged guard, Brian Coll, as other guards looked on.

Coll struck Spear with blows so hard that the Legal Aid Society lawyer Jonathan Chasan later compared them to being hit in the chest over and over again with ninety-mile-per-hour major-league fastballs.

Jail officials tried to cover up the murder with a phony story that Spear had attacked guards first, even planting a cane as the supposed weapon at the scene. It would take three years and a federal investigation for that to finally be unmasked as a lie that was part of the cover-up.

Coll kept a framed *Village Voice* article about Spear's murder in his bedroom as a sick souvenir. He's now doing thirty years in federal prison.

—

NELLIE KELLY, sister of Ronald Spear: My brother's name was Ronald Spear, and people always talked about us like we were twins, because we were eleven months and eighteen days apart. And if you saw him, you saw me. We were always together. At the birth of all three of my little girls, my husband was on one side and he was on the other side. He was a brother and he was an uncle. All the neighborhood children called him Uncle Knowledge.

MICHAEL VELEZ, brother of Matthew Velez: Matt and I grew up at 124th and First Avenue. It still should be called the Wagner Houses, right by the Triborough Bridge. We were three years apart. My mom was a social worker. My dad was not working. Earlier he was in and out of prison. My brother and I just got up and went to school. We had pretty much whatever my mom could afford, which was enough. We played Nintendo. We played basketball for the YMCA. We played baseball together. Then we moved to the Bronx to a one-bedroom apartment.

Nellie Kelly, photographed at home in South Carolina, still hears her late brother Ronald Spear tell her to spice up the spaghetti sauce. Spear was murdered by a correction officer at Rikers in 2012.

NELLIE KELLY: We never referred to him as Ronald. We called him Knowledge, because they always said that between the two of us, we knew everything. So he knew 90 percent of everything. And I knew the other 10 percent. Before they had Google, if the kids were doing homework and didn't know the answer, we'd call Uncle Knowledge. And nine times out of ten, he would know the answer.

MICHAEL VELEZ: When Matt was about fifteen, he went this way with his own friends. As I got older, I started gravitating to my friends. It just so happened that his buddies were living a different lifestyle, selling drugs, and going out.

NELLIE KELLY: Knowledge raised three kids. Well, he didn't raise them to full grown, but my cousin, she got a little mixed up when she had her third child. And he went to that hospital and he picked that little baby girl up from the hospital and he brought her home and he raised her 'til she was five and her two brothers were about maybe seven or eight. That's when their mother was able to take them back. He got awards from the day-care center for "Best Mom."

MICHAEL VELEZ: Had I known what I know now, I would have been more on top of Matt. People are always quick to point out, "Oh, they're running with the wrong crowd." But to that person, those are his buddies. They're going out at night. They're dealing with whatever activities they're dealing with. They're just living a different lifestyle that just wasn't for me. I always saw it as, he'll learn one day, he'll learn one day, he'll learn one day.

NELLIE KELLY: My dad worked construction for fifty years. Ronald tried his hand at construction, but he was up so high, he was just like, "Oh, hey, no, I can't." He really dabbled in everything. He did some acting; he was on this show, *100 Centre Street*.

He tried his hand at elevator mechanics, because I was an elevator mechanic. He did that for a couple of years. He just dabbled in this and that. He started sending Bengay and Tylenol for arthritis over to a country in Africa. They thought he was a miracle worker because they never had Bengay before.

He was told not to go into Rite Aid because they said he was shoplifting. He went into a Rite Aid and it was like a trespassing. That was how he got picked up that last time and went to jail. He was really ill by that time. He was already on dialysis and had been in and out of the hospital for a while.

The last time I spoke to him he said that this Black guard told him to calm down and be quiet because they were out to get him. He said, "They want to kill me." And I said nobody's going to kill you in jail. But he told me he made a fuss about his treatment because when they gave him the dialysis, they were snatching the tube out and his blood was coming out, instead of capping it off. He was writing up complaints against doctors and guards and just making a ruckus.

And he had already put in a lawsuit. And so perhaps that's what he meant. That he was costing them and they would have to go before their bosses or whatever.

Whenever he had a problem, they would always just take him right to Bellevue, and he would get the treatment he needed. But this particular year, they had Hurricane Sandy, and Bellevue was flooded out. So they wasn't taking him to the hospital. He wasn't being able to get proper treatment. And he was fussing about his medication.

He was killed either on a Tuesday or Wednesday. I was putting up displays in the Walmart and I got the phone call.

I didn't know the number, but I answered, and he said, is that Ronald Spear's sister? I say yes. And he said, "I don't know how to tell you this, but they killed your brother." I said, "They *killed* him? Did they give him the wrong medicine?" He said, "No, they beat him to death."

And I screamed, "What? Who is you?" And he says that Knowledge had given him my number that morning because he thought they were going to take him to the hospital.

He said, "Your brother told me to call you to let you know they were taking him to the hospital, but he never got to go." And that was something he would do. He would always let you know.

The guy told me he was dead and that he was still lying there. This was like three o'clock in the afternoon. He was still just lying there. Not in a cell, but in a corridor.

I believed it because I didn't think the guy would call me like that. At the same time, I was like, could this be real? My father was down here with his brother [in South Carolina]. I went to their house and told my dad. My father's wife was still in New York, so we asked if somebody had called her. She said no, she hadn't heard nothing. It wasn't 'til about 7:30 that evening when someone knocked on her door in New York. And I never got a call from them after that. Never.

He was dead five o'clock that morning and I found out at about three in the afternoon because they kept the prisoners where they couldn't get to the phone. And he [Jesse James] was finally able to get to a phone.

Knowledge made sure that I knew exactly what happened to him. There was no doubt about what happened and how it happened or why it happened. He gave me everything I needed through Jesse.

So when we went downtown to DOC, it's two days after what happened, I told them the story that I had. And of course the lady said, "Well, I can't tell you exactly what happened, and I don't know what happened. All I can tell you is that you guys should speak to a lawyer."

Then an article came out in the paper that said Ronald was fighting with a correction officer and he had a cane and he tried to hit the CO with a cane. Then it said he had a heart attack and passed away. I was like, wow, that doesn't even sound close to what happened at all. And it was a small little article too.

I knew in detail what happened. Jesse gave me the names of the people who were involved, plus by him saying that they were out to get him, so that just kind of tied everything together for me.

The district attorney in the Bronx, Robert Johnson, didn't believe anything that we said. He didn't want to give us the information from the autopsy. We had to fight him on every level for that. He didn't want it to come out that it was a homicide. He tried the whole time to keep us from getting that information. But we got everything eventually.

He didn't want it to look like the officers were in the wrong. If we get the autopsy and it said it was a homicide and not a natural cause, we'd go further, which he didn't want us to do. Then they had this mock trial in the Bronx. And of course, they found no wrongdoing at all. None. Nothing.

[DA Johnson declined to charge Coll and the other officers, claiming he couldn't prove "criminal responsibility." The Justice Department then started its own investigation.]

And that is when the officer Coll decided that he was a big, bad man. He got away with murder. He decided since he was a murderer that he should get a teardrop tattoo on his face to show that he had taken a life, like they do in the gangs. Really he was in a gang, the gang of Blues. He mentioned it to his captain.

When the captain was on the stand in the later federal trial, he said he told Coll to get out his office, like, I don't want to hear no more stuff like this.

It was sad, of course, because it's the trial of my murdered brother, but awesome because of the way everything was unveiled. To just sit there and to see that blue wall come down.

When Knowledge was killed, lying there dead on the floor, they call in an investigator to write up a report. He was looking at Knowledge on the floor and writing up what he saw, and someone comes to him and hands him a cane. He says, "What I'm supposed to do with this?" And they said, "This is the cane that he had."

He said, "How do I know this is the cane he had? I can't put that in the report 'cause you handing it to me." Come to find out they had a write-up where whoever is in charge called down to the supply room and was like, send us a cane upstairs.

This came out in the trial. And it's so silly 'cause they had to sign for it, that they are releasing a cane from the supply room that morning. This is after the guy got there to write up the report!

It also came out how one of the officers who was there wasn't supposed to be in that area at that time. And after Knowledge was dead, he told them, "Listen, I'm not here."

But Jesse and them all saw him there. The captain took the reports and threw them away. They had to rewrite the reports until they sounded good to them.

I'm a person of faith. I just couldn't believe that Knowledge was going to let this go. I just kept the faith. I knew Knowledge was not going to rest because he would be tenacious in life. He would wear you down.

I just knew. So when the federal government contacted me through [the lawyer Jonathan] Abady, and they were like, "We're going to pursue every avenue." They uncovered stuff I didn't even know was covered. They had so many people by the cojones that they could do nothing but tell the truth.

When Knowledge died, I wanted the spirit world to be able to come back. I wanted that communication. It was in everything that I saw and touched. When I make spaghetti to this day, I say, "I'm not putting no peppers in it. So I don't care what you say," because Knowledge always wanted peppers in the spaghetti. And I say it out loud because I can feel him talking about "You're going to put peppers in it?" And I go, "No, I'm not going to put peppers in it." I can feel his spirit.

My father is eighty-seven. Until my brother died, my father had never had a loss in the family that close, never. We are the type of people who don't show our hurt. So I couldn't break down in front of him, 'cause I gotta be strong. He couldn't break down in front of me, 'cause he got be strong with me.

It ate at him. Sometimes I would look at him in the first two years, he'd be sitting and thinking, and then he would suddenly say, "They was just stomping him. How could they just stomp him?" And I said, "Daddy, it's going to be okay."

My father now, he doesn't know nothing. He doesn't know anybody. He doesn't remember that this happened. He doesn't feel that pain anymore.

Knowledge is in Neptune, New Jersey, at Mount Prospect Cemetery. They dressed him, anointed him, all the oils, wrapped him in white linen. He was beautiful.

—

MICHAEL VELEZ: Matt would call home from Rikers—my mom would talk to him—say that he needed some stuff. Then she got the call that there was an incident and he was in the hospital.

It was a Saturday. My dad, my mom, myself, and my girlfriend went down to Elmhurst Hospital. The doctors wouldn't let us in. They put us in this room to tell us he had passed away at some point while we were getting there.

I remember being in the prosecutor's office, and there were a bunch of investigators from the gang unit from Rikers. I don't re-member them saying that there should have been more security or the guards that were on duty failed to do their job. It was more like, "We rounded up a bunch of individuals."

I went ahead and identified my brother. My mom was too much of a wreck to do it. I was twenty-one at the time. They kept Matt in Elmhurst, so I went with my best friend. Elmhurst is a very eerie place. There were signs that told us which way to go. I remember a glass window. Someone came out, and I had to tell them who I was there to ID.

They came back with a photo and said, "Who's this?" I didn't even see the actual body. I was like, "Yeah, that's him." I just remember walking into what looked like a dungeon. It was dark and cold.

They made me sign the back of the photo, and they put my initials on it. I don't remember anyone talking to me and telling me what the next steps are or anything like that. It was a "we'll be in touch" kind of thing.

If someone dies under your watch, an adolescent, I would think that the city would have done everything in their power to make it seem that they care. And we never got that.

I don't remember anyone offering us counseling services. Or extending their hand. It's probably because they were at fault. It came out in the civil case that their guard purposely knew that these individuals were going to cause mayhem and didn't do anything about it.

What we were told is, one of the individuals involved in his death had had a run-in with him before. My brother went to the adolescent jail. When you get arrested, they ask you if you are affiliated with a gang. If you say no and you are, and they put you in the wrong house, you're in trouble.

They asked him his affiliation. He said he was affiliated with one gang. They put him in that house. So one kid goes up to my brother, pretends to be friendly, and wants to find out, "Are you affiliated with the gang?" My brother must've said yes. Whatever the language they throw at each other to self-identify that they're part of that specific gang. The guy goes back, tells the rest. The kid he had the previous run-in with didn't believe him. He said, "Let's see how much he knows." He made a comment that they were going to "make it hot."

That information was well known to the COs. They still allowed it to proceed. They lured my brother into the cell. They start asking him questions. He knew the answers to maybe seven or eight of them. And they still felt that they wanted to teach him a lesson. So they jumped him.

The guards weren't around the cell. The Bubble sees the cells. There's always one CO in the Bubble, the other COs supposed to be walking up and down. My brother screamed out. You could tell that there was a ruckus happening. Where was the other guard? I don't know. I just don't know. They turned a blind eye.

The guard involvement wasn't clear to me until I got my attorneys. Until then, all the conversations were geared toward the inmates had attacked Matt. It was never "Hey, we messed up."

My mom went from having motivation to having no motivation, always crying, always praying, constantly praying. It was her youngest child. Even after everything was done, I don't think she ever recuperated from that. She definitely wasn't working. She was just home.

She created a shrine to Matt. It had a lot of pictures, some candles, toys, letters he wrote, a lot of artwork that his friends had created in his memory. There were some rosaries and beads. It was her way of being able to stay connected to him.

Because I was working and going to school, I kind of was at the point where I couldn't continue to try to support her and my father and do my own stuff. It was hard for me to constantly see that. I was upset, upset at the people involved, upset at the city, upset at Matthew himself, upset at my folks, upset at myself.

This was very deliberate and very personal. So it was hard to justify it to myself—like could this have been prevented? Could I have done something? My father hardly ever showed emotion. My mom showed emotion everywhere, no matter who she met.

I remember being at the [criminal] trial and one of them basically trying to turn it around. Some of them turned or snitched. They said what happened. I think one pleaded guilty to moving

Matt's body. The two that were mainly involved in the attack pleaded not guilty, not knowing that the others had already kind of given them up.

When one of them was on the stand, I remember another one having an outburst about how you can't believe a snitch. My dad got up and had some words and had to be escorted out. And that was like the first time I saw my father with a reaction. Most of the time he held it in and consulted my mom. My dad said, "This is bullshit. You killed my son. This is BS. You killed my son. I don't have to listen to this."

I was like, you know what? Let him have this moment. He's upset. He's hurt. We all knew already that they had witnesses who were involved in the attack, who were going to tell them what really happened.

At the sentencing, one of them read a statement which showed no mercy, real BS. I found out later that he was hoping to get like a movie deal. That's ridiculous. He didn't show remorse for what happened. It was more of, he's only there because somebody snitched on him.

The people that are supposed to be there to protect him didn't do their job. So the city should've done more to say, outside the lawsuit, we want to make sure that this doesn't happen again.

My brother had friends that were locked up in different houses at the time of the assault. One of the investigators told me something happened to one of the individuals and that I needed to call off whoever I notified. I said I didn't talk to anybody.

I found it insulting. Call off what? I don't live that lifestyle. I always felt that the city was very insensitive. It's not like they couldn't reach out. My number in New York didn't change until the last day we moved out.

We prepped for the civil trial, we went to trial, and then on the third day or fourth day, when we called our witness to combat the city, the city came back with a third offer of a settlement.

It wasn't about money. It's about them owning up. Sitting in court in the civil case, having to rehash what we already knew from the criminal case . . . We had to call a witness for us who was part of the attack, which really pissed me off. He basically said the guards knew we were going to do this. To have to rehash these things daily and watch my parents, when they offered us that third settlement, I just wanted this to be over.

No amount of money was going to help bring Matt back. We don't know what would have been. We never had that chance. So there's no way of putting a dollar amount or value into what Matt's life would have been had this not happened. And I couldn't sit there watching my folks go through this daily, living the nightmare over and over again.

My mom, based on her downward spiral before we settled, got caught trying to sell pills or something like that—depression pills or something in the street. So she had to do like a week or something. I remember going to visit her.

I was really pissed at my mom because I was like, your husband's been in jail. Matt died in jail. And you're doing something stupid. Now you're in jail. So I'm the only one who hasn't seen jail or been arrested. I want to keep it that way. She was very apologetic.

With the settlement, my parents bought a house in Puerto Rico, where my father's side of the family lived. My mom gave me some money. I used it in Florida to buy property and get married, invested some money. They invested a lot of that money into this house. My mom started really on a worse downward spiral now she had all that money with drugs in Puerto Rico. She wasn't happy there. They just kind of blew their money.

I shouldn't be responsible for my parents' choices. But I probably should have pushed for different lifestyle changes for them. P.R. wasn't a good move for them. I wish they would have just moved to Florida with me and been somewhere where I could help make financial decisions.

My dad died in Puerto Rico in May 2009. My daughter was born in 2009 in June. After my father died, I brought my mom back from Puerto Rico. She lived in Miami until she passed away here in North Carolina from pancreatic cancer. She couldn't take the pain. We put her in hospice and she died two and a half weeks later.

She always, always, always talked about him until the day she passed away. Because of the nature of his death, she never found peace. I think that had my brother passed of being sick, cancer or something like that, she would have accepted it. In the case of what happened to Matt, it could have been prevented. I wouldn't be surprised if in her last breath she called my brother's name out.

I always think of my brother. It's a little bit of everything. What he could have been. The nature of how he died. The fact that the city was negligent in his death. I often wonder where the individuals who were involved are, and I include the COs. I always wonder what kind of lifestyle they're living.

My oldest daughter looks just like him. Spitting image. I often tell her that. "You're tall, you're lanky. You have his eyes." So I always see him, you know. But I have pictures and I show my girls, this is Uncle Matt. I have pictures of Matt. I have a picture in my wallet that I carry around with me. Every time I look at my daughter, I see him.

—

ALFONSO "JUDAH" WASHINGTON, detained 1999, 2002 to 2004, 2011: I was in pretrial hearings in November 2003. I went to court every day for six weeks, from September into November, and my grandmother is in the hospital. I called her every day to get a status update on her.

Her name was Pearl Washington. She was part owner [at one time] of St. Nick's Jazz Pub [in Harlem]. She first came to New York, she worked in a department store, and worked at the department store for many years. When she got laid off, she got angry and she said she would never work for them again. From that point on, she started her own businesses.

On that Wednesday [November 5, 2003], I called and I was told she had passed. When they told me she had passed, I was crushed. My mom, she called the jail to find out what was it gonna take to get me to the funeral. They told her whatever she needed. I spoke to her that Thursday. She took care of everything she had to take care of. She turned in everything she had to turn in Friday. Monday was the funeral. That Monday morning, I remember lying there. And I know when the funeral is. They had already taken care of everything they had to take care of with the jails. So the jails' job now was to just take me to the funeral or the funeral home.

I asked the correction officer, "What's happening? What time are they coming to pick me up?" The CO says she doesn't know. I have to go to social services and find out. She gives me a pass. I went to social services, and the officer working that day, he told me DOC dropped the ball. They didn't send anyone to pick me up. And then I went back to my cell. The only thing I could do is cry. You know, it changed me.

Just as I tell the story, I know I'm going to have to find a time to see someone to talk about it. I remained there in my cell, stayed there and cried and cried; then I got up. I looked in the mirror. I asked myself, what are you crying for? Crying is not going to change anything. It's not going to bring her back. I convinced myself that she wouldn't want me to cry. She wouldn't want me upset. She wouldn't want me angry. I washed my face. She passed just before my thirty-first birthday. The funeral was in Harlem at the Unity Funeral Chapels. She's buried in New Jersey.

[Jail officials sometimes let people behind bars attend funerals of immediate family members. There's a team that takes them to the service. But bureaucracy often gets in the way, and it is hard to coordinate the trip. Many get stuck on Rikers.]

HUMANITY

"When We Lose the Art of Being Human, We Stop Becoming"

Even in a place as depressing as Rikers Island, there are unforgettable moments of light, moments of generosity, and moments of caring that cut through the darkness and make a bad situation just a little bit better than it was before.

—

TOM OPPENHEIM, artistic director, Stella Adler Studio of Acting: There was one program called "Our Circle." And the audience was set in a circle. The piece started, and there was an initial giggling from the women at their friends who were acting, the way people giggle at each other and get sort of embarrassed. And then the women commanded the attention of the audience. They just took over. They had this deep belief in what they were doing. And so suddenly the giggles turned into sighs or sympathetic laughs.

LISETTE BAMENGA, detained 2016: I was on Rikers Island at that time. I had been there for two years. When I heard there's a theater program coming, not only was I thirsty for anything but so overjoyed that it was theater that was being brought. Up to that point

my humanity had completely been stripped from me. My feminin-
ity. It's a place where they tear you down. And so being able to be
in the class really brought life back into me.

TOM OPPENHEIM: There was one really dramatic moment where
Lisette occupied the center of the circle and refused to leave it,
and a CO stepped in. I can't remember the name of that CO. But
she was great. She was ordering her out of the circle, and that was
the tension. It was revolutionary. It was both parties taking off
their masks.

Then the piece ended and there was this thunderous response.
And our students came running down to greet the women. It was
art in jail at the most glorious. It was as though Dionysus just
ripped off this mask of separation for everybody in this space, and
everyone was together, and the barbed wire that you saw outside
the window disappeared, and everyone was free.

LISETTE BAMENGA: I always say, they gave me my voice back. I'm
not shy by nature, but I was kinda quiet and more reserved as a
protective mechanism. In jail you can't make yourself extra. I
made myself small. But when we were in the classes, my personality was able to shine again. I really was able to feel alive and feel
like there are people that don't know me yet love me. They showed
me that love and caring compassion without necessarily knowing
why I was there and how long I'm going to be there.

SUZY PETCHEAM, director of Outreach Field Programs: We did that
pilot program, and we had ten or twelve women participate that
very first time. Programs were really new then, because right before that everything was closed because people have been bringing
in contraband. So they had shut down the island community providers for a while. For the pilot program, the women didn't live
together, they weren't in the same housing, they weren't friends.
Then, all of a sudden, we're in this space together, and we're starting to train, to do intimate things, and to do embarrassing things
and vulnerable things.

Some came with a chip on their shoulders, and some came out of curiosity. That first program was just six weeks but we created a community and a little family, and I remember we had that first sharing. Some women struggled. Some were more nervous than others. But just watching the women support each other wholeheartedly—that's the power of theater. We wanted to shift the culture of Rikers Island.

Suzy Petcheam, an instructor with the Stella Adler Studio of Acting, runs an outreach program that goes into the jails.

JOANNE EDELMANN, Stella Adler instructor: I was originally told that I shouldn't bring in poetry because the women would not understand it. And, boy, was that wrong. Because these women taught me the meaning of the poems. Then I was told that I couldn't bring music again because that would entertain them. That they were not there to be entertained, they were there to be punished. So I said, "I can't teach without the music." It helped them to dig deep inside and move freely.

SUZY PETCHEAM: I worked in this one housing unit where I did the whole class between six inches of Plexiglas. There was no contact. You had to slip the paper between the cracks of the door. Like in the movies when you go in there, you put your hand against the Plexiglas. And that's how you greet somebody. And all you hear is screaming. It's not solitary. But it's for very high classification detainees. They are either very violent or have something in the news.

Even scarier is you see the cages outside, and they're smaller than dog cages. And you have to do the whole class screaming through the door because the detainee can't hear.

I remember we were performing one piece, this guy was writing a poem, and this other guy in the cell next to us, he was just watching us perform the thing. And it came out that he did graffiti. And so I just said, "Yeah, tell me, tell me about how you started doing graffiti." And while he was telling me the story, I just wrote the thing. I just wrote it down. And then I was like, "Congratulations, you have a monologue." And I had somebody perform it for him. He was like, "Oh, shoot. I can't believe I did that." And it was good! That's the magic that happens.

Is he going to take my class again? I don't know. Is he going to be an actor? I don't know. Is he going to be a writer? I don't know. But I know that I made him laugh that day. I made him smile that day.

LISETTE BAMENGA: There was a time when they wanted to provide us T-shirts. It was very important to us that they'd be hot pink, because there's nothing for us here to feel like we are girls. One of our performances, we wanted to wear skirts. So over our institutional uniform, we wore skirts with our hot-pink T-shirt. That was like the first time while I was there that I felt like a woman again.

JOANNE EDELMANN: As far as the skirts were concerned, I knew that we couldn't have costumes. The women had to keep their uniforms on. So we brought in the T-shirts; they allowed that. And then we brought in the skirts and they transformed. The warden at the time was in tears, because she said she didn't realize how beautiful these women were.

So as far as humanity, it did give someone the ability to not have to wear a uniform, which was originally made for men. No room for hips. No room for breasts. No color. I do also remember sneaking in lipstick. I just put it in the room where they were changing. The women came out with bright red lips, and the warden looked over at me with tears streaming down her face and just nodded.

LISETTE BAMENGA: They came to my trial. Every single day. I walked into that courtroom, I would turn around, and there was Tom and Joanne. That would really give me strength. Having performances and being able to speak in front of people. That gave me the courage to take the stand at my trial and tell my story. That was really big for me, because up to that point, for the four years that I was incarcerated, my story was being told by other people who had never even spoken to me. So I was like, "No, no, this is time for me to re-autobiograph and really speak from my truth."

LATANYA JONES, detained early 2000s: The first time I went to Rikers Island was in the early '80s. I was a kid, I was a young, young woman, like twenty-one or twenty-two. If the Stella Adler program had been there then, my whole life would have been different. But it wasn't. And I went through what I went through. And here I am now. It hasn't been easy, but I can second every emotion Lisette talked about.

Being in court and being able to look back and see someone from Stella Adler was huge. Being a human and being an artist are synonymous. I learned so much about being human and loving unconditionally and, as Lisette said, I come into this room and these people love me not knowing my crime. Not knowing how bad I feel about myself.

JOANNE EDELMANN: We didn't talk about what you were accused of, because that wasn't important to us. What was important to us was who's in front of us. Each week it was so hard to get in. I would have an iPod, a drum, and a speaker.

LISETTE BAMENGA: And cookies!

JOANNE EDELMANN: Oh my goodness, cookies! Lisette drove me crazy because she wanted a particular kind of cookie. I would go all over the neighborhood looking for Birthday Cake Oreos. I mean, who over the age of two really likes that?

LISETTE BAMENGA: People who are incarcerated. Something as simple as getting a cookie made me feel alive. They'd bring in a regular Oreo. You know there are other kinds! It never dawned on Joanne that they were a delicacy.

LATANYA JONES: I'm constantly emailing Tom, or texting him, about my neurosis, and he constantly reminds me that I'm creative or smart or resilient because I sometimes need that. Sometimes the folks that's closest to ya can't give it to ya. So sometimes it takes a person on the outside looking in to see that special that it takes to be able to survive and share it.

I went on to prison for five years. They still kept in touch with me. Joanne would send me beautiful poetry. And she would keep me abreast of activities that were going on in the center. And she would send me beautiful things by Sonia Sanchez.

HILTON WEBB, detained 1989 to 1991, 1996: I knew this one guy there. I'll never forget. He was from Barbados, older man. I was in my thirties. He had to be in his fifties, sixties, and we were talking one day. I says, "How did you get here?" He says, "Steering, mahn." I said, "Steering, what the hell is steering?"

And he said he was on his stoop in Brooklyn. A guy came up and says, "You got the crack, man?" He says, "Nah, man, we don't get that shit, that bullshit here. Hey, you want that shit? Go down to the corner. That's where they sell that shit." They arrested him for steering.

And a funny thing about this guy was that he was an ex-cop from Barbados. He did twenty years in Barbados and came to America to retire and be with his daughters and live in this house. So he'd go to court just about every two weeks. And they'd say,

"Time served, you can go home, just admit it." He says, "I do nothing. I admit to nothing."

He was on Rikers Island for almost two years before they just released him. They just dropped the case. 'Cause he wouldn't. He was never going to. He said, "Never, mahn. I never, I never say I did something I didn't do." And I never forgot his words. That's the way I lived for the rest of my bid.

He was a chill dude. He didn't bother nobody and all the officers respected him to cut hair. And he was one of the few guys that would cut your hair and wasn't going to charge you. Most of the guys, they wanted a pack under the table or two packs under the table to do some special cut. And he was a really good barber. So he cut dudes' hair, and he said, "No, mahn, I get paid already. I don't want your money." So everybody wanted him to cut their hair.

GARY HEYWARD, former correction officer and former detainee, 2000s: They made all kinds of dishes. I've seen inmate weddings, using ash for eyeliner, condoms for balloons, toilet tissue to decorate the place, Kool-Aid for hair dye. They buy a radio from commissary, take the speakers apart, and make funnels, and now you can hear the radio throughout the whole dorm.

REV. BERNARD SHEPHERD, senior case manager, Youth Justice Network, 2016 to present: I had a young woman who had her parental rights denied to her at the Rose M. Singer Center [Rosie's] when she was eighteen. She had been in the system since she was nine years of age and had been institutionalized by the totality of the system until she felt completely victimized and without hope for a better outcome for her life.

Trust was difficult for this young woman, but once an atmosphere of safety was established, she would open up about some of her experiences which served as a platform for her rage. She had anger management issues from a wide variety of abuses and shared that she was raped before she was thirteen several times. She was physically abused and, as she said it, thrown away by her mother, who had addiction issues. She was ostracized by her family and felt no true connection issues with her blood relatives.

Before her final incarceration, she became pregnant with twin girls. The twins were the only source of hope that this young woman had, and her world revolved around her daughters. I remember sitting in my office, which was next to a DOC counselor's office. The counselor was telling her about a court's determination that her parental rights had been revoked because she had been in jail too long.

I heard a bloodcurdling scream, the kind that made you cringe. It made me weep. It made my advocate weep, and it made the officer who was there weep. She was so broken that day. I've seen people lose family, I've seen people at their weakest moments, and this experience was a culmination of every hurting experience I had witnessed to that point. It was a resignation of the soul that left me emotionally empty.

For her, this was the only reason she was alive. She was trying hard to get out of jail because she wanted to be a mother for her twins. The kind of mother that she never had. She physically sunk and, through tear-filled and swollen eyes, asked, what am I going to do now? I want to die! In most people, I would have taken that as an idle threat. But coming from her in this unbearable moment, I didn't know. The advocate and I looked at each other. I said, "We're going to wait."

The officer said, "You don't have to stay here." But she was just standing there, violently shaking, refusing to move. She simply couldn't cooperate with what they wanted her to do. She was functionally and emotionally petrified. We silently stood there in the hall with her. That went on for the next two or three hours. We stayed there and let her hurt.

They took her babies because that is part and parcel of child welfare. The biological father gave up his parental rights, but she kept holding on. Hoping. Her cousin, a seemingly emotionally conscientious and responsible adult, was taking care of the children and got attached and did not want to give them up, because

she felt that their future would be bleak with her. Here she is hoping beyond hope to be a mom to them, and it seemed that everything had conspired against her.

She stood there shaking like a leaf in the wind. This woman had melted down and the heat from her melted me. The officer let us stay with her, but said, "I have to get her out of the hall." I think our silent presence convinced the officer to not have her forcibly removed. Later she moved to a bench in front of the office we worked from. We sat there with her. Finally, she said, "I can go to the cell now."

Later, we got to a point where I said if your cousin is going to take care of the children, look at this as being in their best interest. Are you ready to be a mother? With time she eventually understood that she needed to develop herself first.

When she was released from jail, she found a job working in the house's facilities established for homeless people diagnosed with COVID-19. For her, it was a place where she could get a job. She worked as a building facilitator, but it was high risk. The salary was $40,000, which in her mind was more than she could hope to make. She jumped at the chance.

The DOC has to be the penal entity, but when we lose the art of being human, we stop becoming more as a society. The justice—or the injustice system—is not designed to help heal or rehabilitate. It's designed to incarcerate. My job is not to decide who needs help. My job is to help heal the broken. Sometimes, it's just listening. Letting this person silently grieve.

DAVID ROTHENBERG, founder, Fortune Society: In the early days of Fortune, we had a program called Theater for the Forgotten. There was a seventeen-year-old named Stanley Eldridge who wrote poems. I met him in 1968. He was a runaway and he stole food. When he was a runaway, at eight years old, they would put him in the Rockland facility for the insane because they didn't know what else to do with him. He told me he used to hide in the library, and that's how he learned how to read and write.

I met him at Rikers at the Christmas Show, which is one of the

most depressing things I've seen because of the phoniness of it in that setting. He was unlearned, untutored, but he could write poetry. Later, he sent me thirty poems and we published them. The theater gave him a touch of humanity. He never returned to Rikers. He moved to the Caribbean, worked there, and then lived and worked in Jersey City. When he died, I read his poems at his funeral.

RACHEL OPPENHEIM, teacher at Rikers, 2005 to 2010: One of our students, a young woman, had been awaiting sentencing at Rikers for quite a while. She was accused of murder because that's usually the ones who were awaiting sentencing for that long. They had a rule at Rikers against having photographic evidence of yourself.

If you got letters or packages, the officers would go through them. She was in the punk rock scene, so when she was on the outside, she had multicolored hair and braids. She had friends who made a scrapbook for her and sent it to her inside to cheer her up.

She came into class one day really excited to have gotten this gift from her friends and wanted to show it to me and my co-teacher. When she brought it over to us and had us look through it, she was talking through the people in the pictures. Her face was sharpied out in every picture. I don't know if they had made her do that or if they had done that before it came to her. It just really struck me the ways that people's identities are erased in that institution. She was now just in this really drab clothing. No makeup, hair back. She couldn't express herself the way that she did on the outside physically.

She had this evidence of her life, but even there, her face was blacked out. She was going by a number. And yet she was really excited to get this gift and show it to us because it was this relic or remnant of her previous life.

One of the classes that I taught was a math class. We were talking to a couple of the administrators about classes we were going to offer.

One of them said, basically, women are bad at math. "They're

not 'calculating females' over there." And then the other administrator said, "Well, they're calculating in other ways." There was a real narrative that these women will manipulate you. They're manipulative, which again, I think might be a way that people describe women inmates differently than men.

That very week, I had been in a math class with women who had really terrible educational histories, really subpar school-to-prison pipeline. One woman was really struggling, and she said, "I quit. I'm not doing this. I'm bad at math." But there were all these women gathering around her to say you can do this. They really supported and talked her through it. When there was another problem posed, she raised her hand and said, "I'll come, I'll do it." And did it.

So it was so striking to me that within a week this woman had, with the support of her fellow incarcerated women, gotten through a tough math problem. She had *calculated,* despite these administrators stereotyping them all as either bad at math or manipulative.

CAMILLA BRODERICK, former detainee, 2016: I was twenty-six when I went in in 2016. I had been a heroin addict for a while. I lived in Manhattan, and I was arrested for grand larceny and sale of a controlled substance. I was there eight months, a city year, in RMSC [Rose M. Singer Center]. I had been chosen to represent the women at Rosie's in a debate against the men on the Samantha Bee show *Full Frontal.* The debate was about Trump's immigration ban. It was decided by a coin flip, and I got the no-ban side, which was the only reasonable side. I had prepared both sides. They wouldn't let me speak to my partner. I called my parents a lot. They looked up stuff. I spent the whole fifteen minutes I had on the phone asking my parents to look up statistics. The lead debater on the men's side had been winning. But he wasn't prepared and he just flopped.

My dad sent me an outfit, and even after all the approvals they said, you can't wear that, and then gave me crap from the lost and found. I told them, "These clothes don't fit me. I'm going to be on national TV." So, we have to go to the men's facility. We're in intake in the men's facility. The men's intake is so much cleaner. The men are screaming and catcalling at us. Then we get to the big auditorium room and Samantha Bee is there, and I got her to sign something with a jail pencil.

It's really nerve-racking and we sit at the tables and we do the coin toss; we get the good side. I have read my speech over and over and over. I memorized a six-minute speech. The crowd is into it and it's going well. It's over; we get a little interview. I'm telling jokes and she's laughing, and that was awesome. And then we had to go back. When we got back, it was late and we had missed medication and we were trying to get an officer to open the medication window and they were like, "Why should we?" But I was very hyped. I don't think I slept that night.

EDDIE ROSARIO, detained 1990: My first time at Rikers was early 1990. I copped out to six months plus five years' probation. Within fourteen days, I was rearrested. It was all about drugs for me. Their initial proposal for a plea to me was like fifteen years to life. They are throwing crazy numbers at me. I was like, who did I kill? Did I kill the president? I have a warped sense of humor, so I laughed. Fifteen years? I was cracking up.

There was an older Black guy; they called him Pops. This guy was a bunk away. He said, this is not a joke. They are going to put you away.

I said, "I'm a junkie." He goes, "You know the law library? You better go." I went. He happened to be working there. He had done significant time upstate. He knew the system. He saw that I had some smarts. He agreed to help me. He showed me where to look. He said, "This is your case." It was through his help I found out about a law that didn't allow uniformed officers to do drug busts in certain areas. He said, "I think you found something here, kid." I was able to get one charge thrown out.

RACHEL OPPENHEIM: It was Valentine's Day and the second-to-last day of class. The students came in clearly giddy about the fact that it was Valentine's Day. Some of them already had cards, some of them were making cards, and some of them had makeup on. The makeup at Rosie's wasn't actually makeup. It'd be like pens or Wite-Out or things that were maybe supposed to be food or something. But they had fashioned makeup in some way.

One student who normally wore gray sweatpants and an oversize white T-shirt had her hair up in a neat ponytail, and there were a few tiny artificial flowers and a small pink bow at the base of the ponytail. She wore a pair of jeans that looked new, with rhinestones on the back pocket flaps. I had never seen her wear makeup, but she had pink gloss on her lips and she had fashioned shadow and mascara for her eyes.

She had made a card that she said took her three days to make. She used a file folder to simulate the thickness of a real card and drew a pink and red heart on the front using colored pencils and had decorated the heart with rhinestones. She had used toothpaste to glue it together.

I think that's just interesting that it was a special day that people were really excited about and people had partners in our classes. But they just had to cobble together things to make it special, whether it be their own appearance or the cards that they were making or the sort of gifts that they were bringing.

Whatever we had planned for class that day fell on the back burner, which kind of speaks to the purpose of our classes. For some, it was, I want an education. And for some, it was like, I just need to get out of my hot, stinky living space.

Especially on that day, it demonstrated how much love and camaraderie and kinship there was. Rikers, Rosie's jail, prison, is often described as cutthroat and every man for himself. It has to be sometimes, and it is sometimes, but I saw people making connections, friendships. Love.

"If This Comes to Rikers, We're All Screwed"

In March 2020, Kevin del Rosario, a thirty-year-old Bronx man, was one of just under five thousand detainees on Rikers Island and in the city's other borough jails when the first signs of the looming pandemic began to mushroom throughout the city. As the DOC dithered, the virus spread into the confined spaces of the jails. A certain desperation enveloped the system. The jailed sleeping head to toe, three feet apart. Detainees paid as little as $1 an hour to disinfect toilets and sinks. All visits and programs were cut off. It was a crisis like no other experienced in the city jails.

An anguished rush by defendants, aided by a retinue of public defenders, to get out of the system. At its peak, more than fourteen hundred correction officers were out sick with the virus, with at least nine dying. Del Rosario and two other of the jailed never made it out. Another three died within days of their release and never left the hospital.

—

DIMITRI ANTONOV, detained 2020: We heard about it from a broadcast on TV. I'm like, this is nonsense. I mean, swine flu and all this stuff. Number one, this is not even going to come to New York. Number two, even if it does, this is just like another [period of] hysteria by the media. I was wrong. Finally, I was like, okay, there are cases in New York, and if this comes to Rikers, we're all screwed. That's why we were all kinds of paranoid. But I'm like, it's not actually going to come to Rikers. I thought it was just very isolated cases and it'll just kinda swing right through. Right before that, when we were trying to find out that it's there, we noticed that pages were being lifted from the newspaper that talked about anything related to COVID-19 in Rikers. Like that's when it really hit us.

TAHANEE DUNN, lawyer, Bronx Defenders: The last in-person Board of Correction hearing, I believe it was in March 2020. And at that point in time, there was already confirmation that there were COVID cases in New York City. I think one of the first cases that we were able to find out about was actually an attorney from Westchester who had a couple of cases in the Bronx, in the Hall of Justice. There was inevitably going to be cases of our clients in the courthouse, which inevitably meant there were going to be cases at Rikers.

I don't think that we knew on what scale, but I remember us reaching out to the Department of Correction. The DOC just kept ignoring us. And so then the Board of Correction brought it up at their monthly hearing, and the Department of Correction had nothing. They had absolutely no idea what they were going to do. There was also a possibility that there were already active cases at least among the correction officers, but at that point in time testing wasn't widespread enough.

ANNALIZA DEL ROSARIO, mother of Kevin del Rosario: I tried to visit him whenever I could. Until visiting was stopped. And then I was already warning him to keep his hands clean and stay away from people because the pandemic was here. He'd call often. Sometimes even twice a day.

He'd update me. They weren't given masks. No hand sanitizer.

Soap was hard to come by. He described the condition where he was staying. I don't know how exact this is, but he was probably two or three feet away from the next guy in the dorm.

VERONICA DEL ROSARIO, sister of Kevin del Rosario: I think it's worth noting Kevin was only thirty years old and he had Asperger's syndrome. So it was definitely a different experience for him than I think it was for a lot of other people in both getting sick and being in Rikers in general. He had a really different way of perceiving the world and understanding what was happening around him. Socially, it's a scary thought to imagine him there. He didn't really know what he was doing when it came to socializing. So the idea of rubbing someone the wrong way was likely.

With some of that context, he was just a really simple person. He loved anime and comic books and Transformers. And he was very childlike in a lot of ways.

He wrote poetry while he was in there. He loved art and fashioned himself a bit of an artist. He loved food. He loved matcha and bubble tea and ramen and all kinds of food. He lost a lot of weight while he was in. He and my mom were really, really close. She took care of him her whole life.

ANNALIZA DEL ROSARIO: He was starting to get familiar with the place.

VERONICA DEL ROSARIO: He liked routine. So once he started to get used to it, he was getting nervous about having to do it all again, when he'd go upstate.

ANNALIZA DEL ROSARIO: When the visiting was suspended, we heard that they were letting people out. So I called his lawyer and that didn't work. We were told he's not going to be released.

VERONICA DEL ROSARIO: He was really high risk for COVID for a multitude of reasons. He was asthmatic, and he was obese, and he had sleep apnea. So he had a CPAP machine, which was taken away because doctors said it could easily transmit the virus to other detainees in the dorm.

ANNALIZA DEL ROSARIO: Even before they took that away, he told me that he had a fever and that he was sweating a lot and had to change the bedsheets, and that hadn't happened when he got sick at home. He told me that he was tested and that it came back negative. But then his asthma was getting worse. And then the fever was back. He was put in a sick dorm where there were less people but they still shared a dorm. I think there were ten other people there. When he was there, he said he had to clean the bathroom.

Then he was asking for a nebulizer. He wasn't given one. They were just giving him Tylenol. He had his inhaler with him, but he said, "It's so bad. It's not working." I was telling him, "Have you seen the doctor?" And he said, "The nurse came by, and they could only give me Tylenol."

VERONICA DEL ROSARIO: It turned out that that nurse was actually a med tech. Not even a nurse.

ANNALIZA DEL ROSARIO: I said, "Look, you need to demand to see a doctor and say you can't breathe." And that's what he did. That's when the doctors saw him, hours after. This was days after he was in the sick dorm. The doctor said he didn't look good and needed to go to Bellevue.

He called me a couple of times when he was there. Then I got a call from the doctors there saying he needed more and more oxygen and needed to be taken to the ICU.

VERONICA DEL ROSARIO: He was put on a vent. And my mom would FaceTime every day, and there was still a guard just outside the room, as if he was going to go anywhere.

ANNALIZA DEL ROSARIO: I was able to see him twice as a compassionate visit. Both times they told me they would try and wake him up a little bit. They had tried before that, before I came, and he was very, very agitated. So they wanted me there when they tried again so I could calm him down. I ran there; it was my chance to see him and comfort him whether he's conscious or not. Just make him feel that he's not alone. Because Kevin doesn't like the unknown.

Before they intubated him, he said, "Mom, they're going to put me to sleep." And I said, "Yes, they will. And it'll make you feel better. And when you wake up, I'll be there."

VERONICA DEL ROSARIO: When she visited, he seemed confused and in pain. He was looking at her, making eye contact and pointing at the intubation, kind of squirming. Our last experience with him is knowing that he felt scared and alone and confused.

ANNALIZA DEL ROSARIO: I was just trying to reassure him as best I could. But I couldn't give him any comfort.

VERONICA DEL ROSARIO: Because she went in to see him a couple of times, she was exposed. And so when he passed, none of us were able to see her, and she was completely alone for two weeks. And there was this really painful part of the whole process where he actually started to get better over the weekend prior to his passing. He was starting to breathe on his own. And it was just such a relief. But then he got sepsis, actually. And that kind of did it. He was there for about three weeks.

Earlier in his stay at the hospital, she was petitioning for him to be released to her after he got released from the hospital. And the court was putting it off and putting it off. They said he's not going anywhere anyway. Finally, they set a date for April 23. They were going to vacate his sentence. And then he passed April 23 at three in the morning, just hours before they were going to vacate his sentence.

ANNALIZA DEL ROSARIO: I don't understand. First they weren't going to release him, and then they were going to vacate his sentence. There was just no care provided when he was at Rikers before he went to Bellevue.

VERONICA DEL ROSARIO: He knew he was high risk. He did not socialize. He kept largely to himself and played video games. That was pretty much his life. He would have never gotten COVID if he was at home.

ANNALIZA DEL ROSARIO: He had a lot of living to do. Socially he was way behind.

VERONICA DEL ROSARIO: My mom was hopeful. It was a minimal sentence. Once this was through, he could start his life fresh. He was such a late bloomer. He died and it was so avoidable. There wasn't a funeral. It was quite brutal. My mom was asked to identify the body in a picture. Imagine receiving that picture in an email. There was no closure for anybody.

ANNALIZA DEL ROSARIO: You know how they say a loved one passed and he was surrounded with family. It was exactly the opposite for Kevin. He was completely alone and came back to us in a box.

DANIEL RICE, detained in 2021 and currently in state prison: It was like, if we catch it, we are dying. When it finally got here, it was like, whoa. It was devastating. There's nothing we could do physically inside the jail. We never expected it to come inside. It just started spreading all over. We are in a dormitory. We had like forty-three people in here. It went all the way down. A lot of people went home. A lot of people got isolated. They tested and found out everybody had it. A lot of people were scared. Dudes that didn't have it were worried. Even the nurses were coughing. They said, don't worry, it's a regular cold.

TAHANEE DUNN: The correction officers were dropping like flies. And I think at one point in time, they had like three thousand or four thousand correction officers sick. So correctional officers were working three shifts at a time and falling asleep on the job. And it was just chaos, and people were calling our phones, crying, freaking out. All of a sudden they were getting locked in general population, and the dorms were going under quarantine. Nobody knew what that meant. It was just sheer fear and confusion.

DIMITRI ANTONOV: We'd always get the newspaper. And we'd go up to the CO, and we were like, "Hey, what just happened to this page? Why are you cutting the pages out?" That was actually a real thing that was going on. They would just take out pages and not let anybody know that COVID-19 was in Rikers. There were several officers who died from it, and that's when people really started freaking out. Like, remember that guy who was in intake? He's dead.

DANIEL RICE: I got brought to Bellevue to be isolated for two weeks. I stayed for thirteen days. They never tested me again. They said I shouldn't have it no more and shouldn't be able to spread it. That's a lie. We have to beg someone to get hand sanitizer. They are not allowed to give us that, they said. There's nothing to clean the phones or toilets.

TAHANEE DUNN: Something like 88 percent of the housing areas in all the facilities were under quarantine rules or quarantine protocols. But they didn't have access to hand sanitizer. It was still considered contraband. They didn't have access to showers on a regular basis. They were staggering showers. And some people would get showers every other day, because they didn't want to have too many people in the shower area at the same time. They didn't have enough cleaning supplies and weren't allowing for people to access cleaning supplies on their own. So they were rationing that out. In some dorms in like AMKC [Anna M. Kross Center] and OBCC [Otis Bantum Correctional Center], I heard that the CO would just put one or two massive buckets in the middle of the common area with a rag and a little thing of bleach. And that was all they had for twenty-four to forty-eight hours.

They were responsible themselves for cleaning everything. The same thing with the food, in terms of handing it out, they were responsible for trying to figure that out. So it was chaotic.

DAVID CAMPBELL, detained 2019 to 2020: The COs were just like, we don't care. We're not wearing masks. We're not doing what the department was telling us. We're not checking temperatures. Just like, "Stay away. Sleep head to toe." So you got like one guy's head out in the aisle. That was me for a while. I was like, "Oh, this is great." But everybody walking past me was breathing on my fucking head. And they put posters up and to stay six feet away, whatever. But it's just nothing. You can't, it's impossible. Even if I could stay six feet, how vast and prolonged a game of human *Tetris* it would be to stay six feet away from another human being at all times in a dorm with fifty people.

DIMITRI ANTONOV: That's the thing we always kinda laughed about: where's the social distancing? And still we didn't even get masks or anything. That was February all the way up to March. We got masks late in March. I can understand why people were so frustrated and why it caused altercations because if anybody did have COVID, it's like, well, what are we gonna do?

JULIA SOLOMONS, social worker, Bronx Defenders: Early on in the pandemic, the Department of Correction stated that they had hundreds of thousands of masks that they were making available for staff and for clients. I believe it was like 200,095 that were reserved for higher levels of need for protection. And then they had the surgical masks as well. And we had clients reporting that they were never given masks for a while.

DIMITRI ANTONOV: It was not until the spring that we finally got masks, which is crazy.

JULIA SOLOMONS: Maybe two months or so into the pandemic, finally people started having masks, but even then they were wearing the same dirty mask for weeks. They maybe got a new one after a month or two, like it wasn't regular provision of PPE in the way that DOC was purporting that it was.

LEVI MITCHELL, detained 2020: When I got there in May, it was like twenty-five people to the unit. We had a little space. Everybody was about six feet apart. And it wasn't that bad because most of the people wear masks and try to sanitize and keep distance. Now we got thirty-two people in that house. We got people sleeping less than two feet apart. We got people not wearing masks. We got COs that come in and don't wear no mask—the majority of those.

DIMITRI ANTONOV: I was in AMKC. They evacuated everyone. We were the only ones left. People were freaking out. Anytime there was a new person coming in, basically they would yell at the COs not to open the gate for a new person, especially if they were just coming from the street.

DAVID CAMPBELL: Even if you told the COs that if they let COVID run rampant in here again, they could get it and bring it home to their kids . . . like, even with that, with a personal threat involved, they were pretty uninterested in taking care of us.

DIMITRI ANTONOV: Inmates were just like, no, he's not coming in. He's not coming in. That level of paranoia. Especially if somebody came from the hospital, as soon as somebody found out about it, they would flip out. They would say, if he doesn't leave, we're going to beat him up. That's the main thing that was going on during that time, a paranoia of just letting a new person into the house. That this could be somebody who's going to expose you to the virus.

MATT FREY, clinician, 2011 to 2018: They don't have a whole apartment or a house to roam around. It's a living area of thirty other people that are in different types of mental states, different types of stresses. Some of them are not on medications, and they're very violent. It's a very scary place to be. Someone could be in for trespassing and sleeping next to someone who is in for a double homicide. It just doesn't make a whole lot of sense.

DIMITRI ANTONOV: With COVID, it got really ugly. If you had even a suspicion that a newcomer might have it, number one, they would tell him, don't come anywhere toward the back of the room. Always stay in the front, to kind of isolate him. The back of the room was for older members. The first part of the room, when you were just coming in, they would just stick you there.

LEVI MITCHELL: And now they say, "Listen, the virus is down. We only at 3 percent. We're good." They want to put other people in the house. Guys be fighting with each other because they don't want to keep them sleeping on top of each other. We had a fight one morning. A guy said someone sneezed on him. He asked the guy to cover his mouth. It's bad. We all go in a small room to eat. And the food stays out in the open. It's really rough. You have to protect yourself.

DIMITRI ANTONOV: I remember this Asian kid came in from the streets. This other guy is like, well, he's not staying here. I'll let you sleep here one night, but you're not staying here. So on the second day, he's like, "Why the hell is this guy not out of here?" So the Asian kid is lying in bed and the guy comes up on him, slaps him across the face, and pushes him off the bed, like, get the fuck out, I told you already to get the fuck out. The joke is, this guy never even had it.

LEVI MITCHELL: A lot of these guys are going home soon. In a month. Just a [parole] violation of their cases. Some brothers in here don't take any hygiene or pay attention what's going on. Some live day to day. You just try to stay out of their way. Fights break out all the time.

DIMITRI ANTONOV: I definitely saw people get sick, and they would just disappear. I think I may have actually gotten sick myself, but I don't know if that's what it was or if it was another bug because I definitely got sick for about a week while I was there. And I was very scared and I still don't know. That's a problem. When I came in there, there were actual tests, but they wouldn't give me a test.

They said, "Well, unfortunately, we don't really have testing available like that." So I said, "What can you do?" Well, here's some aspirin. I didn't have a running fever, so I didn't go to the hospital, which was good because it might have been minor, and I think I could have gone to the hospital and ended up catching the real thing. So to this day, I don't know.

JULIA SOLOMONS: There's been this very stark contrast between the policy you hear the Department of Correction speak about publicly at Board of Correction meetings, or on their website, and the reality. So drastically different from the reports that we hear from our clients.

There's this clear disconnect between the policies that are supposedly being implemented and the actual practices that are happening in real time.

DANIEL RICE: I'm in a wheelchair. My family is worried. We can't see each other. They have video visits. But my people can't even see me. The handicap video room they said was broken. They put me in a booth visit room, and the screen was up high. My people couldn't see me. They couldn't hear me, because I was next to five other people. The commissary, they bring it to you.

But there's no water. I don't like drinking water out of the faucet, especially from Rikers Island. It used to be a landfill. There's mold, ants, and spiders all over the place. It's unsanitary. The ventilation system is disgusting. You see black stuff everywhere. You have water leaking from the heating pipes. Every day I wake up my nose is dry. There's worms in the shower.

JULIA SOLOMONS: And the Board of Correction actually did an investigation. I think their report came out in early May. They reported that a percentage of people were not wearing masks correctly, both staff and people in custody.

TAHANEE DUNN: I had a client who was actually at MDC [the Tombs] initially. He said that there were a few people on his tier that were sick and they were taken out and a correction officer joked about the fact that it was super contagious and it'll probably kill all of them. And they had heard some other information about the fact that if you say that you have symptoms, they would take you and put you in a single-cell setting where you still had access to the dayroom and stuff, but it was quiet and there were not that many people around.

So he thought, okay, cool. I'll just say that I have symptoms and ended up getting transferred to EMTC [Eric M. Taylor Center] when EMTC had just been reopened for symptomatic and COVID-positive folks. This was in the last two weeks in April 2020.

He called me from EMTC hysterical, saying we don't have any running water here. There are people lying on the floor. There are mice and rats everywhere because they just opened it up and packed everybody in there. And EMTC had been closed for a little over a year at that point in time. There was no heat or hot water. They were not getting food in time. They were not in single cells. It was a dorm situation, but the really, really, really sick were going into cells by choice or other inmates were putting them into cells themselves to isolate them. He was just hysterical.

He was there for about ten days, and every single day he called me hysterical. "Please get me out of here. I'm going to die in here. We're all going to die in here. The correctional officers won't even come in to give us our food, because they're scared that they're going to get COVID from us. CHS [Correctional Health Services] is overwhelmed. They won't come in to give us any treatment. I have a headache. I know I shouldn't have lied and said that I had

COVID or the symptoms, but I didn't know what else to do." It was just awful.

DIMITRI ANTONOV: They kept everything under wraps. They did not want that information out. They realized they can't really censor because we still had the TV. We found out that there was COs who actually did die, but we don't know how many people who died were actually in jail.

LEVI MITCHELL: Anytime we speak about it, they either try to move you to another housing unit or they come through and search the house [to] toss your stuff. So we've been calling 311. The complaint line.

DANIEL RICE: They are trying to put more people in here. They should let more people go home, especially pretrial. I sleep two feet away. The beds are so close. That's why we are trying to keep people out of here. They snuck someone in here while we were sleeping. There's no way to practice social distancing. You can't even get gloves.

JACOBSON

"Nice Jewish Boy Winds Up Correction Commissioner"

When Michael Jacobson took over the Correction Department in 1995, the jail system was plagued by overcrowding, poor conditions, and extreme violence. He persuaded the mayor, Rudy Giuliani, to support additional educational and job training programs and counseling as cost-cutting measures to reduce violence and boost morale.

—

MICHAEL JACOBSON, correction commissioner, 1995 to 1997: The way I wound up there was, I'd been at the budget office a while. [The former mayor David] Dinkins appointed me the probation commissioner. It's probably '92. Then Rudy wins and takes office in '94. So I had always wanted to run an agency, and I loved probation.

I just assumed I was done. With a new mayor, that's how it works. But a number of people I knew pretty well got jobs inside Rudyland. I'm sure at some level they advocated for me. It probably took the mayor a year to even realize probation was a city agency. It's not like people were knocking down his door.

Michael Jacobson served as correction commissioner from 1995 to 1997 during the Giuliani administration.

For whatever reason I was just kept on. I was never quite trusted by the Rudy loyalists, because, to them, I was a Dinkins guy. So I was just doing probation, and then at some point Peter Powers, my boss, called me and said they were replacing Tony Schembri. He was the first correction commissioner for Rudy. He was an investigator at the Brooklyn DA's office. He was the chief of the Rye Police Department [in Westchester County]. Do you remember a show called *The Commish*? It was based on Tony. It was pretty popular. The chief of a small Westchester police department. He was a funny guy.

The tabloids went after him all the time, because he'd leave early, never moved from Westchester. He'd have lights and sirens going back home at four in the afternoon so he could get a haircut. It was all insane.

So Rudy fired him and Peter called me and said, "We're replacing Tony tomorrow; we are making you the acting correction commissioner." I just remember saying, "But I really don't want to be the acting correction commissioner." I think his reply was pretty funny: "I don't remember that being a question." Okay, got it.

So literally the next day I was in city hall, and they were making two announcements. Me as the acting commissioner and Bernie Kerik as the first deputy. I'm sure there were discussions in city hall about just making Bernie the commissioner then, 'cause he was Rudy's driver and he was at DOC; I think he was head of investigations. I'm sure Rudy had people saying just make Bernie the commissioner.

But he was a street cop just a few months earlier, and I'd bet Rudy was advised against it. So I met Bernie right there and then. I spent most of my time on the budget at DOC, which was just a constant battle. The budget was going way up. I was pretty involved in the life of DOC as a budget person. So I knew a lot of the folks. Had a PhD in criminology. I knew that place pretty well, probably as well as you can know it from not being in it.

I said to the chief, Eric Taylor at the time, I should go to city hall and gather everyone together. I don't know how long the acting thing is going to last. I'm not going to act like an "acting." I'm going to make decisions until someone tells me not to. Fine.

So we went to Rikers, the chiefs, deputy chiefs, the wardens. A couple of hundred people. No one said anything when I walked in. Everybody stood up, all at once.

I asked the chief if they were going to sit down. He said, "Well, when you tell them to sit down." I said, "So if I don't tell them to sit down, they're not gonna sit down?" He said no. I said, "What if I say hop on one foot? Will they be hopping?"

So I knew it pretty well but not that well. It's a top-down paramilitary place. I knew the issues. I talked to Rudy before the press conference. Basically his line was, violence in the place was overwhelming and it was out of control. Either the same day or week I was appointed, the cover of *New York* magazine was "Is Rikers About to Explode?"

And I remember that because after it happened, I called my mother, and she said, "Are you out of your mind?" I said, "Well, you know, I saw [the article]." It was just a funny thing. Nice Jewish boy winds up correction commissioner. Rudy said get control of this or you're fired. Fair enough.

And that was, for at least a couple of years, our focus. The issues themselves weren't new. I was still probation commissioner, making the lower salary. And after a couple of years, give or take, someone else became probation commissioner, and then I just became correction commissioner. I did them both for a couple of years. In some ways I didn't really want to give up the probation stuff, even though it's a little insane to do both jobs.

But really the most telling difference was the culture in those places. When I walked into probation, it was, "Eh, schmuck is back." When I walked into corrections, people were saluting me. The first time my wife came to visit me in corrections, I met her at the front door and I walked around and a few officers were walking out and they all saluted me. And my wife said, "Did you just salute him?" "Yes, ma'am."

One of the reasons Schembri was fired was Rudy used to have all these town halls where he'd take all these commissioners. Nobody ever had a probation question. So my task was to just stay awake. Not to nod off.

So at one point the mayor is yakking to someone from the community and Tony needs to go to the bathroom. We are all on the dais. And when he walks down, he's met by his security of like six guys. The earpieces. They walk him right up the middle. It was like a *Saturday Night Live* skit. People were wondering who that guy was. I think that was the last straw for the mayor.

But that's the kind of place it can be. Early on I was going to a meeting and I saw some of the correction guys leaving where I was going. I asked where they were going. "Advance!" That's what they do. They check things out. For what? Who is going to kill me? If you kill me, there's just another one. The only people who probably wanted to kill me were correction officers.

STATS

"They Sit Down and Put Their Little Story Together"

In the Department of Correction, numbers are king. The number of stabbings and slashings is closely watched by everyone from wardens to the mayor. Their careers, and legacies, depend on it. And so, for years, department officials, with the help of rank-and-file staff, figured out ways to juke the figures. The schemes range from ignoring incidents, to changing definitions of violence, to conspiring to create fanciful narratives to cover up that violence, to downgrading serious attacks, to simply not reporting them.

Even after the transition was made from thick paper ledgers to computers and from eyewitness accounts to video surveillance, stats juking continued where it could.

—

ELIAS HUSAMUDEEN, president of the Correction Officers' Benevolent Association, 2016 to 2020: Over the years, have I seen discrepancy in numbers and reporting numbers? Yeah. I've seen one set of numbers provided to the city council, and I've seen another set of numbers provided to the Board of Correction. And I've seen another set of numbers provided to the press, to the public. I've seen it manipulated where you would be given numbers based on the calendar year and somebody else would be given numbers based on the fiscal year.

HELEN TAYLOR, detained 1970s, 1980s: I seen a female officer go up to a female detainee and beat her like she was a man and throw her in the box rather than the clinic. One girl wanted to get into an area, and an officer was just totally ignoring her. When the officer did acknowledge, she came out of the Bubble and spit in the girl's face. The girl said, "Get out of my face," and the officer jumped on her and now they fighting. The girl has to protect herself. The lady officer pulls the button for them to assist her, and when they did come, they jumped on the girl. Somehow, she gets in her cell. Out of fear, she doesn't want to go out of her cell, and they ran up in there.

She's holding onto the bed. She don't want to come out of there. She just didn't want the female officer to spit in her face. They jumped on her and beat her until she got off the bed and dragged her down the hallways. She was bleeding badly. One of her eyes was cut open. She had a big old black eye for months after that. You'd make complaints to the IG [inspector general], but the people running the IG is ex-officers, they just moved up. So you really don't have no help. Everything you told them, they take it right back to the officer. They sit down and put their little story together. You don't come out winning, because they all correction officers, unless you can get help from the outside, like a lawyer. Calling the IG was like going to the warden.

TERRENCE SKINNER, retired deputy warden, 1983 to 2003: In 1983 and 1984, academy training was basically correction law and penal law; here's what you're required to do, like you can use force to have prisoners do certain things and always for self-defense, and you were permitted to use force to stop a prisoner from damaging property. But in those days, force meant you didn't have to explain it. You just had to say I used force to make him do this.

Terrence Skinner fought many battles on the job, and avoided some land mines, in his rise to deputy warden. He now helps care for his grandchildren.

SIDNEY SCHWARTZBAUM, retired deputy warden, union president, 1979 to 2016: In the '80s, the population started to explode. I think crime was on the rise. There were a lot of drugs. I was a captain already when the crack epidemic started. In 1988, Rikers was a lot worse as far as stabbings and slashings. We would have people getting beat up. We'd have a stabbing once in a while from like 1979 to '85 when I was there as an officer. But by 1988, it was fifty. I was there for like eight months as a tour commander. There were fifty slashings a month over there.

On a set of four-by-twelves tour, if I didn't get three or four slashings in four days, it was unusual. They were just cutting each other up. Of course, if you know the guy's got a lung punctured or something, then you would call the warden and they would come in. But then you went to the Giuliani regime.

TERRENCE SKINNER: By 1987, Legal Aid had sued the department, and they came to a deal that you had to explain why you used force and what it was. You had to say you punched him in the face. If you didn't say it, they could check with the doctor, because the doctor would write, for example, "Inmate says he got punched in the face by officer."

At that stage, I was a captain. We were taught the force reports and the injury reports have to be consistent. A lot of guys had a difficult time writing. They were afraid to write. They might have used force when it was necessary, but they couldn't write it. That was a big deal. They might use force and say they didn't, and then they would have severe consequences.

I was an ADW [assistant deputy warden] in 1990, and I was in GMDC. It was wild and out of control. We had had two shootings in the jail, and one or two captains had been stabbed. I was specifically called and asked to go there and write about it properly. There had been a big incident where officers used force, but no one said they used force. They all got in trouble.

I had two incidents early in 1990 where a big prisoner came to a female officer and assaulted her. She hit him in the head with a radio. A captain came to help out. They wrestled him to the floor. In their reports, they made no mention of the radio or of any way he could have gotten the injury. When I said I needed an explanation, they didn't have one. I brought them in, and I said if you're telling me you didn't touch the guy, and the injury is in this square shape of a radio on his head, what happened?

They denied it, saying maybe the floor caused the head injury. It was horrible. I ended up suspending both officers. The witnessing officer got fired because he was on probation. The female officer was suspended and lost vacation days. It didn't have to happen. Their response was justified. They just had to be honest on the report.

SIDNEY SCHWARTZBAUM: I remember my first meeting with [Kerik] in a restaurant and he says we're getting back these jails. They had already started to do a good job. In 1994 and 1995 the violence started to come down, but it was still several hundred a year. And his goal was to get under a hundred slashings a year.

BERNARD KERIK, correction commissioner, 1998 to 2000: They could only get away with it when nobody's looking. So here's the way this works. The commands themselves, they had to collect their numbers and now keep this in mind: we started out with sixteen performance indicators. By the time I left, there were hundreds, and it was violence, vehicle maintenance, facility maintenance, food service, you name it.

SIDNEY SCHWARTZBAUM: Under the Kerik years and after . . . from 1995 to 2009 it was like a renaissance period in the reduction of violence. You take away all the misconduct with the Kerik years and the selective discipline, the officers feeling safe from retaliation, all of that, the inmate violence did come way down. Violence was reduced by a tremendous amount in those years.

TERRENCE SKINNER: In 1993 to '94, in the new administration, the stats weren't manipulated initially. They were searching so much that they did drop violence tremendously. Then there's a split. We didn't drop uses of force. We dropped stabbings and slashings. The argument could have been that you used more force to stop these incidents. There was a small increase in uses of force, incidental in searches. The stabbings and slashings drop was huge. There was more intel gathering. That was all very good.

The budget skyrocketed. Between 1993 and 2000 it must have gone up 50 percent, and the prisoner population went down because we had an administration which supported us and a guy in city hall who supported us. We had more specialized units. We had Tactical Search Operations. And so you're going to find more contraband. That was the beginning. There was a real big push. The stabbings and slashings dropped 50 percent by 1995; then they continued to push on that and continued to put money into surprise searches. That's what led to the decrease.

By 1997, they had created the Gang Intelligence Unit. Prior, it was the gang intelligence task force, and they gathered info and didn't share it. They would tell me it was confidential. They started creating a database. There were two different databases, competing with each other. They reviewed the whole process, and the Gang Intelligence Unit was created. There were weekly meetings with the security captain, the ADWs, and deputy wardens.

What happened was they reached a point where investigations made the arrest in the jail, not the staff. If a prisoner stabbed another prisoner, he got an infraction, but he wasn't arrested. An infraction was like a parking ticket. With the Gang Intelligence Unit, I asked the chief if we could lock inmates up. It took negotiation, but they allowed us to arrest inmates for stabbings and slashings.

Our first big case was a guy who cut someone's throat. He had a two-year sentence. We went to the Bronx DA and we talked with him and they approved the arrest. The guy was being transferred upstate. I ordered my team to stop the bus, get him off the bus. He got eleven years for the throat slashing. It quickly sent a message to all of the gangs that you're going to get hit with a felony charge. That was 1997, March. By 1998, the violence dropped another 50 percent because of all the arrests.

In 1998–99, they turned to uses of force. Legal Aid didn't care about stabbings and slashings. I remember arguing with them that my job wasn't just to take care of officers; we were supposed to take care of inmates too. Prior to 1993–94, because of not getting support and getting in trouble, the mindset was let them stab and cut each other as long as they don't do it to us.

RICHARD KOEHLER, correction commissioner, 1986 to 1989: I saw it at the Police Department and I saw it in correction. I was an [NYPD] sergeant . . . and there was a lot of pressure because the crime was rampant and robberies and burglaries were big. Grand larceny was bad, petit larceny was bad, but robberies and burglaries and assaults were very bad. So I would, as a sergeant, read a crime report and it would say, "The woman was walking down the street and a man ran by and grabbed the necklace from her neck and continued to run. Petit larceny." No, it's grand larceny.

I started inspections divisions in the Police Department and in the Correction Department to look at false stuff like that. I'm getting a lot of pressure, the commissioner says, for use-of-force incidents. Use of force has different categories; it was serious or not serious—A, B, and C or whatever it is.

So if I can change it and make it look like it's less, I'll be okay. The use-of-force report is done by the correctional officer, but the categorization of that is done by a boss somewhere. So that category might be changed. There's a million games that you can play. It's why you need an inspections division. You need somebody who you trust. The investigators from the city have a responsibility to come in and do that.

BERNARD KERIK: You have got to have an inspection team that basically goes out and looks at what the commands are doing. The commands would collect the data and submit it to the borough. The bureau chief submits it to the chief of department's office. The chief of department's office prepares the data, the overall data sheet, and that's what sits in my car at six o'clock in the morning when I get in the car. That's the book that's sitting on my seat next to me. So when I look at that book, that shit was all collected through the night starting at 5:00 a.m. or 4:00 a.m., whatever.

[Kerik founded the TEAMS meetings, which were similar to the NYPD's CompStat model, in which a range of statistical indicators were tracked and chiefs and wardens were held accountable for their numbers.]

BERNARD KERIK: I got that book, but that wasn't the end of it. The TEAMS unit then went out and did systematic unannounced audits of every incident. You couldn't cheat. There was no cheat. You couldn't cheat me. You couldn't fuck around, because if you got caught, you're done.

TERRENCE SKINNER: We made arrests for stabbings that got expanded to arrests for everything, and that meant the Bronx DA started saying we're not going to prosecute for this. DOC officials wanted to increase the arrest numbers. Everything became more and more about the numbers. Gang intelligence in 1998 and 1999, their budget doubled or tripled in those years. You needed more officers to make arrests. They were even arresting them for possession of contraband. If you caught someone smuggling stuff into the jails, they arrested them, but now they were arresting inmates for possession. The DA would either include it in the preexisting case or decline to prosecute.

And then there were the searches. We started out saying that we're going to increase searches; then we started doing random searches with a captain and two COs, one search of ten prisoners. It turned into every captain had to turn in a random search.

I was in CIFM [now the Eric M. Taylor Center]. They were doing three thousand searches a month. If you break that down, you know it's not possible, you can't do that. It's impossible, but because they had the numbers push, they claimed they were doing it.

I called the security captain and said I can't sign all this shit. It took all day. What they were doing was just signing off. They also recorded everything as a search. If you were walking out in a main corridor, there was a pat down. They started calling that a search. They started calling normal routine procedures a search. I said, look, to hell with all these forms. I changed the search procedures. They put together surprise searches, and I dropped the total searches from three thousand to three hundred, but I recovered more contraband. Way more.

At TEAMS, the chief said, what's with this drop in searches? I said, I changed the manner of searches. It wasn't effective. We weren't recovering contraband. I did raids. We're doing different searches but by surprise. It's quick but effective. He said, that's fine.

We went back from the TEAMS meeting, and my secretary got a call from the chief's office. He said, we want your search numbers up. It was a joke because I knew they were false reports. The management report gave you these numbers, and people became fascinated with numbers.

vn. We're saying it's down, and [Jonathan] Chasan and [John] ton [of the Legal Aid Prisoners' Rights Project] are saying, are lying pricks. They knew.

KESSLER: City hall asked me to get some data out of the stat-ans once. They didn't tell me why. So I got it out of the statis-ns. Then the next day they put out this report that said, things o great, blah, blah. I had no idea. The statisticians had no And meanwhile the statisticians looked at the report, which dy had bothered to check back with them, and they saw what obvious mistakes. They're like, "What the fuck?" But that's nd of users city hall was. It was all about burnishing their ation. We were just instruments to them.

ROBERT CRIPPS, retired warden, 1983 to 2013: They would call this TEAMS meeting, and if you're a warden or deputy warden for security and your fights are up and your inmate injuries are up, you're going to get blasted, maybe even get told to retire or what-ever instead of working together and saying, listen, this is the prob-lem. Let's talk about ways we're going to fix this problem. No, they don't want to do that. They want to just get rid of whoever is there and put someone else, like they're miraculously going to fix it. It's not going to work unless you're working together and devise a plan.

So you're basically incentivizing people to come to that meet-ing with numbers that are looking good, because your career is on the line. The threat of being forced into retirement is not a way to run a business. So the person in charge, the deputy warden, had reduced the amount of fights by miscategorizing them as non-fights, when they were clearly inmate-on-inmate fights, and then went to TEAMS with these fudged numbers and was congratu-lated.

FLORENCE FINKLE, DOC deputy commissioner for investigations, 2010 to 2014: All I had to do is take a look at one or two case files to know that they had a broken internal investigation system. They didn't have the staff or the standards and processes set up that would enable them to do high-quality investigations, which sur-prised me because they had just completed a legal settlement with the Legal Aid Society which had mandated certain things be done to improve investigations.

ROBERT CRIPPS: They just came up with a way to do it. Instead of fighting, it was horseplaying. It wasn't a fight. So now it's off the fight list. Oh, they were only horseplaying, you know. We sure have a lot of horseplaying inmates. If you know what you're doing, you'd look at the stats and know they are completely wrong.

They ended up promoting the person that was fudging the stats, who actually continued to fudge the stats in every rank he got. He's no longer with the department, and I don't want to mention his name. But your career's on the line. You're gonna find a way, right?

It's not the way to do things. You shouldn't be nervous to be honest about what's going on. I think now it's done quite a bit differently. Not as brutal as it was in years past. Hopefully, our commanding officers are not afraid to tell the commissioner, listen, I got a problem and this is what I need.

JULIA SOLOMONS, social worker, Bronx Defenders: The *Nunez* Monitor reports [federal court-ordered oversight reports] come out every year. At least the last few years, the uses of force, meaning violence at the hands of officers, have increased. Every time that they produce a report, there's an increase. And so advocates will always ask about that and use it as a point of reference when trying to hold the department accountable to making changes with their staffing and then holding officers accountable for their actions, et cetera.

One thing that's interesting is that the commissioner this past year explained that they changed the definition of "use of force" to be more inclusive. So the change that they made makes them look better, that they're trying to broaden what constitutes unjustifiable violence, because that's a way for them to explain why the use of force has gone up in these reports. They've expanded that definition.

They can explain away numbers with a shift in definition, but you end up skirting the issue, which is still that, regardless of definition, use of force is increasing over time when the work is to reduce it. It's really frustrating because the report is one of the only things we have that concretely says this is a huge problem. The numbers look really bad every time. And it's always explained away as opposed to saying, these are the concrete steps that we're going to take to rectify this the next time.

RICK LOMBARDI, retired DOC gang investigator, 1990 to 2011: The majority of times when I was there, they wouldn't classify slashings

as slashings. They would call them "superficial l[...] the numbers down. When Bloomberg was m[...] arms about numbers. They didn't want to tell [...]

I would have wardens waiting for me at th[...] walked in, and they would beg us, don't com[...] and take a walk with us, we're going to go tak[...] but that's not where I want to go. I want to g[...] He would say, "No, no, no, you're going to[...] would beg us not to uncover what had gone[...] before.

I think under Bloomberg it was the wo[...] The numbers had to be down. A stabbin[...] scratch.

EVE KESSLER, DOC public affairs, 2014 to 2[...] problem, besides the poor condition and [...] being completely inadequate as an admir[...] computerization, record keeping, and da[...] about trying to extract information for [...] because they wanted data. There were l[...] leaguered statisticians. They'd get a sli[...] pletely inadequate computer system.

DOC does everything on paper. It's[...] documentation is literal, tangible pap[...] And that makes it really easy to mispl[...] lot of room for error when everything[...]

TERRENCE SKINNER: A use-of-force[...] meaning serious injuries. They redef[...] class A was also Mace. Then they sw[...] an A; it became a B. The numbers ju[...] the other. We only reported class /[...] redefine it and just totally change[...] reports were clear about that. Tha[...] the department. The real-world [...] happening the way it was. You k[...]

UNIONS

"Serious Violence Is Routinized"

For the last two decades, the union representing rank-and-file correction officers was led by a boisterous former officer. Norman Seabrook, derisively known as Stormin' Norman to some, answered to no one.

In New York City, where nearly all public sector workers are unionized, he stood alone, outlasting at least ten correction commissioners, including one whom he lobbied the former mayor Michael Bloomberg to keep on board when he first came into office. Nearly every single move to reform the department typically first had to get buy-in from the union.

But it wasn't just broad changes Seabrook controlled. He'd frequently flex his power to protect officers accused of heinous abuses and never shied away from a fight with management.

In one example in the early years of the twenty-first century, Seabrook and two other jail union leaders refused to leave the office of a top city pension official who made an unfavorable switch to how some pensions would be calculated. Hours later the change was nixed.

When he didn't get his way, Seabrook made the ultimate flex: shutting down the bridge to Rikers and blocking traffic in the area.

While that was technically illegal, no mayor ever had the courage to arrest him.

In 2013, he slowed the city's entire criminal court system to a crawl as he tried to protect a duo of officers charged with abusing a detainee. At the behest of the union, correction officers refused to drive people to and from court, arguing that the buses failed to meet technical requirements. The detainee set to testify against the officers missed his initial court date. Officials were forced to come up with a new way to make sure he made it to the trial.

Seabrook's outspoken ways, and political alliances, also led to major gains for his membership. During his time atop the union, correction officers bridged the salary and benefits gap between themselves and the city's other uniformed unions like cops and firefighters.

—

DR. HOMER VENTERS, correctional health services chief medical officer, 2015 to 2017: Late on a Friday, [the correction commissioner Joseph] Ponte transferred about thirty people out of mental health units into solitary confinement. And I think it was at the behest of the COBA [Correction Officers' Benevolent Association]. They owed solitary days, and from their perspective they were being pampered in mental observation units.

Chaos ensued over the weekend. People didn't get their medicines. Really dangerous for patients, but also dangerous for the correctional staff. Harmed security and safety.

And then on a Monday we got all the commissioners [Mary Bassett, the health commissioner, and Liz Glazer, the executive director of the Mayor's Office of Criminal Justice] at the chapel on Rikers. Who does Ponte have come in? Norman. He starts yelling and screaming and just completely blows up the meeting. It was really stunning to me that you could have Norman come in and yell profanities at Mary, who was another commissioner.

ELIZABETH GLAZER, director, Mayor's Office of Criminal Justice, 2014 to 2020: Essentially, Seabrook took over and began to lecture Mary with Ponte just standing there. About how she didn't understand anything. That his people were in danger and until she had walked in the shoes of a corrections officer she had no right to say anything. What it seemed to signal was that Norman Seabrook was running Rikers Island. Because who was he to lecture a commissioner of an agency, and why was this happening? And why was the correction commissioner standing by?

HOMER VENTERS: Seabrook yelled, "I have inmates out there, and if you went out there and I wasn't there to protect you, you'd fucking shit your pants." And then, when I went to interrupt him to say, "You've got to just stop," he did this weird thing, which I never understood, he said, "You go fucking blow bubbles. That's what you do." It was really trippy. He was standing at the lectern. We just needed to get out of there. As we were leaving, Ponte gives him a hug. And it was in front of all the DOC brass. It was clear they didn't care one whit about our patients and didn't think they did anything wrong.

RICHARD STEIER, former editor in chief of *The Chief-Leader:* The union's history in a nutshell? Before [the COBA president] Stan Israel, there was Phil Seelig, and Seelig and Stan were sort of an entity. Phil was the crafty guy, and Stan would do some of the dirty work for Phil. They were an anomaly; the union was getting increasingly minority, particularly in terms of Black employees. And these were two white Jewish union officials. Phil would be militant when he thought that it could help his standing there. I remember there was a time when I was working for the *New York Post,* and they were having a meeting in the basement of St. Andrew's Church. It was a nice summer night. They weren't allowing reporters in, but we're standing right outside, there's an open window, and you suddenly hear them talking about what their strategy is going to be when they finally allow reporters in. As soon as they let us in, they started chanting, "We want safe jails! We want safe jails!" as though they were spontaneous outbursts.

Seelig was known as Elvis in those days, and there were two theories about it. One was that it was because he had this air about him that he was the king. And the other was that he was a white person flourishing in a primarily Black field. During his last term in office, Seelig was going to law school rather than negotiating a contract. He got his law degree and retired from COBA under an arrangement that Stan was going to step into the presidency. There was also a plan under which Stan was going to pay Phil to negotiate the contract that he should have been negotiating as part of his duties as president, except that there was opposition, and a good part of the opposition came from Norman Seabrook at his wing of the union, which had been growing in strength. Eventually they got them to shelve that contract.

Seabrook was gaining support within the jail system. He decided to challenge Israel when he ran for his first full term in 1995. It seemed as if this was going to get thwarted by the fact that there were five candidates in the race opposing Israel so that all the anti-Israel vote would be divided, but apparently enough of it coalesced around Norman, and Stan had alienated enough people in the union that Norman won by a big margin. He beat him by close to three to one. Israel didn't even finish second; he wound up third.

And so began the Seabrook era. Along with Elias Husamudeen, who had not been part of Norman's group but at a certain point joined forces, Norman was calling all the shots in the union.

EVE KESSLER, director, DOC public affairs, 2014 to 2017: Now the union, I would say, is one of the more obstreperous ones we have in town. Norman took it to the limit. I would call Norman a cut-rate Malcolm X. He was incredibly charismatic.

RICHARD STEIER: Norman had also tapped Richard Koehler, who was a former correction commissioner, to be his counsel. So he was getting a certain amount of advice from Koehler. One of the first things that he did as president was to endorse the reelection of George Pataki as governor. This was part of a grand plan that Norman had, which was, basically, to show that correction officers are not necessarily your typical Democratic voters.

So it wasn't a great leap to endorse Pataki, but it was somewhat unusual. Pataki was going to be central to Norman's plan to get a variable supplements fund [$12,000-a-year payments for his veteran members]. The variable supplements fund is something that cops and firefighters already had. It's a pension-related benefit that comes out of any particularly good investment years for the pension funds; if there was a profit above a certain amount, part of that money would get skipped to the variable supplements fund.

Police and fire had gotten the variable supplements funds back in the late 1960s, but correction didn't have the kind of leverage that police and fire did.

One of the other pieces that Norman had to put into play was the senate majority leader, Joe Bruno. Norman courted Bruno at every opportunity, contributed money to him, and actually made trips up to not just Albany but Saratoga for the horse races. I saw him and a number of his board members there once. Saratoga was basically Bruno's summer office; you could find him in the clubhouse pretty much any racing day. Norman was going at him hard.

Another person that they really needed was [the city council Speaker] Peter Vallone, because you need a home rule resolution on something that applies only to city employees. Therefore, you had to go through the council. Now, Norman had endorsed Pataki in 1998, when his Democratic opponent was Vallone. So in order to make up for that, Norman endorsed Vallone in his run for mayor in 2001. And he let him know in advance that they were going to be backing him.

So all of this stuff is taking place in 1999 and 2000. And basically, the bill managed to go through. Giuliani objected to it, but not too strenuously, and it basically became law. So something that the other unions had really had to horse-trade in order to be able to get, Norman was able to do just through political relationships. And that really solidified Norman's standing within the union.

It was also just the first of several successes in terms of political endorsements that he made. In 2001, the Democratic nominee for mayor, Mark Green, had talked about wanting to make significant cuts in the Correction Department's budget. So Norman simply endorsed Bloomberg at a time when Bloomberg had no other union endorsements. He brought the captains along with him, and they endorsed Bloomberg. And that probably played a role in Norman being treated more kindly than he might have when he flexed his muscles later, while Bloomberg was mayor.

MARTIN HORN, correction commissioner, 2002 to 2009: Norman was very close to Bloomberg that first term. He had been the first union leader to endorse Bloomberg. He had worked very, very hard on Bloomberg's behalf, and he was very much part of Bloomberg's inner circle. Norman goes to Bloomberg and says, "I only have one ask. And that one ask was that you keep [William J.] Fraser on as commissioner." Bloomberg talks about it with his team. I hear this secondhand; this is all how the story came down to me later. They say, "Look, how can we not give Norman the one thing he's asking for? How can we ever get somebody to support us in the future?" So Fraser kept his job because of Norman.

One day there's some issue, some officer being disciplined in the commissioner's office. Norman yells at Fraser and [Deputy Commissioner Bob] Davoren, "You guys sit in those chairs because I put you there." That's how much Norman felt he could control it. Norman felt that he had tremendous power and clout, and I think my predecessors deferred to him for that reason on many, many things. That was just the reality.

FLORENCE FINKLE, DOC deputy commissioner for investigations, 2010 to 2014: The thing I think that really got the union was when I started referring cases for criminal investigation. They thought everything should be handled internally. I don't think that when you assault an inmate that it should go without a criminal investigative review. Especially if your reports are lies. When officers know that their actions are going to be scrutinized and that there's going to be accountability, then over time, if it's sustained, it can help change the culture. Changing the culture takes years. Having a permanent impact on investigations was going to take longer than four and a half years.

I think [the former correction commissioner] Dora Schriro went into DOC with good intentions like most people do. My impression is that she became intimidated by the union and wanted to maintain a positive relationship with Norman Seabrook.

It's not just about the union advocating for its members. It's about the commissioners who are scared of the union and ceding to their requests or promoting people the union wants promoted and acting against their own instinct to do good. That's my takeaway. They intimidated Commissioner Schriro to an extent that she acted in ways which she knew in her heart that she shouldn't. You don't hire the kind of staff that she hired initially unless you wanted to make improvements. In the area of accountability it runs right up against the union and the interest of the union. And their interest is to have their guys keep their jobs and not have them be prosecuted even if it's unreasonable.

Norman Seabrook basically said he'd make sure I'd pay if I continued to take certain actions. He accused me of doing things that were unfair. The union was the number one obstacle to positive changes when I was there.

ROBERT COHEN, director of the Montefiore Rikers Island Health Services in the 1980s: The department didn't do the work that it needed to do regarding investigations of serious injuries. But it's not just the union. I think it's more fundamental than that. Every union protects its members. It's what unions do. They have to do that. The other part is that it is very hard to investigate yourself. There are union members doing the investigations. In a place like Rikers Island, where serious violence is routinized, it's very hard to have people who know each other investigate and indict each other. That should not be part of the department. It should be a separate entity.

His talks in front of the Board of Correction would encourage violence. He'd say, "By any means necessary." His stump speech, "My brother is in prison, and I want him to get out of prison, and you come to work every day, and I want you to get out of work every day." It's a warrior-versus-guardian analogy. And the camera loved him.

He was very threatening to the board. And really spoke against any efforts to make the place less violent. But I don't think it was a personality issue. It was violent before Norman was there. He wasn't there in the early '80s. This is not about an individual. It's about a culture that has gone on in city jails for a long time. The training is on the job. They go to the academy and learn from captains and other officers how to operate.

Norman helped his members. They have a really hard job. And they certainly deserve what they make. It's great he got the pensions and livable wages.

BERNARD KERIK, correction commissioner, 1998 to 2000: I get a call about three in the morning. Norman closed the bridge at three or four in the morning, and he closed the bridge to all the court vehicles going out at four o'clock, five o'clock, whatever. All the buses are lined up on the fucking bridge, and he ain't letting none go.

So I called Norman and I said, "What the fuck are you doing?" He goes, "Wow, your chief did this." I don't remember his name, but he had given Norman a hard time about something and Norman went off, went out there at fucking four in the morning, stopped every bus. So we had to notify the courts. We had to notify the judges. It was a pain. I had to get everybody in on overtime to do maintenance on the vehicles, make sure they were clean.

He's going, "You tell your fucking guys they better read the SOPs [standard operating procedures] and they'd better read the SOP manual because it says this and this and this and that." And he's telling me all about the buses.

WARNER FREY, retired NYPD captain, 1992 to 2014: In February 2007, my job was as a steady midnight duty captain in Queens North. So my shift started at eleven o'clock the previous night and went until seven o'clock in the morning. Around 5:30 a.m., I received a call from the borough about a possible protest over at Rikers Island. So when I arrived over there, I saw that the Correction Officers' Benevolent Association was having a work slowdown because they were protesting either a contract or some working conditions on Rikers Island.

On the Rikers Island Bridge, the speed limit is five miles an hour going into the facility. Generally, people would go faster than that. On this day, each car was going over the bridge at five miles an hour. And what I quickly learned is that six o'clock in the morning is prime time at Rikers Island. It's change of shift. A lot of administrative people are coming in. A lot of staff is coming in. A lot of correction officers are coming in. So it's a big, big, big population of cars that are going over to Rikers Island. Each one was going at five miles an hour.

By doing so, they backed up the traffic on the Rikers Island Bridge back into Queens onto Ditmars Boulevard. And from Ditmars Boulevard, they backed it up all the way onto the Grand Central Parkway. So you can only imagine the amount of gridlock that was occurring in northern Queens at this time. The temperature was literally about 7 degrees out. It was very sunny that morning. I remember the blue skies, but it was so bitterly cold.

I called a level one [one sergeant and eight cops] to get whatever remaining task force units might be hiding out somewhere. Of course there weren't any. Then I called for a modified level-three mobilization, which means two police officers from each command [roughly eighteen to thirty-six cops]. This raises the eyebrows of One Police Plaza, and operations calls, what's going on. I have a level three going on. I start getting phone calls from some people in the borough saying, do you know what you're asking for?

I said, yeah, I have gridlock going on here in northern Queens. I have to get people to try and relieve this condition because now the Grand Central is stopped up. So there was no highway [NYPD unit] available. I myself was out on Nineteenth Street and Ditmars Boulevard directing traffic. Every person that I could get was out there. I had about ten people, myself included, and we had to spread out, and each one of us took a corner to try and pull the traffic through. I left my driver in the truck to monitor the radio because I couldn't hear it because of all the traffic noise.

There were so many cars that were going very slow. I think Norman was there because it was definitely a protest. I did not see him. He may have already passed me, though. He was probably in a nice warm car. He was smart.

You're hearing on the news reports, there's massive tie-ups in northern Queens on the Grand Central by Ditmars Boulevard, because LaGuardia Airport is only about ten minutes away from there. So it was impacting LaGuardia traffic as well. You had obviously people honking on their horns. I can picture looking east on Ditmars Boulevard and, to this day, seeing all the traffic coming through every which way, all coming into this centralized point.

It was backed up further than LaGuardia Airport. And it hit quick.

It was just completely overwhelming.

I would say I was out there from just before six o'clock in the morning until nine o'clock. It was one of the times of my life that I can honestly say that my body temperature dropped. I could feel my body temperature drop. I couldn't move. I'm filling out my overtime slip. I couldn't really write, because my hands were so cold. The operations lieutenant, Ernie, comes up to me, says, we're putting together an afternoon plan. We're going to be ready for them this time. I looked, I said, Ernie, they're not going to do it in the afternoon. They want to go home. Everybody wants to go home. They're not going to go five miles an hour to go home. You're wasting your time. Sure as the devil, guess what happened? Everybody went home. There were no problems.

BERNARD KERIK: Right before the Super Bowl, that Saturday night, I called five or ten captains. Those are first-line supervisors, like sergeants. I called them to headquarters and I said, starting at 8:00 a.m. tomorrow on Super Bowl Sunday, you're going to do two or three home visits on every correction officer who calls in sick. Every single one. If they're not home, we're suspending them on the spot. If they're drinking, we're suspending them on the spot. If you smell alcohol on them, whatever. I don't remember the number, but we suspended a bunch of guys and Norman went crazy. He called fucking [captain John] Picciano and he was screaming, I could hear him on the phone from my office, and John's office was outside my door. I walked out laughing and Picciano says, he's going crazy.

So I take the phone from John. I said, "Hey, what's up?" He says, "I know you fucking did this 'cause of the buses and I know what you did." I said, "Norman, no, let me tell you what I did." I said, "Remember you told me I should read the SOP? I read that fucking book. I didn't know that correction officers have to be in their house when they call in sick. I had no idea!" He immediately got it, came down to see me a day or two later, and he's like, "That's fucked up what you did. I know it's retaliation." I said, "No, just doing my job, but let me tell you, the next fucking time you have a problem with somebody and you don't come and see me or you go to the press and you don't tell me, I'm going to go back to the book. And that book for you is a big problem. The reason it's a big problem is you don't have eleven thousand angels working for you, right? They get in trouble all the fucking time, right? And they're at my mercy. I'm not asking you for nothing special. Do your job. You have a problem? Come see me and talk to me. If it's real, I'll fix it. If it's not real, don't come and try to bullshit me, because I've done that job."

We did okay. What's funny is when I left and went to the NYPD, I remember [the Police Benevolent Association president] Patty Lynch was talking to Norman. "So what's he like?" Norman said, as long as you don't fucking go to the press and try to fuck him behind his back, as [long as] you tell them up front, he's a good guy. And Patty and I got along well. Really, really well. But that was one of the things with Norman.

MICHAEL JACOBSON, correction commissioner, 1995 to 1997: I was both good friends and colleagues with the city's labor commissioner, Jim Hanley. He was iconic. I'm not sure there will ever be another guy like that in city government. We had our strategy. It happened to be Norman, but it would have been anyone who was the union leader. It was: the union leader talks to us, and even then, not all the time. But there's no direct line to the mayor. We all sort of agreed, especially as Rudy tired of him after a while. It would be a rare event when city hall picked up the phone when he called. If he had issues, we'd deal with them. There were always exceptions. He'd talk to me or Hanley; depending on what the issue was, he'd sometimes set up a labor management meeting where Norman could yell and scream in front of his executive board so they could see he was fighting the good fight.

Norman was a very smart guy, and he would do whatever he could do for his members. Because I guess he was an early supporter of Rudy, he used to say, when I would fight with him, that if he had to, he'd go to Rudy, and maybe I wouldn't have a job. I didn't care if I didn't have the job. That wasn't a threat. It didn't have a lot of leverage over me. He was a very powerful union leader. He had a lot of juice.

He threatened to shut [the bridge] down when I was there. Again, me and Hanley met with the police commissioner at the time. The NYPD gave him a pretty strong message: if you do this, we are going to arrest everyone. I don't even remember what the issue was, if it was a collective bargaining issue or he was pissed about something else.

I had a pretty good relationship. It was hot and cold and we'd hate each other. His threats were always just business. Nothing personal. It was not like I was ever worried for my safety.

RICHARD STEIER: Well, the bridge stuff, that wasn't brand-new. I mean, that had happened when Seelig was president of the union as well. The worst things, though, that Norman did went beyond what Seelig did. There was a dispute in which a guy basically told the captains to go fuck themselves. And it became an issue within the department that Norman basically got management to back away from it. So that they were basically disregarding the chain of command.

There was also the situation in which there were supposed to be a couple of prisoners who were going to be transferred from Rikers Island to the Bronx to testify against a couple of correctional officers who allegedly brutalized them. And Norman basically shut down traffic on the bridge. They eventually opened things up; they let them go. But I think by the time that they got there, it was too late for them to appear on the witness stand. And so that got put off. You had the makings of an improper practice case against the union except that it wasn't brought. And the assumption was that it was because Bloomberg just didn't want to take on the union or Norman.

SIDNEY SCHWARTZBAUM, retired deputy warden, union president, 1979 to 2016: There was a point in NYCERS (New York City Employees' Retirement System) where there was some vague law that if you were under the age of fifty, they were gonna reduce your pension by a significant amount. It was a vague IRS policy that didn't come to light until somebody from the teachers' union brought up something with the pension system and it came up and the city's Office of Labor Relations tried to enforce it. And we had already negotiated a twenty-year pension, which by the way, we paid through our nose, especially the superior officers.

Seabrook said, "Meet me at the NYCERS." So we went up there. It was me and my vice president, Ronnie Whitfield. It was a big room and there were women there. And Norman started to go off. I was cringing in some of the things he was saying, like cursing, "those fucking cocksuckers," like crazy shit. He said, "You're not doing this to my fucking people." That it's not happening. "I'll shut down the city." And then they call the cops on us. And the cops told us that they were gonna have to lock us up.

Norman said, "You're gonna have to throw us out the window. We're not leaving." He said, "Sidney, you with me?" I said, "I'm with you." And I'll never forget, it was like 11:30 at night and

[Deputy Mayor] Peter Madonia called up Norman. And I heard it on the speaker. And he said to him, "Norman, I promise you we're gonna lobby. The city's going to support legislation to change this." And that was my favorite Norman Seabrook story. I said, "You know what? This guy's fucking good."

When he got arrested, it was like a Greek tragedy. He did so many good things for the members.

Sidney Schwartzbaum rose from correction officer in 1979 to become the influential president of the union representing deputy wardens and assistant deputy wardens.

ELIZABETH GLAZER: I mean, look, it's a tough union. But the officers also want to be safe. The officers also would like to have a better environment in which to be working. And one of the things that you hear when you go to institutions in which violence is low is that the officers may just have a different view of what it means to come to work. So I may be a naive optimist, but I think there are common goals here that I would think the union would embrace.

There is the stepchild feeling among the correction officers. The mayor comes and speaks at the Police Department promotion ceremonies, but he doesn't come to ours. PD has this beautiful academy; we don't. And I think it's also tied up in a keen sense of how predominantly the corrections officers are people of color versus PD. And I think part of culture change is treating officers with respect as well. Training and providing them with the kind of training that makes them feel that they are professionals who are being held to a professional standard in the same way that cops are. I think there's a lot of work to be done.

[We repeatedly asked Norman Seabrook to speak with us for the book. He declined because he was in the midst of pressing an appeal of his federal conviction for honest services fraud. He was in federal prison as of August 2022, with a possible 2025 release date.]

CLOSE RIKERS

"Executive Summary: Damned If I Know"

Testifying before the Board of Correction, a forty-nine-year-old city official named Herb Sturz hammered at the social cost of locating the jails on Rikers Island.

"The problems caused by the location of Rikers Island are felt throughout the criminal justice system," he declared. "There are at least two basic things wrong with our corrections system: it is in the wrong place, and it needs about $100 million in capital improvements to make it safe and decent."

At the time, though, Sturz was a deputy mayor under Ed Koch and the year was 1979.

Sturz, who studied under the author John Steinbeck at Columbia's Teachers College in 1953, offered up a more literal kind of modest proposal: lease Rikers to the state to be used as prisons to house people convicted of crimes in the five boroughs, rather than force them into gulags in remote corners of the state. The city's detainees would be housed in new borough jails presumably closer to family.

The idea burned bright for a moment, and then it was snuffed by the familiar old-line institutions—politicians, unions, and the communities where the new jails would be placed.

Nearly forty years later, Sturz, coming toward the end of a long and distinguished career in public policy (the Vera Institute, bail reform), returned to his big idea. He saw a new opportunity in an atmosphere of renewed momentum in favor of deep change in the way we police and the way we incarcerate.

In August 2014, Preet Bharara, the U.S. Attorney in Manhattan, said the Correction Department allowed a "deep-seated culture of violence" against younger detainees that caused staggering numbers of injuries and systematic civil rights violations. Correction staff, he said, employed a "powerful code of silence" to escape accountability.

"Rikers Island is a broken institution," he said. "It is a place where brute force is the first impulse rather than the last resort; where verbal insults are repaid with physical injuries; where beatings are routine while accountability is rare; and where a culture of violence endures even while a code of silence prevails."

The results of the investigation into violence among young detainees forced the city in 2015 to accept a federal monitor to oversee jail operations.

The momentum also came from the activist Glenn Martin's Close Rikers campaign and many other grassroots groups and nonprofits that were conducting lobbying efforts showcasing the decades-old ills of the island's jails. The former chief judge of New York State Jonathan Lippman and other luminaries also got involved.

The campaign gained traction, driven by two very large factors. One, the jail population had dropped below 12,000 and kept going down (to just under 4,000 in 2020 during the pandemic, before going back up to just over 5,400 in 2022). Two, the heavy-handed "tough on crime" approach favored by the Giuliani and Bloomberg administrations had given way to a vast reassessment.

In 2017, Mayor Bill de Blasio announced an $8.16 billion "Borough-Based Jail" plan calling for the building of four new jails in each borough except for Staten Island. It was expected to be finished by 2026 but is already delayed by two years because of the pandemic.

Meanwhile, the deaths and disorder continue on the island in the East River and at the city's other jails in Brooklyn and in lower Manhattan. The federal monitor has issued one report after another finding that the department suffers from a "pervasive level of disorder and chaos," with the use-of-force rate against detainees hitting a five-year high. A sudden and unexpected jump in shootings across the city led to fear of a new crime wave and added fuel to the opponents of closing Rikers.

After six years of the federal monitor, violence continues to rise and the cost per detainee per year crested over $550,000. In other words little was changing.

In September 2021, a massive staffing shortfall—caused by thousands of officers calling in sick—combined with a bump in the jail population led to a rapid and shocking decline in conditions. Men were crammed into intake cells for days at a time. Detainees in effect took over jail units because there were few officers walking the tiers. A group of state legislators called it a humanitarian crisis and dubbed it "horror island."

In January 2022, a new mayor and new commissioner had been installed, but little had changed.

In April 2022, U.S. Attorney Damian Williams became so frustrated with the lack of improvement, he threatened to back an unprecedented federal takeover of the jails with a court-appointed receiver.

Once again, the fate of Rikers Island hung in the balance.

—

ELIZABETH GLAZER, director, Mayor's Office of Criminal Justice, 2014 to 2020: [Herb Sturz] was really visionary, long before anyone else was, and he sort of wore these two hats, both as the criminal justice coordinator and then as the chair of city planning. So he sort of both understood the land aspects of it and the criminal justice reform aspects. And I think he knew that was an incredibly important moment. When he thought, "Why do we have to do it this way?"

That was the first but failed effort to try and move off the island. I think he deserves a lot of credit. And he has always been somebody who was so well respected, both by city officials and by reformers and by a whole range of people. He was always active with a new idea about what to do. I think he saw this as an opportunity. He tried to figure out how to do it large scale, how to get the city to agree to move off the island, and then also how to do it small scale. I would say he's the godfather of the big bold idea to close it down.

MARTIN HORN, correction commissioner, 2002 to 2009: In 1978 actually, Herb convinced Mayor Koch that the city should try to sell Rikers Island to the state. The state needed more prison space. The idea was that it would give the state the opportunity to have state prisons closer to the city where most of the inmates come from. And the city would use the proceeds to build borough-based jails off Rikers. At the time Ben Ward was the state's corrections commissioner. He was a protégé of Herb's. And I worked for Ben in the state corrections system. The state set up a task force to work on a plan. We called it the Rikers Island plan. The state would pay the city, I think it was $25 million. A pittance. We literally flew down to LaGuardia on the governor's helicopter one day. We went and toured all the facilities on Rikers Island. And then we worked for eighteen months on this plan.

MICHAEL MUSHLIN, former Legal Aid Society lawyer: [In the early 1970s,] the Legal Aid Society brought a series of lawsuits, challenging conditions in New York City's jails, and the major one was an attack on conditions at the Tombs. And that branched out then into litigation dealing with every facility that the city was operating.

Judges in the Eastern District and judges in the Southern District were saying publicly in written opinions with court orders that conditions in New York City jails were really unconstitutional and were abysmal.

The attitude of the Beame administration [Mayor Abraham

Beame, 1974–77] was one of total resistance to that litigation. It was an attempt to do everything they could to defeat it, forcing trials at every stage and going up on appeal whenever they could. And they were losing constantly. And it was beginning to get public attention.

When Judge [Morris] Lasker ruled that conditions in the Tombs were unconstitutional, that was a front-page article in *The New York Times*. The city resisted Judge Lasker and in fact closed the Tombs rather than comply with the court order, transferring the entire problem to Rikers Island.

So by the time the Beame administration had ended, Rikers had become much worse than it even was prior to this litigation. The city was attracting a lot of negative attention about the conditions in the jails, and all of this was happening while nationally in the wake of the tragedy in Attica the courts were becoming more involved in establishing constitutional rights for prisoners.

When Koch was elected, one of the first things he did was go to the New York City Bar Association building on Forty-Fourth Street and give a speech. This was 1978 right after he took office, where he said the litigation attacking the conditions was indisputably justifiable. And that the city's response to it had been inappropriate. He said that he as the head of the city was no longer going to engage in this defiance of the court's orders.

He also appointed Herb Sturz as the deputy mayor for criminal justice. This was back in January. I remember meeting Herb Sturz on a very cold day. It was the first time I'd ever met him. He was wearing a heavy ski parka. When he was brought in, he signaled that he was going to carry out this policy that Koch had announced.

And so we embarked on a very long, very complicated year of negotiation that led to a series of consent decrees. My impression is that, in immersing himself into this controversy, Herb Sturz came to see the problem as one that could only be solved by closing Rikers Island.

That was the solution, because that solves the city's problem, that solves the state's problem, but that also solves the problem of how do you deal with people who are New Yorkers who are convicted of crimes. It was a brilliant solution that really made an enormous amount of sense. And it's a real shame that it wasn't implemented.

MARTIN HORN: On the state side, on the staff level, we were never enthusiastic about it. The joke was that there were only two people who thought it was a good idea: one was Ed Koch and the other was Hugh Carey.

On the staff level, on the state's side, we looked at those facilities. Herb thought you could just take them over and put your inmates there. If you've ever been to a state prison, you know that there's a big difference between the facilities on Rikers Island, especially as they were in 1978, and some of the better state prisons. There was not enough program space. There was not enough recreation space. The buildings are what they are today: dingy, confining, and poorly built.

State prisons are built to a much higher degree of security. Just everything from surface finishes to door fasteners to lighting fixtures. Everything is of a more custodial grade. I've always said Rikers Island was built with household-grade fixtures, lighting, and heating.

SIDNEY SCHWARTZBAUM, retired deputy warden, union president, 1979 to 2016: It was about 1980, when they were considering turning Rikers into a state prison and creating community jails. [The Correction Officers' Benevolent Association president] Phil Seelig came out strong with the community saying that you'll have convicted felons in the neighborhood escaping. And he went on a public media blitz, and he got it quashed.

STUART MARQUES, journalist: The communities didn't want it, the correction officers didn't want it. There was some enthusiasm at first, but once the opposition started growing, it couldn't be overcome.

At first they thought that the plan was going to work. They

would spend $200 million for eight smaller jails, and a $100 million upgrade of Rikers. They said that Rikers was dangerous for staff and inmates. And then it grew to $350 million. In October 1979, the Board of Correction held two days of hearings. Sturz told the board the deal would have allowed them to make a new start to "build the best system in the nation."

And then the cost estimates grew to at least $433 million. That's when they just started backing away. Community people testified against it. The head of the National Council on Crime and Delinquency, Diana Gordon, said it was ill-conceived and wouldn't work. Phil Seelig called it a sham and wouldn't even take questions from the board. He just boycotted it.

And then, two years later, Ben Ward tells the city council the plan was "dead and buried." There was a lot of opposition, a lot of the same opposition as in the de Blasio plan. Recently someone asked Herb what happened. His response was that he didn't know.

Once they were unable to do it, they started building more and more jails on the island. By 1986, a report found that injuries and incidents in the facilities were far higher than in the past.

MICHAEL MUSHLIN: I really don't know [why the plan died]. Sometimes the right thing to do is to think outside the box, and then you have to persuade. It's so contrary to the way the system operates that to really pull it off just takes changing a lot of assumptions about how things need to be, and a lot of reliances that people have on the existing way of doing these things. If this had been implemented, you would have closed a lot of prisons upstate, where there's just a tremendous amount of political pressure to keep those prisons upstate for those communities upstate. And there's a lot of political benefits from the system operating the way it does.

The system operates the way it does for a reason, right? It's responding to the political realities, and this proposal challenged those political realities. You have Rikers Island because people don't want pretrial detention facilities in the city. Why do we have prisons upstate? Because people don't want prisons downstate.

What is the solution? One is not having the prisons upstate and having the jails in the communities. So it runs totally counter to the way the system operates. I was more surprised that it was proposed than I was surprised that it didn't happen.

GLENN MARTIN, detained in the 1990s, founder of JustLeadership-USA: Herb made some mistakes. I actually learned from his success, but also learned from his mistakes. The biggest of which is you don't run a campaign about an island that the majority of New Yorkers will never experience without amplifying the voices of people who are harmed by it. And to be fair to him, I don't think there [was] a space for those voices when he was pushing for closure. The world is changing. People are just more willing to hear from people directly impacted, probably because of a lot of pressure from people like me and people who came before me. But I would call him a maverick, a thought leader, somebody who sort of gets out ahead of everyone else. I want to be careful not to take the thunder away from the people who I think actually did create the change.

MARTIN HORN: Herb certainly planted the seed in me in 1979 and [in 2002], when I took over city corrections, it was something that I always had in the back of my mind. I always felt that the location, the public imagination about the place, and the actual physical plan were wrong and not good. And then once I got there and took over DOC, I came to believe that it was worse than that. The actual island contributed to a lot of the cultural and ethical problems that we were having. I used to say Rikers Island is like Las Vegas. What happens on Rikers stays on Rikers. That was sort of the ethic there.

It was an insular environment. It made it very easy for the union to organize. Imagine having all your members in one place for the most part. From Norman Seabrook's point of view, he'd come out to Rikers, walk around a couple of jails, and reach all his members every day. I felt it was a constant political campaign. And if you wanted to shut the system down, you had this choke point at the bridge. I thought from a point of view of running the city, this is a disaster. Why would you want to do it this way?

SOFFIYAH ELIJAH, executive director, Alliance of Families for Justice: The out-of-sight and out-of-mind reality is that you can't ignore the racial dynamics. The overwhelming majority of people who are held at Rikers Island, and whose families are impacted by what happens to them, are Black and brown people in this city. And so we say a lot of people don't know what's happening on Rikers Island or don't care. They have been marginalized and dismissed by a white majority. But many, many Black and brown people in this city know where Rikers Island is, have loved ones there, or have visited people there. And so it is a concern in certain communities, but that concern has not made it to prime-time TV.

Soffiyah Elijah has long campaigned to reduce the number of people sent to jail and improve conditions for people behind bars. She is now executive director of the Alliance of Families for Justice.

MARTIN HORN: Even after the state deal went down, the city had a plan. I think they called it "Jails for the '80s"—to get off Rikers and to develop county-based jails. I would say we are approaching half a century [in the making] that some of us have been talking about this.

GLENN MARTIN: I've known Herb for almost two decades. Met him a long time ago. Heard about his efforts to close Rikers many years ago. That was part of my inspiration. One thing I'll never forget 'til the day I die is Herb marching across Queens with us on the first rally that we did, older than anyone else, with his wife, who has now passed away. Marching all the way to the front line. I remember being onstage with Russell Simmons and all these other celebrity types. And the person I'm looking down and feeling most inspired by was Herb making that march with all these people. It was a great day.

I remember him not just because of his age but the commitment he's had to this issue. And his willingness. I mean, the guy lives on Park Avenue. I went to his house to hang out. And people on Park Avenue don't usually roll up their sleeves and march in the streets for things they care about. They might fund things they care about, they might pontificate about things they care about, you know, but they don't usually do what Herb did, which was get out there and march with people who were directly impacted. Herb seemed to find a way to be comfortable in both worlds. I used to do so many damn panel discussions. He'd be at a lot of those events. That meant a lot to me, at the beginning of the campaign, especially a campaign where most of my other colleagues were telling me I was crazy and that I was going to probably pay a price.

GREG BERMAN, co-founder, Center for Court Innovation (also with the Lippman Commission): My version of [the Lippman Commission story] is that the idea really originated with Herb Sturz. It was something that I think he had in the back of his mind for a while, and then he saw an opportunity and he pitched the idea of a commission, first to the mayor [de Blasio] and the mayor said no. And then he took it to [the then City Council Speaker] Melissa Mark-Viverito, who said yes.

And he had already lined up Judge Lippman to chair the commission. And so those three people that were really crucial to the commission in my estimation were Sturz, Glenn, and Lippman.

JONATHAN LIPPMAN, former chief judge, New York Court of Appeals: I think in this country and in New York City there has been a sweeping under the rug that the criminal justice system does a tremendous racial overlay on the criminal justice system. New York City actually does much better than everybody else, particularly now. We incarcerate far too many people without thinking about it. I knew there's a whole science of criminal justice reform that New York and the country was ignoring. I'm a firm believer that the judiciary has to play a leading role. We don't just say let's throw him in jail and forget it. That's what the law says.

ELIZABETH GLAZER: I do think that, for de Blasio, criminal justice wasn't really a big priority. I know that sounds funny, given that he ran on stop and frisk, and I think that aspect of policing was important to him. But I don't think criminal justice policy as a whole was really at the center of what he was interested in. I think it was really a surprise how bad of shape Rikers was in when the Southern District filed suit about the culture of brutality at Rikers, how violent things were, and how kind of mismanaged it had been. [It] was quite a surprise, and ran very counter to Bloomberg's overall reputation as an excellent manager.

JONATHAN LIPPMAN: Believe me when I say this. I had people on the legislative side saying, "He thinks he's a legislator and he thinks he's either the legislature or the executive branch. He doesn't understand the judiciary." And my answer is, they don't understand the new role of the judiciary in this country. I've talked about that around the country, and when I started doing this, there were maybe a few chiefs [chief judges] in the biggest states who were maybe starting to do something like this. Now there are many chief justices who realize this is the responsibility of the judiciary. We have to be interactive with the society around us.

ELIZABETH GLAZER: There were actually conversations going on for some time to try and figure out what all the options were. I would say it started very early in the administration, with the death of Jerome Murdough [a man who suffered from mental illness who died at Rikers in 2014 of hyperthermia while in solitary in a 100-degree cell]. That was really sort of an elbow in the face. That first summer that the mayor was in office, there was a huge effort, engaging like four hundred groups and formerly incarcerated people and city agencies to come up with a way to address mental health and other issues.

I think it was the first time we ever said that we should get rid of that bail thing. What that did was it sort of set the foundation stone for a lot of strategies that ended up being very effective at reducing the population. The first thing that happened was this realization that these two things driving the jail population, the number of people who came in and how long they stayed, was something that we could actually with intentionality reduce and still maintain safety.

And so following that, maybe six months into this effort, somehow a PowerPoint got leaked to DNAinfo that ended up being the outline for the Lippman Commission report.

GREG BERMAN: If Rikers Island ends up getting closed, I think it's a rare coming together of journalism really very strongly making this case and documenting what was going wrong, a very strong kind of activist push, and all the political forces magically coming together that led to the city making that decision.

But you journalists could have written stories 'til you were blue in the face; Glenn Martin could have had marches 'til he passed out. But if there were still twenty-two thousand people on Rikers Island, no one would be talking about closing Rikers Island. It just would not have been possible.

Over the course of the '90s and the aughts, lots of people were working to change the system and to promote alternatives to incarceration, post-adjudication and pre-adjudication, that were driving the numbers down.

VALERIE YOUNGBLOOD, public defender, 1982 to 1996: I was there really from 1982 to 1996, for the heart and guts of the crack epidemic in New York City anyway. The numbers of cases were staggering. It was common at any given time to have thirty to thirty-five indicted felonies plus like fifty, sixty misdemeanor cases. It was overwhelming. People were getting pleaded out before there was any discovery. There were many, many more trials than there are now. There were many, many, many buy and busts and drug-related cases. Crack tends to produce grandiosity. And so there was a lot of violent crime. I felt like I ate rob 1's for breakfast. It was the Wild West for sure.

GREG BERMAN: Talk about post-traumatic stress disorder. I mean, those people are still haunted by that experience. Just seeing like a parade of zombies coming through the system. And I do think that that experience had a seismic impact that, only in recent days, does it feel like we're past it. 'Cause we have a new generation of people and it's so long ago, but I think that era just has a profound impact on you, if you grew up in the '80s and '90s.

I'm in a book club with a half dozen other guys all our age. We were reading a book that had some criminal justice component. And I asked them how many of them had experienced street crime directly. Every single one of them had been the victim of street crime. I asked them how many of their children had been victims of street crime. Zero. I mean, that's a profound social difference in New York City in the course of thirty years.

ELIZABETH GLAZER: We were deploying these efforts to reduce the jail population. How do we better house people, and where do we better house them? There was a small group that was working very, very hard, both on how could we get the population down without

to be exclusive. But the people don't want borough jails.
make any sense. It'll cost more to build these borough
it would to do the work on Rikers. You can make any-
e; you just have to do it. You give it the resources, the
rovide the staffing levels, treat people humanely, even the
You can use that space to make it more comfortable, to
ze it. And you have the space there to do it. That's what I
o.

fucking judges are the ones that remanded everybody and
em all there. And they didn't have the space to keep them.
ace was falling apart years ago. I believe in jail reform. You
ave to send everybody to jail, prostitutes and all that.
ere should be a smaller inmate ratio to staff. And if you do
you'll be able to control the inmate population, with staff
d in mental health and medical care. They could make a real
cal center there and a real psychiatric center on Rikers. They
do it if they could keep the census down.

GERALD DAVID, retired correction officer, 1987 to 2014: The
PD did these inner-city neighborhoods a very, very dirty injus-
, all in the name of making your police record, making your
called legacy of [the number of arrests you had]. Add up the
ests that were legit and add up the ones that were bullshit.
You have to look at things case by case. Not throw everybody
the same category, because you have people that are smoking
eed or getting high . . . Somebody that's selling major drugs, take
em off the street. I understand that. Somebody is committing
urder or rape, robbery. Take them off the street. But someone
ho has a drug addiction, who's just scored some heroin, scored
ome weed, some coke, or whatever. What the hell are you doing?
What's the point?

MICHAEL MUSHLIN: Prior to the pandemic, I was more optimistic
about it. I was really pleased to see the political support for it,
which didn't happen back in the '70s. I led a community meeting
that was held on it that the borough president held at Pace almost

obviously affecting crime. And then could we repurpose the existing borough facilities? How much would that cost? And how long
would it take? So I think what Close Rikers, and then Lippman
did, is that it sort of made public a lot of that. And it made it impossible for any solution to include anything that would be built
on Rikers. That was the big shift: Rikers itself became taboo, and
the solution had to be found in borough facilities.

So it was very confusing. I really didn't know until the last minute that the mayor was going to agree to close Rikers and move it
off the island. And I think that all happened within a twenty-four-
hour period. I do know that Lippman was talking to him. I think
that there may have been some effort to figure out if there is a way
that we can commit to this plan.

I think [the NYPD commissioner Bill] Bratton was always
against it. Their concern was it seemed unrealistic to reduce the
population to five thousand.

At the time, we were at about ten thousand. I think this was a
year or so into the administration. And the thought was, well, sup-
pose we dropped it by half, like, what would we have to do? So the
number was sort of backed into. It seemed very, very ambitious at
the time because it was going to require a different outlook from
judges and from prosecutors. And they needed to have some confidence that they could, for example, put somebody in an alterna-
tive to incarceration. And that that would still not land them on
the front page of the *New York Post*. Huge sea change.

GREG BERMAN: With the possible exception of Glenn, nobody on
the commission could you characterize as a foaming-at-the-mouth
radical. These were establishment figures. It passed muster with
people and the kind of halo effect of Lippman et al. saying like, oh,
this is not a crazy idea. This is something that mainstream people
can endorse.

SOFFIYAH ELIJAH: I think that the city's plan to shut down Rikers
and overhaul the jail system is a very important step in the right

direction. I'm an abolitionist at heart and a realist in real time. So I don't think that a city of this size is going to completely move to a non-incarcerated system overnight. But I think that this city is proposing some important strides in the right direction. That includes trying to change the culture, which is a huge undertaking, changing the physical space, engaging the community in the processes to what would be a much more humane system.

JOHN BOSTON, retired director, Legal Aid Prisoners' Rights Project: Executive summary: damned if I know. They have a plan to close Rikers, but they're closing jails that are not on Rikers. I have no idea what they're thinking. The wind right now is rather strong and unpredictable. But still, I'd like to know what their plan is. And I suspect that the answer to that is going to be "Er, ah, um."

MARTIN HORN: No mayor has ever gone on to national prominence based on how well they ran their prisons or their jails. And so I think it's unfair to expect any mayor to pay real close attention to the details. And interestingly, I would argue that de Blasio has paid too much attention to the jails. And that's part of the reason they are fucked up.

JACQUELINE MCMICKENS, correction commissioner, 1984 to 1986: Rikers Island, to me, was a very practical place to have a jail since no one wanted a jail in their community. The problem with Rikers Island was it didn't have a very good transportation system. It's very difficult for families to get to Rikers, but that could be overcome by dedicated bus service, and it [could] control who got on it. To me, as commissioner, it didn't pose such a significant problem that would want me to close it.

It seems that it's been spiraling out of control for a while. People should remember that they had a significant riot in the Manhattan House of Detention and in the Brooklyn House of Detention. So violence isn't of its location; it's the nature of the management of the facility. And if anybody thinks that moving our

facility off Rikers Island will cont taken. There's no empirical data t Rikers, it has more violence. That' don't have good management in pla

BERNARD KERIK, correction commissi them, why are you closing it? 'Cause the corruption, the mismanagement. close the facility, you're going to take th the same policies, and you're gonna mo we are in this hotel. You have bad manag busboys, bad cleaners. You know what, buildings for like $1.2 billion and then br do it all over again. That's not the problem

SIDNEY SCHWARTZBAUM: De Blasio says that ough jails, violence goes down. But until de I at the Manhattan House of Detention, I we without a slashing or stabbing. Inmates wante was air-conditioning. It was close to [home] f their family. Now Manhattan House of Deter Now it's one of the worst jails.

So you say if you're gonna just move the in jails, they're going to get better. It's a farce. It's a the biggest fraud that has ever gone on. They're $10 billion on this. It's not going to rehabilitate an

EDWARD GAVIN, retired deputy warden, 1982 to 2(Lippman is a fucking jerkoff. We didn't have the spa he know about corrections? He doesn't know about bolts, how it all happens. What it's like to get arre jerkoffs shouldn't be doing this. Now that they have Rikers, they shouldn't be building jails. They should new jails on Rikers, where you can give quality care.

They're turning it into a real estate thing to make m

two years ago this summer. And I saw at that meeting the opposition. Well, there are a lot of people from that community who are really opposed to a high-rise prison [replacing the Tombs].

There was just a lot of opposition from the Chinatown community. And then there were also abolitionists who are just opposed to building any jails. So there's the potential of a coalition of NIMBY people and abolitionist people defeating this idea of building local jails. I worry about whether this plan will be implemented.

STUART MARQUES: Everybody says get the criminals off the street, but don't put new jails in my neighborhood. But if you close Rikers, they have to go somewhere. You can't just put them on some faraway island and forget about them.

This plan is only four jails rather than eight. Three thousand inmates. But you have to make them skyscraper jails. You gotta create at least three thousand to four thousand beds. You need bigger facilities to hold them.

EDDIE ROSARIO, detained 1990: The "system" isn't broken. Any even cursory inspection of the history of our criminal justice system clearly shows the rules have been rigged—and even created—in order to control Black people and other people of color. Policies intended to reform the system, while sometimes well-intentioned, will always fail. This is because the very foundation of our criminal justice system is rooted in racism and white supremacy. Marginalized communities—mostly Black and Latinx—are de facto open-air detention centers that differ from jails and prisons only in their degree of freedom of movement.

Most attempts to "fix" the system ignore the myriad problems that need to be addressed. And I say this as someone who has engaged in reformist policies that often end up being diluted or never fully implemented.

I often find myself as the sole formerly incarcerated person when hammering out bills, and, outside of the Lippman Commission (to some extent), I have not seen much that attempts to address the fact that incarceration—racialized social control—is the only response society offers. And this is because we have no sight. We are blind. We need to ride that beam of light and imagine a better, more just society. And the fact is that most people engaged in criminal justice reform are dismissive and even hostile to properly addressing the injustices that have created the circumstances we are now trying to address.

As it is, and I say this as someone who has protested and was engaged in the Close Rikers campaign, Rikers Island still stands, and the best we have in terms of vision is billions to build more jails. There's something very wrong here.

GLENN MARTIN: Somebody asked me about this the other day. They said, "Who's the driving force behind closing Rikers now?" I said, fucking Judge Lippman. And they were like, "Oh my God." Like, how fucking depressing is that? That a campaign that started about the people most harmed ended up being driven by a guy like Judge Lippman.

And we started talking about organizing and activism and how it always plays out this way. The most elite people say it can't be done; then grassroots people create the environment for it to be done, shift the political landscape; then it becomes safe. And then elite people come back in and say, "Oh, yeah, it can be done."

And then in the end, the advocates end up killing each other off. And the elite people take the credit at the end. If you don't care who takes the credit, it's all good, but what do I think is going on? I think it's going to be a mediocre version of what we hoped for in the beginning. But that's okay. I mean, it's not okay, but you kind of shoot for the stars. And you land somewhere short of it.

And you know that you ended up getting way more than you anticipated. But it definitely is not my vision. That's for sure. I mean, some other advocates have to come along in twenty years and take another swing at it. But I also don't want to discount where we landed, like, I tell people all the time, they're like, "Well, how do you feel about the fact that it's not shut down yet? How do you feel about the new jails being built?" And I'm like, "Look, man, when we started the campaign, there were like ten thousand people on Rikers during COVID. I think we got down to thirty-five hundred. I know we're back up a bit. But that's a fucking win.

Even if Rikers is never closed, that's a win. And it just proves my theory, which is you might as well go super bold and see where you land.

[Herb Sturz died June 10, 2021.]

LAST DAY

"Don't Ever Look Back or Else You'll Come Back"

The act of departing Rikers often begins with "the pack up"—the assembling of possessions into a black plastic garbage bag—and then there's a predawn wake-up call. And then waiting. And more waiting. For those going "up top," or to state prison, there's a bus standing by. For the vast majority, it's a sheaf of forms, a $2.75 transit pass, and often a ride on the Q100 bus to Queens Plaza and the subway. There, the lonely souls with their garbage bags wait again for a connection home. There's little offered by DOC to prepare detainees for their emergence from jail, even after long pretrial incarcerations. For retiring correction officers, there's the ritual goodbyes and send-offs on the last day, but there's a similar sudden departure and, not uncommonly, a sense of relief.

—

CAMILLA BRODERICK, detained 2016: I had been packing for a while. I was all packed and ready. My parents sent me clothes and books. I gave a lot of books to the library. I got *Fight Club* into jail—that has instructions on how to build a bomb—but they wouldn't let my parents bring in Dante's *Inferno*. Apparently, that was too much. Their rules are so fucking weird. If things are the wrong color gray for clothes, they take them away. I gave my clothes away to the people who were going to be there for a long time. I took my Pumas with me, I had put cheetah decorations on it, and I took my ID and my Corcraft soap.

They wake you at 5:00 a.m. That was the same day an officer was retiring, so they locked me down. Everyone was saying good-bye. It took a long time because he was making his final round of saying goodbye. They put me in a cell with one other girl. I sat in this waiting cell for hours while they were just sitting there talking for hours. I had brought one book, Stephen King's *It*. I knew it was going to take a long time. They were making fun of me too. I had gained quite a bit of weight. I wore a dress coming in, and they were saying, "You think you're going to fit into that?"

I got a lot of mail from my parents. The mail lady didn't like me, because she had to work. I was the inmate rep. I told the warden, "Hey, the mail is taking too long." The warden told the mail officer that I said that. At the end of my stay, officers said, "Any more mail you get, we're throwing in the trash. Next time you come back here, because you will come back here, you junkie bitch." They told me to go eat dog food. So I said, "What makes you sure I'm coming back?" They were like, "You'll be back; everyone comes back." They would call up my unit to yell that I was a junkie and a bitch. "You better not have anyone send any more mail here."

I think they were throwing it away the whole time I was there. I said, I could be dealing drugs in here or fighting, but I'm just getting books. God forbid. The Samantha Bee debate segment had aired, and I had made Rikers look good. The mail lady knew about it. She just shut me down, saying, "Don't use your things on me, Queen Debater." I said, "Do you not think I just made you look very good. I'm sorry, how many positive Rikers stories do you get?"

DONOVAN DRAYTON, detained 2007 to 2012: The first day I got out of Rikers after five years, I got some food. I'm speaking to everybody back and forth around me when I'm about to bail out. I'm like, yo, what's going on with the bail? I'm running numbers, checking in with my dad, my stepmom at the time. My dad is on a tour of Germany at this time. He was on tour with somebody.

I forgot who he was with, but I'm speaking to him internationally. It's like $20, $30 from Rikers Island. And I'm calling my stepmom. Until the point I was released, I'm just calling every couple of hours waiting to get my bail. Running back and forth to the Bubble, asking for the CO, and saying, yo, he ain't call me for bailout yet? But I remember telling my stepmom, she asked me on the phone, what do you want to eat when you first come home? I'm saying, I want some jerk chicken with some peas and rice and some sweet plantains and an ice-cold grape soda. Sure enough, when she came to pick me up, she had that pot of Jamaican food for me and that soda. I was eating that in the car. We drove back to the house.

I ate so much that night. I stayed up and I just watched TV all night. And I ain't gonna lie. I cried, man. I cried like a baby. Like that night when it finally, *finally* settled in, I made it back. I feel that feeling sometimes still to this day. I made it, man, I'm here right here. I just cried on my grandma and my stepmother's couch. I was just sad, I watched TV, and the internet was on. I was listening to music. I'm like, yo, this is technology. Technology just completely just evolved in the five years that I was there, FaceTime and iPhones, like, you know what I'm saying?

My dad called me; I was up mad late. And we were just on the phone crying, like, we made it, bro. Thank you so much. I appreciate you, man. I don't know where I'd be without you, big dog. Yeah. Wow.

Never forget the struggle, man. I never forget that people forget about people in prison all the time. Thank God he gave me a second chance to be here sitting talking to you.

I still to this day have moments where I get on my hands and knees and kiss the ground and just give God all the grace and glory because being free was a far distant memory at one point in time in my life.

DAVID CAMPBELL, detained 2019 to 2020: My last thirty days—time really slowed down, and I had a really tough time sticking to the routine that I developed to pass the time. It was a slog, but I made it through.

It was always kind of a gamble when they were going to pick you up from the dorm. And a lot of times it seemed to be between midnight and 2:00 a.m. on the day of your release. They also pick guys up as late as like 6:00 a.m.

So about quarter to 1:00 a.m., I'm like, man, they're not coming. I'm going to go to bed. As soon as I lie down, they tell me to pack up, coming for you at 1:00. I was like, fuck, yeah, one o'clock. In fifteen minutes, I'll be starting the process. I'll be at intake, who knows how long that'll last, but at least I'm getting the ball rolling. And so one o'clock comes, 1:15, 1:30, 1:45, 2:00, 2:15, 2:30. They're still not there.

I'm fucking bugging out. Every once in a while, I'd be like, "Can you call intake? Like, what's up?" Like, you said they'd be here at one o'clock. And he's like, "They didn't forget about you." Finally, at 2:30, he's going on lunch break. So he escorts me halfway down the hallway, with my big bagful of shit. Most guys take little to nothing home. I wrote like forty legal pads. I didn't want to send them home. So I had them all in a big trash bag. I had a French dictionary the size of a cinder block. I had a whole bunch of paperwork, and it's just like dragging this big bag. He walks me about halfway down the hallway, and the lady that was supposed to pick me up at one is just like chatting in the hallway to some other guard. That's why she didn't pick me up. She's just chatting. It's like, goddamn it, do you not know that these are the longest ninety minutes of my life?

It's incredible. There's no accountability. That was what really fucked with me. They finally get me down to intake. Three in the morning. And I was only there for like an hour and a half. They gave me the weirdest outfit. You can't wear your jail clothes out.

And I had an outfit that I wore for court. The kiosk for your personal property is not gonna open 'til 5:00 a.m. You can wait until 5:00 a.m. I said, nah, just get me out of here. Like, I don't want to be here another hour.

So they're like, all right, well, we got to get some clothing for you. The CO goes and comes back with a tight salmon-colored hoodie. And it's got a white and a black like stripe on each sleeve. And then these skinny jeans that are distressed and they have holes in the knees, and it's got a little tag on the bag. It says, "Royalty, Heroism, and the Streets." Yeah. Supercool.

So that was my look. And I hadn't trimmed my beard in months and my hair's all wild. They put me on a bus with a guy who had done three days on a drunk driving charge. And he was like, I did three days. I'm like, cool, I just did twelve months. That was the last guy I was with. We rode across the bridge together. They dumped me off near the parking lot, where there's the trailers and shit on the Queens side of the bridge.

My friends were waiting there. My brother and my best friend growing up were waiting there, just smoking cigarettes against the car. I came from the opposite direction they were expecting with this weird outfit and a big bag on my shoulder. I came home, smoked a big joint, and took a shower. Then I went to get COVID tested.

EDDIE ROSARIO, detained 1990: The first time on Rikers, I copped a plea for six months plus five years' probation. They put me on a plane. Rikers was so crowded the city was renting space from the state. The facility was right by the St. Lawrence River. They shackle you and put you on a plane; it was a four-engine plane, and guys were freaking out. The guy next to me was asking, what if I have to swim? I was only up there two weeks. They put me back on the plane and sent me down. I ended up doing the rest at Hart Island unloading coffins of unidentified people who died. Even today I can't eat hamburgers. There was the smell of embalming fluid and rotted meat that stayed stuck inside your nostrils. I remember they served sloppy joes all the time. To this day, I can't eat that kind of meat.

The dorm was a trailer. It was lopsided. It was rough. But they would let you roam around because there was nowhere to go. One time a guard took us on a tour. There had been an asylum for the criminally insane there. That was still around. We would see how people would be caged up in there. When they let me go from there, it was like the middle of the night. They tell you you're leaving, and they take you to the ferry, put you on a correction bus, and they drop you right at 125th Street in Harlem. *[Laughs.]* All you heard there was, "I got the good shit right here!" I was high before I got home. It was 2:00 a.m. when they dropped us off. A lot of the street people were right there. They were trying to sell you sex, drugs, whatever.

SADAT X, hip-hop artist, detained 2006: I only told a couple of people, because you never want to tell somebody it's your last day, because a lot of dudes that hate will try to make you do something to keep you there. You understand you don't want to get no ticket or nothing on your last day. So, man, I just chilled out. I woke up, I filled out the whole day, you understand. I watched TV. I went to rec. I ate, you know, I talked to dudes for a little while, and I went to sleep, man. And I was just waiting for them to call me in the morning for the pack up.

It was eight, nine months. I got dropped off downtown, and I remember my man Big Meg and Pat was there. The interesting thing is, we went uptown and they had some smoke for me and I went into the store. This is my first time going in a store in like eight months.

And when I came out, somebody had jumped off the roof right in front of us and landed flat on the ground and killed themselves. Dude had jumped out the window.

CHARLES BARRY, detained 1980s, 1990s, 2000s: My first time I was in Rikers was in 1986. First time I did no problem, no drama, no pressure, but coming home, this old G told me right before I left . . . I'll remember it until the day I die. I could cry. He said, "Youngster, you go home crossing that bridge. Right?" He said, "If you're in the back of that bus, there's one thing you don't do on your first time going home. Do not look back out the window, the back of the bus window, to the bridge. Don't do that." I said, "Okay, I got you." I got on the bus, and I fucking did it. There must have been some curse. I've been coming back and forth for the last thirty-something years. That's some strange shit. The temptation was too much. I looked back. I never saw that old dude again. That's some *Twilight Zone* shit.

JERRY DEAN, detained 1987, 2003: The last day I was leaving Rikers when I was sixteen, I sat in the corner, they drive me upstate [to the Goshen Secure Center], and I remember somebody said, when you leave Rikers, don't ever look back, don't look back in the car or the bus, or else you'll come back. So I didn't want to look back.

JACQUELINE VELEZ, detained 1998: There was no preparation for after Rikers. They would have NA [Narcotics Anonymous] come in once a week or the Women's Prison Association come in. But if anybody helped, the people that worked with those organizations, I would have a conversation on the side with one of them. What do they got outside for us? What resources, like, what can we do? I had no idea, because, although I knew a lot of men that were in and out of prison, I didn't know any women. Or if I did know them, they weren't my friend, then I didn't know their personal experience with them. Do you get what I'm saying? It was almost like there was no information [for] women. That kind of dawned on me while I was there.

In that cell, I lost all of that. I was just determined to be a better mom to my daughter. And in doing that, in holding that, that is what eventually got me where I'm at. Because I'm like, fuck it. If I had to sell my ass for that girl to go to whatever college she wanted to go to, then I was going to do that. That's what it instilled, I guess. I knew I didn't want to be away from my daughter. And I felt like I had to be better. And when she was there in that visit room sniffing on me, I said, I can't do this to this little girl. I just cannot do this. I had to do better.

She just got accepted to the National Honor Society. That's her hard work. She's at a community college, but she's looking to go to a college, college where you live in the dorm. She wants to be part of study-abroad programs. She wants to travel. She's swam with sharks. Some shit I wouldn't do because I'm traumatized from *Jaws*, right? I don't even know how to swim, but I made sure she learned how to swim. She's gone parasailing. She got some balls. I don't know where that came from.

FITZGERALD DAVID, retired correction officer, 1987 to 2014: When I retired, I asked the chief of the department for my good-guy letter, so I can get my firearms. He sent me a letter stating they weren't going to send me my good-guy letter because I was an "unsavory character." Yes, he stated I was an unsavory character because I spoke out against Dora Schriro, the commissioner at the time. And I put Joseph Ponte on blast.

I have the letter to this day that states that I am not qualified to get my good-guy letter because I was an unsavory person. How the hell do you say that to a person?

I asked them, could I get my old shield? They wouldn't give it to me. Just like they didn't want to give me my good-guy letter for my firearms, but I got it anyway, because I went to the Bulova building [DOC HQ] and went off. I told them, I'll expose every one of you that I know something about.

I was told to leave the building and it will be taken care of. I was sitting on my steps at my house, smoking a cigar, having a drink, and a FedEx truck pulled up and my good-guy letter was in there. I had to sign for it.

JAMES MCGOVERN, retired correction captain, 1984 to 2004: My last day, I just drove off the island and said, good, I never have to come back to this place again.

MARTIN CREGG, retired DOC gang investigator, 1996 to 2018: When I wake up in the morning, my wife says, you were yelling in your sleep. "Six upper! You got a problem! You gotta hit the alarm!" So I was like, how would she know that? And the week before that, my alarm clock went off. Bam! It blasted and she started smacking the shit out of me. I wake up and I said, "What are you doing?" She's got a fucking welt on her head. She said you hit me in your sleep.

I'll be honest with you: you see stuff, and yeah, I got a little depressed after I retired. When I went in there, what you said was gospel. You ever seen the movie *A Dog's Purpose* with Dennis Quaid? A dog has to have a purpose. I felt like I had a purpose when I went to the gang unit. I was figuring stuff out. It was like a chess match, and I would find stuff out on the street and give it to the detectives.

SIDNEY SCHWARTZBAUM, retired deputy warden, union president, 1979 to 2016: I had a lot of incidents that I think I blocked out of my head, then they just come up, 'cause I don't even want to think about it.

COLIN ABSOLAM, detained 1993 to 1996: This is something that I experienced, you know, from that day until I was released: the different sounds of prison, like keys jingling. Like that bothers me right now. I have my own keys, and when I go to open the door, they jingle, and that does something to my mind because that's something I've been used to hearing for a long time.

FITZGERALD DAVID: I could've stayed longer. But one of the reasons why I left was I saw the writing on the wall, how the department was going. I stood up and told everyone. I said, I'm leaving December 31, 2014. I won't spend 2015 one day working in jail. So everybody was like, "Don't leave." I said, I'm done. I'm tired of fighting the union. I'm tired of fighting the department. And it's a losing battle.

And December 31 came. I went to work. I went to roll call at seven in the morning, which I didn't work. I worked the one-to-nine tour. Told everybody goodbye, roll call broke. I did the three o'clock roll call.

I told everyone it's time for me to go, bye-bye. I just said, "Listen, I got to go." I went over to the bar called Joey's [Place]. Astoria Boulevard. I got my envelope; I got my plaques. I had a blackened steak with french fries. I had two drinks and a beer. I drove home. That was it. I put my uniforms in a plastic bag before I left, put all my stuff from my locker. I actually didn't get rid of my old uniforms until two years ago. I burned them.

That life is over with. I never want to see it again, and I never want anybody else to go through the hell I went through on that job, because it was a horror show. And the only thing that I kept that's a reminder of DOC is my elected delegate's picture that the officers of OBCC [Otis Bantum Correctional Center], they elected me as a delegate. The only other thing I kept was my plaques, my retired shield, and ID. That's it. It didn't make any sense to me to keep anything else.

KAREN SESSOMS, correction officer, 1991 to 1993: I was injured on the job. I fell down a flight of steps in the facility and suffered an ankle/leg fracture. I was placed on medical leave. Because I was probationary, they didn't want to give me my job back. I ended up being terminated, but I had all the documentation. I never missed a doctor's appointment. I filed an Article 78 [lawsuit]. Nobody really looked at anything factual. I wasn't returned to work.

After that, I matured. I'm more conscious of how I treat individuals. There was a time when I wasn't so patient and so understanding of people's needs. There's a lot of people with mental illness. A lot of people that wander around. If I could leave something with them to let them know there is a way to give them a purpose, to let them know they have purpose. We have different things we can create to be great. We just have to find it.

The way Rikers was run, the perception of inmates, created a lot of damage, physically and spiritually. You can't use the same tactic for everyone. And then you cut programs, and what do they have to do?

If there's nothing to do but go back and forth to the mess hall and the yard and the dayroom and watch TV—most can't read—what are they going to do?

A lot of times, you put a group of people in the same environment, you tend to become that. A lot of these detainees, some of them come in as adolescents, they haven't gone past sixth or seventh grade. You can tell there's no level of college or anything.

There's a better way to do things.

ANNA GRISTINA, detained 2012: I was terrified of leaving. It was bittersweet. I had a bond with people. We became very bonded. There was a group of us, and we shared everything. We actually kept civility. We began a normal life in there. My last day I got approved bail the week before. My friend's package hadn't come through there. I stayed an extra week until her package cleared. On the day they were coming to get me, they said get packed. We're leaving. I started to feel the fear when I got over the bridge. The media trucks following the bus. I had a stress disorder from all the media coverage. I would peel the skin off the heels in my sleep, wearing it away with my fingers. I didn't even know I was doing it. When I walked down the corridor in the morning, you could see the blood behind me.

I often thought, why would anybody ever come back to Rikers? And yet there are people who are there a lot. They lose hope, they do. There are so many beautiful souls that are broken and lost there because the system sets them up to fail. They give them impossible terms to rebuild or build their lives. They've not just lost time being incarcerated, they've lost relationships, kids, they are thrown into halfway houses with nothing. There needs to be total reform like Sweden and Switzerland. It needs to be an educational center instead of a punishment center.

SOFFIYAH ELIJAH, executive director, Alliance of Families for Justice: I did a panel discussion, where I was on a panel with Kalief Browder's mother. This is after he committed suicide. [Kalief Browder died by suicide at age twenty-two after he was arrested for stealing a backpack. He spent three years on Rikers, including two years in solitary.] And we were sitting side by side during the panel where she was trying to speak about her son's suicide, and she reached under the table and reached for my hand. She gripped my hand so tight it hurt. There's no other way to put it. I couldn't think about doing anything except to hold her hand as well as she tried to explain that experience.

And about six months later, she was gone [Venida Browder died in October 2016 of a sudden heart attack]. I always remember that. Even as she was speaking on the panel, how did she find that strength to share it with people? I remember thinking to myself, there's got to be something internal that we never, ever heal. And I think that's part of the reality of the fact that she was gone six months later. Because there's too much pain for everybody to live through.

Casimiro Torres found himself in Rikers many times starting as a teen. He was in the original cast of the off-Broadway play The Castle *and has worked as a counselor. He has two children.*

CASIMIRO TORRES, detained various stints, 1980s to 2000s: I had a girl one time, I used to go to this twenty-four-hour store after I came out of prison, late at night, and after a few times she started calling me Smiley. I said, "Why do you call me that?" And she said, "Because you've never smiled." And it had never occurred to me that I hadn't smiled in years and years. I had my prison face on wherever I went. It's something that clings to you, like the smell of shit.

You have to really wash it off.

AFTER RIKERS

Colin Absolam served more than twenty years in state prison. He was pardoned by Governor Cuomo, preventing his deportation. After his release in 2020, Absolam was hired as a case manager with Exodus Transitional Community.

John Alite was an associate with the Gambino crime family in the eighties. He became a cooperator and writes books and does public appearances.

Charles Barry, whose nickname is MetroCard for the subway system where he hangs out, is trying to turn his life around after more than 160 arrests for low-level subway scams.

Greg Berman was a founder of the Center for Court Innovation, and served on the Lippman Commission, which investigated the closing of Rikers. He is a Guggenheim Fellow and founder of the journal *Vital City*.

John Boston was director of the Legal Aid Society's Prisoners' Rights Project. After a long, distinguished career litigating class action lawsuits on behalf of tens of thousands of detainees, he is enjoying retirement.

Matthew Brockington served three years in state prison. He has worked with Derrick Haynes in an effort to reduce gang violence in Harlem public housing developments.

Camilla Broderick, after Rikers, got her degree in criminology from John Jay College of Criminal Justice and plans a career in law or social work. She still likes to debate.

Barry Campbell spent much of his childhood and early twenties in city jails and upstate prisons during the 1980s. He serves as a top official for the Fortune Society.

David Campbell served one year on Rikers in 2019 and 2020 for punching a Trump supporter in Midtown. He moved to Paris for graduate school to study scientific and technical translation and is involved in prisoner support activism.

Kandra Clark works as the vice president of policy and strategy of Exodus Transitional Community, a nonprofit that helps people "affected by the justice system."

Robert Cohen works as a private practice physician in Manhattan and is a commissioner of the city's Board of Correction. In the 1980s, he served as director of the Montefiore Rikers Island Health Services.

Linus Coraggio continues to make art on the Upper West Side of Manhattan. Ringo Starr is among his collectors. He also still rides his many bikes.

Martin Cregg retired from the DOC after twenty-three years, including ten years as a gang investigator. He founded and runs a private investigation firm.

Robert Cripps retired as a warden after thirty years with the DOC from 1983 to 2013. He splits his time between New York and the Dominican Republic.

Hector "Pastor Benny" Custodio was released from prison in 2011 and got a master's degree from the New York Theological Seminary. He founded a ministry and does mental health and substance abuse counseling.

Sparkle Daniel remains in state prison and is eligible for parole in 2032.

Jerry Dean is an actor and a playwright who has performed a solo show about his life experiences. He appears in the 2022 short film *The Crusaders*.

Donovan Drayton, from age nineteen to twenty-four, served nearly five years on Rikers Island pretrial from 2007 to 2012. Faced with a murder charge, he was eventually acquitted of all but a weapon charge. He lives in Queens, raising his children and working on his music.

Donovan's father, **Ronny Drayton**, toured the world as a lead guitarist, performing with Parliament-Funkadelic, 24-7 Spyz, Living Colour, and Nona Hendryx, among others. He died of cancer in 2020.

Tahanee Dunn is the director of Bronx Defenders Prisoners' Rights Project, where she advocates for detainees.

Martha Grieco works closely with Dunn at Bronx Defenders.

Nestor Eversley was first detained on Rikers in 1969. He lives in Harlem.

Florence Finkle was the Correction Department's deputy commissioner for integrity and policy from 2010 to 2014. She works as a consultant primarily for law enforcement oversight.

Fitzgerald David retired from DOC as a correction officer in 2014. He lives on Long Island with his two beloved dogs and weighs in on correction issues from time to time.

James "Shaquell" Forbes, an early member of the Bloods, served a long stint in state prison, including close to eight years in solitary. Since his 2017 release, he has been active in violence-reduction groups.

Matt Frey was a clinician for the DOC from 2011 to 2018. He currently works at Broadridge, a financial services Fortune 500 company, where he provides therapy and counseling for associates. He's also in private practice.

Warner Frey retired as an NYPD captain in 2014 and works at lawyering and raising his three sons on Long Island.

Robert Gangi was president of the Correctional Association, where he investigated conditions in jails and prisons. He has since founded the Police Reform Organizing Project.

Edward Gavin joined the DOC in 1982 and retired as a deputy warden in 2001. He later worked for the city's child welfare agency and is currently an investigator under contract with a social service agency.

Kenny Gilmore went to prison in 1976 and got out in 2007. He lives in Brooklyn with his partner, Yolanda Cepeda. Gilmore has run programs helping at-risk teens called "True Self–False Self, Love Thyself."

Marcus Grice was in Rikers multiple times. He lives in Manhattan.

Anna Gristina was detained on Rikers in 2012 for four months. In 2021, a movie about her life running a high-end escort service aired on the Lifetime network.

Dupree Harris has been in state prison since 2006. He works in the grievance office and had a parole hearing scheduled in July 2022.

LaSharn Harris has been married to Dupree for five years. She visits him often and recently obtained a master's degree in school counseling.

Derrick Haynes is a retired counselor of juvenile offenders who runs a nonprofit dedicated to improving the lives of youth in several Harlem public housing developments.

Lawrence Henagin served time in prison after Rikers and was living in Harlem working construction.

Devonte Hernandez was sixteen when he was arrested for a fatal shooting in 2015. He is currently serving time in state prison with a possible release date in 2023. He is looking ahead to moving forward with his life.

Shaneika Escartas, Devonte's mom, often drives the four hours upstate to visit her son. She lives in Queens. Doris Osei, Devonte's grandmother, also visits Devonte as often as she can.

William vanden Heuvel was a chair of the Board of Correction in the 1970s. He died in 2021 at the age of ninety-one following a long career in political, government, and legal circles.

Gary Heyward was a correction officer for ten years and then pleaded guilty in 2006 to smuggling contraband. He was released from jail in 2008. He has worked for the city housing authority in the same public housing development where he grew up.

Martin Horn was correction commissioner from 2002 to 2009. He has been a litigation consultant and a professor at John Jay College of Criminal Justice.

Ervin "Easy" Hunt was in Rikers multiple times from the 1970s through the 2000s. He is an actor and comedian who has performed in Shakespeare in the Park. He is "Boompa" to his great-granddaughters.

Elias Husamudeen was a correction officer and then the president of the Correction Officers' Benevolent Association after Norman Seabrook was forced to step down. Husamudeen was voted out of office in 2020. He's president of Eli Global Reform Foundation.

Donna Hylton served twenty-six years in state prison. She is an author and activist on incarceration issues.

Frank Pasqua III was an associate with the Lucchese organized crime family. He served several stints in Rikers. He became a cooperating witness.

Michael Jacobson served as the city's correction commissioner from 1995 to 1998 and the probation commissioner from 1992 to 1996. He's currently director of CUNY Institute for State & Local Governance.

Fat Joe grew up in the Bronx. He continues to record music and perform, and has been active on criminal justice issues.

Nellie Kelly lost her brother, Ronald Spear, on Rikers. Spear was murdered by a correction officer. Kelly lives in South Carolina, where she adores her family and works in the commercial display business.

Bernard Kerik served as NYC correction commissioner from 1998 to 2000 and police commissioner from 2000 to 2001. He was convicted of tax fraud and served time in federal prison. He does security consulting and appears as a cable-TV commentator.

Eve Kessler worked as director of public affairs for DOC from 2014 to 2017. She's an editor and reporter at Streetsblog.

Amin "Minister" King was released from prison in 2010. He has a construction company and works as a personal trainer and bodyguard. He lives in Queens.

Richard Koehler was correction commissioner from 1986 to 1989. He is a lawyer with the firm Koehler & Isaacs, which represents the correction officers union.

Tami Lee retired as a correction officer in 2020. She keeps a world map in her home of all the places she plans to visit.

Rick Lombardi retired from the DOC in 2011 as a gang investigator. He has managed nightclubs and is enjoying life.

Coss Marte served time in prison after Rikers and then founded his own fitness studio called CONBODY on the Lower East Side.

Glenn Martin served time in Rikers starting in 1994. He founded JustLeadershipUSA, which was centrally involved in the Close Rikers movement. He advises nonprofits and flips real estate.

James McGovern retired as a correction captain in 2004. He's in the executive protection business.

Jacqueline McMickens, the DOC's first Black female commissioner, from 1984 to 1986, is a lawyer in private practice who represents correction officers.

Kathy Morse is a co-founder of the Close Rosie's campaign to shut down the Rose M. Singer Center on Rikers. She's a social justice advocate focused on women and adolescents who are locked up.

Michael Mushlin was head of the Legal Aid Society's Prisoners' Rights Projects in the 1970s. He is a law professor with Pace University.

Rachel Oppenheim taught at Rikers from 2005 to 2010. She is a professor at Antioch University in Seattle and continues to work with incarcerated people.

Mario Perez served time in state prison. He lives in the Bronx, raising his children and grandchildren, and works for a construction firm.

Gregory Pierce spent time in state prison and lived in Harlem after his release. He talked about the joy of writing poetry and visiting his grandchildren.

Dr. Robert Powitz is a sanitarian and environmental health expert who conducts investigations of conditions in institutional settings. He is public health consultant for the Bucks County (Pennsylvania) jail.

Grace Price is a freelance writer and also the founder of the Close Rosie's campaign, which advocates for the shuttering of the facility housing women on Rikers.

John Ramsey was released from prison after thirty-three years. He is a private investigator on wrongful conviction cases.

Stanley Richards served several stints in Rikers, then state prison. After his release, he rose to executive vice president of the Fortune Society and served in 2021 as deputy commissioner of operations for the Department of Correction.

Edward-Yemil Rosario was detained on Rikers twice in 1990. He keeps active with freelance work entailing organizational development, as well as criminal justice reform efforts.

David Rothenberg founded the Fortune Society in 1967, a beloved organization that assists some five thousand men and women with criminal justice histories each year. At last check, he was still going strong just shy of ninety.

Dr. Yusef Salaam, one of the Central Park 5, also called the Exonerated 5, is a prison reform activist and motivational speaker.

Sidney Schwartzbaum retired from the DOC in 2016 after a long stint as president of the Assistant Deputy Wardens/Deputy Wardens Association. He is now enjoying time with his twin granddaughters.

Rev. Bernard Shepherd has been a counselor and team leader for the Youth Justice Network in the women's jail on Rikers and is a founder of the Good Samaritans Men's Outreach Ministry.

Terrence Skinner retired as a deputy warden in 2003 and splits his time between New York and Virginia, where he helps out with the grandkids. He still speaks his mind.

Stephanie Smagler retired as a Rikers correction officer in 2015. She has since become a correction officer in Pennsylvania.

Julia Solomons is a social worker in the Criminal Defense Practice of Bronx Defenders.

Sandi Sutton was jailed in the DOC old women's house in Chelsea in 1970. The retired nurse gets around in a smart-looking motorized wheelchair.

Ronald Tackmann, the escape artist, served multiple stints in state prison, where he was known as a master storyteller and artist. He died in 2020 of liver cancer at the age of sixty-six.

Helen Taylor was detained in the old women's house in Chelsea in the 1970s and in Rose M. Singer Center in the eighties. Taylor lives in Harlem, where she works and enjoys her family.

Casimiro Torres is a discharge planner at the Fortune Society helping former detainees get back on their feet.

Angel Tueros served twenty-three years in prison and was released in 2018. He lives in Queens and is grateful to be reunited with his now-grown daughter.

Dr. Susi Vassallo is a toxicologist and emergency room doctor with the NYU Langone hospital network. She is a widely sought expert on heat illness and other medical conditions in U.S. penal institutions.

Michael Velez lost his brother, Matthew Velez, to a fatal beating on Rikers. He lives in North Carolina, where he works for a university in information technology.

Jacqueline Velez lives in Massachusetts, where she works for Massachusetts Jobs with Justice and as a community activist and organizer.

Hazel Figueroa, who had her daughter in Rikers in 1998, lives and works in Puerto Rico. Figueroa and Velez remain close friends. Figueroa's daughter is in college.

Homer Venters served at Rikers from 2008 to 2016 working his way up from deputy medical director to chief medical officer. He's a member of the Biden/Harris COVID-19 Health Equity Task Force. He also serves as a consultant in correctional health.

Judah Washington served time in prison and is a counselor with Exodus Transitional Community.

Hilton Webb awaited trial for two years on Rikers and then served a long stint in state prison. He was released in 2017. He has since gotten a master's degree in social work.

Christine West retired from the Correction Department in 2004. She lives in Louisiana, where she writes and raises her youngest daughter.

Michael "Big Mike" Williams retired in 2008 as a member of DOC's Emergency Services Unit. He lives in upstate New York and works from time to time in the security business when he's not spending time with his grandchildren.

Sadat X, a co-founder of the hip-hop group Brand Nubian, continues to record and perform his music. During the pandemic, he worked in a hospital in North Carolina.

NOTE TO READERS

People who have been in jail have long been described with demeaning terms such as "inmates," "perps," and "skells." Those labels contribute to the dehumanization of people in custody. In this book, we've done our best to move away from such terms wherever possible, while preserving the way people speak in the passages. Some interviews were slightly edited for clarity.

ACKNOWLEDGMENTS

This book took shape in people's homes and offices and cars, in upstate prison visiting rooms, corner cafés, and park benches, and, at the height of the pandemic, in talks through the computer and chats by phone.

We are most grateful to the roughly 130 people who shared their stories with us. Their Rikers experiences were but one part of their lives and do not alone define them. Each in themselves is worthy of a book.

It is not a small thing to talk about such intimate experiences, especially those that begin and end in the darkest of moments, and they did it with courage and humor and thoughtfulness. We tried to do our best to handle their accounts with care and sensitivity.

The project simply wouldn't have happened without Ben Greenberg, executive editor at Random House, whose steady hand kept us on course and was invaluable in shaping the finished product, and Daniel Greenberg, agent extraordinaire, who was always present with the right words at the key moments. Kaeli Subberwal, assistant editor at Random House, offered insight and skill. Photographer Mariela Lombard found a human connection in her portraits for the book, and Tracy Glantz and Rob Zambrano lent us their perceptive eyes in South Carolina and Puerto Rico. Edward-Yemil Rosario both allowed us to interview him and gave us his take on the completed manuscript. Production editor Andy Lefkowitz saved us more than a few times. We'd also like to thank Stacey Stein, our publicist, for her tireless efforts in getting word about the book out.

We couldn't have done this project without our network of friends and relationships built up over many years. One person led us to another and that person led us to someone else. All gave generously of their time, and for that we are eternally grateful.

Former union president Sidney Schwartzbaum's involvement by mere weight of his reputation alone helped open doors. John Boston, the legendary barrister at Legal Aid, freely submitted to three exhaustive interviews spanning his long career fighting for the incarcerated. Ronny Drayton offered his insight on the city's capricious justice system. David Rothenberg, JoAnne Page, Stanley Richards, Colleen Roche, and Jeff Simmons at the Fortune Society helped connect us with people, as did Jonathan Abady, Kenny Gilmore, Pete Gleason, John Gordon, Redmond Haskins, Jeffrey Lichtman, Hawk Newsome, Rich Player, John Ramsey, Stacey Richman, and Ranna Royce. Our bosses at the New York *Daily News* and *The City* kindly gave us time to work on the book.

From Graham

I have been blessed to have had great mentors in my journalism life, none more generous than the journalist Tom Robbins, a treasured friend who always offers wise counsel. A special thanks to Jonathan Chasan, who would set aside time from his much more important work—defending the rights of the jailed—to help me navigate the world that is Rikers.

The words and advice of Les Payne, Leonard Levitt, and Jimmy Breslin still resonate even after their passing.

I owe much to my extraordinary and talented family—my mother, the arts and culture writer Abby Wasserman; Potter Wickware, a scientist, writer, and union welder; my uncle Richey Wasserman, a master carpenter and my first mentor; my philosopher brother Joshua Rayman; and, of course, my amazing sons, Nicholas and William Rayman. Thanks to my good friends who lent an ear or gave the right advice at key moments—including Carl Riedlin, Alix Michel, Terri Rosenblatt, Dan Kyle, Sean Gardiner, Rocco Parascandola, and the late Heather Wainwright. And thanks to the Bluestone group, my friends at The Pauline in Harlem, and those whose names must remain undisclosed.

From Reuven

I'd like to thank Graham for choosing me as a partner for this book. Some meetings are truly life changing, and I'm forever grateful you thought of me when the idea first came up. I'm truly proud of the work we've done together.

I'd also like to acknowledge my college professors, Joe Mancini and Paul Moses, who saw something in a clueless student. Richard Steier, my first boss at The Chief-Leader, who gave me a shot in the business. Your weekly tutorials going over my copy taught me the basics and almost every writing trick I know.

Jere Hester at The City gave me a renewed lease on life as a local reporter. I have never tired of saying how fortunate I've been to get a chance to team up with you and others, like Hasani Gittens and Alyssa Katz. Jere, your kindness and thoughtful edits are unparalleled in an industry filled with sharp elbows. I'd also like to thank John Wotowicz, Nic Dawes, and Richard Kim.

My colleagues at The City have also been absolute lifesavers.

Rosa Goldensohn, your own jail coverage has taught me to never forget about the people behind the stories. No one in the business approaches criminal justice coverage with your level of sensitivity and deep sense of care.

My friendships with Ginger Adams Otis and Lisa Colangelo have kept me sane. I dream of getting a chance to work with both of you again. I'd be nowhere in this business without your cheerleading and endless support. Bruce Diamond has been an incredible sounding board, phantom editor on my local coverage, and a true friend.

The WhatsApp chevra of Chaim Nath, Shmuly Pavel, David Binson, Chaim Plumer, Shmuel Frager, Menashe Roth, and Ely Rappaport have made the world seem like a smaller place. I'm beyond fortunate to call you all friends and have a daily platform to gripe and joke around.

Shai Grabie, your passion for writing and research has been a true inspiration. No one I know has done more to chase their dreams while supporting their family. Koby Oppenheim, your ability to see the big picture has been invaluable. I cherish our talks and am lucky to call you a friend.

Rabbi Marc Spivak has also served as an amazing sounding board and book club partner: I'm truly inspired by your insatiable intellectual curiosity and sermons guided through a prism of kindness and sensitivity.

Dr. Sharon Kofman: your insightful guidance has helped me, and my anxiety, understand the world in ways I never knew possible.

My family has also played a key role in all my successes. My father, Big Chief, has waited years for the book: I'd never have had a chance to pursue a dream career as a journalist without the earlier sacrifices you made to give me a financial backup. Age has done nothing to temper your excitement when it comes to my career and the love you have for me.

As for my mom, Meemer: I'm sorry you were never able to see the final product but hope it gave you some solace, and bragging rights among your friends, before your passing.

My siblings, Judy and Shimy: you've both taken on so much back in Denver and I'm forever grateful. I'd never be able to finish this book without your selfless care of Big Chief.

My in-laws, Roland and Tova, have never questioned my unconventional career choice and cheered this project along since its start. Wonderful Bubbie: your coffees, stories, and unconditional love have brought my world so much light throughout the pandemic. Our breakfast klatches are the highlights of my days.

Same goes for the wonderful aunties and uncles: Atara and Moshe, Shalom and Gila, Michal, Yael, and Henry, and the great Gabi. Moshe, our playground trips have been one of the highlights of our time together.

As for my son, Noam, and his new little sister, Meira: I can't wait until you're each old enough to read this tome. Noam, it has been a true joy seeing you grow and being your dad. I've loved every minute. Sorry so many of the interviews interrupted our bedtime routine.

Acharon acharon chaviv, my wife, Sara Chamama, who has never wavered from the first time I brought up the possibility of this project. I'm haunted by your love and support and sensitive encouragement. I will never forget how you cleared so much of your time so I could put in the work necessary to make this book possible. These pages are a true testament to your love.

CREDITS

221	Mariela Lombard
238	Mariela Lombard
253	Mariela Lombard
266	Mariela Lombard
278	Mariela Lombard
293	Mariela Lombard
307	Tracy Glantz
321	Mariela Lombard
346	Mariela Lombard
351	Mariela Lombard
374	Mariela Lombard
384	Mariela Lombard
407	Mariela Lombard

INDEX

ABOUT THE AUTHORS

Graham Rayman is a journalist who writes mainly about criminal justice and policing. He has won multiple journalism prizes over his thirty-year career. He has worked at the New York *Daily News,* and, before that, *The Village Voice, Newsday,* and *New York Newsday.* He is also the author of *The NYPD Tapes.*

Reuven Blau is a senior reporter at *The City.* He has previously worked at the New York *Daily News,* the *New York Post,* and the *Chief-Leader.* He is known as the dean of Rikers reporters.